THE THEOLOGY
OF RUDOLF BULTMANN

RUDOLF BULTMANN

THE THEOLOGY OF RUDOLF BULTMANN

Edited by Charles W. Kegley

HARPER & ROW, PUBLISHERS

NEW YORK

Grateful acknowledgment is made to the following publishers and individuals for permission to quote from certain of the published works of Rudolf Bultmann, and in some instances of works about him:

Theologische Rundschau, 1954, by J. C. B. Mohr (Paul Siebeck), Tübingen, and especially Walter Baumgartner, Erich Dinkler, and Hans Siebeck, who compiled the Bibliography to 1954.

J. C. B. Mohr (Paul Siebeck), Tübingen, for the material in original and in translation from The Theology of The New Testament, 1951, and from various sections of Glauben und Verstehen, 1933 and subsequent.

Herbert Reich, Evangelischer Verlag, Hamburg, for the material from Kerygma und Mythos.

Charles Scribner's Sons, New York, for the material from Jesus and the Word, by Louise P. Smith and Erminie Huntress, 1934, 1958; Theology of the New Testament, Vol. I, by Kendrick Grobel, 1951, and Vol. II, tr. by Kendrick Grobel, 1955; and Jesus Christ and Mythology, 1958.

S.P.C.K., London, for the material from various sections of Kerygma and Myth, Vol. I, by R. H. Fuller, 1953.

Meridian Books of World Publishing Company, Cleveland, and Prof. Rudolf Bultmann for an extended portion of Autobiographical Reflections, tr. by Schubert M. Ogden, first published in Existence and Faith, 1960.

FIRST EDITION

LIBRARY OF CONGRESS CATALOG CARD NUMBER: 66–11483

A–Q

Acknowledgment

————— ◦•◦ —————

A special statement of gratitude is here made to Mrs. Antje Lemke, of the School of Library Science of Syracuse University, New York, who is Professor Bultmann's daughter. The honored subject of this volume and the editor turned repeatedly to her for advice and help, as did several of the essayists, directly or indirectly. That help was always given graciously and with results showing unerring insight into the many problems of translating into English. She, therefore, is responsible for many of the exceptionally apt renderings, but not for any of the flaws the critic may discover.

C.W.K.

Contents

———— ◆◆◆◆◆◆ ————

v   *Acknowledgment*

xi   *Preface*
       CHARLES W. KEGLEY

xix   *Autobiographical Reflections of Rudolf Bultmann*

       I. ESSSAYS OF INTERPRETATION AND CRITI-
       CISM OF THE WORK OF RUDOLF BULT-
       MANN

3   The Theology of Rudolf Bultmann
       GÜNTHER BORNKAMM

21   The Meaning of Demythologization
       EDWIN M. GOOD

41   Revelation
       H. P. OWEN

51   Rudolf Bultmann's Philosophy of History
       HEINRICH OTT

65   Rudolf Bultmann's Interpretation of New Testament
   Eschatology
       PAUL S. MINEAR

vii

83   The Doctrines of God and Man in the Theology of Rudolf
     Bultmann
         K. E. LØGSTRUP

104 The Significance of Rudolf Bultmann for Contemporary
     Theology
         SCHUBERT M. OGDEN

127 Philosophy and Theology in Bultmann's Thought
         JOHN MACQUARRIE

144 The Theology of Rudolf Bultmann and Its Relation to
     Philosophy
         GÖTZ HARBSMEIER

153 The Role of the Church in the Theology of Rudolf Bultmann
         HANS BOLEWSKI

170 The Event of Salvation and Word in the New Testament
         OTTO MICHEL

183 The Consequences of Bultmann's Theology for Ethics
         HEINZ-HORST SCHREY

201 Bultmann's Relationship to Classical Philology
         FRIEDRICH MÜLLER

211 Bultmann on Judaism
         SAMUEL SANDMEL

221 The Old Testament and Its Significance for Religious
     Instruction
         HANNELIS SCHULTE

236 Contemporary Interpretation of the Gospels as a Challenge to
     Preaching and Religious Education
         MARTIN STALLMANN

II. REPLY TO INTERPRETATION AND CRITICISM

257 Reply
RUDOLF BULTMANN

289 *Bibliography of the Publications of Rudolf Bultmann to 1965*

311 *Subject Index*

315 *Name Index*

Preface

In pondering the present religious situation, one is impressed with the fact that Rudolf Bultmann's thought concentrates attention on most of the unquestionably central issues. The very structure he has chosen to employ for his "Reply to Interpretation and Criticism" constitutes a kind of program for theologians and philosophers of religion in the second half of the twentieth century. That the so-called post-Bultmannian period is largely dominated by the issues he has raised is evident, in part, by considering the interrelated series of problems as he has ordered them: demythologizing, history, philosophy, New Testament interpretation, and the role of the Church as the organ of institutional religion. Bultmann has the distinction of having identified and shaped most of the questions with which contemporary scholars must wrestle.

It is a further sign of Bultmann's vitality and intellectual honesty that, although he has confronted certain of his critics on several issues, and done so *ad hoc* for almost a quarter of a century, once again he is willing to engage in open and critical exchange. The present book (1) brings up-to-date a considerable body of study on the part of scholars throughout the world, (2) offers a structured interpretation of the central elements in his theology, and (3) contains his definitive reply to each and all of the interpreters and critics. One is grateful that another of the giants of the era—in addition to Paul Tillich, Reinhold Niebuhr, Emil Brunner, and Henry Nelson Wieman[1]—is alive, able, and willing to participate vigorously in this kind of stern analysis.

---

[1] An examination of Anders Nygren's philosophy and theology is nearing completion.

It may be of service at this point to ask, in view of Bultmann's role in the whole pattern of contemporary theology and philosophy of religion, in what central and special ways his thought expresses the deeper concerns of our time. Although I realize that other writers might identify different issues from the ones I have chosen or give them differing relative weight, I suggest the following.

Perhaps more than any other contemporary theologian save Tillich and Nygren, Bultmann makes the question of methodology central. Preoccupation with method or way marks all modern thought. For example, existentialism and conceptual analysis, two characteristic and much debated contemporary movements, are *ways* of doing philosophy and theology; they are not sets of doctrines in the manner of previous schools of thought. Indeed what puzzles us about these and other contemporary "ways"—and to some students of history has disturbing significance—is that each of them engages the effort of widely different kinds of thinkers who hold often flatly contradictory positions. Thus, logical empiricism and language analysis have their adherents in almost every stance from radical agnosticism to neo-Thomism. Existentialism, in turn, far from supplying a neat set of answers, offers the conflicting proposals of a Sartre and a Camus on the one hand, and a Bultmann and a Buber on the other.

This characteristic of methodology holds not only for the philosophico-theological scene in general, but applies with special significance to the thought of Rudolf Bultmann. In the central claim that a new *way* must be discovered for interpreting the Bible and communicating its message to contemporary man, namely, that of demythologizing and existential interpretation, two now clearly defined points of view have developed. Method is at issue in both. One group attacks Bultmann's existential method under the banner, "save the kerygma," accusing him of *abandoning* the once-for-all-ness character of the Christ event. Spokesmen for this view hold that Bultmann has carried the line of *liberal* theology too far. On the other hand, there are those who feel that Bultmann has not carried out his method of demythologizing to its logical conclusion. Bultmann, they say, has demythologized miracles, resurrection, eschatology, and the like, but he stops short at the kerygma. They question the combination, in Bultmann's thought, of the kerygmatic element and the principle of demythologizing. John Macquarrie has properly identified the issue: the question at stake is not *whether* demythologizing and existential interpretation are valid and fruitful methods, but what the scope of the method should be. He has described these two points of view, designated above, as the right and the left wing. Macquarrie's cogent criticism of the left-wing tendency to lose the kerygma and to merge theology with a straight philosophy of existence, alleging that existence itself affords a kind of grace, has drawn him into a debate with Schubert Ogden, who feels that Macquarrie has misunderstood the issue.[2] Whether Macquarrie is in error, as Ogden claims, remains in part for Bultmann and contemporary scholars to debate.

Involved in this larger issue of the scope of demythologizing is a more restricted although crucial problem: it is often alleged that Bultmann does not properly describe the nature and role of God. This claim must be distinguished from the question as to whether his analysis of man's nature and destiny is correct. Still further: Is Bultmann's interpretation of man also at fault precisely because all his doctrines about God and God's activity are mutually involved with doctrines about man, his nature and destiny? Here is an area in which the problem of methodology is determinative.

Other related aspects of methodology could be explored, for instance whether Bultmann does arbitrarily or on rational grounds cut short his existential interpretation at two crucial points: (1) grace—or God's saving (acts)—and (2) the unique historical revelation of Jesus. These and similar questions indicate the centrality of the issue of methodology. As we contemplate these questions, it appears that one of the next main theological advances should consist in exploring the relationship between philosophico-theological methodology on the one hand and its content on the other hand.

Nor do all these related questions exhaust the matter, for the whole rapidly growing analysis of religious language is involved the moment one asks whether the method of demythologizing serves to clarify religious language. Ronald Hepburn is the best-known but by no means only critic to allege that Bultmann's definition of myth, because it is too broad, includes almost every kind of "oblique

---

[2] The two main books embodying this controversy are John Macquarrie's *The Scope of Demythologizing* (New York: Harper & Row, 1960) and Schubert Ogden's *Christ Without Myth* (New York: Harper & Row, 1961).

language"[3] and so permits no clear distinction between myth and analogy. In the present volume, H. P. Owen introduces the related problem of the nature and role of symbols into this agitated debate on language by arguing that the difference between miracles, which are alleged facts, and the whole spatiotemporal view of transcendence, which is "a symbolization of fact," is not sufficiently treated by Bultmann. The latter has his defenders, of course, but that is irrelevant to the present point, which is that the methodology of demythologizing brings to the fore the contemporary analysis of the religious language of myth, symbol, analogy, legend, and a host of related terms.

A second major way in which Bultmann's thought concentrates on a central concern of our time is in his treatment of the relation between philosophy and theology. One of the main features of our era is the fresh and vigorous resurgence of philosophy of religion, and inevitably the traditional question arises of the proper relation between philosophy and theology. It is notorious that there are many theologians and religionists who are still strongly *pro* or *anti* concerning this relation of philosophy vis-à-vis theology. Bultmann's contemporaneity and wisdom are seen in part, at least, in the fact that he has gone beyond the antiphilosophy stage in two important respects. For one thing, he rejects the view of those who think that theology can, much less should, maintain a kind of virginal purity and remain uncontaminated by philosophical analysis. For another, he recognizes that philosophy is necessarily at work on theological questions precisely because theology is concerned with meaning and with the articulation of its beliefs. How could it escape linguistic and conceptual analysis? Still further, every theological system involves epistemological, metaphysical, and axiological presuppositions, or, to put it differently, is forced to make assertions which are the subject matter of these philosophical disciplines. The pertinent question, then, is not *whether* but *how* theological issues are related to philosophical concerns.

The excitement really begins when Bultmann, assuming that religious propositions (1) must employ *some* philosophical terminology,

---

[3] See: Flew and MacIntyre (eds.), *New Essays in Philosophical Theology* (London: SCM, 1955), chap. xii.

and (2) ought to be clear and meaningful rather than obscure and meaningless as they so often are, goes beyond this and claims that certain present-day philosophies, and Heidegger's existential analysis especially, offer "a profane philosophical presentation of the New Testament view of human existence."[4] Even more, he has been interpreted as saying that besides furnishing the formal terminology and analysis—the conspicuous example being the distinction between *existential,* or universally describable existence, and *existentiell,* or unique, engaged, decision-making existence—the Heideggerian type of analysis goes so far as to show man what his existence means. It appears to Bultmann to be the best available philosophical framework for the articulation of the kerygma.

This, of course, raises serious questions, and the answers are as yet far from clear. On the one hand, Bultmann wants to reject the criticism that by fitting the kerygma into the framework of Heideggerian existentialism he has distorted and dated it. Theologians have fallen into that kind of trap so often and disastrously that they should not do so again. On the other hand, Bultmann discerningly warns his critics that they may miss the point that philosophy can and has analyzed the nature and condition of man more meaningfully than has much contemporary theology.

Several essential issues are at stake here. I shall try to frame them or identify them without indicating their possible solutions, because that is the task, in part, of this book—in larger part, of the next stage of philosophy and theology.

If the kerygma is not independent of any and all world views, but must select from among those available in any age, how can theologians decide which is the most appropriate and serviceable in its capacity to interpret the kerygma?

What are the criteria to be employed in creating a new terminology —criteria that will safeguard the kerygma?

If the Heideggerian analysis accurately interprets the actual ways in which the decisions leading to authentic existence are made, does not the theologians' talk about the role of faith, revelation, and grace become unnecessary, irrelevant, obscurantist, or all three? Is not Bultmann's characteristically evangelical emphasis on faith, grace,

---

[4] See *Kerygma und Mythos,* I, 32.

and the revelation in Jesus Christ a kind of unnecessary encumbrance?

Granted that Jesus actualized an authentic self-understanding, is man capable of acting freely and responsibly today independent of that historic paradigm?

To pose these questions is not for a moment to seek to turn the theologian's face backward to inadequate and outmoded terminologies and philosophical frameworks. It is to pay the compliment of pointing to the wrestling of one theologian seeking to employ philosophical analyses in the service of rendering the essential New Testament message meaningful. John Macquarrie's judgment deserves repeating, namely, that Bultmann's recognition of the need for an adequate and philosophically sound framework is matched by his conviction that in the philosophy of human existence and the process of demythologizing all must be judged in the light of God's saving action, or, in a word, divine grace.

Another way in which Bultmann's theology embodies a leading contemporary concern is in its wrestling with the nature and role of history and of the religious documents in the Judaeo-Christian tradition. What he has persistently asked concerns the *role* of the historical and how the historical content can be made meaningful and thus useful to modern man. Bultmann is far from alone in this concern with the historical, but he surely has the distinction of being a controversial center of, and a primary contributor to, the effort to state in the language of today the meaning of the events—supremely, of God's action—of the Judaeo-Christian record. His espousal of the existentialist approach is in part an effort to concentrate on these elements in the Christian faith. He hopes thereby to rescue Christian theology, and Christian belief, from dependence upon the constantly changing results of historical criticism.

A fourth way that Bultmann's theology confronts us with the fundamental concerns of our age is in its attitude toward subjectivism versus objectivism and toward the appeal to irrationality.

No educated person today should be unaware of the fact that the claim of reason to be the final criterion or judge in interpreting man's thought and action is challenged as never before. Not only on Freudian grounds, but on existential grounds as well, appeals to subjectivism, to fideism, and finally to crass irrationalism are argued, ironically, with great persuasiveness. In Bultmann, as in a growing number of philosophers and theologians, one encounters a combined repudiation of irrationalistic existentialism and a revolt against subjectivism. In this stance we find a therapeutic factor. It goes to work on much contemporary theological writing that is either superficial or "sick" or both, in part by demanding that it stand up to analysis and to the criterion of coherence—I did not say of rationality. I make this distinction because a theology or philosophy may be free from inconsistencies, and thus "coherent," but nevertheless be antirational. Brand Blanshard's often repeated maxim is "Do not believe beyond the evidence." Now many theologians will quarrel with that, considering it too restrictive, and some will even glory in the intoxication not merely of paradox but paradox which is contradictoriness. Surely Bultmann is correct, and in a sound, evangelically catholic tradition, in saying: Believe only what is in harmony with, even though it goes beyond, but is not flatly contradictory to, the evidence. One of Bultmann's major but usually unremarked distinctions is that he consistently seeks to elicit responsible decision in the light of the evidence available. This demand he applies, moreover, to both the determination of the essence of the kerygma and the personal or existential decisions man makes concerning the meaning of that kerygma for his life.

What is at issue here is a related and characteristically fundamental and contemporary question, i.e., the criterion for determining revelation claims on the one hand, and consequently, the content of belief. This question is often not even faced today, or worse, it is answered in what sounds suspiciously like saying—in Karl Barth's case—that the kerygma is self-authenticating. This very suspicion correctly invites rejection by responsible minds in all fields, philosophers being merely a significant minority today. For it leads inevitably to a subjectivism which, in religious thought and life, makes sense and nonsense shout their claims with equal fanaticism and dogmatism.

Subjectivism—the view that any judgment which involves evaluation (as in ethics, aesthetics, and political philosophy) derives from and has its validity in the *attitude* of some conscious being or beings—stands in contrast to objectivism, which claims that the criteria for judging depend upon some condition, standard, or qualities which exist independent of the person making the judgment (for example, the characteristics, consequences, or qualities of an act or thing, or the will of God and the like). The tendency of subjectivism to dominate contemporary thought has led an astonishing number of people to assume that the corrective—in religious as well as in ethical and political philosophy—lies in some form of absolutism or authoritarianism. The claim that we can frame statements which always and everywhere and without exception are true was never more transparently false and practically more deplorable than it is today. When the propositions are about the essence of religion, that is, God, freedom, life after death, and the like, deep commitment must go hand in hand with criticism. For the twin of absolutism is dogmatism, i.e., the claim of an institution, book, or person to be infallible. Such absolutism Bultmann repudiates. Well he might. For the logical and psychological error which subjectivism entices one to commit is the claim that if one is not a dogmatist or absolutist, one must be a relativist. The relativist says, in effect, that of two or more contradictory assertions, one is as true or false as the other. The choice between them is a matter of taste, opinion, emotional reaction or the like. In theology and in ethics as in political philosophy, this is a disastrous maxim on which to operate. On these matters, as on so many others of crucial consequence—as those who ponder the following pages may discover—Bultmann speaks judiciously, because he assumes that each person must seek through his own responsible self-understanding to know what he believes, why he believes it, and hence why with tolerant determination he proceeds to practice his beliefs in open-minded commitment.

CHARLES W. KEGLEY

Wagner College
Staten Island, New York City

Autobiographical Reflections
of Rudolf Bultmann*

I, Rudolf Karl Bultmann, was born August 20, 1884, in Wiefelstede (at that time a village in the grand duchy of Oldenburg), the eldest son of the Evangelical-Lutheran pastor Arthur Bultmann and his wife Helene (nee Stern). My father came from a farming family near Bremen; his father was a missionary, born in Freetown, Sierra Leone, West Africa. My maternal grandfather was a pastor in Baden.

The first years of my life were spent in the country, and from 1892–1895 I attended the elementary school in Rastede, where my father had been transferred from Wiefelstede. From 1895–1903 I attended the humanistic *Gymnasium* in Oldenburg, where my father served as pastor of the Lamberti Church after 1897. I look back with pleasure on my school years both at the elementary school and the *Gymnasium*. What especially interested me, in addition to the study of religion, was the study of Greek and the history of German literature. I also went to concerts and the theater with great pleasure.

In 1903 I passed the final examination at the *Gymnasium* and began to study theology at Tübingen University. After three semesters I went to Berlin for two semesters, and finally to Marburg for two more. I attended lectures on philosophy and its history as well as those in theology. While in Berlin, I also enjoyed the theater,

---

* In its original form this brief autobiographical statement, which was graciously prepared by Professor Bultmann at our request, is entitled simply "Lebenslauf" and is signed and dated "Marburg, January 28, 1956." A concluding paragraph was added in 1965.

concerts, and museums. The theological teachers to whom I am particularly indebted were: in Tübingen, the church historian, Karl Müller; in Berlin, the Old Testament scholar, Hermann Gunkel, and the historian of dogma, Adolf Harnack; in Marburg, the New Testament scholars, Adolf Jülicher and Johannes Weiss, and the systematic theologian, Wilhelm Herrmann. Johannes Weiss encouraged me to prepare myself for the doctorate and to qualify as a lecturer in the field of New Testament.

Before I actually did so, however, I passed my first theological examination under the High Consistory in Oldenburg in 1907 and, largely for reasons of expediency, remained there for a year (1906–1907) as a teacher in the *Gymnasium*. When, in the autumn of 1907, I received a fellowship for study in Marburg (in the Seminarium Philippinum), it became possible for me to proceed with work toward my degree and my qualification as lecturer. In 1910 I received my degree (*Lic. theol.*) on the basis of a work, *Der Stil der paulinischen Predigt und kynischstoische Diatribe,* the theme for which had been proposed by Johannes Weiss. The subject of my qualification research, *Die Exegese des Theodor von Mopsuestia,* was proposed by Adolf Jülicher. Upon its completion in 1912, I qualified as a lecturer in the field of New Testament at Marburg and taught there as instructor until the autumn of 1916.

In 1908 my teacher, Johannes Weiss, was called to Heidelberg. With his successor, Wilhelm Heitmüller, I soon had a friendly association and I am greatly indebted to him. I spent a great deal of time during these years in the home of Martin Rade. I was a zealous reader of the journal *Die Christliche Welt,* of which he was the editor, and I was also a member of "The Association of the Friends of *Die Christliche Welt,*" regularly attending its annual meetings (as did my father as long as he lived). Here one met the theologians of free Protestantism and was brought into the discussions which stirred theology and the church in the years immediately before and after the First World War. A considerable part of the history which Johannes Rathje has described in his biography of Rade, *Die Welt des freien Protestantismus* (1952), I also personally experienced.

In the autumn of 1916 I was called to Breslau as assistant professor and was active there until 1920. It was there that I was married and that our first two daughters were born. The last years of the war, as well as the ones which immediately followed it were hard times with many privations, during which we saw much need and misery. In 1917 my youngest brother was killed in France. We also experienced much friendship and help. It was in Breslau that I wrote *Die Geschichte der synoptischen Tradition,* which was published in 1921.

In the autumn of 1920 I was called to Giessen as full professor to succeed Wilhelm Bousset. I look back on the time there with particular joy, inasmuch as the friendly exchange with colleagues—and not exclusively within the theological faculty—was especially lively. In fact, it was not easy to leave Giessen, but I was convinced that I could not refuse the call to Marburg, which is, so to speak, my academic home. In the autumn of 1921, therefore, I returned to Marburg as the successor of Wilhelm Heitmüller. I remained in Marburg, having declined a call to Leipzig in 1930, and became professor emeritus in the autumn of 1951.

The years at Marburg were troubled ones as a result of the political developments after 1933, and the outbreak of the Second World War in 1939. During the 1920's the external conditions of life were pleasant, and in 1924 our third daughter was born. The work with students, who were still motivated by the "Youth Movement" of the beginning of the century, was most gratifying. Then came the Hitler regime with its coercion and corrupting methods. Life in the university and in society at large was poisoned by mistrust and denunciations. Only within a small circle of like-minded acquaintances could one enjoy the open and invigorating exchange of the intellectual world. Many Jewish friends were forced to emigrate. During the war, in the course of which my only surviving brother died in a concentration camp, came the worst pressure from the Nazi terror. When the Allies (in Marburg, the Americans) finally marched in, I, along with many friends, greeted the end of Nazi rule as a liberation. In the years of the Hitler regime my work was influenced by the struggle within the church. I belonged to the Confessing Church from the time of its founding in 1934 and, with my friend Hans von Soden, endeavored to see that free scholarly work retained its proper place within it in spite of reactionary tendencies.

The years immediately after 1945 were not easy, although our external needs were considerably lightened by voluntary gifts from abroad, and we always think with gratitude on those—some known to us and some unknown—who sent them. It cannot be denied that at first many blunders on the part of the Occupation authorities made the achievement of a new community life and healthy political relations difficult. A confident cooperation with the American Occupation was, nevertheless, possible, inasmuch as there was never a lack of good will on both sides with which to overcome the difficulties. I will always be especially grateful to the American officials who worked for the reorganization of the University in Marburg. Normal conditions returned gradually, and while the present political situation presents new long-range problems, I will not touch upon them here, especially since I have never directly and actively participated in political affairs. I will simply survey my theological work during the Marburg years.

When I first came to Marburg I taught together with Adolf Jülicher and did so until his retirement in 1923. His successor was Hans von Soden, to whom, until his death in 1945, I was bound in personal friendship and with whom I constantly engaged in scholarly discussions. The same is true of my relationship with Gustav Hölscher, the Old Testament scholar, with whom I had already worked in Giessen and who came to Marburg in 1921 as the successor of Karl Budde. I was likewise close to Walter Baumgartner, who at that time was an instructor. The theological faculty in those days was by no means of one mind, and the various divisions within it, especially the tension between myself and Rudolf Otto (the successor of Wilhelm Herrmann), stirred even the students and led to lively discussions. These became especially animated whenever theologians from other universities, such as Karl Barth and Friedrich Gogarten, were invited to Marburg to lecture. These years were also enriched by the fact that the interchange between theologians and philosophers was very lively —as it had been earlier in the days of Wilhelm Herrmann, Hermann Cohen, and Paul Natorp. This was particularly the case when Martin Heidegger taught in Marburg from 1922 to 1928. I soon engaged in an exchange with him, as I had done previously with Nicolai Hartmann and was to do subsequently with Erich Frank and Julius Ebbinghaus. There was also fruitful work with the instructors in philosophy who were interested in theology—Hans-Georg Gadamer, Gerhard Krüger, and Karl Löwith—in which the New Testament

instructors Heinrich Schlier and Günther Bornkamm also participated. I must make special mention of my friendship with the
classical philologist Paul Friedländer, who was teaching at Marburg
at that time, and to whom I am much indebted. Later the exchange
with the classical scholars H. Dahlmann, Friedrich Müller, and Carl
Becker and the historian Friedrich Täger also became most fruitful
for my work.

The publications which grew out of my work in Marburg are listed
in the bibliography published in *Theologische Rundschau* (1954). In
the years before World War II there were several occasions for
traveling outside Germany. I was invited to give lectures in the
Scandinavian countries, in Holland, and in Switzerland. After the
war, in 1947, I was invited to Sweden for eight weeks by the Swedish
Institute for Cultural Exchange—I think back on this with particular
gratitude. I experienced much human goodness, enjoyed the exchange
with other scholars, and was able to acquaint myself with the
scholarly literature published in other countries from which we had
been cut off during the war. I am especially grateful for my friendship
with Anton Friedrichsen.

In 1951 at the invitation of Yale University I went to the United
States to give the Shaffer Lectures, subsequently published as *Jesus
Christ and Mythology*. Further invitations from various universities
and theological seminaries provided many additional opportunities to
meet American scholars. The exchange that was possible in the
course of this three-month visit was a significant experience. A few
years later, in 1955, I accepted the invitation from Edinburgh
University to give the Gifford Lectures, which later appeared in book
form under the title *The Presence of Eternity*. In 1959 I returned to
the United States at the invitation of Syracuse University to lecture in
the Department of Bible and Religion during the spring semester.
This again was an interesting and rewarding experience.

All of the scholarly exchanges and discussions, both in Marburg
and in other countries, helped me not only in my work with respect to
the New Testament but also in my theological thinking in general. I
have personally lived through an important about-face in the history
of theology and a similar one in the history of modern philosophy—
developments which are in a strange way parallel. In 1919 Karl
Barth's *Der Römerbrief* appeared, and from the beginning of the

1920's his influence on theological work steadily grew. In 1920 Gogarten delivered his lecture, "Die Krisis unserer Kultur," at the annual meeting of "The Friends of *Die Christliche Welt.*" Beginning in 1923 the journal *Zwischen den Zeiten,* edited by Barth, Gogarten, and Thurneysen, appeared as the organ of the new theological movement that soon came to be designated as "dialectical theology." I attempted to enter into discussion with this theology, first in the essay "Die liberale Theologie und die jüngste theologische Bewegung" (1924) and later in the lecture "Die Bedeutung der 'dialektischen Theologie' fur die neutestamentliche Wissenschaft" (1927). I also contributed to the journal *Zwischen den Zeiten.*

It seemed to me that in this new theological movement, as distinguished from the "liberal" theology out of which I had come, it was rightly recognized that the Christian faith is not a phenomenon of the history of religion, that it does not rest on a "religious a priori" (Troeltsch), and that therefore theology does not have to look upon Christian faith as a phenomenon of religious or cultural history. It seemed to me that, distinguished from such a view, the new theology correctly saw that Christian faith is the answer to the Word of the transcendent God which encounters man, and that theology has to deal with this Word and the man who has been encountered by it. This judgment, however, has never led me to a simple condemnation of "liberal" theology; on the contrary I have endeavored throughout my entire work to carry farther the tradition of historical-critical research as it was practiced in "liberal" theology and to make our recent theological knowledge the more fruitful as a result.

In doing so, the work of existential philosophy, which I came to know through my discussions with Martin Heidegger, became of decisive significance for me. I found here the concept through which it became possible to speak adequately of human existence and therefore also of the existence of the believer. In my efforts to make philosophy fruitful for theology, however, I have come more and more into opposition to Karl Barth. I remain grateful to him, however, for the decisive things I have learned from him. I do not believe that a final clarification of our relationship—to which Heinrich Ott has made a good beginning in his book *Geschichte und Heilsgeschichte in der Theologie Rudolf Bultmanns* (1955)—has as yet been reached. On the other hand, a unity in theological intentions between Gogarten and myself has become more and more apparent.

These autobiographical reflections would be incomplete without a reference to the concept of "demythologizing" which has become the focal point of many theological debates. I used this term for the first time in a lecture in 1941, which was later published in the volume *Offenbarung und Heilsgeschehen* (Revelation and the History of Salvation). The "demythologizing" debate is still going on. Since 1948 several volumes of commentaries have been published under the title *Kerygma and Myth,* edited by H. W. Bartsch. Volume VI, 1963, included several lectures from the Roman symposium "Problema della Demitizzazione" which took place in 1961 under the chairmanship of Enrico Castelli. Among the critics of my theology is the philosopher Karl Jaspers. Our exchange was published in 1954 under the title *Die Frage der Entmythologisierung* (The Question of Demythologizing). On the other side of the question, Friedrich Gogarten, a supporter of demythologizing, wrote *Entmythologisierung und Kirche* in 1953, published in English in 1955 as *Demythologizing and History.* In more recent years I have supported the views expressed by Bishop John A. T. Robinson in his book *Honest to God* (1962). The *Honest to God Debate* published in 1963 by Robinson and David L. Edwards includes an excerpt from my contribution to this discussion, written originally for the German weekly *Die Zeit.* Among present developments in theological scholarship, I am glad to observe the fruitful exchange between those who work in the area of historical interpretation of the New Testament and those in the field of systematic theology. In this connection I follow with special interest the work of American theologians, as represented by the contributions of James M. Robinson, Schubert Ogden, and Van Harvey.

R. B.

I

ESSAYS OF INTERPRETATION AND CRITICISM OF THE WORK OF RUDOLF BULTMANN

I

The Theology of Rudolf Bultmann*

GÜNTHER BORNKAMM

Heidelberg University
Heidelberg, Germany

For many years the theology of Rudolf Bultmann has engaged the minds of men throughout the world. In Germany, to be sure, especially in Protestant theological circles, one gathers that the initially lively debate, stimulated above all by Bultmann's programmatic essay *Neues Testament und Mythologie,* has abated. At any rate, the number of publications on this subject has decreased considerably— in itself not a bad thing. The problems raised by Bultmann have yielded place to other, apparently more important topics. His theology has continued to be a favorite subject for doctoral dissertations, but even these are not as numerous as in earlier decades. Not a few people have come to the conclusion that these problems and their solutions are the internal concern of the so-called "Bultmann school," and meanwhile there has developed an increasingly firm front against this school in official church circles. But no matter how much one might welcome the end of the excited current debate with its profusion of inept comments, it would be highly disastrous if the problems this position poses for theology were laid aside *ab acta* and considered settled.

Fortunately a different picture is presented by the way the debate is

---

* Translated by Arne Unhjem.

going in non-German and non-Protestant circles—especially within
Roman Catholicism, but also in philosophical literature. As the many
essays and monographs from widely different parts of the world
show, the discussion there is in full swing and has produced results
that may well put Protestant German theology to shame. It has
already become evident that we are here confronted with problems
that are not at all peculiar to Bultmann and his disciples.

I

The historical roots of Bultmann's theology can be found in two
movements, both of which have been highly significant down to the
present time. The first of these is the historical-critical theology
whose leader was Bultmann's own teacher. Bultmann has carried on
the tradition and task of this theology in a number of scholarly
studies, especially on the Synoptics, John, and Paul, in such comprehensive works as his *Theologie des Neuen Testamentes, Das Urchristentum im Rahmen der antiken Religionen,* and many others. This
work has been done with such distinction that even his opponents
count his books among the standard writings in the field.

But if Bultmann has earned a solid reputation for himself in the
field of New Testament scholarship, he differs nevertheless from his
colleagues in the radical questions he asks concerning the meaning,
foundation, and consequences of the historical method. Since 1920
Bultmann has asked such questions in a new and comprehensive
manner under the influence of so-called dialectic theology, especially
with Karl Barth and Friedrich Gogarten. This is the other root of the
wider theological position that Bultmann has maintained and constantly elaborated ever since.

These sources of Bultmann's theology ought not to be forgotten.
They made him quite consistently take the way followed by the
Confessional Church during the Third Reich, and remained decisive
for him even though his initial partnership with Karl Barth came to a
painful end and the two became hopelessly divided in their understanding of theology. It would be wrong to say that a temporary
misunderstanding led Bultmann at one time to join dialectic theologians in a common front against so-called liberal theology.   The
fundamental principles of dialectic theology have never lost their

validity for Bultmann and have been further developed in his theological work even though this work has frequently been misunderstood to mean the abandonment of these principles.

Among these principles is the insight of a qualitative difference between God and the world, between God and man—which means that the human being is radically lost. There is also a recognition of the paradoxical character of a revelation that can never be authenticated in the historical-empirical realm but can only be encountered in the Word event and grasped in faith.[1] Consonant with these principles is Bultmann's understanding of faith as an obedient decision, bereft of all worldly assurance, concerned only with the Word and its liberating message to man about God's saving act in Christ. For Bultmann these insights include, now as formerly, the defense against the Catholic doctrine of *analogia entis* and the Reformation understanding of *sola gratia, sola fide*.

This, however, merely gives a preliminary outline of the themes and problems to which Bultmann's own theological work has been devoted. We must now give closer attention to the path he has followed in seeking clarification of these problems. As is well known, this path took him in a direction quite different from that followed by Karl Barth, and it has evoked sharp criticism from Barth and others. Here we shall limit ourselves for the present to a primary set of questions for which Bultmann sought new answers, namely, the problem of history and the possibility of historical understanding in general.

II

The question posed here is a universal one and not unique to theology. For all the virtuosity of liberal theology since Ferdinand Christian Baur, the question had largely eluded this theology; and where it was really an object of philosophical and theological thought, as in Ernst Troeltsch, it had become involved in positivistic relativism.

This question became a central theme in all of Bultmann's work, as

---

[1] It hardly needs to be pointed out that in recognizing this Bultmann has been deeply influenced by Kierkegaard, who also influenced him in his further development of this central idea.

is shown by the many scattered or connected statements in which he gives an account of his understanding of history and challenges others to render a similar account. The basic idea of his concept of history was articulated in his *Jesus* of 1926, and since that time has been elaborated and defended in a great number of published works. For Bultmann the character of history is such that it cannot be regarded as an empirical object. If history is treated as an empirical object there are doubtless facts and events that can be established and chronologically arranged; but history becomes, so to speak, a mass of news items that reveals nothing new. From this perspective and in this kind of inquiry the historian necessarily brings with him a set of categories and coordinates that becomes the basis for his judgments —such as when he makes a value distinction between "historical" and "suprahistorical" data. In Bultmann's view the unique meaning of history cannot be understood so long as the historian remains just an observer, for he who endeavors to understand history is himself in the nature of an historical being and can succeed in understanding history only as he responds to the challenge of history. This means that the possibilities pertaining to the human understanding of existence become internalized, challenging the interpreter himself to make decisions. In fundamental contrast to the neutral view of history where the historian believes himself to follow strictly "objective" procedures in which he plays no subjective part, Bultmann holds that a truly proper relation to history can only be in the form of a dialogue with history. In other words, the encounter with history must be in the form of word and response, challenge and decision. The traditional subject-object scheme, adopted uncritically from the natural sciences and applied to the science of history, turns out to be highly deceptive and disastrous, "for the facts of the past become historical phenomena only as they become meaningful to a subject who stands within history and participates in it, i.e., as they speak—which they can do only to a subject who understands them."[2]

For Bultmann the problem of history thus leads necessarily to the problem of man and can be clarified only from this vantage point. This by no means implies that history—or, more concretely, the texts that bear witness to history—imposes an existential model and that it

---

[2] *Glauben und Verstehen*, II (1952), 229.

must be judged in terms of this model. This would mean the surrender of history to subjectivism. The concern here is to discover the condition under which any historical understanding is possible. According to Bultmann this condition consists in the bearing of the interpreter's life on the matter in the text that is under discussion or subject to investigation.[3] This essential bearing of life Bultmann calls "preunderstanding," and without it no understanding is possible. Only the bearing of life on relevant matters that makes itself felt in preunderstanding can establish communication between the text and the interpreter and make possible a proper examination of the text, allowing the interpreter to ask himself about the text and to revise it on the basis of his own self-understanding.

There could thus be no cruder misunderstanding of Bultmann's concept of preunderstanding than to accuse him—as has unfortunately very often happened—of equating "preunderstanding" with "prejudgment." Prejudgment not only forces all understanding of history into a Procrustean bed, but makes the very encounter with history impossible from the outset, and Bultmann has often been reproached for doing this.[4] It is hardly necessary to call attention to the theological confusion that such a misunderstanding inspires in the view of man's relation to revelation, the sovereign authority of which Bultmann has ostensibly destroyed. In defense against this criticism, however, one need only point out that it ignores the question of what revelation means and always assumes that a blanket answer has been given, whereas Bultmann's hermeneutical reflections are aimed directly at this question and seek to make an answer to it possible.

The preunderstanding which man brings with him necessarily and unavoidably to his encounter with history does not need to be explicit. It is *de facto* inherent in man, inasmuch as he is human and not just a thing or an animal. Man is not just something that happens in the world and in time, but is always aware of himself and concerned about himself. This is what constitutes his unique relationship to his world and to time—the past, the future, and the present. This is what makes his memory possible and makes him look

---

[3] *Ibid.*, p. 217.

[4] For a refutation of this criticism see the able and clear discussion by H. Ott, *Geschichte und Heilsgeschichte in der Theologie R. Bultmanns* (1955), pp. 60 ff.

hopefully to the future. But this is also what makes him feel guilty and aware of the voice of his conscience. All this is quite independent of whether he thinks about it and is able to conceptualize his understanding of himself.

A conceptual explication of his understanding of existence nevertheless helps the interpreter to examine history properly and critically. This is the reason why Bultmann has made Martin Heidegger's philosophical analysis of existence his own and, as his book *Geschichte und Eschatologie* shows especially, has made the examination of theories pertaining to the philosophy of history part of his work. Following Heidegger, he gives the name of *existential interpretation* to the kind of interpretation which, according to the essential nature of history, inquires about the possibilities for the understanding of human nature that are disclosed and encountered in history. In this view, existence is understood strictly as the specifically human mode of being which, as has already been indicated, is not simply something that appears in nature, that can be objectively perceived and is subsumed under the law of causality. Rather, the nature of man consists in the fact that, regardless of how clearly or dimly he knows himself, he has had to take charge of his own being and thus is responsible for himself.[5] For this very reason the physical concept of time is not, according to Bultmann, adequate for the nature of history as "the field of human decisions."[6]

Seen in relation to this fundamental hermeneutical insight, Bultmann's much debated program of *demythologization* of the New Testament message also becomes understandable. As Bultmann himself has stressed, the demand for demythologization as such is nothing new. It has long been recognized as proper and necessary and has been practiced, albeit without adequate methodological or hermeneutical consideration and without the required consistency. Bultmann can speak of a *testimonium paupertatis* in that he has had to call attention to this unsolved problem and ask how the demand it entails can be properly met.[7] Furthermore, the programmatic term "demythologization" designates a general task rather than a specifi-

---

[5] Cf. R. Bultmann, *Zum Problem der Entmythologisierung,* in *Il Problema della Demitizzazione* (Rome: Istituto di Studi), Filosofici (1961), pp. 19 ff.

[6] *Ibid.,* p. 20.

[7] "Neues Testament und Mythologie," in *Kerygma und Mythos,* §14, p. 23.

cally theological assignment, no matter how urgently it may confront the theologian. In reality the New Testament becomes part of this task only because it involves a mode of thinking that has become impossible for contemporary man. This is a mode of thinking in which divine and human elements, otherworldly and mundane components, as well as nature and man, are as yet completely undifferentiated; hence it can speak about God and man only mythologically, i.e., in terms of mundane, objectifying representations. An interpretation in which these representations and modes of thinking tend to encumber the myth fails to appreciate the true nature of the myth, for in spite of its mundane representations the myth cannot really be understood in terms of these at all but only in terms of what transcends the world and nature. According to Bultmann, the myth demands and justifies an interpretation that examines it in terms of the human self-understanding to which it gives expression. In this sense the demand for demythologization and the hermeneutical principle of existential interpretation are inseparable for Bultmann.

In the meantime the concept of the myth presupposed by Bultmann's thesis has itself let loose a voluminous debate—except where its application to New Testament statements has been rejected outright, mostly with purely Biblicistic arguments. Many of Bultmann's critics have not rejected the myth concept altogether, but they have recognized it only where it does not touch directly upon statements that pertain to salvation, although the scope of the latter has been subject to highly varied definition. Still others have questioned Bultmann's view that the myth is an unsuitable mode of expression that tends to conceal its purpose. They have maintained that no religious language can do without the myth. Particularly instructive is the view, frequently encountered in Catholic theology especially, which grants that the myth has a preliminary, figurative significance for revelation and must be retained, in the sense that revelation has realized and fulfilled what the myth has anticipated and projected. This is a conception that clearly reflects the Scholastic view of the relation between a natural and a supernatural knowledge of God.

Bultmann himself has remained aloof and critical toward all these trains of thought and has not found it necessary to modify or adapt his concept of the myth to suit his critics. Indeed he does not assign the importance to the question that many others do. The reason for his position here is clear: these arguments, which admittedly have a long and venerable history,[8] only tend to obscure the contemporary task of critical, demythologizing interpretation, even though the arguments are for the most part manifest—albeit not fully explicit and not hermeneutically adequate—attempts to solve the problem of demythologization. The soundness of this opinion can hardly be questioned. All discussion of myths does in fact assume a certain distance separating the contemporary interpreter from mythological man, even when the interpreter emphatically defends mythical representations and modes of thinking. This distance, which no amount of reflection can eliminate (reflection only makes it more obvious!), cannot be ignored or obscured. According to Bultmann, this distance makes possible and demands an existential interpretation of the myth rather than the elimination of the myth.[9]

III

His strict commitment to the basic hermeneutical insight that the primary bearing of the interpreter's life on the meaning conveyed by the text is the condition for all understanding, and hence within the context of existential interpretation, prevents Bultmann from making direct use of the statements about God, the world, Christ, and man contained in the objectified language of the New Testament in his exegesis of the New Testament texts. Rather, he asks primarily about the possibilities for human self-understanding that find expression in these texts. Just how is man understood in the New Testament writings?

Bultmann finds this question answered most clearly in Paul and John, and the answer has two parts. The human being appears here

---

[8] Cf. Plato's thoughts on the relationship between *mythos* and *logos;* see also G. Krüger, *Einsicht und Leidenschaft* (1939), pp. 29 ff., 56 ff. There is also Goethe's concept of the symbol. He saw the relationship between appearance, idea, and image in the following way: "The idea always remains infinitely effective and inapproachable in the image, present in all language yet itself ineffable" (*Maximen und Reflexionen*).

[9] Since the myth concept is no longer dealt with in the more recent Bible scholarship in terms of a mere rationalistic devaluation, it cannot really be understood in any other way; cf. C. Hartlich and W. Sachs, *Der Ursprung des Mythesbegriffs in der modernen Bibelwissenschaft* (1952).

as one who has forfeited his unique role and is radically lost in respect to God. He has become the slave of sin, sorrow, self-glorification, anxiety, the world, and death. In Pauline language, he has become carnal. But in contrast to this unredeemed man, the believer is one who has surrendered himself, who has renounced all security and has abandoned all his resources. Trusting in the grace of God alone, he exists in critical detachment from the world, and in this way he attains to his uniqueness, i.e., his real role. His formerly corrupted existence has become open to the future.

Bultmann uses a rather mystical-sounding term, "desecularization," to designate such an existence. But in reality he means nothing more than what the New Testament itself describes as eschatological existence, i.e., an existence that has been freed from the dead freight of representations. Faith does not achieve this existence through an adventitious or ascetic flight from the world, but by remaining *in* the world and by being called to the position of *os me* (I Cor. 7:29 ff.). All of these statements by Bultmann become understandable only when, and to the degree that, the existence of man himself is understood historically—in other words, when man is not simply conceived as something that just is, but is seen as someone whose existence is determined by possibilities that he can either grasp or fail to realize. This concept of man implies that he is by nature always involved in decisions and always summoned to make choices. Without this insight—to which a proper analysis of human existence will lead soon enough—all theological discussion of sin and redemption is meaningless, according to Bultmann.

The New Testament message does indeed maintain that in his state of radical perdition man himself is unable to realize his true destiny even though he never ceases to hear its call. This is the main concern of the Pauline teaching about the law and the failure of Jewish righteousness by law. This is the only perspective from which the *skandalon* of the message of salvation can be understood, and it is also the position to which contemporary man truly belongs. The character of the *skandalon* is not that it demands a *sacrificium intellectus* from the hearer, but solely that it asks the hearer to believe that God *has* done in Christ what man himself has been unable to accomplish. This, and nothing else, is the saving event proclaimed by the New Testament.

Faith is the obedient reception of this message. Faith signifies an
acceptance of the once-for-all (*ephapax*) character of God's saving
act in Christ. The eschatological meaning of *ephapax* is misunderstood if one attempts to ascertain and account for it as an
ordinary historical fact somewhat analogous to the *res gestae Au-
gusti*. This traditional error, whose disastrous effects are still felt,
mistakenly interprets the *ephapax* as a saving event that engages man
existentially in the Word that is preached again and again. The saving
event and the kerygma therefore are inseparable: not as if the
kerygma were to replace the saving event (this is the constantly
repeated objection of the "fact-of-salvation theology" to the so-called
"kerygma theology"), nor as if the kerygma were merely a consequent report on the saving event applied by the hearer. Both of these
mistakes are avoided in Bultmann's assertion that the Now of the
saving event is concurrent with the Now of preaching and faith.[10]

Bultmann's critical interpretation, in which he demythologizes the
objectifications of both the New Testament and church doctrine (the
mythological statements of apocalyptic or Gnostic origin, the miracle
stories of the New Testament, the representations of an earthly-
futuristic eschatology, etc.), is therefore obviously an attempt to
bring to bear universally the Reformation principle of *pro me*. This is
the meaning of his thesis: "Radical demythologization is a parallel to
the Pauline and Lutheran doctrine of justification without the works
of the law, through faith alone. Or rather: demythologization is the
consistent application of this doctrine to the realm of cognition. Just
like the doctrine of justification, demythologization destroys every
specious human certainty and every specious demand for certainty,
be this certainty based on man's good works or on his cognitive
ability."[11] It is significant that Catholic critics of Bultmann have,
obviously without condoning it, fully recognized this Reformation
element in him and have acknowledged him as the legitimate custodian
of the Lutheran heritage.[12]

---

[10] Compare here the excellent book by J. Körner, *Eschatologie und
Geschichte* (1957).

[11] This is the final position taken by Bultmann in *Kerygma und Mythos*,
II, 207.

[12] The same conclusion has been reached, and just as critically, by Karl
Barth in *R. Bultmann: ein Versuch ihn zu verstehen* (1952), pp. 46 ff., 12 ff.

I V

It has not yet been possible to survey the infinitely extended debate on Bultmann's theology, especially since it is widely scattered in monographs and essays on New Testament theology, systematic and practical theology, and in general works on religion and philosophy—written in many different languages. In itself this is encouraging, for it disposes of the impression that one is dealing here with a special "Bultmann problem." For this reason it is also impossible at present to have a complete bibliography. The fact is that Bultmann's theology does not deal only with particular problems in the traditional manner —problems that can be described and delimited in terms of the conventional definitions of historical theology or the usual *loci* of dogmatics—but is concerned with more fundamental questions, the answers to which have made their impact felt in many different directions. For this reason the discussion of Bultmann's position has broken up into a great number of special investigations, all seeking to clarify some aspect of his theology, but dealing with such different topics as his hermeneutics, his relation to philosophy, his understanding of history, his concepts of revelation, salvation, faith, and a number of other subjects. After the initial debate, which was stormy and downright tumultuous at times, considerable depth and clarity in the understanding of Bultmann were achieved. But unfortunately the results of this work were largely inaccessible to the people most seriously affected by them, i.e., the contemporary preachers of the Christian message, and so the issues have been the special concern of scholars and theological "schools."

It appears to me, however, that a complete review of all the topics dealt with in this discussion is hardly necessary here. Furthermore, such a review is bound to be quite repetitious, for the literature shows quite clearly that there are some fundamental questions that turn up again and again. For this reason I will limit myself to a brief account of certain characteristic critical objections to Bultmann's theology, particularly in regard to his program of demythologization and his insistence on an existential interpretation. They are important, even though they vary greatly in their conceptual clarity and the scholarly level on which they have been conducted. These more important, more or less frequently recurring criticisms can, it seems to me, be summarized somewhat as follows.

(1) Bultmann's assertion that all understanding is contingent on a preunderstanding, and that all genuine interpretation must be guided by the question about what understanding of existence is disclosed and expressed in history and its texts, is from the outset a violation of the Biblical texts. It is maintained that he makes the preunderstanding and self-understanding of the interpreter into a norm and a canon and that the text is thus under censorship in regard to what it may or may not say as the Word of God—in other words, the text has had its mouth stopped—even before it is read. Such an erroneous hermeneutics, deadly to all understanding and making *a priori* impossible the dialogue with history that Bultmann calls for, is completely disastrous for the understanding of Biblical texts that speak in a strange language and must be so understood, since they challenge radically all human self-understanding. Karl Barth, who has voiced this criticism of Bultmann with particular sharpness on many occasions, has vented his whole wrath in the charge that Bultmann makes man's understanding of his existence into a "catalyst"[13] for Biblical statements and engages in "disaster tactics"[14] in his criticism of the Biblical texts. He furiously accuses Bultmann of assuming a "pre-Copernican"[15] position in his hermeneutics and of having returned to that from which dialetic theology broke away. Bultmann, he claims, has undone the protest that this new theological movement raised against every philosophical stranglehold on the Word of God and has thus surrendered the only legitimate kind of "demythologization," namely, the destruction of "the myth of the man who takes himself as the measure of his understanding of himself and everything else."[16]

(2) This criticism of Barth's, in which he is only the spokesman for many others who are not for the most part so well armed with eristic skills, is directed toward a great many particular problems. The persistent idea of his criticism is nevertheless the same: the authoritative primacy of revelation in regard to all preaching, faith, and understanding has been surrendered; theology has been swal-

---

13 *Ibid.*, pp. 49 f.
14 *Kirchliche Dogmatik*, Vol. III, §2, p. 536.
15 *R. Bultmann*, p. 53.
16 *Ibid.*, p. 52.

lowed up by an anthropology that is not based on revelation; theology has thus lost its trinitarian element, Christology is completely absorbed by soteriology, kerygma and faith are no longer subsumed under the saving event but take on constitutive meaning for the saving event; one can no longer ask in a fundamental sense what God and Christ are in themselves, but only about their significance from the all-pervasive "for-us" perspective. Thus all natural and historical dimensions are lost from Bultmann's theology.

The misunderstandings that are evident in this criticism of Bultmann have not been sufficiently broached in the discussion to date. Bultmann has rightly defended himself against these charges, and has defended and explained the intent of "existential interpretation" in a number of statements. He has no desire to elevate the modern interpreter's understanding of existence to the role of critical norm and thus to assign validity to the text only to the extent that it confirms his understanding. He has often and emphatically stressed "the element of strangeness in the Christian message," the problem of "contact and contradiction," the "offense" [17] of a gospel that radically denies man's own ability to realize his "true role" and refers him to a saving act of God in Christ that is accomplished apart from him and encountered in an historical event.

However, he denies just as emphatically that it is possible to encounter the saving event as a saving event—to hear the message and in the obedience of faith surrender all self-assertion before God—unless man faces the question concerning himself earnestly and clearly. So long as this hermeneutical principle is rejected, man may hear what is said a thousand times, may possibly accept what is presented in objectified representations through a *sacrificium intellectus,* or—as is more likely—may reject it, without seeing himself in the least challenged or affected by it. The paradox of the Word that becomes flesh in the sense of John 1:14, the scandal of the Pauline message of the Cross, have no chance at all, for they remain sheer absurdities to the hearer. Bultmann has never tired of bringing this truth to bear wherever it applies.

And just as he has had to defend himself against his critics on the "right," he has also joined battle against his opponents on the "left,"

---

[17] *Glauben und Verstehen,* II (1952), 117 ff.; III (1960), 197 ff.

notably Karl Jaspers and his disciple, F. Buri—as Barth himself has had to acknowledge. This left flank has charged that Bultmann's insistence on a saving event encountered in history is a form of orthodoxy and, as in the case of Buri, has demanded that the demythologization program be carried out radically and consistently in the direction of a dekerygmatization. Karl Barth's statement, which on the one hand praises Bultmann for his firm stand against his opponents on the left, but on the other hand is unwilling to recognize that Bultmann's stand here is grounded on his principles, shows clearly that Barth has not understood what for Bultmann is in fact an essential distinction between a potentiality for genuine existence that is not entirely excluded from human understanding, and the actualization of this existence.[18] For Bultmann this distinction follows necessarily both from the insight—learned in his historical studies of the New Testament—regarding the difference between Biblical and contemporary modes of representation and thinking, and from the analysis of understanding and faith in systematic theology.

There is really more than misunderstanding involved here. There are factual disagreements as well, for Bultmann cannot accept any "objective" revelatory realm of being that can be recognized, established, and understood in and by itself prior to its relation to faith. In this he claims, appealing to the Reformers as well as to W. Hermann, that he is faithful to the basic position that "we can say nothing about what God is in himself, but only what he does for us."[19] To speak about the acts of God is, therefore, according to Bultmann, to "speak of my existence."[20] But this in no way implies that for him revelation becomes completely subjective. If this were so, he could not insist so stubbornly that faith is not a subjective experience but obedience to the proclaimed Word, and is thus always faith *in* something. If this appears to make him agree with his dialectic opponents, there is yet a profound difference, for this position implies for Bultmann a surrender of the ontology taken over from the Greeks and the Scholastics and hence the surrender of the conventional subject-object

---

[18] This is the reason for Barth's reduction of the question concerning correct "translation" into the trivial form: "How shall I say it to my children?" (*R. Bultmann*, pp. 9 f.), and his mockery of Bultmann's conceptual distinction between "existential" and "existentialist" (*ibid.*, p. 35).

[19] *Kerygma und Mythos,* II (1954), 185.

[20] *Ibid.*, p. 196.

scheme in all thinking and speaking that deals with Biblical revelation.

The question of a "Copernican reversal" must in this case refer to
the Reformation understanding of theology and must thus be returned
to Bultmann's opponents. How little this question has made itself felt
among Bultmann's Protestant critics is unfortunately more than
evident. In a more or less summary fashion they talk, troubled neither
by history nor by Reformation insights, about revelation as a fixed
value and about the establishment of a formal concept of Scriptures
and canon. There is no room left for Luther's free evaluation of the
Old and New Testament writings. Furthermore, preaching is understood once more as communication and application of facts, and faith
is understood as the consequent reception of these facts. Bultmann
often quotes a statement from Melanchthon's first *Loci,* a well-known
statement that undoubtedly reflects the original spirit of the Reformation: *Hoc est Christum cognoscere, beneficia eius cognoscere, non,
quod isti* (*sc. scholastici theologistae*) *docent, eius natura, modos
incarnationis contueri.* It is symptomatic that this statement, as well
as the Reformation principle *pro me, pro nobis,* are not often quoted
for their own sake, but usually as illustrations of dangerous subjectivism and not with approval of the basic theological meaning that is
here conveyed. Hand in hand with this is the fact that the Reformers'
simul peccator et iustus is still retained more or less as a basic
Reformation principle but that hardly a question is asked concerning
the implications of this principle for theological cognition.

It is quite significant that in their argumentations Catholic and
Protestant opponents of Bultmann have come surprisingly close to
each other. Catholic critics differ from their Protestant cohorts,
however, in one respect: they seem to be far better equipped by their
own tradition to analyze the relation between theology and philosophy, and they are surprisingly ready and able to understand Bultmann's theological concern and to recognize that he has consistently
carried on the Reformation heritage, even though from the Catholic
viewpoint he has carried this *ad absurdum.* This is the reason for
their insistence that one must first accept a metaphysical order of
being that encompasses both nature and supernature, both the creative and the redemptive orders. Only within such a metaphysics and
ontology, they insist, can any talk of God and man, of revelation and

faith, be meaningful. It is not strange that they welcome—as a sound reaction, no longer compatible with the unique principles of Protestantism—both the Barthian doctrine in *Kirchliche Dogmatik* of an *analogia fidei* (which they regard as a step on the way back to *analogia entis*) and the views of others who recognize the constitutive significance of church tradition for the exegesis of the Scriptures.[21]

Bultmann has, especially in his reply to Marlé, admitted the legitimacy of wanting to involve both the *imago Dei* character of man that has not been lost and the continuity of creation and redemption. But he has rejected the demand that one must have recourse to an "order of reality" (*ordre de réalité, ordre ontologique*) "on the basis of which . . . the dialectic interplay of sin and grace comes to an end."[22] The continuity of creation and redemption, and thus the *imago Dei* being of man, are involved, he suggests, in the fact that the redemption of man leads to his true role, the latter possibility having never been denied man altogether, no matter how clearly or consciously he has been aware of it. Were it not for this fact, there could be no hearing and no understanding of the message. This is why Bultmann can say that "man in his existence, in his total being, is the point of contact."[23] Yet he associates with this the other proposition, namely, that God's action stands in opposition even to this man considered in terms of his highest possibility, because man is altogether a sinner. Thus it is also true for Bultmann that "the sin of man is the point of contact for the contradicting Word of grace."[24] This means, however, that one can speak of creation, redemption, and the image of God only in terms of the dialectical *simul peccator et iustus* of Paul and the Reformation, and not in the sense of a given and permanently accessible ontology that delimits sin.

Protestant theology is thus, now as formerly, confronted with important questions. The aim here is not to engage in hasty and mutual accusations of heresy in which the charge of a return to Catholic theology flies back and forth with unfortunate regularity.

---

[21] R. Marlé in the German edition of *Bultmann et l'interprétation du Nouveau Testament* (Paris, 1956), p. 34, n. 106; cf. Bultmann, *Glauben und Verstehen*, II, 102 ff.

[22] Marlé, *op. cit.*, pp. 138 f.

[23] *Glauben und Verstehen*, II, 120.

[24] *Ibid.*, III, 186.

The question is, rather, how Protestant theology can manage to escape the demand, which from the Catholic viewpoint is a legitimate one, that it return to a metaphysics of being if it insists on making the aseity of God and a fixed revelation its objects and denies the constitutive relations of the saving event, the Word, and faith. To be sure, this development took place in the interest of preserving the inviolable given (*extra nos*) and once-for-all (*ephapax*) character of God's saving act in Christ, and to avoid a definition of faith as intentionality or, in other words, the notion of faith as an answer. But can and will this be achieved by separating the ground and content of faith and through surrendering the Reformation *punctum mathematicum* of revelation as the phenomenon of the Word and faith?

This should make it quite clear that the position of contemporary man in regard to the message of the New Testament, about which Bultmann inquires so energetically and about which he speaks in ways so shocking to many people, is of interest not only for the purposes of self-understanding and to account for the human being who is concerned about his intellectual integrity (although in itself this is no small matter). Rather, one is here confronted with a theological question of profound significance comparable to the questions with which the Reformers were faced. Far from setting aside the *skandalon* of the message, this question aims to confront the hearer with the message in all its offensiveness as a message of judgment and salvation; for this question arises from the fundamental insight that the Word of God cannot be received by man as he is in any preliminary fashion but only in the manner of one confronting a Word that has a work to do in him. This actually happens when, from the basis of a false understanding of revelation (false even if it is enunciated in Biblicistically traditional and dogmatically correct terms), man is forced to leap over his own shadow and is forced to surrender to this supposed "revelation" his world view and his self-understanding, as odds or as a bonus, so to speak, with a *sacrificium intellectus* to faith.

So long as this question is not really answered, one cannot dismiss as superfluous Bultmann's *ceterum censeo,* even though it is offensive to many and far too many people now believe they can leave it behind as something that has already been "settled." His questions will therefore continue to disturb and stimulate Protestant theology.

This includes also a broader, more insistent question which, it seems to me, Bultmann has not answered adequately thus far and may largely have avoided. This is the question of whether his Reformation theology, which no longer moves within traditional metaphysics and ontology and offers no specious securities, does indeed open up new dimensions and horizons in regard to the world, time, and history which have been preserved in the message of the primitive church and in the confession of faith and are waiting to be rediscovered.

The Meaning of Demythologization

EDWIN M. GOOD

Stanford University
Stanford, California

The most recent epoch of Protestant theology may profitably be described as a recovery of grace. Out of the uneasy coexistence of liberalism and fundamentalism—both progressively growing sterile—has appeared not a synthesis but a recovery, symbolized in the widely used but imprecise term "neo-orthodoxy." Whatever the term may mean, the movement has certainly meant a recovery of grace, and therefore of the gospel. Concurrently has come a return to Biblical theology. One need not detail the specifics of this return; they are there. And although we have by no means solved all the problems connected with it, we have at least taken them up, and that is something.

Grace, the gospel, and Biblical theology: there in a nutshell is the problem confronting contemporary Protestant theology, a problem that comes down finally to interpretation. For we stand on the Biblical witness; we proclaim the gospel; and we live by grace. But what are these? How shall they be interpreted? To these questions the present and following generations of theology will continue to address themselves in unmeasured and possibly immeasurable gratitude to Rudolf Bultmann. He, more than any other theologian of our era, has put the questions in the sharpest possible form and has sought to indicate directions for their answer. Perhaps the subject of this essay,

21

"demythologization," will be the "tag" by which generations of historians of theology in the future will remember Bultmann. If it becomes nothing but a tag, we will be back where we were before. If those future generations go on demythologizing—whatever they may call it—with the clarity and devotion of Bultmann, Christendom may retain the freshness of that faith by which we live.

What is demythologization? A brief definition is in order here, so that we may have a starting point. In its broadest sense, demythologization is the interpretation of the New Testament in terms that contemporary man can comprehend. In the more specific way that Bultmann means the term, it is a method of interpreting the mythological understanding of man held by the New Testament so that it becomes understandable to its contemporary hearer and compels him to make a decision for himself with regard to it.

Demythologization, then, is interpretation, reinterpretation if you like. We must therefore at the outset pay particular attention to the subject of hermeneutics.

THE PROBLEM OF HERMENEUTICS[1]

American theology has never gone in much for hermeneutics, either the word or the enterprise. It is our loss. For hermeneutics— the delineation of the principles of interpretation—is the effort to take the chaos out of the process of interpretation, to discipline it, and to send it out refreshed to do the job demanded of it. In a document like the New Testament, grammar of *koine* Greek is a necessity, historical knowledge is a requirement, acquaintance with the pervasive style and the pivotal words and concepts of the time is a prerequisite for interpretation.

But for a document like the New Testament, mere detached knowledge and the ability to parse a Greek verbal form are not enough. The New Testament itself insists clamorously on more. What more? To this question Bultmann has addressed himself in his essay

---

[1] See the essay of that title in Bultmann's *Essays, Philosophical and Theological* (New York: The Macmillan Company, 1955), pp. 234–61. The comprehension of this essay is, in my opinion, absolutely essential to understanding Bultmann.

on hermeneutics. Two things, he thinks, are necessary for an interpretation that is more than mere scholarly routine: *Vorverständnis* and an openness to the meaning of man. Having thus summarily reduced a long, complicated essay to two short phrases, we may try to do Bultmann better justice.

Vorverständnis is probably untranslatable, but the English phrase "prior understanding" is as good a place as any from which to start.

"A comprehension—an interpretation—is, it follows, *constantly orientated to a particular formulation of a question, a particular 'objective.'* But included in this, therefore, is the fact that it is never without its own presuppositions; or, to put it more precisely, that it is *governed always by a prior understanding of the subject,* in accordance with which it investigates the text. The formulation of a question, and an interpretation, is possible at all only on the basis of such a prior understanding."[2]

What the "subject" is we will consider again. We may note here that what is involved is emphatically not a "presuppositionless exegesis."[3] Exegesis refuses presuppositions only with regard to its conclusion; the exegete must not decide beforehand what the meaning of the text is. But he does stand before the text with a question formulated out of his own experience and history, a question to which the text may or may not have an answer. Perhaps Bultmann does not reckon sufficiently with the fact that the Bible is sometimes forced to show us not only the answer but also the right question.[4] At the same time, although the question may be wrong, the inquiry is not, and the inquiry itself is the main question. But we have a question only because we have a "prior understanding," a prior relationship in life to the subject. We approach the text in order to hear what it says of the subject, not in order to maintain our own opinions.

That brings us to the second point about hermeneutics. We must be

---

[2] "The Problem of Hermeneutics," p. 239 (italics Bultmann's).

[3] Cf. Bultmann, "Ist voraussetzungslos Exegese möglich?" *ThZ,* XIII (1957), 409–17.

[4] I may sound here like a Barthian, although I am not. The trouble with Barth, perhaps, is that he doubts that we can *ever* of ourselves ask the right question. But, Dr. Bultmann, do we not sometimes in all honesty ask the wrong one?

open to what the text has to say about man's meaning, what understanding it has of *"human being in its possibilities as the possibilities that belong specifically to the one who understands."*[5] That is to say, the basic meaning of any piece of literature is what it has to say about man. To be sure, some texts, mathematics, for example, may have nothing specific or even indirect to say about man, and such texts must be studied in accord with their own purposes and limitations. But the New Testament, in which Bultmann is interested, does speak about man. Yet what it says is not simply descriptive of man. It amounts to the setting forth of an understanding of man in terms of potentiality, "human being in its possibilities"; but more yet: "as the possibilities that belong specifically to the one who understands." The text conveys demand and promise, not only for itself but also for the interpreter. He must be open to what it has to say *to him,* not only about human potential in general but about him in particular.

This, then, is the "subject" of the text: the question of man. It is the question of man in his actuality and in his potentiality. It is, to come right down to it, the question about *me* and about *you.* And this is a quest not merely for information about man but for the existential significance of human life.

The word is out: "existential." Is it a bad word? The fact that it has become all but jargon in theological circles need not debilitate it unduly. We may perhaps be grateful that in English we do not have two words to confuse us, as they have confused some of the German participants in the debate.[6] The ambiguity of our one word may be sufficient guarantee of our confusion. What Bultmann intends by it is that we be existentially concerned with the question of man in our approach to the text, and that the business of interpretation be carried out in existentialist terms. We must *understand* in order to

---

[5] "The Problem of Hermeneutics," p. 246 (italics Bultmann's). In this passage, Bultmann is referring to poetic works, but the rest of the essay demonstrates that he means this definition to apply more widely.

[6] The two words, of course, are *existential* and *existentiell.* The former has to do with the methods of existentialist philosophy and should perhaps be translated "existentialist." The latter means that which is involved with one's own existence and should be translated "existential." Others suggest that *existential* could be translated "ontological," and *existentiell,* "ontic," as the difference between being and philosophizing about being.

interpret.[7] And the interpretation must go on to be *understandable,* that is, to convey the meaning of the text to the hearer or reader so that he too is summoned to decision with regard to the meaning of his own existence.

LITERALISM, LIBERALISM, AND MYTHOLOGY

When we come to the New Testament, the matter of interpretation becomes complicated. *How* do we go about interpreting? In what terms can we cast the thought of the New Testament so as to preserve at once its bursting vitality and its theological intention?

As anyone who takes seriously the problem of communicating the gospel knows very well, the terms in which the New Testament speaks are alien to our culture, or, at least, our culture in selectively preserving New Testament terms tends quickly to distort them from their New Testament meaning. For the New Testament speaks from within the world picture of the first-century Hellenistic Orient. It speaks with the mythology of its own day and age, a mythology that modern culture has left behind as obsolete.[8] Thus, while angels, miracles, demons, spirits, and the rest were an integral part of the

---

[7] Cf. "The Problem of Hermeneutics," p. 261: "The problem of interpretation is precisely that of understanding." I have the impression that by "understanding" Bultmann means more than intellectual comprehension. The word seems to have the connotation of decision, with its intellectual component. Cf. the relevant section in Bultmann's reply to Jaspers, "The Case for Demythologization," in *Myth and Christianity* (New York: Noonday Press, 1958), pp. 58–66.

[8] For Bultmann's thumbnail sketch of the New Testament mythological world view, see H. W. Bartsch (ed.), *Kerygma and Myth* (London: S.P.C.K., 1953), pp. 1–2 (hereafter referred to as *KM*). This essay, "New Testament and Mythology," was the first overt expression of Bultmann's demythologizing endeavor, and it landed like a bombshell in the German theological world of 1942. The so-called "Confessional Church movement" felt that its only weapon against Nazi inroads was the Bible. Since Bultmann has been a leader in the movement, the dismay aroused by the article can be well imagined. For it seemed to many, who had reacted to the exigencies of the situation by falling into a rather dogmatic Biblicism, to undercut the whole Christian proclamation. The repercussions have continued through five volumes of *Kerygma und Mythos* (Hamburg: Herbert Reich–Evangelischer Verlag). Barth has added his own somewhat caustic expression in *Kirchliche Dogmatik,* Vol. III, §2, pp. 531–538, and in a pamphlet, *Rudolf Bultmann: ein Versuch ihn zu verstehen* (Zürich: Evangelischer Verlag, 1952 [Theologische Studien, Heft 34]).

intellectual trappings of first-century man, modern science has pretty thoroughly demolished them for man in the twentieth century.[9] Bultmann stands, therefore, against every kind of literalism. The proclamation of the New Testament's gospel does not involve the proclamation of the New Testament's world view. Faith must not be confused with *Weltanschauung*.[10] It is not only unnecessary but positively undesirable to expect Christian people to swallow the New Testament's picture of the world along with the perspective on the meaning of man which the gospel implies, for that would involve what Paul Tillich calls "intellectual asceticism."[11] Therefore, the angels, demons, miracles, and so forth, which play such a significant role in the world view of the New Testament, must be interpreted in terms of their contribution to the New Testament's understanding of human existence.

But, steadfastly as Bultmann stands against literalism, he is no happier with liberalism.[12] To be sure, he stands closer to liberalism than to fundamentalism. He can say of Harnack that "this 'liberal' understanding, at the very least, contains active impulses which though now obscured nonetheless preserve their legitimacy and will recover their validity."[13] At the same time, his complaint with liberalism, quite the opposite of that with literalism, is that it sought to eliminate the mythology, thereby throwing out the baby with the

---

[9] I am aware that there are pockets of resistance to a world view dominated by the scientific outlook, but they seem rather pitiful remnants of medieval credulity. I am also aware that some critics have argued that modern science views the "miraculous" much more sanguinely than it did a few years ago (cf., e.g., Austin Farrer's comments in *KM*, p. 222; A. Oepke, "Entmythologisierung des Christentums," *Kerygma und Mythos*, III [1954], 171 f.; see the refutation of this position by L. Malevez, S.J., *The Christian Message and Myth* [London: SCM Press, 1958], pp. 133 f.). To this it must be said that such a viewpoint, which I for one have been unable to find among scientists at my own university, is no guarantee of the New Testament miracles, none of which has anything to do with the kind of "miraculous" occurrences which modern science allegedly views so complacently. To define "miraculous" as "the unexplained" is one thing; to define it as "the unexplainable" is quite another.

[10] This point is cogently made in "The Crisis in Belief," *Essays*, pp. 7–9.

[11] Note Bultmann's strictures against Barth on the *sacrificium intellectus* in "The Problem of Hermeneutics," pp. 260 f.; and cf. *KM*, pp. 3–5.

[12] This is one of Jaspers' complaints; cf. *Myth and Christianity*, pp. 49–50.

[13] Quoted from Bultmann's introduction to Harnack, *What Is Christianity?* (New York: Harper Torchbooks, 1957), p. viii.

bath. Surely the mythology gives the gospel its power; yet the power is obscured for us by the fact that the gospel as it stands in the New Testament is clothed in an antiquated mythology. Bultmann insists that our business is not the *elimination* of the mythology but its *interpretation*.[14]

It is time, then, to consider the question of myth. At one point, Bultmann says that this problem is not the most germane to the issue.[15] At the same time, it is important to know what he means by it, because if one is going to demythologize, he ought to know what mythology is. The definition is straightforward enough: "Mythology is the use of imagery to express the other-worldly in terms of this world and the divine in terms of human life, the other side in terms of this side."[16] Or again, "Myth is the report of an event or occurrence in which supernatural, superhuman powers or persons are at work (thereby often simply defined as a narrative of the gods)."[17] The mythological deals with the life of man *sub specie Dei,* understands man's existence in terms of his relationship with the divine, and presents the divine power in action within the human sphere. It is, therefore, a mode of expression for "man's understanding of himself in the world in which he lives."[18] But the difficulty is that mythological imagery could be and has been taken as descriptive of the world, as a scientific (or functionally scientific) analysis of the structure of reality. This, says Bultmann, it was never meant to be, and to insist on interpreting it as literal in any sense is to do it violence. To be sure, to reject it out of hand as nonsense because it reflects a prescientific viewpoint is to do it equal injustice. The problem is to penetrate the mythology in order to discover the understanding of human existence enshrined there, and then to discover the contemporary terms in which that understanding may be interpreted. To Bultmann, those terms are the terms hammered out by existentialist

---

[14] Cf. *KM,* pp. 9–15.

[15] Cf. "Der Sinn des Mythos und der Entmythologisierung," *Kerygma und Mythos,* II (1952), 180: "I do not consider that the question about the concept of myth belongs to the most important questions." He continues in the same paragraph: "If anyone wants to find my concept of myth questionable and to understand something different by myth, he is welcome to do so."

[16] *KM,* p. 10, n. 2.

[17] "Der Sinn des Mythos," etc., *Kerygma und Mythos,* II, 180.

[18] *KM,* p. 10.

philosophy, a philosophy which itself is interested and involved in human existence. It is this that constitutes "demythologization," the use of nonmythological terms to express for the modern day the mythological understanding of human existence contained in the New Testament.

THE DEMYTHOLOGIZATION PROCESS

In what has gone before, I have several times referred to processes which are *not* involved in demythologization. It is perhaps easiest to review these first.

Demythologization is not a reductionism. We cannot, in the manner of much of the nineteenth century and too much of the twentieth, simply ignore as irrelevant those elements in the New Testament that do not appeal to us. There is point, it seems, in the fact that the Church submits itself to a canonical Scripture. Too much criticism of Bultmann, particularly from what can be called "evangelical" American circles, [19] has proceeded from the (false) assumption that he was seeking to reduce the relevant material in the New Testament—that *de*mythologization meant an outright rejection of the mythological materials. That this is not so can be categorically stated and illustrated from any number of passages, both from Bultmann's original article and from the reactions to it.[20] If people persist in misunderstanding what Bultmann is up to, the criticisms they make from their misunderstanding can be dismissed.

Second, the program of demythologization, in which Bultmann wants to express the New Testament understanding of human existence in existentialist terms, is not simply Heidegger's philosophy baptized. The confusion is understandable. Long before Bultmann wrote his essay, "New Testament and Mythology," he was using the categories of Heidegger's *Sein und Zeit* to interpret the New Testament. He refers to criticisms leveled at him for this in "New

---

[19] "Evangelical" is their own word, and we may hope that the rest of American Protestantism will not permit them to pre-empt the word. I have in mind the position represented by *Christianity Today*. See Philip Edgcumbe Hughes, "Myth in Modern Theology," *Christianity Today*, Vol. III, No. 13 (March 30, 1959), pp. 7–9.

[20] Cf. *KM*, pp. 9, 12, 144–145, 176, etc.

Testament and Mythology," [21] with a remark that leaves him open to criticism: "Heidegger's existentialist analysis of the ontological structure of being would seem to be no more than a secularized, philosophical version of the New Testament view of human life."[22] But this is a criticism which, in the longer view of Bultmann's work, is not validated. He makes great use of Heidegger's philosophical analysis when he discusses man outside of faith, [23] but Bultmann is too close to the New Testament to take over Heidegger uncritically. Indeed, he himself has said so,[24] and if that were not enough, others have said it, too.[25] Though Bultmann does use Heidegger's category of decision, the setting of the Christian decision in faith within the context of grace completely seals off Bultmann's Christian solution of the human condition from Heidegger's humanist one. The *analysis* of the existential predicament is not also the *answer*. And all Bultmann claims to do with Heidegger is to use his phenomenology of man, his ontological analysis.[26] At the same time, a theological query is in order and will be put below.

It is time now to move to what demythologization *does* involve. It revolves around two poles: interpretation, which is the articulation of an ancient message in modern terminology, and the question about human existence, its potentiality and its meaning. For demythologization is the interpretation of New Testament faith in terms of the understanding of human existence. It rests on exegesis, and therefore on the principles of hermeneutics, and the question it raises is: What does New Testament faith say of human existence?

Tua res agitur. Fundamentally, this is the New Testament message. "This concerns you." To be sure, the New Testament proceeds to fill

---

[21] Cf. *KM,* pp. 24–25.

[22] Cf. the strictures of Karl Jaspers on this point, *Myth and Christianity,* pp. 8–9.

[23] This is evident in his interpretation of Paul in *Theology of the New Testament,* Vol. I, Part II.

[24] Cf. *Myth and Christianity,* p. 58.

[25] The very useful and stimulating book of John Macquarrie, *An Existentialist Theology* (New York: The Macmillan Company, 1955), is an explicit comparison of Bultmann and Heidegger, and Macquarrie makes very clear the points at which Bultmann departs from Heidegger. Cf. also Friedrich Gogarten, *Demythologizing and History* (New York: Charles Scribner's Sons, 1955).

[26] Cf. *Jesus Christ and Mythology* (New York: Charles Scribner's Sons, 1958), chap. iv, esp. pp. 55–59.

in the "this" with its Christian content. But it is the formal consideration that New Testament faith is neither speculative nor merely
descriptive that drives Bultmann to his existentialist interpretation.
The New Testament, if it is not *existential,* is certainly *existentiell.*

It is the function of myth to articulate the *existentiell* in a
comprehensible way. But, says Bultmann, as the New Testament has
been interpreted through the centuries, its mythology has been used
as if it were descriptive, it has ceased to be existential and has
become dogma, its originally fresh articulation of human existence
has degenerated into statements of external fact. The Church has
tended to lose sight of the mythological dynamics of the New Testament and has treated it as the source book of theological systematization. "Mythological thought . . . objectifies the divine activity and
projects it on to the plane of worldly happenings."[27] That is the
trouble. The miracle then demands a rational explanation, for it must
conform to "history" in the positivistic sense. And by a curious twist
of mentality, the fundamentalist proceeds to force the allegedly
"historical" miracle on the unbeliever as demonstration of the truth
of his message, feeling that if his miracle is called in question, the
truth of his message is shaken to the foundation.

Bultmann prefers to bypass that question and to concentrate on the
New Testament's focal point. In this connection, an observation of
Ian Henderson is useful.[28] He points out that there are three ways in
which we can talk about Christ. There is the *historic* mode, in which
Jesus was a rabbi who lived in the early years of the first century A.D.
and "suffered under Pontius Pilate." Second, there is the *mythological*
mode, in which Christ is "the Lamb of God who takes away the sin of
the world" (John 1:29), or in which he is the pre-existent Logos who
can say, "Before Abraham was, I am" (John 8:58). The third way is
the *existential,* in which Christ is present to our existence, e.g., "I
have been crucified with Christ" (Gal. 2:20).[29] Here the eschato-

---

[27] *KM,* p. 197.

[28] *Myth in the New Testament* (London: SCM Press, 1952 [Studies in
Biblical Theology, No. 7]), pp. 41 f.

[29] Another term has been used by Bultmann instead of existential, namely
"eschatological." Cf. esp. *The Presence of Eternity* (New York: Harper &
Row, 1957), chaps. iii–v, x. For Bultmann, the Christ event is the eschatologi-

logical fact has become actualized in one's own life.[30] He is in the "new age." He has left behind the "world" and the "flesh." He has received "forgiveness of sins," and "the power of sin" no longer has any hold over him. The Christ event has been taken out of the purely historic realm, where it can never be more than the tragic death of a great man. It has been taken out of the mythological realm, where we must imagine a cosmic transaction between God and Christ or between God and Satan. It has become the encounter of the self with God himself, in which one's own past and security give place to the past of the Christ event and to faith.

This drives on to the decision of faith in the present toward the future, another reason why the existential mode is necessary and correct. Eschatology, Bultman feels, is the inbreaking of the future upon the present, and the decision of faith in the present is a decision pointed toward the meaning of the future.[31] But no decision can leave us at rest about the future. There is no objective security about decision, for decision is precisely *in faith,* apart from the certitudes of doctrine or the possession of truth. Such possessions and certainties live in the past, while existential decision drives to the future. To this the existential-eschatological Christ event points, and to this Bultmann's program of demythologization seeks to point. He is a great believer in *sola fide,* which to him means the encounter with the living God himself and with his grace. So decision in faith is decision in

---

cal event, inaugurating the new age. When, therefore, one participates in the event in faith, he is taken up into the new age—the *eschaton*—and his existence is now eschatological existence. This is not, however, the same as C. H. Dodd's "realized eschatology," as Bultmann makes quite clear in his essay, " 'The Bible Today' und die Eschatologie," in the Dodd *Festschrift, The Background of the New Testament and its Eschatology.* Dodd objectifies the eschatology; Bultmann existentializes it (or, as he would prefer, recognizes its intrinsically existential nature).

[30] Note Luther's words in the *Treatise on Christian Liberty:* "It is not enough, nor is it Christian, to preach the works, life, and words of Christ as historical facts, as if the knowledge of these would suffice for the conduct of life. . . . . Rather ought Christ be preached to the end that he may not only be Christ but be Christ for thee and for me, and that what is said of Him and what His name denotes may be effectual in us." This is surely a case of demythologizing, and it provides an excellent commentary on what Bultmann is doing.

[31] Cf. *The Presence of Eternity,* pp. 140 f.

obedience and under grace.[32] But this decision is not, for Bultmann, dependent upon the accuracy of the Biblical narrative—i.e., upon either the historical or the mythological aspects—although grace is to be sought in the Church's preaching of the Christ. Indeed, unless the Biblical narrative is preached as gospel, i.e., unless it is preached existentially to man's condition, it is irrelevant.

This brings us to the core of demythologization: the interpretation of the Cross and the Resurrection. To these the Church always points in its effort to give an account of itself.[33] The Cross, first of all,

---

[32] At this point, among others, Bultmann departs basically from Heidegger. Decision is possible only with grace, whereas for Heidegger man is capable of decision solely on the basis of analysis of human existence. A rather long passage from "Der Sinn des Mythos," etc., in *Kerygma und Mythos,* II, 190, points this up: "Demythologization, as an existentialist interpretation, seeks to make clear, to make understandable, exactly the real mystery of God in its peculiar intangibility. To understand is something different from rational explanation. I can understand what friendship, love, and truth are; and precisely when I understand them rightly, I know that the friendship, love, and truth which manifest themselves to me are and continually remain a gratefully welcomed mystery. I do not grasp them by my rational thought, nor by logical deduction from the behavior of the other, nor by psychological analysis, nor even by existentialist analysis, but only in the existential openness of my self for the encounter. I also understand in such openness what friendship, love, and truth are before they are granted to me, since my existence requires them; I understand them, then, in the question about them. Thus I can also understand what God's grace means; otherwise I could not speak of it at all. But that this grace encounters me, that the God of grace is *my* God, is always a mystery, precisely in its revelation. It is not, however, a mystery because God is an irrational being, or because he does something which disturbs (*durch-löchert*) the course of the world in an incomprehensible way, but because it is inconceivable that he encounters me." (Almost the same passage occurs in *Jesus Christ and Mythology,* pp. 43–44; I have translated the above without reference to the latter passage.) Cf. also *The Presence of Eternity,* p. 150: "Christian faith believes that man does not have the freedom which is presupposed for historical decisions." This is surely a direct contradiction of Heidegger. The essay, "Grace and Freedom," *Essays,* pp. 168–81, gives an extended and eloquent discussion of the whole problem.

[33] It could be argued that the Church actually points to more than this, to the Incarnation, for example, or to Pentecost. At the same time, the Incarnation cannot be viewed apart from the Cross and Resurrection, while the reverse is possible. And Pentecost depends on the Holy Week narrative to make any sense at all, for out of Pentecost comes the *kerygma* of the Church, which centers on the Cross and Resurrection. And surely we must admit that Bultmann is in the Pauline-Johannine line in his emphasis. In this connection, of course, the problem of the historic Jesus arises, but that can best be raised in the final portion of this essay.

viewed historically—of which no one denies the possibility—is simply one fact beside others, which can be observed in detachment. But when the Cross is viewed mythologically, it receives the power of faith's interpretation, as the Cross of the "Lamb of God" or of *Christus Victor,* who overcomes Death and Satan and their hosts. But the sacrificial mythology is no longer significant in our day, and the notion of a triumph over Satan has become absurd in a culture which believes neither in Satan nor in his hosts. How can we preserve the *intention* of the mythology and still proclaim an intelligible message? The Cross stands clearly as the twofold action of judgment and grace. It is judgment on sin and guilt, on the self-centeredness of man, and it is also the possibility of deliverance from sin and guilt. But the Cross is this action—not as the mythological past accomplishment of God, but as the confrontation of the hearer of the gospel by the requirement that he appropriate this judgment and deliverance. The importance of the Cross is not that it happened once, but that when it happened once it inaugurated a new historic situation of judgment and redemption which, in preaching, in sacraments, in life, is always challenging its hearers.[34]

And this can be so because of the immediately related Resurrection. The Resurrection cannot be separated off from the Cross, as if it were a "happy ending," a vindication of what had seemed to be tragedy. If the power of the Cross lies in its presenting us with our "death to the flesh" and to "the world," then the power of the Resurrection lies in its being our "new life."[35] Indeed, more than this cannot be said. Historical research cannot establish the credibility of this event as it can the Cross.[36] The only objective fact to which we

---

[34] Cf. *KM,* p. 37; see also *Theology of the New Testament,* I, 282–306; II, 49–55.

[35] Cf. Rom. 6:3–11.

[36] *Theology of the New Testament,* I, 295: "For the resurrection, of course, simply cannot be a visible fact in the realm of human history." And cf. *KM,* pp. 38–43. We must appreciate Bultmann's rigorous honesty in exposing his presuppositions. The impossibility of the resuscitation of a corpse *is* a presupposition for Bultmann, and some others would not find such a thing incredible. But the case for demythologization does not rest on this presupposition. Historical skepticism does not provide the motivation for any flight to dogma in the effort to salvage something from radical criticism. Cf. *Glauben und Verstehen,* I (1927), 101: "I have never felt uncomfortable in my critical radicalism, but instead quite comfortable. But I often have the impression that

can point is the Church's proclamation of the Risen Lord. The Church and its preaching are part of the Resurrection; faith itself is the life of the Resurrection, and the Church stands on that new life as an article and ingredient of its faith.[37] As faith, the Resurrection is not amenable to proof. Nor can it be adduced as demonstration of faith's truth, for it constitutes faith and the life of faith. Just as we are "crucified with Christ," we are "risen with him." The Cross and Resurrection are not mythological but existential, in that they lie at the foundation of our existence. They are not merely past tales or facts, but present facts which enter into consciousness at every moment of life, and in which we make the decisions of life which lead us in responsibility and love to action.

Such, in too brief outline, is what Bultmann is trying to do.

COMMENTS AND QUERIES

I have been instructed by the editor that part of my task is to see that the battle of demythologization is fought out here once and for all. Yet if I am right in my understanding of Bultmann, this battle is to be fought out in every generation. The problem, I think, is not *whether* we demythologize, but *how* we demythologize. Has Bultmann done the job or showed the way to doing it? Or is he barking up the wrong tree?[38]

---

my conservative colleagues in New Testament feel quite uncomfortable; for I see them always involved in salvage operations. I quietly let it burn; for I see that what is there burning are all the phantasies of the life-of-Jesus-theology, the *Christos kata sarka* itself." (Quoted in J. M. Robinson, *A New Quest of the Historical Jesus* [Naperville, Ill.: A. R. Allenson, 1959], p. 74, n. 2.) Bultmann is seriously criticized for this view of history by Richard R. Niebuhr, *Resurrection and Historical Reason* (New York: Charles Scribner's Sons, 1957). I cannot see that Niebuhr presents a better alternative.

[37] These conclusions on the Resurrection have caused the greatest uproar. There have been many who thought that Bultmann had taken away their Easter sermons, and they knew not where he had laid them!

[38] It seems somewhat bootless to bring up the arguments against the whole business here. Bultmann could reply only by saying again what he has said. An example is Jaspers' plea for the retention of the mythological "ciphers," as he calls them (*Myth and Christianity*, pp. 15–21). It is too late in the day for us to say, "But Dr. Bultmann, do you really think we ought to demythologize?" And I fail to see that Jaspers has brought a decisive criticism to bear. The only issue with which we can deal is whether Bultmann has projected the

1. *The Character of Myth.* Bultmann's definition of myth has been quoted above, and we have quoted him as saying that this is a secondary question. Yet the question needs to be probed further. Does this definition fit his own task?

An interesting objection has been raised on the basis of the so-called "linguistic analysis" in contemporary philosophy. Ronald Hepburn, writing on the problem of validity, accuses Bultmann of riding two horses at once, of defining mythology in different ways.[39] On the one hand, Bultmann's definition of mythology is purely formal, treating it as *a kind of language* that uses images to describe the unimaged. On the other hand, when Bultmann makes statements like: "Mythological thought regards the divine activity . . . as an interference with the course of nature, history, or the life of the soul,"[40] then he is investing mythology with *a particular content*. In another place, Bultmann says, "There are certain concepts which are fundamentally mythological, and with which we shall never be able to dispense—e.g. the idea of transcendence."[41] The question Hepburn raises is, Can we talk directly about God, or can we only talk obliquely about him?[42] The danger present in the talk necessarily involved in demythologizing is that we make the very mistake that mythological thinking is prone to, namely to regard the talk as direct. In terms of the formal definition of myth, referred to above, is it possible to *de*mythologize? The matter thus interpreted may, to be sure, not be mythological. No one would claim that what binds Rudolf Bultmann to God is a myth; his own testimony is that it is not. But as soon as he talks about it, he must use what is *formally* mythological language for it, "imagery to express the other-worldly in

---

task rightly and at what points he has failed to make himself clear or to stick to his own direction. I should, however, make a confession: I cannot claim to have controlled all the literature on this subject. Hence there may be points which ought to be raised here but are not, either because I am ignorant of their existence or because I am not bright enough to think of them myself.

[39] "Demythologizing and the Problem of Validity," in Flew & MacIntyre (eds.), *New Essays in Philosophical Theology* (London: SCM Press, 1955), pp. 227–42.

[40] *KM,* p. 197. Cf. Hepburn, *op. cit.,* p. 229.

[41] *KM,* pp. 102–103. Cf. Hepburn, *op. cit.,* pp. 236–37.

[42] *Ibid.,* pp. 237–39. This question from Hepburn's essay seems to me a valid one. Some of his other problems, however, remain remote from the heart of the matter.

terms of this world and the divine in terms of human lives. . . ." We
have no terms but those of this world and of human life, and unless
we are prepared to assert a thoroughgoing immanentism, we can only
talk in mythological terms about that which of itself is not myth. At
this point—although at very few others—I find myself in agreement
with Thielicke: "If there is to be no demythologizing, let us at least
have remythologizing!"[43] We must talk about the faith, but our talk
is not the precise equivalent of what we are interpreting thereby. The
point is small but germane.

2. *Faith and Phenomenology.* It was pointed out above that
Bultmann uses Heidegger's analysis of existence to illuminate the
case of man outside of faith, but that at the fundamental point of the
Christian existential decision, he leaves Heidegger's humanist option
and enters the realm of grace. The theological query mentioned there
is this: what is the relation between existence in Christ and existence
in "the flesh"? Is it really possible to analyze existence outside of
faith without reference to faith? Does not the stance within the realm
of faith alone make it possible to comprehend the true character of
life without faith?

I do not mean to say that "natural man" is unable to reflect upon
himself. But it appears to me that faith affirms that only *in faith* can
man see himself as he really is. Only in faith can we see the true
extent of the human predicament outside of faith. An analysis of
human existence (e.g. Heidegger's) that does not involve and include
the decision of faith under grace, which alone restores our lost
manhood, is both incomplete and positively misleading. This is not to
say that faith gives us information to fill in gaps in phenomenology.
But faith makes it possible for us to gaze unafraid on those aspects
of existence upon which, without it, we dare not look.

I think I am asking about methodology. When Bultmann says,
"Every assertion about God is simultaneously an assertion about man
and vice versa,"[44] does he not say this very thing? Only under God

---

[43] "The Restatement of New Testament Mythology," *KM,* p. 162. I have
the feeling that Thielicke says this for the wrong reason. That does not vitiate
the aptness of the remark.

[44] *Theology of the New Testament,* I, 191.

can man apprehend an adequate phenomenology. What then is the criterion by which we make use of some existentialist categories and reject others? Or do we make use of them solely as terminological conveniences, filling them in the process with new meanings? I do not know the answer. But it does raise the question, I think, whether the discussion of phenomenology properly precedes or follows the discussion of faith. It can be argued that man outside of faith does not know who he is, does not know what is good for him, cannot analyze his own predicament. Paul could write Romans 7 only after he had come to life in Christ.[45]

3. *Myth and History.* Bultmann's aversion to the *Christos kata sarka* is well known. Though he could write a book on Jesus' teaching,[46] he could also refer to it somewhat condescendingly as not being kerygma.[47] He, along with Paul, is not interested in Jesus "as a phenomenon of the past."[48] "How things looked in Jesus' heart I do not know and do not wish to know."[49]

But recent work by former pupils of Bultmann moves in a different direction. Where Bultmann is theologically interested only in the Atonement, these scholars view the career of Jesus as having more positive importance to the kerygma than Bultmann will allow.[50] This raises, I believe, a legitimate and important question: If myth is the interpretation by the early Church of what can properly be called historic experience, what is the importance of the history thus interpreted? Indeed, what is the history to which we must look for

---

[45] I am aware of the question whether Paul is speaking in Rom. 7 of man under the law or of his own discovery that life under grace is itself no simple matter. For the purposes of this particular question, I do not believe that it matters which way the passage is interpreted.

[46] *Jesus and the Word* (New York: Charles Scribner's Sons, 1934). Cf. also the sections of *Primitive Christianity* (New York: Living Age Books, 1956) on the preaching of Jesus, pp. 71–79, 86–93, and note that they are in the context of a discussion of Judaism.

[47] *KM*, p. 117: "The Jesus of history is not kerygma, any more than my book was."

[48] *Ibid.* Cf. also *Theology of the New Testament*, I, 293 f.

[49] *Glauben und Verstehen*, I, 101.

[50] The work of Käsemann, Fuchs, Bornkamm, and Conzelmann, among others, is conveniently summarized by James M. Robinson, *A New Quest of the Historical Jesus.*

our comprehension of the New Testament's mythology? To Bultmann it seems to be reduced to two factors: the event of the Cross and the Church's reception of redemption. Yet he can say, "The word of God is not some mysterious oracle, but a sober, factual account of a human life, of Jesus of Nazareth, possessing saving efficacy for man."[51] Or again, *"Thus the relation to history is a constitutive character of the Word of God in the OT."*[52] The myth could not, therefore, have arisen without the history. Yet, not the historic but the present proclamation is determinative for Bultmann: "Jesus Christ is the eschatological event not as an established fact of past time but as repeatedly present, as addressing you and me here and now in preaching."[53] We can see an analogue to this in Bultmann's fairly widely accepted understanding that the gospel materials have been informed by the Resurrection faith, and at some points Resurrection narratives have been placed in Jesus' career and the teaching of Jesus has been altered by the Church's knowledge of the Resurrection. The awareness of being kerygmatically addressed determines the viewpoint on the historic material. But *how* does it determine the viewpoint? By what criterion do we say that the Jesus of history either is or is not kerygma? Clearly the compilers of the Synoptics—and John as well—thought that he was.[54]

4. *Individual and Community.* One gets the impression from Bultmann that faith is always a matter of individual encounter between God and man.[55] History is personal history, and the quest

---

[51] *KM.*, p. 44.

[52] *Glauben und Verstehen*, I, 287 (italics Bultmann's). It is clear that this statement applies equally to the New Testament.

[53] *The Presence of Eternity*, pp. 151–52; cf. also *KM*, p. 209.

[54] I confess myself to be somewhat uneasy at the new study of the historical Jesus. My first reading of James Robinson's book left me greatly excited, for it seemed that a valid approach had been found. The second reading made me twitch in my chair, for it seemed to me that the net result of the "new quest" was the old one dressed up in existentialist terminology. Robinson refers—all too briefly, I believe—to "The Methodological Impasse" (pp. 100–104), which has been overleaped by a virtual *tour de force*. I have no suggestions to make on this point, but I feel that Bultmann has not been answered on the problem. Perhaps a more significant philosophical criticism is made by Richard R. Niebuhr, *Resurrection and Historical Reason.*

[55] Cf. *Presence of Eternity*, pp. 149–55, all of which is cast in the first person singular.

for meaning in history is the individual's quest for his own personal meaning.[56]

Is this, however, adequate for the communal aspect of the Christian understanding of man? Surely there is more to the "new understanding of myself" than my endowment with my "new self."[57] To be sure, Bultmann understands this new self as being "unreservedly for one's neighbour."[58] But it is more. It is not simply that I as an individual may now act in love toward other individuals. I am incorporated into a body, within which and from which I act. Personal history is taken up into redemptive history, and the Church's history becomes our history. Only on the basis of this history are we given the possibility of responsible decision.

I communicated this criticism to Dr. Bultmann, and he generously responded in a letter on May 22, 1959: "According to my understanding it goes without saying that personal history is related to community. History always goes through encounters, and without encounters I do not have a personal history."

I do not believe that this answers the criticism. To be sure, only through encounters with others does the individual gain a glimpse of the requirements of his humanity. But the decisive encounter for the Christian is that with God in Jesus Christ, and this encounter takes place only in the community where the faith in God in Jesus Christ is held and proclaimed. And this encounter is not merely the meeting between me and God, but, much more crucially, the meeting between the Church and God. *Extra ecclesiam nulla salus.* The paradoxical fact remains: we neither come to faith nor continue in faith outside the Church.[59] I am certain that Bultmann would agree with this,

---

[56] *Ibid.*, p. 155: "Man who complains: 'I cannot see meaning in history, and therefore my life, interwoven in history, is meaningless,' is to be admonished: do not look around yourself into universal history, *you must look into your own personal history.* Always in your present lies the meaning in history, and you cannot see it as a spectator, but only in your responsible decisions" (italics Bultmann's). Shades of Heidegger! Of course, no one would quarrel with the contention that individual meaning comes, not from the contemplation of man in general or of oneself in detachment, but from personal involvement in decision and in action.

[57] *Presence of Eternity,* p. 152.

[58] *Ibid.*

[59] Cf. B. H. Throckmorton, Jr., *The New Testament and Mythology* (Philadelphia: Westminster Press, 1959), pp. 111 f.

particularly in view of his insistence on the centrality of preaching. I say it simply to set it down as a point that needs clarification by him.

The late Charles Williams, a lay British theologian of great power and insight, suggested that the history of Christendom could be organized around the two points of view, the negation of images and the affirmation of images.[60] Bultmann, strangely, sees both ways. He belongs emphatically, on the one hand, to the way of negation. Jaspers can say with great justice: "It seems to me that you are at home in imagelessness."[61] Bultmann negates the images because they are not the equivalent of that which they image. On the other hand, we must also say, "It seems to me that you are at home among images." For Bultmann affirms the images by the very fact that he interprets them. He affirms them because what they image is centrally true and profoundly of concern to his life and ours. Dangers there are in too exclusive a concentration on either of the two ways, and perhaps Bultmann can properly be criticized for his tendency to negate more than to affirm. But for all that, I for one must tender him profound thanks for opening the New Testament to me as no one else has done.

[60] Cf. *The Descent of the Dove* (New York: Pellegrini & Cudahy, 1939).
[61] *Myth and Christianity*, p. 90.

Revelation

——— ·◆· ———

H. P. OWEN
King's College
The University of London

The concept of revelation is central in Bultmann's thought. Fortunately, he has presented his views on the subject in a thorough, consistent, and lucid way. But he has not presented them systematically. I hope that my own attempt at systematization will not distort his perspective or misrepresent his aim.[1]

I shall base my analysis on Bultmann's earlier writings, translated in the volume entitled *Existence and Faith*.[2] I choose these as my chief documents because I consider it important to show that his theory of revelation was not determined (though it may have been sharpened) by the later demands of *Entmythologisierung* for which he has become disproportionately known.

The two early essays in *Existence and Faith* show that, from the beginning of his literary career, Bultmann (if I may so put it) has ascribed five characteristics to the revelation of God in Christ.

---

[1] I have attempted to examine Bultmann's theology as a whole in my book *Revelation and Existence* (Cardiff, 1957).

[2] These have been selected, translated, and introduced by Schubert M. Ogden. I shall quote from the British edition (London: Hodder & Stoughton, 1961). All my references (unless otherwise indicated) will be to this volume, and especially to the two articles in it entitled "Concerning the Hidden and the Revealed God" (1917) and "The Concept of Revelation in the New Testament" (1929).

(1) His basic axiom is that the subject and object of revelation is not a series of propositions or body of dogma; it is neither more nor less than the living God himself. Hence Bultmann rejects the view, which he regards as the typically Catholic one, that revelation consists in "the communication of knowledge or of doctrine" (p. 66). Taking his stand on the New Testament he affirms that the primary content of revelation is the divine life which Christ conveys. This affirmation has been made by a multitude of recent theologians, among whom one need mention only Temple, Hebert, Bulgakoff, Barth, and Brunner.[3] Bultmann's distinctive contribution is to be found in the succeeding characteristics.

(2) God's act of revelation is simultaneously concealed in the events that mediate it. He is always present (to use the inevitable word) "incognito." This truth is indicated by the title of Bultmann's essay "The Hidden and the Revealed God." Here we are told that the "hiddenness" of God is congruous with both the irreducible mystery of his being and the lesser but analogous mystery inherent in every finite person:

> God has to be hidden and mysterious if we are to approach him in humility and reverence. Indeed, this is so even among men. We often feel with pain that we are mysteries to one another. And yet, when we rightly reflect on it, there is something precious in our being mysteries to ourselves, in our never being completely known to one another, in our being unable ever to see through even the person who is closest to our heart and to reckon with him as though he were a logical proposition or a problem in accounting [p. 28].

This characteristic of the divine self-disclosure is increasingly emphasized in Bultmann's later writings. No one can ever isolate God's act and present it as an object for observation. "God's handiwork cannot be labelled and docketed like the work of an artist or an engineer."[4] "To every other eye than the eye of faith the action of God is hidden. Only the 'natural' happening is generally visible and ascertainable. In it is accomplished the hidden act of God."[5]

---

[3] The history of the view that revelation means primarily the self-disclosure of God's personal presence, and only secondarily the formulation of doctrine, is given by John Baillie in *The Idea of Revelation in Recent Thought* (1956).

[4] *Kerygma and Myth*, trans. R. H. Fuller (London: S.P.C.K., 1953), p. 121. I shall refer to this as *KM*.

[5] *KM*, p. 197.

(3) Revelation occurs in an "encounter" with the Word of preaching. The preacher does not simply point to revelation or discourse about it. Preaching, by mediating an encounter in which God addresses man and man answers God, is itself revelation. This is how Bultmann puts it on page 78:

> The preaching is itself revelation and does not merely speak about it, so that it mediates a content that one can understand or to which he can relate himself through knowledge and thereby "have" the revelation. If preaching communicates a content, it at the same time addresses us; it speaks to our consciences, and whoever refuses to let himself be addressed likewise does not understand what is communicated. He is blind (II Cor. 4:4), and for him the revelation is veiled (II Cor. 4:3).

This rigid interpretation of the divine-human relationship in terms of an encounter with the Word of preaching (the *kerygma*) explains the precise meaning that Bultmann attaches to his constantly repeated view that revelation, so far from being a system of dogma, is an *act*. It is not *any* kind of act. It is specifically God acting here and now in addressing to man his decisive eschatological Word of salvation.

(4) God's act of self-disclosure in the proclamation of the gospel would not be complete—could not indeed occur—unless it met with self-knowledge (or self-understanding) in the hearer. If a man is to receive and then to obey God's Word, he must see it in relation to his own existence. Revelation does not unveil the Speaker only. It also unveils the hearer by showing what he is and what he can become.

> What, then, has been revealed? Nothing at all, so far as the question concerning revelation asks for doctrines—doctrines, say, that no man could have discovered for himself—or for mysteries that become known once and for all as soon as they are communicated. On the other hand, however, *everything has been revealed, insofar as man's eyes are opened concerning his own existence and he is once again able to understand himself*. It is as Luther says: "Thus, in going out of himself, God brings it about that we go into ourselves; and through knowledge of him he brings us to knowledge of ourselves" [pp. 85–6].

Revelation is never a theory about the universe and man's place in it. It is always the disclosure of our standing before God in a particular situation; and the situation is always unique. Any attempt to use it as the basis for a speculative *Weltanschauung* is bound to destroy its nature.

Then there is indeed a *knowledge* that is also given in revelation, however little the latter is a supernatural arrangement for communicating
remarkable doctrines. I am given a knowledge, namely, of myself, of my
immediate now, in which and for which the word of proclamation is
spoken to me. Thus it is not an observer's knowledge, not a world-view
in which man is interpreted as a phenomenon within the world on the
basis of certain general principles of explanation, but rather a knowledge
that is only opened up to me in laying hold of the possibility for understanding myself that is disclosed in the proclamation; it is a knowledge
that is only real in the act of faith and love [p. 88].

(5) It follows that God's revelation is always in the *present*. To
locate it in the past would be to remove it from the sphere of self-
understanding. Therefore it is impossible to perceive a divine significance in "the historical Jesus." Christ becomes the Revealer only in
so far as God speaks to us through him in a present encounter.

Just as preaching, if thought of merely as a mediating communication
about the past, would be completely misunderstood, so also, on the other
hand, would the fact of salvation be misunderstood if it were thought of
as an isolated fact that happened in some place and at some time and that
requires to be mediated to the present through a communication. As the
preaching itself belongs to the fact of salvation, so also is this fact not
what it is without the preaching. Thus there also is no way whereby the
hearer of the preaching can get behind it, whether in order to find a
"historical Jesus" or to find some cosmic process that has occurred in a
certain place and at a certain time. Rather everything that is decisive for
him takes place in his present; *"now* is the day of salvation" [p. 79].

In his later writings Bultmann intensifies this contrast between "the
Jesus of history" and "the Christ of faith." He denies outright that
faith can derive support from historical inquiry. The *kerygma* is
wholly self-authenticating. "I still deny," he writes in answer to
Schniewind, "that historical research can ever encounter any traces of
the epiphany of God in Christ."[6] He forbids us even to ask why it is
through Jesus (and not, say, Socrates or the Buddha) that God
reveals his saving Word. "Now it also becomes clear that the
Revealer is nothing but a definite historical man, Jesus of Nazareth.
Why this specific man? That is a question that must not, may not, be

---

6 *KM,* p. 117.

answered—for to do so would destroy the offense which belongs ineradicably to the Revelation."[7]

These five characterisitcs that Bultmann ascribes to revelation explain the meaning that he attaches to "myth." Many of his critics interpret his use of this admittedly flexible word in a superficial way. They take it to signify those images of God, and of his activity in the world, that have been outmoded (so it is said) by post-Copernican cosmology. To demythologize the gospel then means either to omit or to restate these archaic elements.

While I do not wish to deny the existence of an apologetic concern in Bultmann's later writings I have a clear impression that the basic sense which he gives to myth is determined by his concept of revelation, not by the so-called "problem of communication." A statement belongs to the category of "myth" if it describes God as an "object" outside the sphere of encounter and self-understanding. Truth concerning God must always be, in Kierkegaard's sense of the word, "subjective." It must be a truth illumining my own existence and inviting my own decision here and now. Thus in 1929 Bultmann wrote that the revelation occurrence "cannot be a cosmic process which takes place outside of us and of which the word would merely bring a report (*so that it would be nothing other than a myth*)" (p. 78; italics mine).

This, then, is the basic structure of God's revelation in Christ. To complete my account I shall glance at two further questions: the relation between Christian revelation and secular philosophy, and the relation between Christian and so-called "general" revelation.

It is well known that Bultmann uses the terms of existentialist philosophy in order to expound the nature of self-understanding. His defense is double.

First, he claims that Christian thinkers have always been compelled to adopt philosophical categories in elucidating revelation. "*Every* theology is dependent for the clarification of its concepts upon a pretheological understanding of man that, as a rule, is determined by some philosophical tradition" (p. 98).

Second, he draws a sharp dividing line between philosophy and revelation. Philosophy can throw light on the nature of existence. It

---

[7] *Theology of the New Testament,* II (Eng. trans., London: 1955), 69.

can even propose a goal at which man must strive. But it cannot actualize the ideal. In Heidegger's terminology, it can disclose the form of "authentic" being; but only God in Christ can give the form content.[8]

Bultmann's views on general, or natural, revelation are made explicit in an essay dated 1941.[9] According to this essay non-Christians can know God as a power transcending their own existence, but they cannot know anything that is positively true about him. They positively know only that they are finite, limited beings who are controlled by an altogether higher being; but Christianity alone can tell them what (or rather who) this being is.

The Christian belief therefore criticizes on the basis of its knowledge *not the non-Christian inquiry about God—it can only penetrate into it and illuminate it—but first of all the answer which the non-Christian inquiry constructs.* It asserts indeed that man apart from Christianity could not arrive at an answer at all, even if he carried on to the end in the clarity and seriousness of his inquiry. It asserts that *all answers* apart from the Christian answer are illusions.[10]

I shall now comment on Bultmann's concept of revelation according to the five characteristics I have described.

(1) I should certainly wish to agree with Bultmann in considering it to be axiomatic that revelation means, primarily, God's personal self-disclosure in Christ. This axiom (explicitly shared, as I have said, by so many theologians today) is demanded by the Bible. According to the Biblical writers God is not a remote, impersonal *Summum Bonum* or First Cause; he is the *living* God who acts to redeem the world that he created. More precisely, the axiom is required by the New Testament's use of *apocalypsis* and *apocalyptein*. These words normally have an eschatological meaning; they refer to the second coming of Christ. But the second coming will be cosubstantial with the first. Therefore the essence of the first apocalypse must be (as Jesus himself declared)[11] the unveiling of the Father's nature in the Son.

---

[8] See *KM,* pp. 27–28.

[9] Translated in *Essays, Philosophical and Theological* (London: SCM Press, 1955), pp. 90–118.

[10] *Ibid.,* p. 98.

[11] Matt. 11:25–27. Luke 10:21–22.

It is often said that a personal understanding of Christianity has been obscured by the Roman Catholic tendency to equate revelation with the "revealed truths" of dogma. But it is salutary to remember that Newman charged English Protestants of his day with substituting "notional assent" to a narrow range of arbitrarily selected doctrines for "real assent" to the divine Person whom all doctrines directly or indirectly signify.

(2) It seems to me that Bultmann is also right in insisting that God's act of revelation is simultaneously concealed. Here again he is faithful to the Bible where the "revealed" is always also the "hidden" God. Even in Christ, the incarnate Son, God's presence cannot be known apart from faith. This concealment of God in the events that mediate him may have been ignored by cruder forms of the old-fashioned arguments from prophecy and miracles; but it is so widely recognized today that I do not think it needs to be further discussed.

There are, however, certain criticisms which I feel bound to make with reference to point 1 (the basic axiom). While I fully endorse Bultmann's view that revelation means primarily the self-disclosure of God's personal presence in historical events, I doubt whether he realizes the secondary importance of doctrinal formulations. "Believing in" is impossible without some measure of "believing that." Even the New Testament (as Cullmann has shown) contains nuclear creeds. Furthermore, once the Church began to reflect on revealed data, it was bound (in order both to check heresy and to clarify its own awareness) to engage in those speculations which culminated in the conciliar creeds.

Bultmann's insensitivity to dogma is easily explained in terms of his philosophical and theological background. Liberal Protestantism descends through Herrmann, Ritschl, and Schleiermacher from Kant. It rests philosophically on Kant's severance of noumena from phenomena and the speculative from the practical reason. The only statements we can safely make about Christian revelation are those which show its moral effect. Thus we cannot know whether Christ *really* is divine; the most we can say is that he is God "for us." The inadequacy of Ritschlian restatements of doctrine (and their contradictoriness—for after all they *are* speculations that go beyond the given data) have often been exposed. The same inadequacy (and the same contradictoriness) attends Bultmann's rejection of speculative dogma on the basis of the absolute contrast that he posits between "objective" reason and "subjective" faith.

Yet this contrast is not dictated merely by the liberal tradition interpreted through a diffused existentialism. It is made irrevocable by the third, fourth, and fifth of the characteristics I described. If revelation is restricted to a present encounter, and if it must be systematically correlated to self-understanding, there can be no place for doctrines which attempt to speak of God and his actions "in themselves." Hence, in the essay on "The Christological Confession of the World Council of Churches," Bultmann writes:

The decisive question might now be this: whether and how far the titles at any time intend to tell us something about the nature of Jesus— how far they describe him, so to speak, objectifying him in his being in himself, or whether and how far they speak of him in his significance for man, for faith? Do they speak—I can formulate it this way too—of his *physis* or of the *Christus pro me*? How far is a christological pronounce- ment about him also a pronouncement about me? Does he help me be- cause he is God's Son, or is he the Son of God because he helps me?[12]

It is clear that a critique of Bultmann's views on revelation must consider the third, fourth, and fifth characteristics; for these deter- mine the particular form that he gives to the Kantian dichotomies that liberal Protestantism presupposes.

(3) It seems to me self-evident that while "encounter" is a possible (and perhaps for Lutherans a congenial) image for depicting the relation between God and man, it is not the only image. It cannot do justice to (for example) the intellectually toned faith of the Cambridge Platonists or the experience of mystical union. Further- more, preaching (which is the normal precondition of an encounter) is only one among the many elements that constitute the true and spiritual worship through which God reveals himself to believers.

Bultmann departs radically from both scriptural and patristic

---

[12] *Essays*, p. 280. Note the disparaging reference to *physis*. Bultmann con- stantly opposes Greek to Hebrew modes of thought in an exaggerated and mis- leading way. Furthermore, "because" in the last sentence is ambiguous. It may be that in the *ordo cognoscendi* Christ is God's Son because he helps me. So it was through the atoning power of Christ's death that Paul perceived in him the incarnation of God's love. But in the *ordo essendi* Christ helps me because he is God's Son; for it was through his divine (as well as through his human) nature that he was able to offer a perfect sacrifice.

thought; and in so doing he loses the theological comprehensiveness that the deepest insights of existentialism require. According to the orthodox doctrine (derived from the Johannine prologue), Christ is the pre-existent Word through whom all things were made. Bultmann has no place for a creative and indwelling Word. Lacking any concept of divine immanence he cannot conserve the truth (so splendidly expressed by Augustine and Pascal) that God is drawing men to himself in the very act by which they seek him. This denial of God's immanence by nature involves the denial of his immanence by grace. Scriptural references to the indwelling Spirit cannot be allowed to retain their original force. Bultmann is bound to recast ("demythologize") them in the language of encounter.

(4) Bultmann's claim that knowledge of God also involves knowledge of oneself is more plausible; and I doubt whether it has been given the attention it deserves. He certainly does not wish to *identify* revelation with self-awareness. Rather he says that self-awareness is the human element in revelation. In this he is surely right. The believer cannot regard God with the detached, theoretical, interest with which the physicist regards an atom. To know God is to know oneself as the object of his providential and redemptive care.

The term "self-understanding" (and the existentialist categories through which it is articulated) are new; but the idea is intrinsic to Christianity and was expressed succinctly as follows by Calvin at the beginning of his *Institutes*. "Our wisdom, in so far as it ought to be deemed true and solid wisdom, consists almost entirely of two parts: the knowledge of God and of ourselves. But as these are connected together by many ties, it is not easy to determine which of the two precedes, and gives birth to the other."

Yet the thesis requires qualification. Every theological statement need not make an *immediate* appeal to self-understanding. Surely it is proper for a Christian to contemplate the doctrine of the Trinity without expecting it to have an immediately perceptible effect on his existence. Such contemplation will indeed have an effect—but of an indirect kind which might not be fully describable in existentialist terms. How far our knowledge and love of God can be disinterested is a vexed question into which I cannot enter; but they need not *always* be *directly* tied to *practical* interests in the uniform way that Bultmann's talk about self-understanding implies.

(5) Perhaps the most calamitous (as it is the most notorious) consequence that follows from Bultmann's restriction of revelation to a present encounter is his refusal to find any divine epiphany in the historical Jesus. I find his position incredible. Doubtless God could have given a final revelation in many ways. In fact he chose to give it through the manhood he assumed from a virgin in ancient Palestine. He thus placed himself at the disposal of men; and so he was crucified. By comparison it is surely congruous (and by comparison too it is surely a small "offense") that he should place the legitimization of belief in his saving acts (to the extent and in the form that may from time to time be necessary) in the hands of fallible historians and their fallible crafts. The historical nature of his revelation demands that we accept historical knowledge (with all its particular uncertainties) as *one* among the many elements that constitute the total evidence for faith.

Two subsidiary points remain: Bultmann's use of philosophical concepts in elucidating revelation, and his views on general (or natural) revelation. I shall not speak of the first, which will be covered in other essays; but in closing I shall indicate my attitude to the second.

Bultmann's denial of any positive revelation outside Christianity shows his strong affinity with Barth. The denial seems to me to be untenable. If we define true religion as the acknowledgment of one God who possesses moral properties and is capable of entering into some kind of personal relationship with his worshippers—and this suffices as a *minimal* definition from the Christian standpoint—I do not see how we can deny that God has revealed himself positively through (for example) well-known phases of Greek and Hindu thought. Of course the revelation is incomplete and insecure. Yet it remains, in its limited mode and degree, a revelation of the one, ineffable God whom Christians know as the Father of Jesus Christ.

Rudolf Bultmann's Philosophy of History*

HEINRICH OTT

The University of Basel
Basel, Switzerland

Over a period of years, I have had the privilege of being able to discuss the philosophy of history with Rudolf Bultmann personally, both orally and in writing. I would like to regard the following comments as a continuation of this exchange. It is not my intention to develop a "position" over against Bultmann's and then to defend it. I trust that on this question neither Bultmann nor I have a definitive position which can only be "attacked" or "defended." Together with him—certainly not in mere passive acceptance of his view—I am attempting to penetrate a bit further into the mystery of history, and into an understanding of its nature.

As a historian, as a man, and as a Christian, Bultmann is concerned with the problem of history. Perhaps we may say that it is *the* one great theme which claims his thought. The most eloquent witness to his deep concern is indeed his Gifford Lectures, *History and Eschatology*,[1] given in Edinburgh; the lectures represent a mature

---

* Translated by Niels C. Nielsen, Jr.

[1] German edition, *Geschichte und Eschatologie* (Tübingen: J. C. B. Mohr [Siebeck], 1958); original English edition, *History and Eschatology* (Edinburgh: The University Press, 1957). In the references to this work that follow, numbers in parentheses will refer to pages in the original English edition.

summary of his experience, questions, and insights in this matter. I shall draw on them more than on any other source.

Bultmann understands man in his radical historicity, in his being delivered over to history (*Ausgeliefertsein*). In earlier times, "human nature" could still be thought of as an unchanging substratum underlying all the changes of history. The accidents of man's being, but not the substance, alter with the movement of history. Today, however, we know from our own experience that man *himself* changes with history. Absolutely no area of his existence can avoid it and none is safe from it. "His historicity does not consist in the fact that he is an individual who passes through history, who experiences history, who meets with history. No, man is nothing but history, for he is, so to speak, not an active being but someone to whom things happen. Man is only a process without 'true existence.' The end, it seems, is nihilism."[2] Bultmann understands the historical consciousness to have developed such an outlook today. The question has become urgent: "Can there be deliverance from nihilism?"

Bultmann's *provisional* answer or working hypothesis runs as follows: "Must we say that the historicity of man is not yet understood in a sufficiently radical way but must be worked out to its ultimate consequences in order to overcome the conclusion of nihilism? Such questions can be answered only when we recognize clearly the essence, the idea of history. It seems to me that the real problem is veiled by the one-sided question about meaning in history."[3] His *definitive* answer, given from the Christian faith, is as follows:

The meaning in history lies always in the present, and when the present is conceived as the eschatological present by Christian faith, the meaning in history is realized. Anyone who complains: "I cannot see meaning in history, and therefore my life, which is interwoven in history, is meaningless," is to be admonished: "Do not look around yourself into universal history, you must look into your own personal history. Always in your present lies the meaning in history. . . . In every moment slumbers the possibility of being the eschatological moment. You must awaken it."[4]

---

[2] *Ibid.*, p. 11 (11).
[3] *Ibid.*, p. 12 (11).
[4] *Ibid.*, p. 184 (155).

These two answers already reveal the content side of Bultmann's philosophy of history (or theology of history—the expression does not matter here!). Bultmann radicalizes the modern consciousness of historicity, that man is delivered over (*Ausgeliefertsein*) to history. It is this radicalization which enables him to overcome the threatening dangers of relativism and nihilism. Above all he achieves this in dialogue with the English philosopher of history, R. G. Collingwood. According to Collingwood, the act of historical insight is a re-enactment of history; through it, one achieves knowledge of both himself and his own possibilities. Every moment of history is one of possible human self-knowledge and as such has its own intrinsic meaning; the question of a "meaning of history" does not need to be pursued further. Collingwood has radicalized the historicity of man— the fact that he cannot avoid historical change—to such an extent that every historical event appears meaningful in itself.

Without contradicting Collingwood, Bultmann wishes to take this radicalization one step further: What is the intent of self-knowledge, he inquires? Is it not an act of decision in consciousness of responsibility with regard to the future? And does it not include also what happens to man, his sufferings (and not only his actions), reactions, and therefore decision and responsibility? It is on this ground that Bultmann not only affirms man's radical historicity with Collingwood, but interprets it from the standpoint of Christian faith. The self of man in its radical historicity, in its being delivered over to history (*Ausgeliefertsein*—not in the sense that the past is determinative for me, but that every decision is necessarily made in view of the future), is ultimately the self in a situation of decision before God. The freedom which I need in order to maintain myself effectively in history I do not have of myself. It comes to me only as a gift which I grasp in faith. Christian faith knows this: that freedom is a gift. This is the specific character of Christianity!

Bultmann presents the historical consciousness of modern man for our examination. He analyzes it to its lowest depths and concludes that the historical consciousness is taken with more radical serious-ness by Christian faith than it ever could have been by itself. On this premise, Christianity appears plausible from the point of view of modern historical experience, but of course that does not mean that an historical "proof" for the truth of Christianity is being advanced. At this point, an objection could be raised against Bultmann on the grounds that he does not understand Christianity as developing primarily from itself but as the crown of a structure of historical-philosophical development—as a philosophy of radical historicity. I would not accept this objection as justified. Rather, it seems to me that the method which he follows is necessary in all theological thought. To be sure, Bultmann develops a "worldly phenomenon" in dialogue with science and philosophy, but also with immediate experience (in this case, the phenomenon of radical historicity). He thus points out that this phenomenon is best interpreted from the standpoint of Christian faith, because it gives an answer to the question which necessarily arises from the phenomenon itself. Christian faith not only gives the answer to a question with which an immanental view of history is already finished; it radicalizes the question itself. Indeed, it goes so far as to radicalize the already radical historical understanding of modern thought forms. This is not a variety of natural theology, which is here applied not to nature but to history. Instead, it is simply an indication that the Christian faith is in contact with the experience of reality, in that the revelation of the gospel actually encounters the reality in which we live, and to that extent it actually is *revelation*. By its light, this reality can be understood more deeply.

If, for reasons which will be stated later, I come to somewhat different conclusions than Bultmann about the content, I nonetheless wish to affirm the main lines of his method without reservation. It is in fact the task of all serious theology to show that the revelation of God encounters reality and that it is therefore actually revelation.

Besides the question of content, Bultmann's philosophy of history also has a very essential formal or theory-of-knowledge (epistemological) aspect. This is the aspect of *hermeneutics,* which Bultmann divides into two questions:[5] (1) How is it possible to understand historical documents transmitted by tradition? (2) Is it in general possible to reach an objective knowledge of history?

Bultmann understands that these primary hermeneutical questions are closely related. When I ask to what extent historical knowledge in general is possible—for example, in the understanding of historical texts and other documents—and what are the presuppositions of

---

[5] Cf. *History and Eschatology*, chap. viii.

historical knowledge, the answer will accordingly give an indication of the range and limits of this knowledge. At the same time the hermeneutical questions which we have already characterized as formal (i.e., epistemological) are linked most closely with the content aspect of the theology of history, that is, with the question about the essence or meaning of history. What is characteristic of history is that "an ultimate distinction between the knower and his object cannot be maintained."[6] The hermeneutical question about the nature of historical *knowledge* and the material historical-philosophical question concerning historical *being* ultimately reach the same goal.

Bultmann answers the first hermeneutical question concerning the understanding of historical documents transmitted by the tradition with his now famous concept of "preunderstanding" (*Vorverständniss*). This preunderstanding, which the interpreter must bring to his work in order to arrive at an understanding, is a special living relation to the subject in which the author who is being interpreted has a stake. There must be a certain commonality between the author and his interpreter, therefore: a common interest in a common subject. This interest can assume a very different form in the author and his interpreter. Yet, without a living relation to the contents of his text, the interpreter can never understand it.

Now an interpreter can, of course, approach the same text with a variety of different interests and questions. He can, for example, have a purely scientific-historical interest simply in past facts. He can try to represent the preceding psychological and psychic factors which led to the emergence of such documents. He can see and evaluate the document as an aesthetic phenomenon. Finally, he can also bring out the question of the truth of the text and become interested in the understanding of man and his possibilities which it offers. This complex of possible interests and viewpoints on the part of the historian corresponds to the complexity of man himself. "He (or man) is a complex being. He consists of body and soul, or if one prefers, of body, soul, and mind." Therefore "from each viewpoint something objectively true will appear. The picture is falsified only if a single viewpoint is made an absolute one, if it comes to be a dogma."[7]

---

[6] Bultmann cites Erich Frank as agreeing to this effect, *ibid.*, p. 134 (119–120).

[7] *Ibid.*, p. 132 (118).

Bultmann answers the second hermeneutical question—whether we can obtain objective knowledge of history—by considering the extent to which it is possible to bring to light crude historical facts.

Indeed, strict methodical research can recognize objectively a certain part of the historical process, namely, events in so far as they are nothing but occurrences which happened at a certain place in space and time. It is possible, for instance, to fix objectively the fact and the time at which Socrates drank the cup of hemlock, the fact and the time when Caesar crossed the Rubicon, the fact and the time when Luther affixed his ninety-five theses to the doors of the Castle-Church of Wittenberg, or to know objectively the fact that and the time when a certain battle was fought or a certain empire was founded or a certain catastrophe happened.[8]

This, however, is not Bultmann's complete answer. And I agree emphatically that only "a part of the historical process," never the whole, can be known objectively. He explains with justification: "We must ask whether history is sufficiently comprehended when it is only seen as a field of such events and actions as can be fixed in space and time."[9] By denying that such is the case, Bultmann rejects and overcomes an historical positivism which holds that the whole of history—what happened in the past—can be known with objective certainty "as it really happened." He denies the positivist claim that a neutral, disinterested, and therefore universally valid viewpoint can be achieved. Instead, he affirms that history is an interrelation and not merely the totality of events that can be determined as to space and time. "In any case history is a movement, a process, in which the single events are not without connection but are connected by the chain of cause and effect. Such connection presupposes powers at work in the historical process. . . . Furthermore, everyone can recognize how economic and social needs and distresses are factors in the historical process, but that is also true of ideas and ideals. Of course, the understanding and appreciation and valuation of such factors is different, and there is no court which can give a final judgment."[10]

But above all, and in this I see Bultmann's decisive contribution, "historical events and actions are what they are—that is, historical—

---

8 *Ibid.*, pp. 129 f. (116).
9 *Ibid.*, p. 130 (116).
10 *Ibid.*, pp. 129–130 (116–117).

only together with their meaning or importance. What is the importance of the fact that Socrates drank the cup of hemlock; the importance for the history of Athens; even for the history of the human mind? What is the importance of the fact that Caesar crossed the Rubicon . . . ?"[11] The meaning of an historical event which belongs integrally to the reality of the event discloses itself only in the future. It is on this ground that Bultmann can say: "To each historical phenomenon belongs its future, a future in which alone it will appear as that which it really is—to speak precisely we must say: the future in which it evermore clearly appears as that which it is. For ultimately it will show itself in its very essence only when history has reached its end."[12]

Bultmann does not state explicitly, but I assume he would consider it a matter of course, that the meaning of an historical event in the future can also be darkened by misunderstainding. In this case, it is up to an even later time to restore a proper understanding (which of course also can be only a provisional understanding). Although I agree with Bultmann on the main points, I miss two factors: (1) With respect to historical causality Bultmann holds, I believe correctly, that no objectively certain statements can be made. However, he fails to undertake any detailed investigation about the nature of historical causality. In my judgment, this is a central problem in the philosophy of history. There is a clearly worked-out concept of causality in natural science (at least for classical physics) but there is as yet none in the area of history. It is clear that "causality" is something very different in these two cases. In history an element of freedom is implicit in all causal relations, and it remains to be shown in which sense it is still possible to speak of "causality" at all. In order to comprehend the nature of the causal relations of particular historical circumstances, the historian must seek to place himself precisely and with empathy in the position of earlier men in their freedom. Furthermore, it is clear that this is an act of understanding encounter in a situation of personal involvement, and that it cannot be carried out simply with a method of coercive objective universal validity. It is Bultmann's contribution already at this point to have

---

[11] Etc., *ibid.*, p. 131 (117).
[12] *Ibid.*, p. 135 (120).

shown the limits of historical positivism in relation to the possibility of comprehending historical causality and continuity. The reason that he does not probe the question of causality further may be connected with the way he approaches the problem. I believe it is because he asks what is possible and impossi^le for the historian (he himself is a historian) in relation to his object and gives less attention to the ontological nature of history as such.

(2) Bultmann speaks of the future of historical events as belonging to the reality of these events, and of the end of history when for the first time the final meaning of all historical phenomena will be made known. Is this end of history, in which the meaning of all historical events will be disclosed and all history seen fully, a mere hypothesis for the sake of illustration? Is the concept merely peripheral? Or must such a qualified end of history be reckoned with ontically—even if it obviously cannot enter into the range of vision of the historian? If one does not reckon with it, that is, if language concerning it is a mere illustration for purposes of perception without ontic significance, an expression which intends no meaningful assertion, then this question must be faced: How can one still speak at all of a "meaning" of historical events? How can one say that an historical event has a meaning if the place where this meaning becomes known is nonexistent not only for the historian but *in principle?* I accept most emphatically Bultmann's conception of the future dimension of historical phenomena. However, from this I must conclude that there is such a thing as an end of history, a "last judgment" in which all that is hidden will be revealed. Of course this end does not enter into the perspective of the historian. But it forms the ontological presupposition of the historical-ontological language used in the description of the essentially intrinsic future dimension of all historical events. This judgment, which is in my opinion unavoidable, I cannot find anywhere in Bultmann. Rather he excludes the conception of a last judgment as mythological. I must therefore ask him how he proposes to handle the ontological problem that he raises with his own interpretation. Of course, one can say that an historical event is already concluded and settled in a certain way. Yet, future generations can find incalculable unforeseen meanings in it, re-evaluate it and "make something else of it." In this respect, its future remains open. For all that, such a way of viewing the matter seems too

trivial to me. What happens in the future with respect to meaning remains as merely external to the event itself. In this case there would be no reason to say that the future belongs to the event itself. Moreover, with respect to such external and abiding factors of future meaning, there would be no basis on which to distinguish between understanding and misunderstanding of an historical phenomenon.

I shall now attempt to summarize Bultmann's philosophy of history as we have thus far characterized it. Knowledge of history in the proper sense exists only as there is encounter with history itself. Moreover, the moments of encounter are not only moments of insight into history; rather, the meaning which is grasped is already implicit in the events of encounter themselves. The act in which I encounter history (some event of history) thus has at the same time both noetic and ontic meaning: Noetic in that here (and only here) I really know history; ontic because here (and only here) is the meaning of historical events at all recognizable. The "meaning of history" exists only in a given moment and not in any comprehensive historical sweep, only in encounter and not in any being in itself. "The question of meaning in history (the course of history) has become meaningless."[13] The real problem, namely the question of the essence of history, has become "veiled by the one-sided question about the meaning of history (i.e., the whole course of history)."[14] The nature of history, rightly understood, is as follows: that every historical moment has its own meaning in itself in that it implies openness to God and that it has the possibility of becoming the eschatological moment.

I agree with most of Bultmann's essential claims. I have already stated my reasons for accepting his general method and his approach to the relation between modern historical consciousness and Christian understanding of history. Above all, I concur in his attack on historical positivism and objectivism, in his designation of true historical knowledge as encounter with history, and in his view that to the reality of an historical event belongs its future. I can agree with Bultmann's tendency to take seriously the radicalism of the modern historical consciousness: there is no metaphysical substratum of

---

[13] *Ibid.*, p. 135 (120).
[14] *Ibid.*, p. 12 (11).

humanity which remains undisturbed through the changes of history. I can also agree to a great extent with his statement that objective knowledge of history is possible in principle, in so far as it refers merely to facts which can be located in space-time (this is with certin minor reservations, which I shall not now explain in detail; they are most appropriately related to what was said earlier about the particular character of historical causality). I agree with what Bultmann says about the structure of the historical moment as openness to God, as well as about the gift of freedom in which man in his historical existence is granted a share by God. Also, I accept Bultmann's claim that there is no "meaning of history" in a "natural being in itself." "This 'being in itself' is an illusion of an objectivising type of thinking which is proper in natural science but not in history."[15] Indeed, "every present is called in question and challenged through its future."[16] There is no knowledge of a meaning of history apart from engagement, from being challenged and being claimed, from the existential participation by man.

Finally, it appears to me important and relevant when Bultmann extends the horizon of his inquiry about history toward the tradition of the philosophy of history and includes the dimension which he calls *personality*. The object of our inquiry about the essence of history and the being of man in history is not just the great historical processes which disclose themselves to the historian. We must

. . . ask whether the decisions through which life runs are solely decisions demanded by historical tasks. Decisions within personal encounters, decisions of friendship and love, or of indifference and hatred— can these be called positively or negatively answers to historical problems? Are gratitude or fidelity answers to historical problems? Certainly such relationships and actions have historical consequences. Can the choice of a way of life which develops out of one's situation and personal encounters be called an answer to a historical problem? . . . Is patience in the endurance of sufferings or joy in beauty an answer to the historical problems? Can one equate self-knowledge into which one is led through personal destiny, whether through blessings or distresses or the threatening nearness of death, with self-knowledge which is gained through historical reflection . . . ? It seems to me that the self in question has another

15 *Ibid.*, p. 136 (121).
16 *Ibid.*, p. 167 (152).

dimension than those which Croce and Collingwood take into account. We may call this the dimension of *Personality*.[17]

Following all this agreement, it is not easy to state with sufficient clarity the decisive point at which Bultmann's conception of the philosophy or theology of history appears questionable to me. This point was already touched upon in what was said about the concept of the end of history. It raises an issue on which, in spite of all agreement, I am obliged to believe differently from Bultmann.

I wish to explain my question by applying it to what Bultmann says about the knowledge of single historical epochs. Indeed, according to Bultmann, we can no longer ask legitimately about the meaning of history as a whole, or the course of history. Because man is at the mercy of history (*Ausgeliefertsein*) and unable to occupy a position outside it, such a question has become meaningless. On this point Christian faith must agree with radical modern historical consciousness. Likewise, for him there is no universal meaning of history, since world history in its multifarious complications belongs to the old aeon. It can be safely excluded from faith's question of meaning. If there is a meaning of history from the viewpoint of faith, it can only be that meaning, solely and uniquely, which is bound up in its eschatological moment of faith decision. (And this moment of faith decision indeed is much more likely to occur in the dimension of personality than in the dimension of world history which is relevant for the historian. Of course, we must make it clear that both dimensions interpenetrate in many different ways.)

After Bultmann has discussed the question of the meaning of history as a whole from the point of view of the modern historical consciousness as well as of Christian faith, he nevertheless remarks as follows:

But there still remains the question of the meaning of single historical phenomena and single historical epochs. To speak more exactly: there remains the question of the importance of single historical events and deeds of our past for our present, a present which is charged with responsibility for our future. For instance: what is the meaning and importance of the decay of the uniform medieval culture in face of the problem of the relationship of the Christian confessional groups, especially with regard

---

[17] *Ibid.*, p. 174 (145–46).

to religious education? Or what is the meaning and importance of the
French Revolution for the problem of the organization and authority of
the state? Or what is the meaning and importance of the rise of capitalism
and socialism for the problem of economic organization? and so on. In
all these cases the analysis of motives and consequences gives light for
the demands of our future. Judgments concerning the past and the present
belong together, and each is clarified by the other. It is by such historical
interaction that the phenomena of the past become real historical phenomena and begin to disclose their meaning. I say they begin—that is to
say, objectivity of historical knowledge is not attainable in the sense of
absolute ultimate knowledge, nor in the sense that the phenomena could
be known in their "being in themselves" which the historian could perceive in pure receptivity.[18]

For three reasons this citation seems to me to be very important
for the discussion of Bultmann's philosophy of history:

(1) Here Bultmann introduces a new, important viewpoint: that
of responsibility for the future, and with it, the responsible shaping of
history. It is no longer merely a viewpoint of detached observation by
the historian who may enter the complex patterns of history with *his*
interests and ask *his* questions. The stance of the one who shapes
history is deeper and in a certain way more comprehensive than that
of one who engages in historical reflection. But, of course, again both
of these viewpoints and approaches to intercourse with history
are closely related. "The historian recognizes himself as historical,
and in that he is thereby confronted with the question as to the
meaning of historical observation, he comes to know the meaning
of historicity in a deeper sense. . . . Historicity now gains the meaning of responsibility in the face of the future, which is at the same
time the responsibility for the heritage of the past in view of the
future."[19]

(2) Thus is overcome the very strongly individualistic punctiliar
perspective in which Bultmann's historical thinking seemed at first to
be caught. Bultmann could say that the proper meaning of history is
to be found only in the moment of individual decision. But he
includes as well the idea of a responsibility which reaches from a
"space" of the historical past to a "space" of the historical future.

---

18 *Ibid.* pp. 135 f. (120–21).
19 *Ibid.*, p. 172 (143).

Drawing on the heritage of the past, it shapes the future creatively. Drawing on the meaning of the past, it gets the power to impart creatively new meaning to the future.

(3) Bultmann appears to me to concede, in the first cited passage, that historical phenomena, past epochs, and individual experience all have a meaning in themselves. They "begin to disclose their meaning." But they do so only (and never conclusively) in encounter where man is engaged responsibly and bears responsibility for the future. However, man himself does not determine this meaning. He does not invent it. But it comes to him out of history; it challenges him and he must respond.

These three thoughts which can be explicated from the text are interrelated. Now, I believe that Bultmann should pursue this line further. Whoever structures history, and so bears responsibility for the future, in my opinion must believe in a meaning of history, a meaning which is realized not alone in the individual moment, but also in the course of history. Also, if one holds the opinion that this meaning is realized only through man himself and not from necessity, one need not refrain from speaking of a meaning of history. And this meaning must in every moment appear as meaning of history as a whole, since, as is the case today, we are gaining a world-wide view which encompasses all mankind. Today, if one seeks to see the goal for which we strive (to which we are creatively committed, and for which we feel responsibility) in the progress of humanity, of righteousness and freedom in the relations of men and peoples, this would imply an idea of the meaning of history as a whole as well as a belief in this meaning. In this case, one will examine the course of past history in order to see to what extent it reveals fixed points en route and evidence of progress.

These thoughts which we must frame on the basis of Bultmann's own statements lead to the conclusion that the dimension of the meaning of history as a whole must be kept open. I cannot agree with Bultmann's view that "the question of the meaning of history has become meaningless." It is true that such "meaning" cannot signify something detached from man, something given in itself outside him. But is this not self-evident? Already implicit in the concept of "meaning" as such is the consideration that it is not given as a natural fact but must be appropriated with understanding and so, in a certain way, realized by man. How much this realization occurs with a certain necessity, as Hegel or the Marxists believe, is of course another question. At any rate, from the point of view of Christian faith, a concept must also be taken into consideration which I have not yet been able to discover in connection with Bultmann's theology of history: the concept of God's providence. In his historical conduct and his shaping of the future, the believer regards himself not only as responsible to God, but as supported or hindered by God. God guides him without taking away his responsibility or the possibility of failure.

A Christian theology or philosophy of history must consider this interplay of divine providence and human freedom, divine wisdom and human failure and achievement, more carefully. (But this problem is indeed extremely old in theology and has been discussed under various dogmatic headings. It has not been sufficiently clarified even to the present, but instinctively we have seen again and again that neither the divine determination nor human responsibility can be surrendered—that one may not become either Pelagian or fatalist.) Finally an ultimate relation between salvation-history and world history begins to dawn, in the sense that earthly conduct and occurrences are not in vain or forgotten before God. On the other hand, God's eschatological action will not be objectivized to a this-worldly dimension. The questionable nature of all that is historical remains. Therefore, it is impossible to identify the plan of divine providence in history or to pronounce a final judgment on past epochs or present events. This consideration does not hinder us from believing in a hidden meaning of all history in God's sight or from making ourselves available in our own sphere as tools of God—in the risk of faith and by responsible action—for the realization of this meaning. We may do so in awareness of the questionable nature of our action and the possibility of failure; yet we do so trusting in God's wisdom and forgiveness.

These wholly introductory evaluations and questions are not intended as a criticism of Bultmann but to renew and develop further the discussion on history which he has led with such illuminating power.

Rudolf Bultmann's Interpretation
of New Testament Eschatology

PAUL S. MINEAR
Yale University Divinity School
New Haven, Connecticut

Eschatology has exerted a strange fascination upon Professor Bultmann throughout his productive career. His writings, the first of which appeared in 1909, began immediately following the epoch-making books by Johannes Weiss and Albert Schweitzer. In 1914 he was reviewing those books and by 1917 he had published an essay of his own—"Die Bedeutung der Eschatologie für die Religion des Neues Testament."[1] The four intervening decades have marked a steady acceleration not only in his own personal interest in this topic, but also in the corresponding interest of virtually all modern theologians. His work thus coincides with the epoch of eschatological concentration in both historical and theological disciplines. A thorough review of this topic would therefore involve a complete history of contemporary theology. For this essay we must be content with much more modest objectives. We will seek to epitomize his more recent thought on the topic and to appraise its strength.

I. An Epitome

The restricted scope of our first objective, i.e., Rudolf Bultmann's more recent thought, might well involve distortion if there had been

---

[1] *ZThK*, XXVII, 76–87.

drastic changes in his viewpoint over the five decades. But of such changes there is surprisingly little evidence. For example, his early essay on the eschatology of the Fourth Gospel[2] undergoes little significant modification in the later *Theology* and *Commentary*. The dangers of distortion are also reduced by the fact that Professor Bultmann has provided his own summaries of previous work in this area in his more recent books: *Theology of the New Testament, Primitive Christianity in Its Contemporary Setting,* and *History and Eschatology.* Our epitome will therefore follow the recurrent motifs in these books.

A choice must be made whether to focus attention on this scholar's own eschatology or on his reconstruction of early Christian eschatology. I have chosen the latter course because Rudolf Bultmann is primarily a historian, both in intent and in methodology. His own theological position, however, will appear quite clearly in the presuppositions of his exegesis and in the norms by which he evaluates the various ancient outlooks.

If I may suggest two of these norms at the outset it will perhaps clarify the later analysis. The first norm is a negative one and might be phrased as follows: an eschatological viewpoint is non-valid and must be rejected to the degree that it embodies cosmological ingredients. A cosmological eschatology is *per se* mythological. It inevitably confuses history with nature and reduces human existence to the realm of cosmic objectivity. The second norm is positive: an eschatology is valid to the degree that it produces and is in accord with "the complete genuine historicity of man." We will see later how this norm is applied. Here it will suffice to say that the standpoint is that of an existential anthropology which locates meaning in history in the present moment of decision, through which a man achieves authentic selfhood. The term "historicity" is Bultmann's favorite word for this realization of manhood. As parallel to the famous Kierkegaardian dictum, his motto might read: "Historicity is the truth." Because these are the dominant norms by which the successive types of eschatology are weighed, our summary of these types must include at every step the double reference to cosmology and historicity.

---

2 In *Zwischen den Zeiten* (1928), VI, 4–22. Reprinted in *Glauben und Verstehen,* I (Tübingen: J. C. B. Mohr, 1958), 134 ff.

It is typical of Professor Bultmann's work as a historian that he invariably presents his survey of types in chronological order, even though as a theologian he recognizes that the truth of a type does not depend upon its place in the history of ideas. The methodological structure of his writings and of his strictly historical research is determined very largely by the canons of *religionsgeschichtliche* study. A thinker's situation in history is defined first of all in terms of cultural and chronological succession. This means that the meaning of each of his major concepts is assumed to be derived from the previous history of that concept in the contiguous cultures. He inherits a word and an idea from Judaism or Hellenism or Gnosticism. He combines it with other words or ideas from the same or from other traditions. His thought is therefore by nature a syncretistic amalgam that must be dissolved into its original components before it can be fully grasped. And in the process of dissolution his views must be carefully distinguished from those of other thinkers. The method for logical appraisal and evaluation is quite different. Here the self-knowledge of the historian and his full recognition of what historicity means produce another concept of history, and thereby a quite distinctive vantage point from which to measure the truth of the various eschatologies. As Professor Bultmann puts it, the chief question becomes one not of research but of interpretation. "What understanding of human existence is enshrined in primitive Christianity?"[3]

The whole range of Biblical eschatologies is constantly seen in contrast to characteristic Greek views. The Greek understood history in the same way as he understood cosmic movements. In such movements all change is simply "the same thing in new constellations." Because history is understood "by analogy with nature,"[4] the task of historiography becomes analogous to the task of natural science. Inevitably therefore the doctrine of the end of the world grew out of the observed periodicity of the seasons and the ecliptic of the sun. "A cosmic mythology" developed, correlative to cyclical time. Eschatology was subordinated to concepts of universal natural law

---

[3] Rudolf Bultmann, *Primitive Christianity in Its Contemporary Setting,* trans. R. H. Fuller (London: Thames and Hudson, 1956), p. 12.

[4] Rudolf Bultmann, *History and Eschatology* (Edinburgh: The University Press, 1957), pp. 15–16.

and cosmic harmony.[5] Although various thinkers rationalized and historicized this doctrine, it remained basically a cosmological, and hence a mythological eschatology.

Professor Bultmann appears to reject virtually all Greek views, not only on the grounds just mentioned, but also because of the resultant anthropology. Man's individuality is ignored; he is "an instance of universal human Being, which in its turn is seen to be an instance of cosmic Being in general."[6] As an historical agent he is a being whose substance does not change. His character is not basically affected by his decisions, experiences, or actions. In fact, history is not understood as a field wherein man has intrinsic responsibility for the future, because the future is determined by natural processes. In short, man is "not understood in his historicity."[7]

In the perspectives of Israel under the old covenant, by contrast, there is no sensitivity to the laws of history and no tendency to view historical developments as determined by natural forces. History is ruled by a Creator God who has a goal for it. The cycle of rebellion and return is more decisive than the cycle of the seasons. The unity of history derives from the unity of God's promise; historiography is therefore not scientific but homiletical. Each situation embodies a call to the covenant people to accept their responsibility in the face of the future.[8] This call produces critical self-knowledge, an awareness of the past and a hope for the future which transforms the present. "God is always a God who comes. Every moment points to that coming."[9] Consequently Bultmann can write that the Old Testament shows a definite "preoccupation with eschatology."[10]

This judgment seems to contradict his contention in another place that there is no eschatology in Old Testament prophecy.[11] In this negation, of course, he has defined eschatology more narrowly, as a doctrine of the end of the world followed by a time of salvation. The

---

[5] *Ibid.*, pp. 23–24.
[6] *Primitive Christianity in Its Contemporary Setting*, p. 180.
[7] *History and Eschatology*, p. 18.
[8] *Ibid.*, pp. 18 ff.
[9] *Primitive Christianity in Its Contemporary Setting*, p. 34.
[10] *Ibid.*, p. 22.
[11] *History and Eschatology*, pp. 27 f.

prophets viewed God's judgments as taking place within history and not at its end. Nevertheless, in terms of the anthropological structure of the prophetic word, that authoritative proclamation of coming historical catastrophes was eschatological, because it produced knowledge of the past and an openness toward the future.

This anthropology was the essence of the Biblical outlook. It made genuine history the real center of things, effectively historicizing cosmology. It made human will the central reality in history. Because its God is always a coming God, man is recognized as a being always open to the future. "Man is always what his past has made him. He always brings his past along with him into his present (where) . . . confession and forgiveness can make him a new man."[12]

Nevertheless this anthropology had serious defects which weakened the prophetic eschatology. The subject of history was the people, not the individual; hence the future remained the future of the nation alone. Should fulfillment come within history, it would include only those who were then alive. But fulfillment never came, and never could come within history, so long as the destiny of the nation was the content of the promise. The objective historical fortunes of Israel became an inescapable refutation of the eschatology. Israel was thus prepared to shift its hope to the distant future, and to a mythical future at that.[13] We are led to suppose that a more adequate understanding of historicity would have made such an evasion unnecessary.

With late Judaism in its apocalyptic form we arrive at "eschatology in the real sense." This real sense developed only as Jewish thinkers adopted the pessimistic dualism of Iranian speculation. Now the whole of previous history was seen as an epoch of evil, and accordingly the end must be grasped not as an historical crisis but as a "purely supranatural event, realised by a cosmic catastrophe."[14] Now the last things (*ta eschata*) signified the end of the cosmos and the beginning of a new and endless cosmos. God became "a

---

[12] *Primitive Christianity in Its Contemporary Setting*, pp. 180–82; cf. also *History and Eschatology*, p. 28.

[13] *History and Eschatology*, p. 21.; *Primitive Christianity in Its Contemporary Setting*, pp. 35–41.

[14] *History and Eschatology*, p. 29.

superior cosmic power, spatially distant and ontologically distinct from all worldly phenomena."[15] The Messiah became a "figure of cosmic eschatology, the archetypal man as the head of a new humanity."[16] Redemption was assigned to a future which embodied no real historical events but which was a fantastic affair whose advent depended solely upon the time determined by God. Israel lost its historical moorings, and historical time was evacuated of any meaning whatsoever. In short, history was cosmologized. Events in nature were again made determinative of events in history. Apocalyptic thus represented a drastic retrogression toward a cosmic eschatology. Yet it marked a distinct progress in anthropological insight in that the individual was released from his bondage to the people (Israel), and upon him was placed a final sense of responsibility for his own decisions.[17]

Jesus is "placed" by Professor Bultmann in the context of late Jewish apocalyptic, for his sense of mission was oriented around the reign of God as the fulfillment of the cosmic hopes of the apocalyptists. With them, Jesus viewed the whole of previous history as an old and evil age. To him all judgment was concentrated in the hands of a heavenly savior, a supernatural, not a historical figure. He gave no promise for Israel, no hope for the future of the people as a people. With many of his contemporaries he anticipated an immediate world's end, and was therein mistaken. As an apocalyptist the form of his expectation was mythological and cosmic.[18]

Yet when one asks concerning Jesus' understanding of human existence (his anthropology) one discovers that it did not depend upon this cosmic mythology. He restored the earlier Jewish view of God, rejecting a "false cosmic transcendence" by redefining God as always the coming God who defines the present moment of time as one of radical decision. God's cosmic future was translated into his historical nearness; his cosmic transcendence was translated into

---

[15] *Primitive Christianity in Its Contemporary Setting*, p. 61.

[16] *Ibid.*, p. 86.

[17] *History and Eschatology*, p. 31.

[18] *Ibid.*, p. 32; see also *Primitive Christianity in Its Contemporary Setting*, p. 87; *New Testament Theology*, I, trans. K. Grobel (New York: Charles Scribner's Sons, 1951), 4–5.

the demand for an immediate and absolute choice. Individuals and not the nation became central; the wills of the individuals became the fulcrum of historical existence. An ultimate weight was placed on the Now, and this Now was seen in terms of today's encounter with the neighbor; therefore love became the mode of repentance and obedience.[19]

The God-knowledge which produced this self-knowledge was relatively independent of the apocalyptic fantasy. Accordingly, Jesus reduced and modified the latter until the anthropological component became primary. For example, he showed no concern for speculations concerning the date of the Day or the shape of the coming bliss.[20] The radical dualism between the two ages was simply the occasion for grasping the absoluteness of man's choice: either the world or God's reign.

After the death of Jesus, however, the earliest Christian church adopted an eschatology which was more cosmological than anthropological. It heightened the cosmic elements in Jesus' message with themes drawn from Jewish apocalyptic. So it visualized the end of the cosmos as imminent. It viewed itself not as an historical community but as a community belonging only to the new age, in sharpest cleavage with the world, including historical Israel. So it viewed the death of Jesus not as an historical event; the new covenant must be grounded on a cosmic, supernatural event. Thus, to the degree that eschatology was cosmologized, it "swallowed up" history.[21]

Nevertheless, the process of historical life continued inexorably. The church which viewed itself as belonging only to the new aeon became again an historical phenomenon. The faith became a new religion, dependent upon the past, reliant upon inherited tradition, inseparable from formal doctrines, from moral codes, from cultus, sacrament, and priesthood. The contradiction between the cosmic myth and continuing historical time created the critical problem: how long can hope in the Parousia last when the world whose end it celebrates does not end? Of this problem, Professor Bultmann finds

---

[19] *Primitive Christianity in Its Contemporary Setting*, pp. 77–79, 88–93; *New Testament Theology*, I, 6–25.
[20] *History and Eschatology*, p. 32.
[21] *Ibid.*, p. 37.

in early Christianity many temporizing solutions, none of them having, in the nature of the case, the possibility of permanence.[22] No way was open by which the genuine historicity of man could be grounded in a cosmological mythology.

Yet a solution of the problem was achieved by the anthropological theologies of Paul and John. As the Old Testament prophets had articulated an eschatology superior to that of the Greeks, as Jesus had transmuted the cosmic mythology of the Iranian-Jewish apocalyptists, so Paul solved the problem of a delayed Parousia by transmuting the primitive Christian apocalyptic. His new understanding of historical existence "contains the solution."[23]

In some ways, of course, the eschatology which the apostle inherited determined his view of historical process. He retained the expectation of future cosmic events. Viewing the past story of mankind from this anticipated end, he saw it as a single story, comprised within the sin of Adam. The end of this story would come soon, not as a result of immanent forces, but as a decisive termination by God, a termination representing the power of his grace.[24]

Yet the significant thing about Paul's thought was his view of man. It was this view which altered decisively the apocalyptic myth, in effect historicizing its cosmic components and making it the instrument for understanding what true historicity consists of. With the Jewish prophets, Paul understood history as centered in God's rule and man's response. Man again becomes the subject of history; his very essence is to live in his actions. The power of the will to make decisions is essential. With Jesus, Paul freed the individual from his bondage to Israel and to the past, and he used the message of God's transcendence to give an absolute ultimacy to the decisions of man today. With the primitive Christian believers, Paul understood that the eschatological event has happened and that the new community lives already in the end-time. To Paul, as to them, "the history of the nation and the world had lost interest."[25] But to him this dawning of the new age produced a new situation in which, through God's grace, the true historicity of man could be realized. By the decision of faith

22 *Ibid.*
23 *Ibid.*, p. 47.
24 *Ibid.*, p. 40.
25 *Ibid.*, p. 43.

man can become truly himself, free from the past and free for the future. God's call claims him as a free man and sets him free "for a real historical life in free decisions."[26] This produces a radical and full individualizing of man. It makes each moment of decision an eschatological occasion for losing life and finding it, for becoming what in God's grace he already is—a new man. The proclamation of God's forgiveness in Christ's death sets him free from a past in which he was not and could never become free from the past. It sets him in a position of choosing to be himself, by making him responsible for the future which now is a perpetually open future. It sets him wholly free from himself in love for his neighbor. Henceforth his historicity becomes an embodiment in the present moment of faith, hope, and love. It becomes a dialectical matter of "a continual being on the way, between the no longer and the not yet." It is thus that every man "gains his real essence."[27] This essence, this historicity, is rightly called eschatological existence, but this eschatology is historicized eschatology. Its chief obstacle remains the continued or recurrent intrusion of cosmological eschatology.[28]

This obstacle is fully removed in the Fourth Gospel, at least after the scholar's knife has cut out of the original document the later redactions. The original author consciously and intentionally rejected all expectations of future cosmic events. The resurrection of the dead and the final judgment were both present in the coming of Jesus among men. The eschatological event begins with his manifestation, and in continuity with that manifestation the eschatological event occurs again and again in history. This event, of course, is not subject to such historical development as "can be confirmed by any historian." Yet salvation happens only within "concrete worldly existence and nowhere else."[29] "Jesus Christ is the eschatological event not as an established fact of past time but as repeatedly present, as addressing you and me here and now in preaching."[30] Accordingly, life becomes a dynamic movement for the time between, a dialectic of the indicative and the imperative. For this dialectic a future is needed,

---

[26] *Ibid.*, p. 45.
[27] *Ibid.*, p. 43.
[28] *Primitive Christianity in Its Contemporary Setting*, p. 186.
[29] *History and Eschatology*, p. 154.
[30] *Ibid.*, pp. 151–152.

but it must be God's pure future uncontaminated with cosmic description. It is the continuing future which offers to men the possibility of full and genuine historicity. "Every instant has the possibility of being an eschatological instant and in Christian faith this possibility is realised."[31] Man does not and cannot know the meaning *of* history, but he can appropriate the meaning *in* history when history is understood as a divine "call to historicity."[32]

Measuring valid eschatology by this standard, Professor Bultmann can apply the adjective "eschatological" to every aspect of man's existence under faith, i.e., to the death and Resurrection of Christ as a salvation event appropriated by today's decision of the new man. Righteousness becomes "the essence of salvation."[33] It has its origin in God's transcendent grace which is his "eschatological deed."[34] This grace transforms the Now into the acceptable time. Although this event is "lifted out of all temporal limitation, it continues to take place in any present moment, both in the proclaiming word and in the sacraments."[35] Therefore the apostles, the congregations, the whole Church belong to the one eschatological event. Therefore also the life in faith, hope, and love participates in that event and is determined by it at every moment. This life, of course, is "no phenomenon of nature,"[36] but a work of the Holy Spirit of the end-time, which renews the inward self day by day. Thus every cosmic dimension in eschatology becomes in reality a historic dimension, i.e., it has its locus "in the actual living of men which is true 'history.' "[37]

Professor Bultmann raises the important question whether this understanding by which Paul and John appropriated the true significance of eschatology could be retained. The answer is, "It could not."[38] Inevitably the Church as an historical phenomenon led Christians to accept status as a religious group, an entity of world history.[39] Christians relapsed into a normal secular manner of life. Where eschatological interest continued, it supported the doctrine of

---

31 *Ibid.*, p. 154.
32 *Ibid.*, p. 136.
33 *New Testament Theology*, I, 271 f.
34 *Ibid.*, p. 289.
35 *Ibid.*, p. 303.
36 *Ibid.*, p. 331.
37 *Ibid.*, p. 305, also pp. 331–36.
38 *History and Eschatology*, p. 49.
39 *New Testament Theology*, I, 116–120.

salvation by works at the world's end. During the lengthening interim, man's quest for perfection would depend upon his own resources.[40] He would need the objectivized Church as an institution of salvation and by the same token he would rely upon ecclesiastical officers and upon the sacraments which must be placed under their control. Writers who utilized the traditions of Jewish apocalyptic allowed those traditions more and more to submerge historicity beneath cosmology. Writers who used Gnostic traditions allowed the Gnostic terminology in an unconverted form to dictate a cosmologized anthropology (e.g., Colossians, Ephesians).

It had not been so with Paul and John. They had freely used Gnostic terminology, but they had transformed it. They had always transposed cosmic categories into an historical key. In doing this they were aided by the Gnostic "discovery of the absolute distinction between humanity and its objective environment."[41] Gnostics themselves freely recognized this distinction, but they nullified their recognition of this "absolute distinction" by defining humanity "in ontological terms."[42] They persisted in thinking of human existence in "the categories of natural Being" and therefore could only conceive of deliverance from the world in terms of "being saved by nature." For the Gnostics, God's transcendence can only be conceived as metaphysical distance, not as the sovereignty of grace. Consequently their pictures of the future require an objective grounding in cosmic events. In the light of God's deed in Christ, by contrast, Christian hope visualizes only "the permanent futurity of God which is already there before man arrives, wherever it be, even in the darkness of death."[43] Paul and John were enabled to apprehend this true eschatology, which is "the full genuine historicity" of man, by transposing all cosmic elements, whether apocalyptic or Gnostic in origin, into historical (or anthropological or existential) categories. But on their monuments the sad epitaph must be inscribed: their true eschatology, i.e., their understanding of man's true nature, could not be retained either in the second century or in the nineteenth.

---

[40] *History and Eschatology*, pp. 51–55; cf. also *New Testament Theology*, II, 95–236.
[41] *Primitive Christianity in Its Contemporary Setting*, p. 202.
[42] *Ibid.*
[43] *Ibid.*, p. 208.

This postscript for the nineteenth century and the twentieth is compressed within a few pages of the Gifford Lectures.[44] Here Professor Bultmann traces current nihilism back to its parent relativism and traces relativism, in turn, back to romanticism. Throughout this genealogy he finds the reduction of anthropology to biology, of humanity to the life of nature, of human history to natural history. Salvation from such nihilism, he contends, is possible only through a fuller understanding of the historicity of man. Salvation is impossible unless the question about the meaning in history is put in a different sense than the question about the meaning in nature or in the cosmos.

II. An Appraisal

Having epitomized Professor Bultmann's reconstruction of various types of eschatology, we can turn now to an appraisal of his position vis-à-vis the eschatological problem. In our reconstruction we have followed the historical sequence because we were considering him primarily as a historian. It may be that we should devote our attention to testing the accuracy of his research as a historian. This would mean determining whether his description of the eschatological position of the early Christian authors is valid. Should our essay follow that course, the present writer would be impelled to raise exegetical questions all along the line. The interest of this volume as a whole, however, centers in Professor Bultmann's work as theologian. In our critique, therefore, we will outline primarily the issues which he raises not so much in his historical exposition as in his interpretation. It so happens that my reluctance in adopting his exegesis of New Testament texts arises at points where that exegesis is conditioned largely by his theological presuppositions and convictions. Our reaction to his understanding of the New Testament will depend largely on how valid we judge his central norms to be. More precisely, the central issue is whether Professor Bultmann's basic distinction between nature and history is valid, whether it can be maintained, and whether it does not ultimately endanger his own "ultimate concern."

I believe that it is accurate to say that such a distinction is basic to both his exegesis of particular epochs of ancient thought and his interpretation of his own role in the contemporary situation. I also

---

[44] *History and Eschatology*, pp. 7–11.

believe that it appears so frequently that we are right in concluding that the distinction springs from a primal perception of reality that is dualistic in form. The formulas may change: nature versus history, being versus existence, cosmology versus anthropology, cosmologized history versus historicized cosmology. The primarily dualistic perception of reality, however, does not change. From beginning to end, Professor Bultmann's thinking presupposes an accent upon the *versus* in the formulations noted above. Each represents an antithesis which compels us to make an exclusive choice. The options are reduced to two mutually exclusive propositions. To be sure, if the only alternative is to endorse either an eschatology in which cosmology has swallowed historicity or an eschatology in which historicity is preserved by the repudiation of cosmology, I would prefer the latter. But when the formulation of an antithesis is faulty, the resolution of it is bound to be equally so. When a question has not been rightly phrased and when it demands a no or a yes, one can legitimately refuse to say either. This is the case, I believe, with the dualism which conditions both the historical reconstructions and the theological interpretations of Professor Bultmann.

In attacking such a dualism it is well for the critic to adopt a self-denying ordinance. He must resist the temptation to form an aggressive alliance with all other critics, regardless of the diverse systems which they are defending. To mount an attack from a dozen mutually incompatible points of view may be outwardly impressive, but it is not an example of fair play. Nor is it helpful in clarifying the multiple battle lines. My respect for Professor Bultmann's service to contemporary thought it too great to permit such an indiscriminate treaty with all his theological opponents. My own critical comments will be motivated by a desire to buttress his own central concern: salvation from nihilism by way of a fuller understanding of the historicity of man.[45]

Considering the dualism which has been mentioned, I am convinced that it reflects an inherently modern perception of the nature of the cosmos and of man. More than this, the formulation of this perception into a radical antithesis is itself a positive factor in the sequence—romanticism, relativism, nihilism—which characterizes

---

[45] *History and Eschatology,* p. 11.

recent intellectual history. Where reality has been bifurcated into a war between a cosmology, from which by definition historicity has been exluded, and an anthropology, from which cosmology has been excluded, the war can never be won (and eschatology must by definition include its end) by an assertion of the total existentialist transposition of cosmology into anthropology. This may, in fact, guarantee the victory for the enemy. The course of human history is full of such ironies.

Considering the same dualism, I think it plays havoc with New Testament exegesis. It provides an oversimplified and an overrationalized mold into which to force the eschatological visions of prophets and apostles. Those visions require their own context if they are to retain their full power. That context includes perceptions of the interdependence of *cosmos* and *anthropos* which are destroyed alike by the objectivistic cosmologies and by the existentialist anthropologies of modern man. In a period when objectivist cosmologies have destroyed the native integrity of Biblical thinking, we must be grateful for Professor Bultmann's valiant restatement of the anthropological constituents in Biblical eschatology. But Biblical thought will not stay quiescent under this either-or dichotomy. For Paul and John the cosmological and the anthropological were not incompatible components but intrinsically interdependent. It is this very interdependence which safeguards their understanding of man's historicity against dangers to which Professor Bultmann's existentialism would be vulnerable. Let us attempt to clarify this point.

A good point of attack is offered in his appraisal of the position of Paul and John vis-à-vis Gnosticism. They adopted the Gnostic concept of an "absolute distinction between humanity and its objective environment." In this adoption Dr. Bultmann concurs.[46] But the Gnostics ultimately negated this distinction. They were unable in the last resort to think of man in any but ontological terms, "in the categories of natural Being." As a result, salvation remained for the Gnostics a salvation "by nature." Accordingly God's transcendence continued to be a matter of metaphysical distance and not of gracious action. Paul and John rejected this negation of the distinction,[47] and

---

[46] *Primitive Christianity in Its Contemporary Setting*, p. 202.
[47] *Ibid.*

in their rejection Dr. Bultmann concurs. Now what are the implications of holding firmly to this "absolute distinction"? Is the distinction itself truly an absolute one? Must it be maintained with absolute rigor? If so, the distinction itself is automatically exalted to the status of metaphysical truth. We have absolutized our own dualistic postulate. We have rejected in advance any eschatology in which the dualism is transcended. We have imprisoned ourselves within an eschatology in which the "objective environment" ("natural Being" or the world) remains forever unchanged and unchanging, impermeable and unconquerable. However sovereign we may reckon God's grace to be, we cannot attribute to it the requisite power to modify the "absolute distinction" or to resolve the dualism. Such a resolution would require the inclusion of some kind of cosmic event, some picture of a coming cosmic denouement. But by definition such an event would violate "the full genuine historicity of man." It would give faith an objectivist crutch rather than instill in it an existentialist strength. We are therefore in the name of faith (and of our dualistic presuppositions) limited to a form of eschatology in which all cosmological terms are fully transposed into anthropological categories. This transposition, when complete, gives us as the object of Christian hope only "the permanent futurity of God."[48] This futurity is such that "every instant has the possibility of being an eschatological instant and in Christian faith this possibility is realized."[49]

I cannot believe that Paul and John would consent to an eschatology so limited. I cannot believe that so total a transposition of cosmology into anthropology would secure "the full genuine historicity of man." If this transposition is possible, it is possible only as an exercise of thought. The chasm between nature and man would remain unbridged. The dualism would remain as an ultimate metaphysical fact. God would forever be bound by it, and so would man. Struggling for authentic freedom against his objective environment, man would be doomed to defeat, to despair and death. It may be that before man arrives "in the darkness of death," God would be there. God and man would meet in that darkness.[50] But man could know in advance that death's sovereignty would not be ended, at least over

---

[48] *Ibid.*, p. 208.
[49] *History and Eschatology*, p. 154.
[50] *Primitive Christianity in Its Contemporary Setting*, p. 208.

the realm of nature. The Gnostics were assuredly wrong in holding that man can be "saved by nature"; but the only alternative is not damnation by nature. The Christian apostles were right in this: unless in the end God overcomes and banishes death and Hell, man is forever condemned to be their slave. This is why no New Testament writer, not even the Fourth Evangelist, utterly jettisoned the cosmological component in eschatology: its elimination would deny the sovereignty of God's grace over the whole creation. Since faith is a response to grace and since the realization of historicity is a corollary of faith, a grace which is unable to redeem man's objective environment will at most produce a humanity which remains alien to an unredeemable world.

How, then, could Paul and John recognize a distinction between *anthropos* and *cosmos* without making that distinction absolute? How could they retain a cosmological eschatology which did not contradict a historicized eschatology? Many cosmological eschatologies are, in fact, destructive of human freedom. But not all. Why could Paul and John so tenaciously hold to faith in Christ's redemption of both nature and man? They could do so because they had not absolutized the nature-man antithesis. For them the major categories of thought were neither cosmological nor anthropological, but theological. Both nature and man, both the world and history, have beginning and end in God, however inconceivable this may be. If our thought begins with the dualism, then the one category is bound to swallow the other. But God's activity in Christ destroyed the ultimacy of this dualism. It replaced the absoluteness of a man-drawn distinction with the unrestricted sovereignty of God's grace.

The real problem in eschatology lies here: Which categories are to be made basic? Paul could freely and confusingly transpose cosmic and human elements because to him other categories were more primal. One such category was the warfare between Christ and Satan. This distinction was more strategic than the opposition between man and his objective environment, because both commanders carried on their battle simultaneously in both realms. But even this dualism was penultimate, not ultimate. The victory of Christ over principalities and powers had already begun the subjugation of both nature and history. Another category of primary significance to Paul was God's promise and election. Promise and election were not designed to insure a permanently open future for man at the expense of a permanently closed future for the world. The promise rather assured a full future of freedom in sonship for the whole *ktisis* (Rom. 8). And this promise transcended the distinctions between Israel and the individual, between tradition and the moment of faith, which permeate Professor Bultmann's exegesis. What is at issue here is not so much the exposition of individual texts as the selection of the basic categories. The categories which Paul considered primary (God, Jesus Christ, the Spirit, principalities, promise, Israel, grace, etc.) are distorted if we insist upon forcing them into an alien set of categories, especially if these alien categories covertly establish a final metaphysical dualism.

If we begin with the "absolute distinction" between nature and man, we seem to limit the eschatological options to two: a cosmologized history or a historicized cosmology. But if we begin with distinctions which are more basic to Biblical theology, other options enter the field. One of these might be called a Christological eschatology which is cosmological by virtue of the truth that this Messiah is Lord of heaven and earth and which is anthropological by virtue of the truth that this Messiah is the man in whom a new humanity is called into existence. Not only does this Messiah redeem the cosmos, he radically changes man's conception of the cosmos. Not only does he redeem man, he gives to man a radically new understanding of his own historicity. This Messiah gives a wholly new meaning to the phrases "the end of history" and "the end of the world" by redefining both time and space. Faith in his power to free man from the past and for the future is inseparable from faith in his power to redeem *ta panta*. Faith, therefore, itself destroys any absolute distinction between nature and man.

It is in his penetrating analysis of Pauline faith that Professor Bultmann has placed us all in his debt. He is right in stressing the eschatological character of life in Christ: its forgiveness, its obedience, its peace, its freedom, its hope. He is right in resisting all those appeals to objective, cosmic facticity which would undercut the radical dimensions of obedient response to God's word. But there are cosmological components in the Christian gospel which do not undercut those dimensions. To recognize those components would sharpen, not dull, the weapons of the existentialist interpreter. The confession that Christ has taken captivity captive is not necessarily a pretext for again enslaving the genuine historicity of man to the cosmic. The confession that the last enemy's death will be subjected to God is not necessarily a denial of faith. It may, in fact, make faith more difficult and demanding, more totally dependent upon the sovereignty of grace and more fully a sign of God's redemption of the world. Even those sections in the Fourth Gospel which embody a reference to future cosmic events, sections which have been attributed to a redactor, may be far more necessary than antagonistic to a truly existential anthropology.

In his reinterpretation of New Testament eschatology, Professor Bultmann has been motivated by the responsibility of communicating the word of God in Christ to modern men. With many modern men he has succeeded, if my own theological students can be called modern. But in any such effort at communication, a curious dialectic may be observed. On the one hand the categories for communication must be chosen from the repertoire intelligible to those men. On the other hand those categories will be infected by the very disease which requires to be healed. Before health is restored, the doctor must both utilize the current idioms *and* substitute new idioms. Dr. Bultmann has succeeded in the first, because his basic category has been the antinomy between history and nature, an antinomy which is deeply imbedded in the consciousness of us all. Any scholar whose interpretation of Christian eschatology thus renews in us a hope which is freed from the colossal weight of a godless cosmology is to be thanked. But if his success does not extend to the point of giving us a new perception of both nature and history, a new doctrine of the cosmos itself in all its exhilarating and terrifying aspects, then the achievement of freedom may be partial rather than total, temporary rather than permanent. This is simply to say that a historicized eschatology which does not include a new cosmology and a new ontology does not as yet fully merit the term eschatology. And it is to say that the most adequate cosmology and ontology will undoubtedly utilize categories which do not appear modern enough to be relevant. Yet that very irrelevance may be an added reason for adopting again some of the basic ontological and cosmological perceptions by which the New Testament writers sought to express faith's confidence in the ultimate lordship of Christ.

The Doctrines of God and Man in the Theology of Rudolf Bultmann*

K. E. LØGSTRUP
Aarhus University
Aarhus, Denmark

I. FAITH AND NIHILISM

One of the focal points in Professor Bultmann's theology is his idea that the true alternative to the Christian faith is nihilism, the latter to be defined as the will to take all the consequences of the limitations of our existence and of the darkness by which our life is encompassed on all sides.

In which respects are the Christian faith and nihilism alike, so that it will be meaningful and instructive both to compare and contrast them? The answer to this question is that in a certain sense their relation to the world is the same. A nihilist expects nothing from the world—neither fulfillment, nor meaning, nor explanation. He boldly faces and admits the nothingness both of the world and of his own endeavors.

Christian belief corresponds to this in renouncing the world. The world is alien, anything but "homelike." This fact is not changed even by an abundant and splendid civilization. The reason for this can be found in the Christian belief in the transcendency of God, whose eternity differs from anything found in this temporal world. Thus,

* Translated by Professor Johanne M. Stochholm.

only by setting himself free from this world can man enter into relationship with God.

Bultmann is obviously not interested in setting faith and nihilism as far apart from each other as possible. Two things prevent him. In the first place he believes that a recognition of the Beyond presupposes despair leading to nihilism. The humility and susceptibility necessary to apprehend and recognize the existence of a power beyond man and his world can today be achieved by man only if he has in a radical sense recognized the nothingness of everything.

If it should be asked why this is true even today, the most likely answer would be that there have been periods in history when the Beyond was part of man's world view, but at the present time this is not the case. Therefore there is now no other way to an understanding and a recognition of the Beyond than through nihilism. The question of the Beyond does not arise until the nothingness of the world and of one's own existence has been fully apprehended. The individual must be deprived of everything; he must be absolutely alone before the question can appear. As long as we rely on the world and on ourselves, the Beyond is no problem to us, for it is no part of the present world view. This must not, however, be misinterpreted and taken to mean that the importance of nihilism, when regarded in the light of the Christian faith, is, as it were, merely pedagogical. Nihilism is not a thing of the past that has been left behind; on the contrary, it has been accepted as an established element of the Christian faith. This is the second and decisive reason why Bultmann is not interested in contrasting Christian faith and nihilism. The Christian faith is based on a fundamental realization of God as transcendent and also on a fundamental realization of the perdition of man. To the Christian faith, God is always a mystery and always ever-coming, self-disclosing. It is impossible to fuse the worldly life and the Beyond into a cosmic unity. Man's realization of God involves his readiness to enter the darkness.

Faith and nihilism thus have in common a realization of the darkness encompassing our existence on all sides. Everywhere, wheresoever man turns, he finds himself limited, with no possibility of transcendence. Everywhere he finds himself butting against walls. And everywhere his limitation spells annihilation. However, this darkness is not unambiguous. We are obliged to interpret it, and we can interpret it either as nothingness or as God. Does this imply that the interpretation is arbitrary, so that the faith in God may be voluntarism (the Roman Catholic objection to Protestantism)? Bultmann denies this, for if we name the dark limiting power, "nothingness," we turn our life into an existence without meaning from beginning to end; whereas faith in God affirms the meaning of life in its interpretation of the dark power as our God and offers a revelation of our existence which we recognize as true. For a man's life will become authentic by his renunciation of his own demands on life and by his surrender to the power encompassing our life in the belief that it is God who gives us our life and who is our Lord.

But would not a man's life also become authentic if he accepted in a purely nihilistic sense all the consequences of its nothingness? The question is futile, for no human being is capable of doing so. Whatever man does to liberate himself will merely imprison him more deeply within himself. Man is not capable of renouncing his own demands on life, nor is he capable of surrender. God alone, in his forgiveness, can lead man to this. That man by his own efforts alone cannot renounce the world is not due to his sinfulness but to his fear, which is really a fear of eternity. Why? Because to man, who insists on holding on to his being, eternity means annihilation. Thus his fear indicates a veiled knowledge of eternity, because to man eternity always means a negation of his demands on life.

But then can it be said that the Christian faith is nothing but a rebellious attitude? The answer is, it believes in forgiveness and that this is related to an event. In the New Testament, God's forgiveness is not a concept belonging to a world view but an act performed by God—an act which we encounter in history, namely, in the concrete historical man, Jesus of Nazareth.

II. CHRISTIANITY AND RELIGION

It is not, however, in the Christian faith alone that the dark power encompassing our life on all sides is interpreted as God, for the same happens in the non-Christian religions. Their interpretation is achieved in the following way. We know what we are not and what we do not have, since wherever we turn we are limited by nothingness. But to know what we are not and what we do not have is tantamount

to knowing what we should like to be and should like to have. The
two kinds of knowledge correspond to each other—are simply two
aspects of one and the same knowledge. If a man is willing to admit
to himself that no fulfillment is final—that all happiness is fleeting—
then to this knowledge corresponds the concept of an eternity where
nothing is temporary or transitory, but where everything holds perfection, fulfillment, and permanency. To our knowledge of our own and
of our world's limitations corresponds our concept of God who is
beyond us and our world and who breaks down our limitations. When
man knows that his life has been delivered up to the powers of
nature, history, fate, and death, then because of this knowledge he
seeks a benevolent power on whom to rely in his distress, a power
who upon confrontation with death will annihilate it. Out of our
knowledge of the mystery and uncertainty of our existence arises the
question of a power that can bring light into the darkness and life in
death. To our knowledge of our own impotence corresponds our
concept of God's omnipotence.

But what does the Christian faith have to say to all this? Does it
ally itself with the religions against nihilism? Does it concede that the
religions in their attitude toward God may be conditionally right, in
order at all costs to avert nihilism? No, it is the other way around.
The Christian faith allies itself with nihilism against the religions. It
maintains that all non-Christian belief in God is illusory. For man
will not be content with just asking for God, because his knowledge of
his own impotence and temporality originates in fear, anxiety, and
despair. Therefore the corresponding concept of God's omnipotence
and eternity represents at attempt to overcome the worry, fear,
anxiety, and despair in some way or other by participating in the
omnipotence, making sure of it, and exploiting it.

Because the concept of God has been created by our fears, no
wonder an answer is sought which will make the fears subside. That is
why the incomprehensibility and mystery encompassing our existence
is objectivized and hypostatized into an omnipotent deity by whom
the mystery and obscurity of our existence can be held in check.

Thus the Christian faith maintains that the only knowledge which,
upon close examination, is to be found in the non-Christian concept of
God merely proves to be knowledge of man's own limited existence.
The idea of an omnipotent God is derived from that concept. And all

the answers to the questions posed by the limitations of our existence
are nothing but attempts to exorcize the darkness and mystery of our
existence and all the anxiety connected with it. For this reason any
speculation as to whether the transcendency of God is tantamount to
eternity becomes illusory if it sets itself up to be more than an
admission that the existence of man, as it is actually experienced, is
empty of God. From the worldly life's emptiness of God no conclusions can be drawn as to the divine richness of the Beyond.

Because man wants to avert with his religion the threat from the
power that limits his life on all sides, God's revelation, when considered from a Christian point of view, is one long contradiction of
the religion of man. However, that does not mean that man's religion
is without connecting links to God's words and acts. This can be
found in the very contradiction itself. A contradiction can only exist
where there is a relationship, and a reversed relationship is still a
relationship. Man's contradiction of God provides the basis for God's
contradiction of man. Bultmann's view that a reversed relationship to
God is found in the religions presupposes that as long as there has
been religion, God has been in relationship with man and has spoken
to him directly, apart from Christ.

Religion is a fight against God's acts and words, a fight that
consists in man destroying the works of God and distorting his
words. Does Bultmann fully understand this presupposition? He certainly does. It is his opinion that in the created universe God speaks,
wanting to teach man to comprehend that his life is a gift and is demanded of him. Unfortunately man cannot comprehend this, because
he is filled with the desire to take care of and hold on to himself. Thus
we misinterpret the demand, taking it as a challenge to our strength
and to our ability to give and to achieve. When we do not hear God,
it is not because God does not speak to us, but because of our
answer. It is true that our answer is caused by God's speech; but
nevertheless we do not hear the latter, for we reply to something
other than God's words; so we hear only our own answer, which is
always a belief in our own obedience—unless despair has replaced
our will to obedience.

But how does God speak in the created universe? Bultmann's
understanding is characterized by the close relationship which, in his
opinion, exists between faith and nihilism; his answer is as follows:

God speaks in the limitation of man's existence. The limitation of nothingness is God's limitation. Therefore, when in religion and philosophy man fights his limitation—and because it is total and fundamental, he is able to fight it only with conjurations and illusions —it is God's power that man is fighting. Thus the revelation of God's power in Christ becomes a real contradiction of man's religious and philosophical conjurations.

III. ETHICAL DEMAND

We have seen that by his own endeavors man does not enter into a relationship with God himself. But then perhaps he achieves this when he knows himself to be under the ethical demand? According to Bultmann, the answer of the Christian faith is again "No." The voice of conscience is not God's voice. To enter the fight against evil, to realize that the demand continues to exist, heroically to confess his guilt, to fight his own past in order to set himself free from its determination—all this does not mean man's recognition of God's demand and judgment.

To recognize the demand and judgment as God's can mean only one of two things. It can mean that man's will is at one with God's, so that no contradiction at all exists (only obedience based on total surrender is true obedience; to consider obedience as an achievement to be proud of makes it untrue, for then one really is independent and not dependent in so doing). Or it means that in his despair man recognizes that all his endeavors, his struggle, his conquest over himself and his moral conquests, no less than his defeats, are all manifestations of his self-assertive defiance of God. But in the latter case he recognizes that the demand, such as he admits it to be in his own merely ethical existence, is for this very reason not God's demand.

Thus, just as man by his own endeavors cannot enter into relationship with God, no more can he do so when he submits himself to the ethical demand; for the two things are connected in the closest possible way. Man will never want to give up his own demands on life, and therefore he can have no relation to God himself. Here we find the real reason why man's own answer to the question about God always assumes the nature of a delusion. Man thinks that he is

capable of admitting his own impotence, of accepting the consequences of that admission, and of surrendering before God's omnipotence. But that is a delusion, and because it is a delusion that the
individual is able to submit himself to the omnipotent, the omnipotent
to whom man imagines that he is submitting becomes a delusion.

IV. ANALOGOUS SITUATIONS

A theology that is one-sidedly dominated by a conception of
nihilism as a true alternative to faith would divide in half the
anthropology implied by faith and be satisfied with only one half. It
would acknowledge only that anthropology which recognizes that
God's power lies in the limitation of man; but it would ignore the
anthropology which recognizes that God's power manifests itself
precisely in the human life that is limited.

Thus the question arises whether the conception of nihilism as the
true alternative to faith dominates Bultmann's theology to such an
extent that it contains only one half of the anthropology implied in
the Christian faith. The answer is "No." The other half is also there,
especially in his account of what he terms "analogous situations."

Before approaching the latter, it will be necessary to examine
further Bultmann's view of the ethical demand, for it is closely
related to his view of the relationship between faith and nihilism. God
makes his demands by his limitation of us, and he demands that we
accept the limitation as his. To obey the demand would thus mean to
give up all demands on life in order to surrender to the power that
limits our life in a belief that it is God who gives us our life and who is
our Lord. The demand is more closely determined when we observe
that any attempt to extend the boundaries of one's life is always paid
for by one's fellow man. For my fellow man, with whom I am
connected, will always also be the limitation of my life. To make
one's own decisions, to wish to form one's own life, is a sin because it
shows lack of charity. To allow oneself to be impelled by willfulness
into forcing the limitations of one's life—always with regard to one's
relationship to one's fellow man—is to be guilty of hardness and
ingratitude, of lies and acts of meanness, of frivolous destruction of
the other man's joys, of standoffishness, of harping on one's rights.
And therefore the surrender to the power limiting my life does not

consist in a merely abstract recognition of my life's limitations, but in a concrete recognition of the fact that, although the demands of my fellow-man will limit my life, yet at the same time they will fulfill it. The surrender not only consists in a negative recognition that I am not my own master, but also in a positive recognition that I exist for the sake of my fellow man.

This is Bultmann's view. A decisive question here presents itself. Is it correct to say, in reference to relationships with other human beings, that accepting rather than forcing the limitations of one's life is tantamount to the assertion that my life shall find its fulfillment in my love of my fellow man? Does the latter not draw on knowledge gained elsewhere? Can the essence of love really be defind by saying that in one's relationship to one's fellow man love means the acceptance and not the forcing of the limitations of one's life? Does love not mean the taking of the other man into one's own world, so that the other's happiness and unhappiness become one's own happiness and unhappiness? Is the source of *lex creationis* to be found only in our life's limitation with the demand to accept it, as Kierkegaard had asserted? Is the source of *lex creationis* not also to be found in a recognition that human beings have been given into the hands of one another, because we constitute one another's world and fate (as Luther asserted)? Does the demand not also find its content in the created goodness of human life, so that from natural love we know something about what love of our fellow man is (as Luther maintained but Kierkegaard denied)? And that does not lessen the understanding that the demand will always be limiting too, because the will of the individual is evil and is continuously distorting the goodness of his given life.

Is it not also true that we understand the demand through the created good realities in our human life, and the more so because those are the very ones that are required of us? Is the individual not required to surrender himself with that simple trust in which his life has been created to exist? And is the individual not likewise required to bring his fellow man into his own world by virtue of the love on which his existence has been founded?

If the questions raised are answered in the affirmative, this indicates that the power of God is manifest not only in the limitations of our life but also in the unfolding of our life—to use a challenging term.

This may be illustrated by choosing a simple situation as an example, namely, that the power of God is present in parents' expression of love for their children, in all its manifestations—in their determination to provide security for them, in their joy when their love is returned, and in any other way in which it finds an expression.

But because the parents' love of their children is good, they will admit of no limitations to it. No limits must be set to the security which their love desires to provide for the child. The child's existence is unreasonably protected and fenced in, and if the child escapes, the concern of the parents takes on an aspect of persecution. Nor do they recognize, as a limit to their love, that reciprocity in love should be voluntary; they demand it, and often let the children know in the most annoying fashion how grateful they ought to be for their good home. In numerous other ways the parents will ignore the fact that their love is in all respects a limited one. It assumes the aspect of self-centeredness, egotism, and self-pity.

Love can exist only when its limitations are recognized, namely with the understanding that we possess love only as the receivers of it.

To return to Bultmann's theology, a question can be asked here in the following terms: Does it, in short, contain the concept of the created goodness of human life? The answer to this is "Yes." His account of "analogous situations" shows that. A number of these situations will be discussed below.

(a) When forgiven, the forgiven person will no longer be bound by his past. This holds good for all forgiveness, including forgiveness among human beings. It is a phenomenological determination and not merely a philosophical one.

(b) Man cannot by means of self-reformation, be it ever so thorough, restore his relationship to God after having destroyed it through the desertion which makes him guilty. Only through the promise of forgiveness will man be forgiven.

The same holds good for the relationship of man to man. The offender cannot restore his relationship to the other man by self-reformation, for he must experience the other's forgiveness, whether expressed or unexpressed. Forgiveness exists as an event only.

(c) Faith requires man to abandon his personal pride and without support or guarantees of any kind to expect everything from God. Yet what would seem to be the most natural thing in the world has become the most difficult, precisely because man is proud.

The situation is no different where the relationship of man to man is concerned. Many people yearn for friendship and love and want to devote themselves to others, in the realization that only thereby will they obtain fulfillment in life, and yet they cannot accomplish this. They are unable to trust others unconditionally, without any guarantees. For this very reason friendships and marriages are wrecked.

(d) Belief is founded on man's voluntary decision, but a decision in which he has acknowledged his dependence on God. His freedom is not determined by his independence; on the contrary, by his voluntary decision to believe, man receives a new existence in forgiveness.

The same applies in the relationship of man to man. In friendship and love the trustful surrender is genuine only when it is voluntary. But it is at the same time entirely dependent on the other person. If one's love is returned so that free surrender eventuates, one knows that the very act of surrender is due to the other person, so that one's existence stems from him or her.

(e) Man's will to assert himself is one that leads him into situations which will show that he is right, and confirm him to himself in the face of all his uncertainty and doubts about himself by which he is incessantly assailed. This will is in itself not evil. The crux of the matter lies in man's own relation to it. And here it is a case of his wanting to make himself worthy of praise before God and justified by his own deeds. But faith requires a recognition of the fact that the validity which is to make man certain with regard both to himself and to God can only be a gift. Thus faith requires man to give up the attempt to obtain praise and to be accepted on the basis of his own achievements—self-education and self-conquest, effort and sacrifice—and instead receive his honor, validity, and righteousness from God.

An analogous situation exists among human beings. Nobody can exist without being taken into account by other people and without consciously or unconsciously being happy about this. Behind man's desire to assert himself lies a knowledge of his dependence on others, a knowledge that he is subject to their judgment of him. But here too the crux of the matter lies in the fact that it is a misconception to believe that man can force his acceptance, demand it on the basis of his achievements, for it can only be given. The others will give it voluntarily for what one is, and not for one's achievements. In the relation of man to man it holds true that man can only live by grace. Thus if a man insists on asserting himself, he will only obtain the exact opposite of what he intended; he is found to be insufferable.

The acceptance we give to another person, we give only of our own free will. And the more natural and trusting a human being is in his devotion, the more his acceptance becomes a matter of course.

What significance can be ascribed to the analogous situations in Bultmann's theology? The answer is to be found in their designation, namely, that they are analogous. Through them the individual is able to understand the Christian message. If the individual had no knowledge of love, forgiveness, devotion, trust, community, etc., from the created life of human beings, the promise of grace would be incomprehensible.

Is it, however, clearly stated that it is through the analogous situations that we understand the demand, especially because it is precisely those that are demanded? As far as I can judge, this is not the case. No more is said about the content of the demand than is apparent from our encountering it in and with the limitations of our life, as has been explained at the beginning of this section.

To summarize, it may perhaps be said that Bultmann develops that anthropology which is implied in the faith in God as the one who limits my life. In so far as man in his endless endeavors—whether the endlessness consists in perfect economic security or the fulfillment of his life in love, recognition, or morality—is obsessed by the will himself to be God, God is the one who says nay. God's power exists in the limitations of my existence—and God's demand lies in my fellow man's limitation of it.

The anthropology implied in the faith in the manifestation of God's power in the human life that is limited is also found in Bultmann's theology in his discussion of the analogous situations. Only the noteworthy point here is that by analogous situations is understood the promise of grace but not the demand. The demand is not apprehended as a contradiction between the created goodness in human life and the individual's evil will.

How can that be? Is it mere chance, in the sense that one man's reflections cannot branch out in all directions? Some of them he must disregard, leaving them for others to deal with. But it may be questioned whether this is not determined by the way in which Bultmann accounts for the nature of faith as requiring decision.

v. Decision, Faith, and World View

When nihilism is taken to be the true alternative to faith, there is a choice of letting the darkness be nothingness, and our life utterly meaningless, or calling the darkness God so that our existence acquires a meaning through our renunciation of all our own demands on life in order to let God rule. And in so far as this is the choice, nothing distracts our attention from the fact that the decision will be made by the individual. In this connection it is unmistakably so.

In general, it can be said about a decision that by making it I change my situation. But as far as Bultmann is concerned, it is proper to use the term only when the change results in an incomprehensible situation becoming comprehensible. And again: the situation in which my life is encompassed by darkness on all sides is incomprehensible, so that understanding will occur only by my renouncing every attempt to penetrate the darkness, and instead accepting its limiting and ruling power, because the truth of my life consists in my being limited and ruled by God.

Bultmann determines the nature of faith by contrasting it with that of a world view. The latter provides in advance an understanding of my life, its situations and happenings, which are turned into examples of the concepts, values, and laws embodied in the world view. In that respect it gives me certainty and helps me to flee from my own existence and the conditions on which it depends.

In a world view we are confronted with a misconceived, esthetic-speculative conquest of the incomprehensible and a flight from the decision and its uncertainty.

On the other hand the concept of God as the power ruling and limiting my life is incomprehensible and cannot be preconceived. Therefore faith exists only when it is achieved in the moment of decision.

Does this indicate that Bultmann thinks that faith is not to be understood? By no means; but there are different kinds of understanding. One kind is the preconceived understanding which man has at his disposal and may use, and which therefore assumes the nature of a point of view. This kind is the enemy of faith.

But there is another kind of understanding which does not conquer the darkness by claiming an insight gained independently, but which comes into being at the moment when the individual, accepting the power which both limits and rules him, gives up his own demands on life. For thereby an understanding is revealed that only in this way can my life become true.

Faith can never become part of my nature, at my disposal, or useful. For my nature is and remains one of willfulness which always is opposed to faith. Therefore the crisis of faith is constant, and faith exists only as decision.

Now it seems to me that in order to arrive at a conclusion with regard to Bultmann's statement, a distinction must be made.

That which exists already is not necessarily at our disposal. It may be so, as is the case with a world view, which both exists in advance and is at our disposal. But the two things are not necessarily identical, and they certainly are not so as far as the fundamental demand and the Christian faith are concerned. They imply realities which already exist but are not at our disposal. Which are they? Precisely those mentioned by Bultmann in his statements about the analogous situations which we summarized as the goodness of our life—for instance, trust and love. If it is true that Christian faith implies an anthropology that includes the evil will of the individual giving the goodness of his life its distorted form, then the Christian faith implies given realities; but these are not at man's disposal precisely because in the life of the individual they exist only as realities that are not due to himself. If we accept them as though they were due to our own efforts, as though they were our own virtues and deeds, we will inevitably destroy them—directly, for instance, by self-righteousness and self-complacency, and indirectly (that is to say in our relationship to others) by resentment and wrangling. When expressed in a slightly different way, it becomes a matter of whether our comprehension of what is meant by the expression that the demanded realities exist "in advance" be biased or unprejudiced. With biased understanding we imagine that when they exist in advance it is because they are due to ourselves; they exist not only in advance but are also at our disposal. But such a conception is nothing but a self-contradiction, because their destruction is caused by our acceptance of them as if they were due to ourselves. On the other hand, an unprejudiced understanding of their existing in advance stresses that they are not due to ourselves, but that they are created and given. In other words, the fact that they are realities existing in advance becomes meaningful only in relation to our faith in God.

Yet this does not abrogate the decision. For the demand appears because the will of the individual is evil, causing incessant destruction of the goodness of his life. In this struggle, and conditioned by it, the demand makes itself known—thereby making the struggle decisive. Decision is not prevented by the fact that the realities demanded, and their understanding, exist in advance; only if they were at our disposal would they prevent a decision.

In my opinion Bultmann does not discriminate between the pre-existence of something and its being at our disposal, and this is a consequence of the dominant position ascribed in his theology to the relationship between faith and nihilism. The understanding implied in faith in God must not be an understanding of preconceived realities. When we attempt to cling to something "in advance," it proves to be nothing but darkness, mystery, incomprehensibility, and death. When we attempt to get hold of realities, we find that nothingness rules, limits, and encompasses our life. The understanding therefore belongs to the decision alone in which the individual finds the truth of his life by letting himself be limited and ruled, because the power encompassing his life on all sides is not that of nothingness but of God.

But ought not both anthropologies—the one based on God's limitation of my life, the other on his creation of my life—be developed at the same time? Do they not throw light on each other? Bultmann does deal with both anthropologies, but stresses one at the expense of the other in his discussion of decision. They are not fused into true unity. When this does not happen, could it possibly be ascribed to Bultmann's fear that, during the unfolding of the understanding of life which is implied in faith, it will be transformed into a world veiw and that the nature of faith as decision will be effaced?

If this is the reason, then it appears to me that two points can be made. On the one hand it is a legitimate theological task to establish our view of life as unified and coherent and, on the other hand, to maintain that it is not the limitation of our life only upon which we have to decide. This does not lessen the goodness existing in our human life. We accept this, as due to our own achievement, in many different ways, such as with self-complacency, grievance, revenge;

whereas we are required to accept it as a gift, for that is what it is, so that our life can only become an authentic one if lived in acceptance of it.

VI. THE RELATION TO THE WORLD

Another trend of thought is important for a point of view based on and taken from Bultmann's theology. It appears that because man's will is evil, God's creation will become a destructive force because of that evil will. Only the forgiveness of man's sins can annihilate this force which turns the world into an inimical power; for in this forgiveness the world reappears as the creation of God.

Thus, through his faith, man acquires a peculiar and decisive distance from the world; without this distance there is no faith. Does this mean that man's relation to the world must not absorb his mind—that he should not lose himself in his work, nor allow himself to be carried away by natural love or absorbed by his own interests, etc.? No, something different is meant, namely, that the individual will not allow what absorbs his mind to become an absolute fulfillment so that it becomes a religion to him, which is what happens to a man without faith. Therefore, by his agonized longing, anxiety, and frivolousness, every man without faith is tied to the world in self-deception and vanity. For without faith, man has nothing but the world from which to expect all good things in his existence, but his expectations cannot be fulfilled; so that man, tied to the world in the before-mentioned as well as in other ways, will no longer be free. In his existence there is no room for a decision. But thanks to the distance of faith, the longing loses its agony, for faith sets the longing free from the illusion that it can be assuaged here and now. In faith, longing understands itself as a longing for eternity. And owing to the distance mentioned, man acquires space to think and act freely and to give serious consideration to the decision.

Bultmann finds a key word in I Corinthians 7:29–31. He quotes it repeatedly: "But this I say, brethren, the time is short: it remaineth, that both they that have wives be as though they had none; And they that weep, as though they wept not; and they that rejoice, as though they rejoiced not; and they that buy, as though they possessed not; And they that use this world, as not abusing it: for the fashion of this world passeth away." And Bultmann adds: yet without their ceasing to live in marriage, nor ceasing to weep, to rejoice, to buy, and to use the world. The individual's relation to love, joy, sorrow, and use of the world is changed without the cessation of love, joy, sorrow, and use of the world. The individual remains in the given and created condition in which he has previously lived.

If we now continue to follow Bultmann's trend of thought, we must acknowledge that if the one who loves, weeps, rejoices, and uses the world does not stop doing so, then it will not be the essence of love, sorrow, joy, and use of the world that will be changed by the decision. But then what will be changed? Something must be changed unless I Corinthians 7:29–31 means only pretending to live under the given and created conditions. What is actually changed must be the selfish character that the individual gives to love, sorrow, joy, and use of the world.

But in distinguishing between the essence of love, sorrow, joy, and use of the world and the selfish forms we give to them, we encounter the anthropology implied in the understanding of the presence of God's power in created life. We realize once more that the second half of the anthropology of the Christian faith is found in Bultmann's work.This is obviously so, because the essence of marriage, friendship, sorrow, joy, and use of the world has been described by Bultmann in discussing what he calls the analogous situations. He also mentions the ambiguity of the created world in connection with the relation of the world. And in so far as we give our created life the character of our own egotism, we make it ambiguous. We give trust the character of reservation, natural love the character of self-righteousness, resentment, and sentimentality. We distort the innate goodness in our life and are not ready to accept trust and natural love as realities given to us. We have destroyed that which we should have understood, so that there is no need to seek the cause of our lack of understanding in a mistake in our point of view. It is, however, an indication that the ambiguity characteristic of the world is not created. The ambiguity is the result of the evil work of our will. Bultmann also understands the ambiguity in this way, as shown by his discussions of God's creation of the universe and of man, and the relation of faith to this world.

But now the following question arises: Is this in consonance with

Bultmann's conception of the decision as stated before? It appears to me, as mentioned above, that in his discussion of decision Bultmann ignores the fact that what is demanded is the goodness of human life, which already exists and is being destroyed continually by our will. If that point is ignored, is there not then a tendency to reduce the created universe to neutral matter that will only become good or evil according to the decision of the individual? Or in other words, the ambiguity in the created universe and in the created human life calls for a distinction between the innate goodness of human life and the evil of our will. For because the ambiguity is the result of the destruction of the created life by our will, it can be comprehended only if that distinction is made, whereas if created human life is understood without distinguishing between its innate goodness and the evil of our will, it will inevitably become neutral matter that the decision alone makes good or evil.

VII. PREACHING AND PHILOSOPHY

Bultmann's emphasis on faith as decision also manifests itself in his view of the relation of preaching to philosophy. He maintains that the relationship between God and man is not one that falls within the scope of philosophy (philosophy in the sense of analysis of human existence) because the relation can exist only as a concrete event in man's meeting with God, but it is precisely the concrete meeting in which existence at any time realizes itself that is disregarded by philosophy. That apart from the concrete meeting man cannot find God in his existence is determined by the individual's existential (German: *existentiell*) self-recognition which is constantly present in the philosophical (German: *existential*) analysis, and for this reason man's relation to God must be beyond its scope.

The following question might, however, be raised with Bultmann: When we persist in the argument that man's relation to God is beyond the scope of philosophy, then ought not many other questions, such as any meeting between human beings, also be considered to be beyond the scope of philosophy? In that case, neither the trust without which we cannot live together nor the forgiveness existing between human beings can be said to be proper subjects for philosophical investigation; for these very questions are analogous to that of man's relation to God. Trust and forgiveness exist only as concrete events in one man's meeting with his fellow man.

It is certainly correct that when we consider a present-day philosophical analysis, such as Heidegger's for instance, neither trust itself nor forgiveness itself is analyzed, but only their presuppositions in the character of human life as being one of togetherness. However, that is not due to the difference between existential (*existentiell*) self-recognition and a philosophical analysis, but it is caused by the formal ontological character of the analysis as distinct from what has been called a philosophical psychology or anthropology. But is the difference between the two types of problems that the philosophers can raise of any importance to Bultmann? It is in my opinion irrelevant to his theology.

If I should content myself with asking Bultmann the question in the above-mentioned way, he might justifiably answer that I had missed a very important distinction. With regard to the difference between the individual's own existential (*existentiell*) self-recognition and a philosophical analysis of human existence, there is definitely one respect in which man's relation to God differs from man's relation to man. For while the concepts of trust and forgiveness are at our disposal, the concept of God is not. There Bultmann also expresses his thought by saying that when we formulate a theory about our existence, a concept of God is not at our disposal, because man, as mentioned above, enters into relationship with God only at the concrete meeting.

In order to bring the difference to a point and to elucidate it, let us suppose that the relationship would be as follows. Even if man never at any time in a concrete meeting with his fellow man has had the experience of showing trust or being trusted, of forgiving and being forgiven, nevertheless he is aware of trust and forgiveness as possibilities, and they are at his disposal as concepts when he is formulating a hypothesis concerning human existence or undertaking a philosophical analysis of it. However, the circumstances are different where faith in God is concerned. Man does not by himself alone recognize that as a possibility, but does so only when God in a moment of human existence meets man. For this reason the concept of God does not fall within the scope of philosophy.

But is this correct? If the meeting between man and his fellow man is known, if trust and forgiveness are recognized as possibilities, then the fundamental ethical demand to succor that part of the other man's life with which the meeting confronts one must also be known as a possibility. Thus the concept of the fundamental ethical demand is within the scope of philosophy precisely in the same way as are the concepts of trust and forgiveness.

Just as the individual in his actual meeting with his fellow man will experience trust and love, he will, through the same concrete meeting, experience his existence as demanded and given. A concrete meeting is necessary to experience this, but not necessary for recognizing it as a possibility. Just as trust and love are known both as possibilities and concepts, so is there the possibility of the character of existence being one that is both demanded and given. In other words, the fundamental ethical demand, or to use Luther's expression, "God's words to us apart from Christ," is also within the scope of philosophy.

It is possible to shape my question to Bultmann in a slightly different way. The difference between what man has or does not have at his disposal, which is so important to Bultmann's way of thinking, is used in this connection, in my opinion, in two different ways. He uses it to separate the objective from the personal. We have the objective at our disposal, we have control of it practically and technically, as well as in our methodological recognition of it; whereas we can neither change a personal relationship into one that is at our disposal, nor can we dominate our fellow man without depersonalizing and externalizing the relationship, for instance, by making it a mere question of law or using the other person as a means, that is to say, as an object which will serve our own ends.

The distinction of what is and what is not at our disposal is used by Bultmann not only to separate the objective from the personal, but also to distinguish the relation of man to his fellow man from man's relation to God, who both demands and gives us our existence. But can this be done? Can a philosophical discrimination be made between having at my disposal the love offered me by my fellow man and having at my disposal my existence which I, by the acceptance of the fundamental ethical demand, understand to be given me?

It is, however, true that in a philosophy such as Heidegger's no concept of God occurs. But is that not so because Heidegger commits the philosophical error of regarding every demand as objective?

Heidegger believes that no other demands belong to human existence than those made by contemporary morality and law and these are objective. Thus if man comprehends himself on the basis of the demands to which he is subjected, then he comprehends his own existence as being just as objective as the demands and therefore lives unrealistically (German: *uneigentlich*) in an ontological mis-interpretation of his own existence. Only in relation to death, and not in relation to any demand, does man's existence become an existence in reality; but in my opinion this is a philosophical distor-tion of the ethical existence.

In contradistinction to Heidegger, Kierkegaard takes it for granted that the demand is infinite and eternal, that is to say, anything but objective. Would it be possible to eliminate the contradiction between Heidegger and Kierkegaard by referring to philosophy Heidegger's statement that the demands are always finite, temporal, and objective, and referring to preaching Kierkegaard's statement that it is the infinite and eternal demand that makes man into an ego and a spirit and turns existence into movement and becoming? I do not think so, for Kierkegaard's understanding of the infinitude of the demand is not only preaching but also philosophy. Kierkegaard applies a method similar to that used by modern existentialists; for instance, in the early part of *The Sickness unto Death* he analyzes the syntheses of human existence, discriminating between the synthesis of soul-body and that of finite-infinite, recognizing the infinite as demand. It is an investigation parallel to Heidegger's in *Sein und Zeit*. And either Heidegger's statement that the demand is objective or Kierkegaard's statement that the demand is infinite must be the correct one. Both men cannot be right.

But still another—and this my last—consideration is of decisive importance for Bultmann's claim that the concept of God is beyond the scope of philosophy. He maintains that if man is to speak of God, he must speak as one who is himself being addressed, namely, as one upon whose existence God in his omnipotence has an absolute demand; whereas any philosophical discussion of God as a possibility and a concept is only a contradiction, because, while discussing God and his omnipotence, man pretends to be beyond God's omnipotence and in a way denies this situation by the analytical and conceptual character of his very discussion. By the analytical position assumed, the omnipotence that is an integral part of the analysis is denied.

In my opinion the following objection can be raised to this. The concept of God does not become self-contradictory by becoming part of an analysis in which man pretends to be beyond God's demand and omnipotence, but on the contrary, what does become self-contradictory is my existence. In other words, when there is no link between the individual's thought and his existence, then the content of his thought will not prove to be incorrect for that reason, but instead his existence will become untrue. For the linking of thought and existence depends on the individual's existence only and not on his thought.

The Significance of Rudolf Bultmann
for Contemporary Theology

SCHUBERT M. OGDEN
Perkins School of Theology
Southern Methodist University
Dallas, Texas

I

By common consent, Rudolf Bultmann is one of the most significant figures on the contemporary theological scene. By whatever criteria one judges such significance—whether quantitative or qualitative, whether with reference to the specific fields of theological inquiry or to theology as a whole—his contribution is unchallengeably among the most important of our time. Through a long and productive scholarly career, which already spans over half a century and still continues with unabated power, he has come to be one of the most decisive influences on the direction of Protestant theology in the twentieth century. Thus James M. Robinson has rightly written that "Germany is just as nearly 'Bultmannian' today as it was 'Barthian' a generation ago, 'Ritschlian' half a century or more ago, and 'Hegelian' still earlier; and Bultmann's works and ideas have become Germany's dominant theological export throughout the world."[1]

Robinson also claims, to be sure, that there are mounting signs that the Bultmannian epoch in theology is now coming to an end. Instead of any expected period of "Bultmannian scholasticism," the

---

[1] James M. Robinson, *A New Quest of the Historical Jesus* (London: SCM Press, 1959), pp. 11 f.

most recent developments in Continental theology—many of which are being carried forward by Bultmann's leading students—seem to be pointing toward a distinctively "post-Bultmannian" theology.[2] That this should to some extent be the case is, as Robinson recognizes, hardly surprising. An important measure of Bultmann's greatness is that he has not created epigones after his own image, but has inspired within his students the kind of critical independence of mind that he himself so marvelously exemplifies and that could never eventuate in any merely scholastic following of a master. But, even given these recent developments, it is questionable whether the post-Bultmannian period in theology is as certainly upon us as it sometimes appears and as is sometimes claimed. The differences between Bultmann and his students can be only too easily exaggerated as the latter struggle to find their own places in the theological sun; and even where the differences often seem most acute, Bultmann's shadow still hovers over the scene as the dominant influence over their thinking. In spite, or, perhaps, just because of the creative work of his followers, Bultmann stands forth as one of the most significant influences on the present theological situation, and, from all indications, this promises to be true in the years immediately before us.

The important question has to do with the *reasons* for this significance. Why is it that Bultmann's work has come to have such importance for those who are laboring at the present theological task?

The obvious reasons for his significance have already been indicated: the quantity and quality of his production and the potential scope of his insights, which are relevant not only for the field of exegetical and historical theology in which he primarily labors, but for the fields of systematic and practical theology as well. My question, however, is intended to reach beneath such obvious reasons toward a more profound explanation of the importance of Bultmann's work. Perhaps he himself has provided the requisite insight for a deeper understanding of his significance.

It is axiomatic with him that all historical events of the past are what they are only in relation to their future, to some present moment

---

[2] *Ibid.*, p. 12.

or moments in which their true meaning is first disclosed.[3] A past figure or event is significant just to the extent that it continues to speak to some present in such a way as to clarify and answer the questions with which men in that present approach the past. Bultmann assumes that we ourselves here and now in the present are faced with all sorts of questions posed for us by our particular station and responsibility in history and that it is in our attempts to get answers to these questions that the figures and events of the past become meaningful for us. Just because or in so far as the past continues to speak relevantly to our own tasks and questions as historical beings, it takes on real historical significance and thus becomes history in the only full sense of the word.

If this insight is followed up, it suggests the deeper reason for Bultmann's own historical significance is that he speaks with a unique relevance to our present situation as men in history who are driven to ask questions to which his work in some sense provides answers. He is important to us because he has clarified and attempted to solve the crucial problem of the contemporary theological generation and has done so, moreover, by creatively appropriating at least some of the major resources for solving it that this generation has provided.

Unlike some of his contemporaries, he has not simply turned his back on the main theological developments of the nineteenth century, but has recognized that the basic problem to which these developments were the response is still a problem for contemporary theology. Furthermore, he has also been unique among his contemporaries in exploiting to the full one of the distinctive philosophical resources of the twentieth century—namely, existentialist philosophy—in trying to solve this basic theological problem. Other contemporary theologians, naturally, are also indebted to the work of the existentialist philosophers, and so in one way or another can properly be spoken of as "existentialist" theologians. But probably none of them so justly deserves the label as Bultmann. Like Thomas Aquinas in the thirteenth century, he has uniquely sensed the theological importance of a new and in some ways threatening philosophy and has turned it to the advantage of a more adequate restatement of the Christian faith for our time.

---

[3] Cf., e.g., Schubert M. Ogden (ed.), *Existence and Faith: Shorter Writings of Rudolf Bultmann* (New York: Meridian Books, 1960), p. 295.

It may be said, therefore, that the deeper reason for Bultmann's theological importance is that he is the contemporary theologian *par excellence*. In a way that distinguishes him from most of his contemporaries, he has profoundly involved himself in the present historical situation of Protestant Christianity in the West and has endeavored to work out a new theological synthesis within the limits and the opportunities of that situation.

But this may seem to overstate the matter, since there may appear to be other contemporary theologians who could with as much right lay claim to the same distinction. Add to this, then, that some of these figures—for example, Paul Tillich or Reinhold Niebuhr—are quite close to Bultmann in their substantive theological positions, and the claim I am making may seem exaggerated indeed. Maybe it is; but there is another factor in Bultmann's work as yet unemphasized that may make the claim seem more justified.

Perhaps more than any other contemporary Protestant theologian, Bultmann has given thorough and extended reflection to the problem of theological method. He has not only done theology, but has been unusually self-conscious about what he has done and has tried to work out a mode of procedure—a theological program—that could serve to point directions for the work of an entire generation. In this sense, he is not only the contemporary theologian *par excellence,* but, if I may say so, also the contemporary theologian's theologian *par excellence*. It is not that his works are written in the esoteric language of the theological shop or that they are especially difficult to understand. As a matter of fact, in comparison with some contemporary theologians, his style is simplicity itself, and even the layman can readily grasp his approach to the theological task. But where he is different from most other present-day theologians is in his high degree of self-consciousness about theological methodology. He has clearly recognized the central theological task of our time and has tried to work out a method whereby this task can be approached with some hope of bringing it to successful completion. If I may adapt, somewhat, words that were originally applied to Albert Camus when he was awarded the Nobel Prize for literature, Bultmann is the methodological conscience of his theological generation; and this is the deepest reason why his work is so significant for everyone who is seriously concerned with the present theological task.

If this line of thought is valid, the next step toward understanding Bultmann's significance is to focus the contemporary theological problem he has tried to solve and the solution he has proposed as the most likely method for solving it. Against this background, then, I may make some critical comments directed toward assessing the precise measure of his significance. This second task is unavoidable, given the very character of what we mean by such significance. For a theologian's work is important, finally, not simply because he grasps the fundamental problem of his generation and proposes a method for solving it, but because his solution is really adequate—both in itself, in the sense of being logically self-consistent, and in relation to other possible solutions to the same problem. The responsibility of this essay will not be fully discharged until an attempt is made to assess Bultmann's work against criteria such as these.

II

It has been noted that one of the distinctive characteristics of Bultmann's theology is that he has continued to be sensitive to the problem that in one way or another was behind the Protestant liberal theology of the nineteenth century. Although he has fully participated in the criticisms of liberalism initiated by the epoch-making work of Karl Barth's commentary on Romans of 1919, he has never been led to any simple condemnation of the liberal theological tradition in which he was originally trained.[4] His theology, rather, is a unique attempt at a genuinely postliberal theology. If he has transcended liberalism—and he undoubtedly has[5]—he has done so not by simply repudiating it, but by dialectically preserving its understanding of the central theological problem and trying to find a more adequate way of solving this problem than liberalism itself succeeded in finding.

The basic problem of liberal theology was the problem posed by the evident irreconcilability of the scientific and critical-historical outlook of modern Western culture and the prescientific forms in

---

4 *Ibid.*, p. 288.

5 It is unfortunately still necessary to insist on this in view of the recent publication in English translation of such one-sided interpretations as those of Ernst Kinder and Walter Künneth. Cf. C. E. Braaten and R. A. Harrisville (eds.), *Kerygma and History: A Symposium on the Theology of Rudolf Bultmann* (Nashville: Abingdon Press, 1962), pp. 55–119.

which Christian faith found its classical expressions.[6] The destiny of the liberal theologians was to experience most sharply the tensions that had been steadily mounting ever since the beginning of the Renaissance between the distinctively modern cultural consciousness and the classical theological heritage. Unlike their orthodox contemporaries, they could not ignore the radical transformation in man's picture of himself and his world taking place through the development of science and technology and the emergence of a genuinely critical attitude to the historical past. They recognized that theology had no alternative but to accept this transformation, with all it implied by way of a thoroughgoing criticism of traditional theological formulations and procedures, and then try to find new ways of thinking and speaking through which the Christian faith could be given adequate contemporary expression.

From our vantage point today, with all its benefits of hindsight, it seems evident that the liberal theologians were less than completely successful in finding the new theological forms and methods for which they were searching. Only too often they succeeded in disengaging the Christian faith from its earlier antiquated expressions only to accommodate it much too uncritically to the insights and values of an increasingly secularist culture. But the significance of their work lies less in their constructive solutions—although even they are far from valueless, as we are now more and more coming to realize[7]—than in their clear grasp of the overriding problem of all modern theology. The lesson they are there to teach us is that no theology today can possibly be adequate that does not squarely confront the difficulty posed by the triumph of modern science and critical historiography over traditional theological forms and procedures.

---

[6] Cf., e.g., Wilhelm Herrmann, *Der Verkehr des Christen mit Gott im Anschluss an Luther dargestellt* (6th ed.; Stuttgart and Berlin: J. G. Cotta, 1908), pp. 1–14 (Eng. trans. J. Sandys Stanyon in Wilhelm Herrmann, *The Communion of the Christian With God Described on the Basis of Luther's Statements* [3rd ed.; New York: G. P. Putnam's Sons, 1913], pp. 1–18. The parallels between Herrmann's analysis of the theological problem and Bultmann's later analysis in "Neues Testament und Mythologie" are, to say the least, striking.

[7] Cf., e.g., the Christological position outlined in Gerhard Ebeling, *Theologie und Verkündigung: ein Gespräch mit Rudolf Bultmann* (Tübingen: J. C. B. Mohr, 1962), in which the central motives of Herrmann's work are taken up and re-expressed.

It is just this lesson that Bultmann thoroughly learned from liberal theology and has never forgotten.[8] In a period in which theologians have been only too easily beguiled by what Karl Barth once spoke of as "the strange new world within the Bible," Bultmann has continued to remind us of the ambiguity of that "strangeness." He has insisted that the Bible is strange to men today not only because its central message radically calls in question their usual self-understanding as men who have turned away from God to seek their own self-contrived securities, but also because the conceptual forms in which this message is expressed are those of an earlier and to us alien age. Specifically, he argues, the concepts of the New Testament, and thus also of the theological tradition, are "mythical," and therefore presuppose a picture of man and his world that men today not only do not but cannot share. Because contemporary men are so thoroughly dominated by a scientific outlook toward themselves and their world, mythological formulations of the meaning of Christian faith cannot but strike them as incredible and irrelevant. Therefore, Bultmann concludes, just to the extent that theology has no alternative but to return to the Bible as the only normative source of Christian faith, it is faced all the more urgently with the problem that confronted the liberal theologians of the last century. It also has no alternative but to engage in the task of a radical "demythologizing" of the mythological formulations in whith the Biblical message is expressed.

"Demythologizing," of course, is the term by which Bultmann's theology is most widely known and identified. Although he did not introduce the word as such until his programmatic essay of 1941[9] he had actually been practicing demythologizing for at least a decade and a half before, [10] and so the term is not an inappropriate label for

---

[8] H. W. Bartsch (ed.), *Kerygma und Mythos*, I (2nd ed.; Hamburg: Herbert Reich-Evangelischer Verlag, 1951), 24: "The critical work of earlier generations may not simply be thrown out, but must be positively accepted. If that does not happen, sooner or later—providing the church and theology continue to exist at all—the old battles between orthodoxy and liberalism must be fought all over" (Eng. trans. R. H. Fuller in H. W. Bartsch [ed.], *Kerygma and Myth* [2nd ed.; New York: Harper Torchbooks, 1961], p. 12).

[9] *Ibid.*, pp. 15–48 (Eng. trans., pp. 1–44).

[10] Cf., e.g., *Jesus*, which first appeared in 1926 (3rd ed.; Tübingen: J. C. B. Mohr, 1951), pp. 46–51 (Eng. trans. L. P. Smith and E. H. Lanterno in Rudolf Bultmann, *Jesus and the Word* [2nd ed.; New York: Charles Scribner's Sons, 1958], pp. 51–56).

identifying at least one main thrust of his work. True, some interpreters have held that the essentially negative sound of the word
inadequately expresses the primarily positive intention of his method,
and he himself has conceded, for reasons that will presently become
evident, that it is not an entirely satisfactory term.[11] Nevertheless, it
is not accidental that he should have chosen this word—and should
continue to use it even up to the present time[12]—to describe the task
of contemporary theology. Precisely because the central problem to
which his work is directed is the same problem that also confronted
liberal theology, he could hardly have chosen any other way of describing the task this problem poses. Or, to turn the point around, the
fact that he has chosen this expression is the surest evidence that his
work stands in continuity, as well as discontinuity, with that of the
earlier liberal theology.

This is not the place to analyze in detail the meaning of the
concept "demythologizing" and of the more basic concept of "myth"
with which it is cognate and in relation to which it has to be
understood.[13] But there are two observations that seem to me crucial
if one is to understand what Bultmann is about.

First of all, his use of the word "myth" (or "mythology"), and
thus also of "demythologizing," is not simply the same as that of
many other contemporary theologians. A good deal of wasted time
and ink could have been saved if interpreters and critics of Bultmann
had given more care than they generally have to his use of these
terms.[14] In his usage, "myth" emphatically does not mean every
form of oblique or analogical discourse about God. Rather, he makes

---

[11] *Jesus Christ and Mythology* (New York: Charles Scribner's Sons,
1958), p. 18.

[12] "On the Problem of Demythologizing," *The Journal of Religion*, XLII
(1962), pp. 96–102.

[13] Cf., however, my discussion in *Christ Without Myth: A Study Based on
the Theology of Rudolf Bultmann* (New York: Harper & Row, 1961), pp.
22–94.

[14] E.g., Reinhold Niebuhr's reservations about "demythologizing" in C. W.
Kegley and R. W. Bretall (eds.), *Reinhold Niebuhr: His Religious, Social, and
Political Thought* (New York: The Macmillan Company, 1956), pp. 438 f.
and 446, rest on a failure to understand *Bultmann's* use of the word. The same
must be said of the criticisms of Bultmann implied by Paul Tillich in *Systematic Theology*, II (Chicago: The University of Chicago Press, 1957), 29 and
152, and *Dynamics of Faith* (New York: Harper & Row, 1957), pp. 50 f.

clear that, in his sense of the term, "myth" refers to only one particular way in which the divine may be spoken about in concepts ordinarily used to speak of what is non-divine.[15] Specifically, myth is that way of speaking in which the realm of the divine is conceptualized as though it were the object of the kind of thinking appropriate to science. To use one of his own favorite examples, myth speaks of God's transcendence over the world as if it were a matter of spatial distance and thus pictures him as located in a heaven situated somewhere above the world of mundane occurrences. The result of such speaking is that myth sooner or later comes into conflict with the thinking of science and, being no match for its adversary, inevitably gives way before it. Because it has the logical and grammatical form of objective scientific discourse, and yet intends to speak of a reality of which science in principle cannot speak, it can only be regarded by the scientist as a kind of primitive thinking that no longer has any reason for being.

In *this* sense, however, "myth" is something more restricted in scope than what is meant by the word as used, say, by Reinhold Niebuhr and Paul Tillich. It does not include *all* discourse about the divine, but solely that type of such discourse in which God is spoken of in the categories of science, and the propositions of which, therefore, are open to verification or falsification by their coherence or incoherence with the propositions of genuine scientific thinking.

The second observation I would make is by way of correcting a possible misunderstanding of some of my earlier statements. The reason Bultmann calls for demythologizing, finally, is not the problem posed by the irreconcilability of myth and a scientific picture of the world. This, to be sure, is a problem, and he in no way tries to avoid it or the task of demythologizing it so sharply poses. But he is also aware that a program of demythologizing would be illegitimate if the only reason for undertaking it was that a mythological picture of the world cannot be reconciled with the very different picture of modern

---

[15] Cf. the distinction between "mythology" and "analogy" in H. W. Bartsch (ed.), *Kerygma und Mythos,* II (Hamburg: Herbert Reich-Evangelischer Verlag, 1952), 196 f. (Eng. trans. R. H. Fuller in H. W. Bartsch [ed.], *Kerygma and Myth* [2nd ed.; New York: Harper Torchbooks, 1961], pp. 196 f.). Bultmann also distinguishes between "myth" and "symbol" (or "figure," "image," or "cipher") in a way that directly parallels Tillich's distinction between "unbroken" and "broken" myth.

science. Real as this problem is, he recognizes it can be but the occasion for inquiring whether there is not something about myth itself, and especially about the New Testament's use of myth, that provides a much more fundamental reason for critically interpreting it.

This point requires emphasis because Bultmann continues to be interpreted as essentially an apologist, that is, as a theologian whose primary concern is to state the Christian faith so that it can be understood by men who live in the present historical situation.[16] As he himself regards the matter, however, such apologetic interest is finally but a secondary element in his theological program. The real reason for demythologizing, he says, is the New Testament message itself.[17] By this he means that, just when one understands myth in general and specifically in its use to express the faith of the New Testament, it becomes evident that myth itself demands a critical interpretation such as the contemporary historical situation also makes imperative.

This, however, is already to move beyond Bultmann's analysis of the theological problem and task to his proposed method for dealing with them. The clue to the whole constructive thrust of his work is his insight that myth itself inadequately expresses what it intends to say.[18] Although it speaks in the categories appropriate solely to the objectifying thinking of science, its real intention is to speak of something utterly transcending the limits of scientific thought— namely, the ultimate existential ground and end of man's being as a historical person and of the environing world of fellow beings. While the logical and grammatical form of myth is that of the objectifying thinking of science, its "use" or function is not scientific at all, but existential. Its purpose is not to add to man's scientific knowledge of himself and his world, but rather to address him as a person who is continually confronted by an ultimate gift and demand that constrain him to decide how he will understand his existence.

Bultmann believes this existential intention of myth is made especially clear by the writings of the New Testament.[19] If these writings

---

[16] Cf., e.g., Braaten and Harrisville (eds.), *op. cit.*, pp. 212–228.

[17] *Kerygma und Mythos*, II, 207 f. (Eng. trans., pp. 210 f.).

[18] "On the Problem of Demythologizing," *The Journal of Religion*, XLII (1962), 96, 99 ff.

[19] *Kerygma und Mythos*, I, 23 (Eng. trans., pp. 11 f.).

are carefully studied, it is evident their true meaning is not at all what one might suppose simply from the objective mythological concepts in which they are for the most part expressed. So far from intending to speak scientifically, they are, so to say, transparently concerned to speak to the question of man's existence and to confront him with the possibilities for understanding himself before God and in relation to the world. Thus, for example, the New Testament's talk about God as the Creator is intended to be something entirely different from a cosmological theory concerning the origin of the world in some remote cosmic occurrence. What such talk really wants to say is that man and his world here and now have their ultimate ground not in themselves, but in the free decision of God, and that it is in understanding himself accordingly that man realizes his authentic existence. Likewise, Bultmann argues, the meaning of all the talk about the end of the world, about the last judgment and the resurrection of the dead, has a very different purpose than modern scientific theories about the eventual development of the physical universe. Its real intention is to remind man that his ultimate end as a historical being who must continually decide his own existence is not in himself or in his world, but in the gracious judgment of God, which even now confronts him with a definitive decision.

In a word, both myth in general and the New Testament in particular make clear that the positive meaning of demythologizing must be what Bultmann calls "existentialist interpretation"—that is, the kind of interpretation in which the basic intention of myth to speak of God and of man's existence before him is taken as the key to myth's meaning. To interpret mythological statements existentially is simply to ask for the understanding of human life, or the possibility for deciding man's existence as a historical being, that they basically intend to express.

From this, however, it should be easy to see why "demythologizing" is not a wholly satisfactory term for identifying Bultmann's solution to the theological problem. The method for theology he proposes is less a method for *eliminating* mythology than for *understanding* it. It is, as he puts it, a "hermeneutical procedure."[20] This means that the task of the theologian is not to subtract, but to interpret—to interpret the New Testament's original mythological

---

[20] "On the Problem of Demythologizing," p. 96. Cf. also *Jesus Christ and Mythology,* pp. 18, 45.

statements in terms of the understanding of human existence before God they inadequately express.

It is at this point that Bultmann's difference from the liberal theology whose problem he takes so seriously is most clearly evident. Whereas the liberal theologians tended simply to eliminate the mythological elements in the New Testament and located its true meaning in certain timeless religious and moral ideals, Bultmann's attitude toward myth is rather that of the interpreter who simply wants to understand it in its true intention. True, in one sense, his existentialist interpretation also involves an elimination of myth because mythological statements are no longer understood in terms of their objective contents, but solely in terms of their fundamental intention to speak of man's existence. To this extent, therefore, the word "demythologizing" is undoubtedly descriptive of Bultmann's procedure. But the primary emphasis of his theological method does not have the negative implication this word only too readily suggests. His attitude toward myth is not that of one who wants to get rid of it, but rather that of one who wants correctly to understand it, so as to be able to express its true meaning as adequately as possible. Hence he can say without hesitation that theology may by all means still make use of mythological concepts, provided only that they are always interpreted in such a way as to make clear their real existential meaning.[21]

It seems to me, therefore, that Bultmann's position on the question of myth is not really as different from Reinhold Niebuhr's or Paul Tillich's as is commonly assumed. Bultmann could subscribe without any difficulty whatever to Niebuhr's famous dictum that, while myth must never be taken literally, it must always be taken seriously. The first requirement in Niebuhr's dictum is exactly what Bultmann tries to express in demanding radical demythologizing; and his whole project of existentialist interpretation is simply his way of formulating the second demand Niebuhr lays down. Perhaps the main difference between Bultmann and Niebuhr in this respect is that Bultmann makes clear in a way Niebuhr hardly does[22] just what it means to take myth seriously. By interpreting all mythological statements on the basis of a clearly defined and self-consciously followed

---

[21] *Jesus Christ and Mythology*, pp. 68 ff.

[22] Cf. Emil Brunner's criticism of Niebuhr in Kegley and Bretall (eds.), *op. cit.*, pp. 31 f.

hermeneutical procedure, Bultmann gives precise content to Nie-buhr's demand and thus avoids the ambiguities of Niebuhr's own demythologizing.

To this brief analysis of the essential structure and movement of Bultmann's theology can be added only that what he means by existentialist interpretation is not fully realized until it culminates in a nonmythological restatement or translation of the understanding of human existence expressed in the New Testament. Bultmann believes the best way to make such a translation is by employing the concepts of the early Martin Heidegger's existentialist philosophy. What Hei-degger provides is a formal ontological analysis of the phenomenon of human existence, that is, an analysis that enables the theologian to state in a conceptually clear and precise way the possibility of self-understanding given in, and with faith, in the Christian proclamation.

Bultmann does not mean by this, naturally, that the New Testa-ment is to be abandoned in favor of Heidegger's *Sein und Zeit* or that the minister in the pulpit is to preach his sermons in the abstruse technical terms of Heidegger's analysis.[23] His point, rather, is that every theologian is necessarily dependent upon some philosophy for conceptualizing his understanding of the New Testament message and that no preaching can be really adequate unless it is framed under the guidance, although not in the terms, of such a precise philosophical clarification.[24] The merit of Heidegger's philosophy, as compared with others used by theologians, is that it provides concepts in which faith can be adequately clarified in the way faith itself demands. For while Heidegger speaks of man in a technically clear and precise way, he does so neither in the mythological concepts of the New Testament and the theological tradition nor in the inappropriate categories of an objectifying science. Hence by employing his concepts, the theologian can bring to more appropriate and understandable expression the real existential meaning of the Christian faith and proclamation.

---

[23] Cf. John Macquarrie, *An Existentialist Theology: a Comparison of Heidegger and Bultmann* (London: SCM Press, 1955), pp. 175 f.

[24] Significantly, Bultmann's own sermons are completely free of Heidegger's *termini technici,* although, as one would expect, his rich use of ordinary language and *belles-lettres* is everywhere disciplined by existentialist analysis. Cf. *This World and the Beyond: Marburg Sermons* (New York: Charles Scribner's Sons, 1960).

III

Reference was made above to Professor Robinson's claim that the Bultmannian epoch in theology seems to be coming to an end by giving way to theological developments that can only be described as "post-Bultmannian." I want now to develop two theses that will clarify my own position in relation to this claim and, in this somewhat indirect way, to offer a critical assessment of Bultmann's contribution that should add yet a further necessary element to our consideration of his significance for contemporary theology.

The first thesis is that much of the current talk about a post-Bultmannian theology is either premature or, in some instances, actually an attempt to resurrect *pre*-Bultmannian modes of thought.

If, as I believe, Bultmann's theology represents a unique attempt to formulate the program for a genuinely postliberal theology, then it is at least doubtful that his work can be easily transcended by the Protestant theology of the present and the near future. I do not see that the stage in theological history that his work marks—and here I am thinking primarily of his demand for demythologizing and his method of existentialist interpretation—is as yet behind us. On the contrary, my impression, at least of English-speaking theology, is that we still have quite a way to go before we even reach it. And from my limited knowledge of current Continental theology, the various claims to have moved beyond Bultmann seem to me to depend too much for their plausibility upon mistakenly confining his work within limits that he himself has long since transcended, if indeed he was ever bound by them.

This is not to suggest, of course, that these new tendencies do not contain elements that do go beyond some of the positions Bultmann has held. The point is simply that their novelty often appears far less impressive when they are viewed against a correct understanding of his work such as too frequently is lacking. This is true to a large extent, for example, of what Robinson has taught us to call the "new quest of the historical Jesus," in which so many of Bultmann's former students have been recently engaged. I seriously question whether the differences between Bultmann's own *Jesus* of 1926 and Günther Bornkamm's *Jesus von Nazareth* of 1956 are as great as some have claimed who have patently misunderstood the scope and limits of Bultmann's work on the problem of the historical Jesus. The usual image of Bultmann's position on this problem that one encounters among English-speaking theologians is that it represents a strange mixture of historical skepticism and existentialist disinterest in history that together make a quest for the historical Jesus both impossible and unnecessary. In my judgment, this image is at best seriously distorted and completely fails to do justice to Bultmann's own constructive proposal for an approach to the Jesus of history that would be at once historically possible and by no means theologically illegitimate.[25]

Likewise, Henrich Ott's recent attempt to apply the insights of the later Heidegger to overcome Bultmann's understanding of theology in its relation to faith fails to establish a real post-Bultmannian alternative. Although the basic direction of Ott's thinking indeed points away from Bultmann's position—less, however, in my judgment, *beyond* it than *behind* it—the argument he presents in support of his view is convincing only against a one-sided interpretation of Bultmann's work.[26]

Other examples could be cited, but these may serve to suggest that much of the talk about a post-Bultmannian theology is premature. More than some of the post-Bultmannian theologians seem to realize, their most creative and significant insights are due primarily to Bultmann's influence and do not really advance beyond his own position.

In other instances, however, the claims to have gone beyond Bultmann are not only premature, and in that sense false, but even more seriously false. So far from going beyond Bultmann, some contemporary tendencies go *behind* him—that is, are reactionary

---

[25] This judgment is developed and supported in my essay, "Bultmann and the 'New Quest,' " *The Journal of Bible and Religion,* XXX (1962), 209–18. Cf. also Van A. Harvey and Schubert M. Ogden, "Wie neu ist die 'Neue Frage nach dem historischen Jesus,' " *ZfTuK.,* LIX (1962), 50–68. For a discriminating discussion of some of the *real* limitations of Bultmann's treatment of the historical Jesus, cf. Ebeling, *op. cit.,* pp. 19–82.

[26] The criticism expressed here is worked out in detail in my essay, "The Understanding of Theology in Ott and Bultmann," in J. M. Robinson and J. B. Cobb, Jr. (eds.), *The Later Heidegger and Theology* (New York: Harper & Row, 1963), pp. 157–73.

attempts to resurrect modes of thought that he as much as anyone has helped us to break through. I have already indicated that this is the tendency, perhaps unintentional, of Ott's attempt to qualify Bultmann's dialectical interpretation of theology in its relation to faith. And Bultmann himself has pointed out that a principal difference between the old quest of the historical Jesus of the nineteenth century and the new one is that, whereas the former was the project of a liberal movement in theological thinking, the latter is beloved by many who are in fact anything but liberal in their theology. In their case, as he slyly puts it, it represents one more attempt to pluck some brands from the burning.[27]

Also, it is sometimes claimed that Bultmann's understanding of modern science and of the problem it poses in relation to myth reflects a pre-twentieth century perspective that more recent theoretical developments in science have called in question. Thus, in the name of an allegedly post-Bultmannian view of science, the attempt is made to make room once again for a very pre-Bultmannian approach to the problem of miracle.[28] It is evident, however, as Bultmann points out, that this kind of tactic completely misreads the meaning of more recent scientific developments and, in the bargain, avoids the real challenge of his demand for demythologizing.[29]

From only this brief discussion, it should be clear why my enthusiasm about the current proposals to go beyond Bultmann in the direction of a post-Bultmannian theology must be qualified. Both because his work is so rich in insights as not easily to be superseded and because some of the attempts to go beyond him seem to represent anything else but theological progress, I should prefer to see us stay with him a while longer and to appropriate more fully than we have as yet done the contribution he has made to a postliberal theology. This is especially my feeling about what I understand to be the vital center of his contribution. I see no other path to a theology that will

---

[27] "Das Verhältnis der urchristlichen Christusbotschaft zum historischen Jesus" (Heidelberg: Carl Winter–Universitätsverlag, 1960), pp. 10 f. Ebeling is, of course, quite right in warning against an illicit conversion here. Not *all* those who are engaged in the new quest can be dismissed as having such an apologetic interest (cf. *op. cit.*, p. 60, n. 2).

[28] Cf., e.g., Walter Künneth's argument to just this effect in Braaten and Harrisville (eds.), *op. cit.*, p. 104.

[29] *Kerygma und Mythos*, II, 181.

be adequate for our time than the path of thoroughgoing demythologizing and existentialist interpretation.

I indicated, however, that I also have a second thesis. Perhaps
when I have stated it, it will appear that I do not take the first one as
seriously as I have pretended or that I am simply confused in my
assessment of Bultmann's significance. I recognize this may be the
only honest conclusion that can be drawn. But, in defense of my
position, I would emphasize something we ought always to remember
when we try to judge a theologian's work.

There is always a gap—a larger or smaller gap—between what a
theologian *intends* to do and what he in fact *succeeds in doing*. None
of us is entirely successful in closing this gap, and this as much as
anything reminds us that in our work as theologians, just as in all
other aspects of our life in the church, we are members one of
another, and constantly require the help of others beyond ourselves in
all we attempt to do. Bultmann himself has explicitly disavowed that
his work does anything more than point a direction, and he has made
quite clear that the fulfillment of the program he lays down will
require nothing less than the time and labor of an entire theological
generation. My point—and this is my second thesis—is that part of
the reason why such additional work will be required is because he
himself has only partially and, as I believe, inconsistently, carried out
the program he has proposed for contemporary theology. Our task,
therefore, is to criticize his actual achievement in the light of his own
basic intention and thus to bring to fruition the general development
of which he, more than any other, is the contemporary representative.

In a sense, this, too, is a summons to go beyond Bultmann toward
a post-Bultmannian position. But I prefer to think of it as a call to
the full and consistent development of the view he himself represents.
I am less interested that we should claim any novelty for what we are
to do than that we try to develop the ground that he has already
claimed and that requires of us the humbler, but no less important
task of full and complete development.

There are two points in particular where it seems to me Bultmann's
position demands such development. The first of these is at the
crucial point of Christology. If there is anything about which his
various critics have agreed, it is that his demand for radical demythologizing and existentialist interpretation is fundamentally

inconsistent with his claim that authentic human existence is factually possible solely in consequence of God's act in Jesus Christ.[30] Bultmann has always maintained that the real possibility of man's actualizing his true life is entirely dependent on the historical event of Jesus of Nazareth, in which God's gracious judgment is uniquely actualized. Although all men, simply as men, have the "possibility in principle" of such authentic life, this possibility becomes a "possibility in fact" for them exclusively in the event of Jesus Christ and in the proclamation of the Christian Church in which that event is again and again re-presented.[31] But, according to the widespread consensus among Bultmann's critics, this claim for the exclusive significance of Jesus Christ is irreconcilable with Bultmann's program of thoroughgoing existentialist interpretation of the New Testament message. The critics disagree, of course, about how this inconsistency should be resolved. Some hold—and theirs is the majority opinion— that the inconsistency is incontrovertible evidence that demythologizing and existentialist interpretation must be rejected or at least limited, so that the claim for the exclusive significance of Jesus Christ can be maintained. Others, however, take the minority position that this claim itself must be sacrificed, at least in the sense in which it has often been understood, so that the program of existentialist interpretation can be thoroughly and consistently carried out.

My own view is that the second group of critics is essentially correct—and this not simply because otherwise the problem posed by mythology is not really solved, although this is one reason, but because the New Testament itself gives no real warrant for the kind of exclusivism that Bultmann, together with much conventional Christianity, has claimed for the event of Jesus Christ. The arguments for this view cannot be developed here, but perhaps I can clarify a bit further what the view itself involves.

As I read the New Testament, it knows of no basis for man's authentic existence except the primordial love of God, which is, indeed, decisively manifested in Jesus of Nazareth, but is in no sense

---

30 I have attempted to document this consensus in *Christ Without Myth*, pp. 95–111. Additional evidence for it, if such is required, is amply provided by several of the essays in Braaten and Harrisville, *op. cit.* Cf. also the essays now available in H. W. Bartsch (ed.), *Kerygma and Myth*, Vol. II, trans. R. H. Fuller (London: S.P.C.K., 1962).

31 *Kerygma und Mythos*, I, 31–40 (Eng. trans., pp. 22–33).

exhausted in him. Therefore, Bultmann seems to me to be wrong when he says that in the event of Jesus our salvation first becomes possible.[32] Jesus' significance is not that he constitutes God's grace, as though God were not or could not be a gracious God apart from him, but rather that he transparently re-presents God' grace with all the force of final revelation and as a possibility demanding decision. This is the reason the New Testament can in places completely abstract from the event of Jesus in setting forth the conditions of man's salvation, as, for example, in the parable of the Last Judgment in Matthew 25:31–46, where a confession of faith in Jesus Christ in no way figures as an essential element in the life of the blessed.

To be sure, the New Testament also claims again and again that there is no other way whereby men can be saved than through faith in Jesus Christ. But clearly this claim as such is just as mythological as any of the other elements to which Bultmann directs attention and therefore also has to be interpreted in terms of its existential meaning if it is to be properly understood. If Bultmann's basic method is valid, then we must ask what it means existentially to affirm that men can realize their authentic existence solely through Jesus Christ. The answer, I believe, is this: men can realize their true life as men, and thus enjoy essential salvation, only if they understand themselves in the way concretely re-presented to them in Jesus' word and deed and tragic destiny. Only by radically surrendering every form of self-contrived security and trusting solely in the grace of God, which transcends the world as its final ground and end, can men achieve an authentic human existence.[33]

In other words, the New Testament claim "only in Jesus Christ" must be interpreted to mean not that God acts to redeem only in the event of Jesus and in no other event, but that the only God who acts to redeem any event—*although he in fact redeems every event*—is the God whose redemptive action is decisively revealed in the word that Jesus speaks and is. In *this* sense, we may indeed say with the apostle, "there is no other name under heaven among men whereby we must be saved" (Acts 4:12).[34]

---

[32] Tillich argues the point here most effectively in *Systematic Theology*, II 175 f.; cf. also 169 f.

[33] Cf. my essay, "The Lordship of Jesus Christ: The Meaning of Our Affirmation," *Encounter*, XXI (1960), 408–422.

[34] Cf. the parallel position in John Baillie, *The Sense of the Presence of God* (New York: Charles Scribner's Sons, 1962), pp. 189–212.

Bultmann's theology seems to me to require development in some such way as this if its essential intention is to be realized in the matter of Christology.[35] That such a position has its own problems—and, indeed, some very difficult ones—I am quite aware. It is hardly a small matter to hold that what many Christians have regarded as the central claim of their faith is but a mythological way of expressing an even more central and fundamental claim. Even so, I believe there is ample reason to argue that the other alternative raises difficulties even more serious—both from the standpoint of an understandable proclamation of the gospel in our contemporary situation and, far more important, from the standpoint of an appropriate explication of the Christian faith itself.

The second point where I believe Bultmann's position stands in need of development is its philosophical foundations.[36] Bultmann himself has recognized that the chief criticism of his demand for existentialist interpretation is that it finally makes impossible any direct speaking of God and his action.[37] By apparently urging the complete theological adequacy of the early Heidegger's existentialist analysis, Bultmann seems to hold that God can be spoken of only indirectly, through speaking about man and his possibilities of existence.

That there is much in Bultmann's writings that makes this criticism plausible can hardly be denied by anyone who had studied them. But that it fairly describes his *intention*—to say nothing of much of his actual practice—cannot be maintained. He has explicitly stated that he in no way intends to deny that theology must speak directly of God no less than of man. And, beginning with his reply to his critics

---

[35] It may not be out of place to emphasize, in view of some misunderstandings of my previous formulations (cf. Braaten and Harrisville [eds.], *op. cit.,* pp. 13 f., n. 2), that my issue with Bultmann is not *whether* Christology, but *what* Christology. Of course Bultmann's Christology does not enter into his work as a "misplaced afterthought." (Nor, I may add, can Christology ever be anything but the chief concern in any Christian theology, including, I would hope, my own.) But this does not settle the question of whether the Christology Bultmann presents is at all points consistent with his basic theological intention.

[36] Cf. my essay, "Bultmann's Demythologizing and Hartshorne's Dipolar Theism," in W. L. Reese and E. Freeman (eds.), *Process and Divinity: The Hartshorne Festschrift* (LaSalle, Ill.: The Open Court Publishing Co., 1964), pp. 493–513.

[37] *Kerygma und Mythos,* II, 196 (Eng. trans., p. 196).

of 1952,[38] he has again and again affirmed the possibility of an "analogical," as distinct from a mythological, way of speaking directly of the divine. He holds that the theologian can and must speak directly of God as well as of man, and that he should do so by means of analogies constructed in the terms of Heidegger's existentialist analysis.

The difficulty, however, is that, for all of its obvious importance, Bultmann nowhere fully works out the rationale for this way of analogy. This may at first seem strange until one reflects on the peculiar limitations of the philosophical background of his work. Specifically, there are two closely related reasons that seem to account for his neglect of this important point.

First, like many other existentialists, he is acutely sensitive to the dangers of direct speaking about God. He knows that again and again in the history of theology God has been spoken of directly only at the price of reducing him to a hypostatized abstraction, thus obscuring his reality as the living personal God witnessed to by Scripture. Correlative with this misunderstanding of God, faith in God also has been misinterpreted as a form of intellectual knowledge, as the acceptance of certain beliefs or doctrines, rather than as existential understanding of oneself in relation to the reality of God's gift and demand. Just because Bultmann is so concerned to avoid this kind of illicit objectification of God and faith, he displays a marked reluctance to engage in any direct speaking of God at all. He chooses, rather, to speak of God primarily indirectly, through speaking of man and his possibilities of self-understanding in relation to God. In this way, it can be made clear that God is not an object of intellectual knowledge, but the divine Subject who confronts man with the free personal decision of faith.

The second reason, presumably, that Bultmann fails to develop his theory of analogy is that he has not had available to him the kind of philosophical resource which would facilitate and encourage such development. The only kinds of philosophical theology with which he betrays any acquaintance—classical theism and the idealistic theology of nineteenth-century German philosophy—speak of God only by falsely objectifying him and thus obscure the truth that Bultmann

---

[38] *Ibid.*, pp. 196 f. (Eng. trans., pp. 196 f.). Cf. also *Jesus Christ and Mythology,* pp. 60–70, and "On the Problem of Demythologizing," p. 101.

is most concerned to express. To be sure, the merit of the early Heidegger is that he succeeds in speaking about man in a technically precise way without falsely objectifying his being as a free historical subject. And it is evident to Bultmann that the terms of Heidegger's existentialist analysis can be used to construct analogies in which God also may be appropriately conceptualized without being reduced to nothing more than an object of theoretical knowledge. But neither the early Heidegger himself nor anyone else of Bultmann's acquaintance has fully worked out the details of such an existentialist philosophical theology, and so Bultmann has had no conceptual resource, comparable to Heidegger's analysis of man, by means of which God and his action can be directly spoken of, while at the same time being in no way falsely objectified.

For both of these reasons, then, which have a common basis in Bultmann's too exclusive dependence upon a somewhat truncated existentialist philosophy, he has failed to develop the philosophical theology to which his theory and practice of analogy clearly point. Therefore, the second thing his position requires is just such a fully elaborated philosophical framework that will provide for our necessary speaking of God the same kind of resource that Heidegger's existentialist analysis provides for our speaking of man. My conviction is that such a resource is to be found in the kind of philosophical theology of which the American thinker, Charles Hartshorne, is the best exponent. The genius of Hartshorne's view is that it takes with real seriousness the Biblical understanding of God as genuinely personal without concluding, as the existentialists tend to do, that this precludes the possibility of constructing a full-blown philosophical theology. Hartshorne rightly insists that, although God in his full concrete actuality is always Subject and never object, it is nevertheless possible to objectify the essential structure of God's nature in a way that directly parallels the early Heidegger's analysis of the nature of man.[39] Thus Hartshorne in effect provides a much needed sup-

---

[39] *The Divine Relativity* (New Haven: Yale University Press, 1948), pp. xi f. Among Hartshorne's many other writings, cf. especially *Man's Vision of God and the Logic of Theism* (New York: Harper & Brothers, 1941); *Reality as Social Process* (Glencoe, Ill.: The Free Press, 1953); and *The Logic of Perfection and Other Essays in Neoclassical Metaphysics* (LaSalle, Ill.: The Open Court Publishing Co., 1962).

plement to Bultmann's work at the point of the philosophical foundations of an adequate theology.

Implicit in this attempt at a critical assessment of Bultmann's work are two major questions that may now be summarily posed:

(1) How does Bultmann propose to deal with the widespread consensus among his critics that his attempt to hold together unlimited demythologizing and existentialist interpretation with an exclusivistic Christocentrism involves his theology in a structural inconsistency? If his critics are mistaken, how can this be shown by making clearer than he has yet done that his position is, after all, consistent? On the other hand, if the critics are right, how would Bultmann attempt to remove the inconsistency? By limiting the scope of demythologizing? Or by qualifying the claim that authentic existence becomes factually possible solely through the event of Jesus Christ?

(2) If, as seems evident, Bultmann wants to leave open the possibility of an "analogical" (as distinct from a mythological) way of speaking of God and his action, is it not necessary to work out much more fully than he has ever done the rationale for such a way of analogy? And, to do this, will it not be necessary to appeal to philosophical resources that go beyond the early Heidegger's existentialist analysis—specifically, to a fully developed philosophical theology in which the meaning of "God" is conceptually clarified in nonmythological terms?

I trust I do not have to emphasize that the immense significance of Bultmann's work does not stand or fall with his answers to these questions. Whatever the difficulties his position may involve, he has performed the inestimable service of clearly focusing the fundamental problem of contemporary theology and providing the basic method by which this problem can be successfully solved. Thus I have tried to make clear that our task as the beneficiaries of his contribution is not so much to go beyond him to some essentially new position as to advance along the lines he has already laid down by his theory and practice of radical demythologizing and existentialist interpretation. In this way, we may hope to realize in its fullness that genuinely postliberal theology to which he has so significantly contributed.

Philosophy and Theology in Bultmann's Thought

JOHN MACQUARRIE

Union Theological Seminary
New York City, New York

When we ask what has in fact been the relation of Christian theology to secular philosophy during the history of the Church, we find that this relation has varied very greatly. The variations have ranged from close alliance through mutual indifference to open warfare. And when we ask the further question of what this relation ought to be, we find that this has been a matter for continual debate in the Church. Some early Christian thinkers, like Justin the Martyr and Clement of Alexandria, rejoiced to find an affinity between their faith and the teaching of philosophy, and tended to regard Christianity as itself a philosophy. Others, like Tatian and Tertullian, stressed the distinctiveness of Christianity and its incompatibility with the wisdom of this world.

The debate has continued down to modern times. In the nineteenth century many theologians fell under the spell of Hegel's philosophy, but there were not lacking others who vigorously contended that Christianity has nothing to do with such a speculative system, and can only be distorted by being forced into relationships with it. In the present century, it might seem as if the tide has set definitely against any close association of theology with philosophy. The revival of theology which has been inspired by the work of Karl Barth has put forward as one of its main emphases the distinctive character of the

127

Christian revelation and its distance from human speculations. Moreover, the separation of theology from philosophy has been accelerated by developments within philosophy itself. Contemporary philosophy, both existentialism and logical empiricism, tends to be analytical. It confines itself to the investigation of limited problems and has for the most part renounced the ambition to construct an all-embracing world view, such as earlier philosophies often sought to provide. Thus theology has ceased to turn to philosophy for "confirmation" of religious truth in the form of those theistic world views which philosophers once provided; and even if theology were to turn to philosophy for this kind of thing, it would be disappointed, for the philosophers are much too busy talking about more modest problems. Each discipline prides itself on its autonomy, and autonomy has come to mean isolation. As one of our leading British philosophers has remarked, the two disciplines have, in the past half century, ceased to be on speaking terms.

Where does Rudolf Bultmann fit into this picture? At first sight, it might seem that he is trying to reverse the process which we have described, and to re-establish the bond between theology and philosophy, for, as everyone knows, his theological thinking is strongly influenced by existentialist philosophy. Thus Karl Barth has expressed the fear that theology, after having spent a generation in liberating itself, may be led back by Bultmann into "an Egyptian bondage in which a philosophy lays down what the Holy Spirit is permitted to say."[1] Bultmann, however, would strenuously deny the charge that he is subordinating Christian theology to a philosophy. And over against Barth's estimate, we may set quite a different reading of the situation by Fritz Buri, who remarks that while Bultmann may look like a philosopher to the kerygmatic theologian, he looks very definitely like a theologian to the philosopher.[2]

The relation of theology and philosophy in Bultmann is indeed by no means simple. It would be wrong to suppose that he has put the clock back and returned to the practice of those earlier theologians

---

[1] *Rudolf Bultmann: ein Versuch ihn zu verstehen* (Zürich: Evangelischer Verlag, 1952), pp. 52–53.

[2] "Entmythologisierung oder Entkerygmatisierung der Theologie," in H. W. Bartsch (ed.), *Kerygma und Mythos,* II (Hamburg: Evangelischer Verlag, 1952), 94.

who tried to make Christianity conform to the Procrustean bed of a secular system of thought. Yet Bultmann does recognize the dangers that arise if Christian thought is isolated from the general thinking of our time. He has lived through, participated in, and learned from the revival of kerygmatic theology. But he asks how the Christian message can be heard and understood if the stress on its distinctiveness is allowed to lead to its encapsulation.

The tendencies which are at work in Bultmann's attitude to philosophy may be illustrated from a recent short article[3] in which he tells us about the books which have been most influential for his work as a theologian and student of the New Testament. Of the half-dozen titles which he mentions, only one is that of a purely philosophical work. As we might expect, it is Martin Heidegger's *Sein und Zeit*. "Instructed by this book," writes Bultmann, "I attained a deeper understanding of the historical character of human existence, and thereby at the same time the conceptual framework in which theology too can operate in order to bring faith to appropriate expression as an existential attitude." But neighbor to *Sein und Zeit* on the list is Karl Barth's *Römerbrief*. "From this book," writes Bultmann, "it became decisively clear to me that the essence of Christian faith does not consist in an attitude of the soul, but in its relation to its object, God's revelation."

The juxtaposition of these two books, with Bultmann's accompanying statements, may well puzzle us. He holds out one hand to the philosophers, but with the other he holds firmly to the distinctive Christian revelation. For this reason he incurs the wrath of both parties. Barth accuses him of bringing theology into bondage to a philosophy; Buri accuses him of a certain arrogance, in so far as he meets the philosophers on their own ground only to break off the conversation with an appeal to the kerygma. Is there a fundamental inconsistency in Bultmann's thinking here? Or is it that he is trying to overcome in a new synthesis that long-standing quarrel between the prophilosophical and the antiphilosophical theologians, and to avoid those dangerous extremes in which Christianity is either subordinated to a philosophy or is so isolated that it becomes unintelligible?

What is the *positive* tendency in Bultmann's attitude to philoso-

---

[3] "Milestones in Books," in *The Expository Times* (Edinburgh: T. & T. Clark), LXX, 125.

phy? We may say at the outset that he is just as firmly opposed as anyone to making Christianity conform to any particular philosophical world view. We may say also that he is not merely concerned to find a fashionable terminology in which to express his theology. His positive attitude to philosophy is based on his recognition that the theologian, whether he likes it or not and whether he is conscious of it or not, always works within a conceptual framework, and the concepts which he employs carry with them their philosophical implications. Now the analysis and clarification of the categories of our human thinking are not a theological but a philosophical task. The theologian may indeed have to turn philosopher and work himself at this task, but he cannot afford to ignore what the philosopher has to say on the subject. Bultmann's attitude may perhaps be best expressed by saying that he finds certain *zones of common interest* between the theologian and the philosopher and that he is prepared to learn from the philosopher about those conceptual structures within which, as a theologian, he must work.

In particular, Bultmann finds such a zone of common interest in the field of human existence. It is not with any and every philosophy that he is concerned, but with existentialism as that philosophy which offers a conceptual analysis of the structures of human existence. Why should this zone of common interest be of special importance? This depends upon Bultmann's belief that the basic religious questions are questions about our own existence, about which we all have to decide. Thus he maintains quite bluntly that the work of exegesis depends upon the work of philosophy. "The 'right' philosophy is, quite simply, that kind of philosophical work which endeavours to develop in suitable concepts that understanding of existence which is given with human existence."[4] This philosophical work does not prejudice the content of the answers which we get to our questions— these answers come from the Bible itself. But it does provide the theologian with the conceptual framework which he needs if his work is to have transparency and if it is to be carried out in full awareness of what his questions and answers involve.

What, on the other hand, is the *negative* tendency in Bultmann's attitude to philosophy? He himself asks the question about the possi-

---

[4] "Zum Problem der Entmythologisierung," in *Kerygma und Mythos*, II, 192.

bility of theology being swallowed up in a philosophy of existence. "Is theology simply the precursor of existentialism?" he asks. "Is it no more than an antiquated survival and an unnecessary incubus?"[5] But to these questions he replies with a firm and uncompromising negative. The existential approach to the New Testament lays bare not another philosophy of existence but a kerygma, the proclamation of God's saving acts in Christ. This kerygma is entirely different from a philosophy. The existentialist philosopher may know that man's existence is a fallen one, he may even be able to conceive of an authentic existence, but it is the New Testament which knows of God's gracious act which can lift men out of their fallen state, and of the divine love which can empower men to love. Theology cannot be absorbed into philosophy because it knows and proclaims what God has done about that human situation which philosophy can only analyze. Thus Bultmann draws the dividing line between theology and philosophy, and sets an immense distance between them.

These two aspects of Bultmann's attitude to philosophy, the positive and the negative, may now be considered in greater detail. In order to do this concretely, we consider his relations with two eminent contemporary philosophers: for the positive aspect, his relations with Martin Heidegger; and for the negative aspect, his debates with Karl Jaspers.

Bultmann makes no secret of his indebtedness to Heidegger.[6] It is Heidegger more than any other philosopher who provides Bultmann with the conceptual framework for his theology. Here we can give only a bare outline of Heidegger's leading ideas.[7]

Strictly speaking, Heidegger has always been an ontologist rather than an existentialist. His interest is in the problem of Being in general (*das Sein überhaupt*). He maintains that the ontological question precedes the ontical questions of any particular branch of inquiry, for every science starts off with some presuppositions about the Being of the entities which it investigates. This is evident from the

---

[5] "New Testament and Mythology," in H. W. Bartsch (ed.), *Kerygma and Myth,* trans. R. H. Fuller (London: S.P.C.K., 1953), p. 23.

[6] For a detailed study of the relation between them, the present writer may be permitted to refer to his book, *An Existentialist Theology: a Comparison of Heidegger and Bultmann* (New York: The Macmillan Company, 1955).

[7] See *Sein und Zeit* (6th ed.; Tübingen: Niemeyer, 1949).

fact that we divide up the totality of entities into distinct areas which
we assign to particular sciences—for instance, we assign the area of
living things to biology. We can do this only because we already have
some rough notion of what life is, and can distinguish between living
and nonliving. This means that biology is from the beginning guided
by a basic concept which is itself prescientific in its origin. Progress in
this, or in any other science, according to Heidegger, consists in the
continual clarification of its basic concepts. And this, in turn, can be
attained only through a clearer understanding of the kind of Being
which belongs to the entities in this particular field, and ultimately
from an understanding of Being in general. Among the sciences which
stand in need of such ontological clarification, Heidegger mentions
theology.[8]

But how do we approach the ontological question? We must begin
from the things which *are*—entities—and inquire about their Being.
But there is an almost endless variety of entities. Is there any one of
them which has a privileged position in the ontological inquiry?
Heidegger thinks that there is. The entity which has ontological priority is man himself. Man differs in his Being from things like rivers
and desks in a very special way—he not only is, but has always some
understanding that he is. Heidegger speaks of him in one passage as
like a clearing in a forest[9]—that is to say, he is the *locus* where Being
gets lit up, as it were, and becomes transparent to itself. For man, to
be is at the same time to have some understanding of Being. This
peculiar kind of Being which belongs to man, Heidegger calls "existence." The first step in the ontological inquiry is therefore to clarify
and conceptualize by philosophical analysis the understanding of
existence which is given with existence itself. And Heidegger believes—or believed[10]—that there is a way from the understanding of
man's Being—existence—to the understanding of Being in general.

---

[8] *Ibid.*, p. 10.

[9] *Ibid.*, p. 133.

[10] He has always, of course, recognized that there is something of a circle
in this procedure—see *ibid.*, pp. 7–8. Can we properly understand man's Being
without a prior understanding of Being in general? And if we cannot, how
can we use the understanding of man's Being as the approach to the understanding of Being in general? In his later works, Heidegger seems to believe
that we can have a direct mystical awareness of Being as such. Since, however, it is the Heidegger of *Sein und Zeit* who has influenced Bultmann, we can
for the moment leave aside these complications.

What is the picture which emerges from Heidegger's philosophical analysis of existence? He thinks that the categories which we employ in describing objects "within the world" (*innerweltlich*) are inappropriate for the understanding of human existence as "Being-in-the-world" (*In-der-Welt-sein*). Man is not like a thing with fixed properties. So long as he is, he stands before possibilities among which he must decide. Thus Heidegger sets out to construct a new set of categories—or *existentialia,* as he prefers to call them—which will provide a framework for describing not the properties which characterize things, but *the possible ways in which man can be.* Here again we must content ourselves with a bare summary. The Being of man is disclosed as care, which has a threefold structure. It is constituted by the *possibilities* of existence, which a man may let slip or upon which he may lay hold; by the *facticity* of existence, which reminds us that man's possibilities are limited and finite, for he never starts from scratch but is always "thrown" into a situation, and ultimately into the situation of death; and by *fallenness,* by which Heidegger means man's absorption in concern with the world of things.

There are two fundamental ways in which man can exist. His existence can be authentic or inauthentic. An inauthentic existence is one in which the self is lost and scattered in its immediate concerns with the world and in which its possibilities are decided for it by the collective depersonalized mass of mankind—*das Man,* as Heidegger calls this phenomenon. The individual's responsibility is taken away from him, he is deprived of his potentiality for Being, he is alienated from his genuine self. An authentic existence is attained through hearing and responding to conscience, which Heidegger describes as the call of the authentic self to the inauthentic self. Resolutely accepting his "thrownness," man takes upon himself responsibility for his existence, is liberated from the tyranny of things and of *das Man,* and projects himself upon his genuine possibilities.

As far as its content is concerned, this interpretation of human existence might seem to have little in common with the teaching of the New Testament. Bultmann's interest, however, is directed upon the formal structure revealed by Heidegger's analysis. The distinction between authentic and inauthentic existence suggests a framework within which the concrete ideas of the New Testament can be exhibited in their interconnections. The New Testament distinguishes

between the "natural" man and the "spiritual" man. The first is the
man whose horizons are limited to earthly things, the second is the
man who through dying to the world finds his true life. Salvation is
the transition from the one kind of existence to the other, a passing
"from death into life." Heidegger's concept of *das Man* with its
tyrannical power becomes concrete in the New Testament idea of the
"world," which rarely means the physical world but usually designates the whole body of fallen mankind, supposed to be subject to
dark cosmic powers. The possibility of fallenness likewise finds concrete expression in the New Testament concepts of the "flesh," which
represents the realm of the earthly, and of "sin," which implies in
Christian teaching not merely man's alienation from his own authentic existence but from God as the source of his existence. The
resoluteness which, in Heidegger's view, brings a man into authentic
existence, has its counterpart in the New Testament concept of
"faith." Here Bultmann stresses the elements of decision for and
commitment to the new life which God offers to men in Christ.

We have given only the merest outline of Bultmann's interpretation
of the New Testament teaching in terms of a philosophy of existence,[11] but enough has been said to make clear what his relation to
Heidegger is. Heidegger's formal scheme of existence provides Bultmann with precisely that conceptual apparatus which he holds to be
the prerequisite for any systematic exegetical work upon the New
Testament. Even Bultmann's most severe critics can scarcely deny
that he has had remarkable success, especially with the Pauline and
Johannine writings, in showing how the various ideas hang together
in a closely knit intelligible scheme. Yet he has been able to do this
only because of his employment of the conceptual scheme which
Heidegger's philosophy provides. And we may ask whether he would
have been able to do this if there were not an affinity, as he himself
claims that there is, between the concept of existence implicit in the
New Testament writers and that which is made explicit in Heidegger's
analysis. The result of Bultmann's work is that New Testament concepts like "faith," the "flesh," the "world," the "spirit," which, as
every preacher knows, are so remote from the ordinary man of our

---

[11] For Bultmann's detailed analysis of the New Testament concepts, see his
Theology of the New Testament, trans. K. Grobel (New York: Charles Scribner's Sons, 1951).

time, have been refurbished and given a fresh relevance and currency.

Since Bultmann has specifically mentioned his debt to Heidegger for the understanding of History, [12] a few words may be added on this important subject. Since history is concerned with man, then it follows that for Heidegger it must be understood not in terms of categories such as cause and effect but in terms of the *existentialia*. This leads us to the somewhat paradoxical view that historical study is concerned not so much with facts as with possibility, for man himself is the primary historical, and his existence is constituted by possibility. We study man as he has been in order to know what the possibilities of his Being are. But we can study man as he has been only because we ourselves are men and are historical in our Being. To understand the possibilities of history is at the same time to have our own possibilities disclosed to us. This view of history is decisive for Bultmann's interpretation of the historical elements in the New Testament. We may consider as an example the Cross of Christ. How is it possible that an event which took place long ago and in another place could be an atonement for our sins or a means of salvation for us today? The answer to this question is that the Cross can have atoning power in the present when we think of it not as past event but as the disclosure of a possibility of existence, which can be a possibility for us now. According to Bultmann, to believe in the Cross of Christ means to make that Cross one's own. In "dying with" Christ, we also "rise with" him. When we take up the Cross, we experience it as atonement, we become "at one" with ourselves and with God, we enter on the new life. Bultmann's attitude to the historical element in the New Testament has proved to be one of the most controversial items in his theology, but from what has been said here, we can see clearly that it is a necessary consequence of his existential exegesis, and that once again Heidegger's philosophy of existence has provided the groundwork for the theological interpretation.

We must leave aside for the present the questions and criticisms which are bound to arise in our minds after this survey of Bultmann's relation to Heidegger, and turn our attention to his exchanges with Karl Jaspers. In doing this, we shall be able to get a clearer view of the negative element in Bultmann's attitude toward philosophy.

---

[12] See above, p. 129.

First of all, it may be said that the very fact that a philosopher of Jaspers' eminence has been drawn into a theological discussion is to be welcomed.[13] It gives further evidence that with the advent of Bultmann's demythologizing, some of the barriers that had been erected between theology and philosophy are being broken down, and the exchange of ideas between the two disciplines is being resumed. One might have supposed that Jaspers would display a certain sympathy toward Bultmann's endeavour to link theology with existentialism, for Jaspers himself is the advocate of what he calls "philosophical faith."[14] This faith, which is offered as a middle way between a shallow secularism on the one hand and a hidebound orthodoxy on the other, is based upon Jaspers' philosophy of existence, but it finds room for the tradition of Biblical religion in which, as Jaspers recognizes, we in the Western world "have our specific roots."[15] It would, therefore, be not unreasonable to expect that Jaspers, moving toward religion from the side of existentialist philosophy, and Bultmann, moving toward existentialism from the side of religion, would find some common ground, and that there would be a certain affinity between the philosophical faith of the one and the demythologized Christianity of the other. But this expectation gets disappointed, for Jaspers' attitude to Bultmann's demythologizing turns out to be almost entirely negative. In a wide-ranging critique of the subject, Jaspers can find scarcely anything that is of merit.

Why should this be so? We may see the answer to this question if we select from Jaspers' many criticisms of Bultmann two which are particularly relevant to our task of trying to throw light on Bultmann's conception of the relation between theology and philosophy.

The first criticism is that Bultmann is prejudiced in philosophy.[16] He has based his theological work upon the views of a single philosopher, Martin Heidegger. More than that, he has confined himself mainly to a single early book by that philosopher, *Sein und Zeit*, and has virtually ignored all that Heidegger has written since. Worse still,

---

[13] For the complete debate, see K. Jaspers and R. Bultmann, *Die Frage der Entmythologisierung* (Munich: R. Piper, 1954). A shorter version consisting of Jaspers' first paper and Bultmann's reply to it is published in *Kerygma und Mythos*, Vol. III (1954).

[14] See especially his book, *The Perennial Scope of Philosophy*, trans. Ralph Manheim (London: Routledge & Kegan Paul, 1950).

[15] *Ibid.*, p. 41.

[16] See *Die Frage der Entmythologisierung*, pp. 11 ff.

Jaspers doubts whether Bultmann has properly understood this single philosophical work to which he attaches such importance. He has developed his theology upon his own dubious interpretation of a single work by a single philosopher and this, according to Jaspers, is enough to put Bultmann outside the field of philosophy altogether. For, as Jaspers sees it, the essence of philosophy lies in its openness, its freedom from prejudice, its willingness to give genuine consideration to alternatives. The true philosopher must expose himself to divergent currents of thought, and the man who is open for one current only is no true philosopher. Jaspers contrasts Bultmann's work as a historian of Christian origins with his work as a theologian. As a historian, Bultmann did have this openness which is so prized by Jaspers, he was willing to follow wherever his investigations might lead him. Jaspers acknowledges that he himself has learned much from Bultmann's researches into the New Testament. But as a theologian, Bultmann is said to have lost this openness, and to be misleading us altogether. His apparent interest in philosophy is not a genuine one, but is superficial and deceptive.

In the context of this essay we are less interested in assessing the weight of Jaspers' criticism than in seeing what it implies about Bultmann's attitude to philosophy. Even if some conservative theologians fear that Bultmann is subjecting theology to philosophy, it is abundantly clear from what Jaspers says that the professional philosopher does not for a moment believe that Bultmann has become a brother philosopher. This means that Bultmann has important reservations in his attitude to philosophy. It confirms what was said above—that Bultmann is not interested in trying to bring Christianity into line with philosophy, nor is he willing to let himself be blown about by every wind of fashionable philosophical doctrine. His interest is confined to zones of common interest, as we called them, and it is for this reason that he has selected so narrow an area of the philosophical field. Just what the nature of his reservations are becomes clearer when we look at a second criticism offered by Jaspers.

This second criticism which Jaspers makes of Bultmann is more far-reaching than the first. It is, in effect, that Bultmann gives a special place in his scheme of thought to the revelation of God in Jesus Christ.[17] Of course, we should scarcely expect to find anything

---

[17] See *Die Frage der Entmythologisierung*, pp. 41 ff.

else in a Christian theologian. But Jaspers' complaint is that Bultmann associates divine revelation exclusively with the event of Jesus Christ, and such a procedure offends once more against the openness of philosophy. In Jaspers' view, the knowledge of God is not mediated by any one event or series of events. Indeed, to say that it is would be to place an arrogant restriction upon God. There are ways to God without Christ and without the Bible. Asians have found them in their great religions, and any man who is willing to learn of God can do so. Jaspers' doctrine of limit-situations teaches that if we have eyes to see and ears to hear, we can become aware of the transcendent amid the situations of our own existence. Revelation must be here and now, and cannot lie in an event which is distant from us in space and time. It is doubtful if Jaspers has fully appreciated Bultmann's intentions, for Bultmann also believes that a revelatory act must be here and now, and his existentialist interpretation of history is designed to show that the event of Jesus Christ, as proclaimed in the kerygma, is not tied to any point in time or space but is presented to the hearer as a present possibility of decision. It is an eschatological event, as Bultmann calls it. Nevertheless, revelation is always associated in Bultmann's thought with Jesus Christ, the crucified and risen one, and Jaspers will not accept this. As he sees it, Bultmann's apparent concession to philosophy is really a veil for an illiberal and even intolerant orthodoxy. The philosopher, whose horizons are open, cannot come to grips with an opponent who interrupts a philosophical conversation in order to appeal to a unique and absolute act of God. Long before his debate with Bultmann, Jaspers wrote these words: "It is among the sorrows of my life, spent in the search for truth, that discussion with theologians always dries up at crucial points. . . . No one who is in definitive possession of the truth can speak properly with someone else—he breaks off authentic communication in favour of the belief he holds."[18] In spite of Bultmann's apparent willingness to meet the philosophers on their own ground and to talk about Christianity as a possibility of human existence, he falls into the same condemnation—from Jaspers' point of view—as other theologians, because he finds a place in his thinking for the kerygma, the proclamation of God's saving act in Christ.

Once more, we are less interested for the purposes of this essay in

---

[18] *The Perennial Scope of Philosophy*, pp. 77–78.

determining whether Bultmann or Jaspers is right, than in asking what light their debate throws on Bultmann's attitude to philosophy. It has become abundantly clear that in spite of all his existentialist terminology and all his admiration for Heidegger, the place which Bultmann assigns to philosophy in the theological enterprise is a subordinate one. Though he maintains that the philosophical work precedes the work of exegesis,[19] the philosophical analysis has, for the theologian, only a propaedeutic function. This function is to elucidate the kerygma, as a word of God addressed to our human existence. But the kerygma itself lies beyond the horizons of philosophy. Indeed, as Jaspers' comments indicate, it presents a scandal to the philosopher, who cannot find a place for it in the categories of his thinking. Thus the kerygma, which is the heart of the Christian message, is inaccessible to the philosopher.

Why then does Bultmann wish to bring philosophy into the picture at all? He does so because he believes that we can hear the kerygma only if we already have some understanding of what it is all about. In order to understand anything, we must already have some preunderstanding (*Vorverständnis*) of the subject matter.[20] Since the kerygma is addressed to human existence, the preunderstanding which we require is self-understanding, the understanding of our own existence, and this is the kind of understanding which is clarified and conceptualized in the philosophy of existence. Yet however important this philosophical work may be for the theologian, it is only preliminary in its function. It leads to the kerygma of which no philosophy can conceive, for the kerygma is the proclamation of God's gracious act, addressed *to* human existence but coming *from beyond* it. Thus Bultmann places a powerful restriction upon the place of philosophy in theological work. He does not hesitate to suggest that when philosophy goes beyond its legitimate function, we have a form of sin. Just as Saint Paul perceived a certain arrogance in the wisdom of the Greeks, so Bultmann condemns the self-sufficiency (*Eigenständigkeit*) of a philosophy which seeks to solve all human problems out of human resources.[21]

---

19 See above, p. 130.
20 See Bultmann's essay, "The Problem of Hermeneutics," in *Essays, Philosophical and Theological*, trans. J. C. G. Greig (New York: The Macmillan Company, 1955), pp. 234 ff.
21 See *Kerygma and Myth*, pp. 23 ff.

We now see how complex and even paradoxical is Bultmann's conception of the relation between theology and philosophy. On the one hand, he finds a zone of common interest where he is willing to learn from the philosopher—the field of human existence, where Heidegger's existential analytic provides a conceptual framework for the elucidation of New Testament teaching. On the other hand, he stresses the distinctiveness of the gospel as the proclamation of God's saving act in Christ, which lies beyond the scope of any possible philosophy. He sees that without philosophy Christianity cannot be made intelligible; yet it cannot be assimilated to philosophy without ceasing to be what it distinctively is—the affirmation of God's act of redeeming love. However difficult it may be to hold together the two sides, we have suggested that Bultmann may here be reaching toward a synthesis of those rival attitudes toward philosophy which have characterized Christian theology in the past. Neither the indiscriminate embracing of philosophy nor the wholesale repudiation of it has proved satisfactory, and Bultmann shows genuine insight in striving to find a middle way. Yet, however laudable his endeavour, it still leaves us with unsolved problems on our hands, and we must now direct our attention to some of the difficulties and ambiguities in his position.

The first point which we must notice is the *anthropological bias* which Bultmann's employment of existentialist concepts gives to his account of Christianity. We may reject out of hand, as a gross misunderstanding, the objections of those critics of Bultmann who accuse him of subjectivizing the gospel and of putting in its place a mere description of the religious consciousness. Such critics have failed to grasp the concept of existence, which is never the existence of a bare subject, but always refers to the concrete encounters of the self with the world, with other selves, and with God. Nevertheless, Bultmann's approach to the problems of theology is very much an anthropological one, taking its rise in the natural self-understanding and proceeding subsequently to the kerygma. Karl Barth wonders whether we can really know about sin until we know what God has done about it.[22] Father Malevez insists that "the Bible is not primarily a treatise on anthropology: its whole aim is the knowledge of God and the

---

[22] *Rudolf Bultmann: ein Versuch ihn zu verstehen*, p. 14.

contemplation of God."[23] We may see a different aspect of the same problem in the work of Martin Heidegger, who took human existence as the starting point for an investigation into Being, but who now seems to understand human existence in the light of Being. We may put the question thus: does not the existentialist framework of concepts within which Bultmann works require a more definite ontological setting (as we find, for instance, in Paul Tillich) before it can be considered adequate?

A second point concerns more specifically the *existentialist philosophy of history*. To think of history in terms of possibilities of existence is most enlightening theologically, and enables us to understand how, for instance, the Cross of Christ can be understood as an atonement. But can the question of historical factuality be simply bracketed, so that the theological question and the questions of historical research have nothing whatever to do with each other? Or does the philosophy of history which theology employs require to be broadened, so as to find some room for the factual questions? Does it, for instance, make sense to talk of "dying and rising with Christ" without an assurance that, in some sense, Christ actually died and rose? Can men be summoned to a possibility without the assurance that it has been verified in actual happening? R. G. Collingwood, whose views of history approximate in some ways Heidegger's, and for whom Bultmann has a great admiration, once put it this way: if Jesus never lived, it might be as foolish to urge men to follow his way of life as it would be to urge an athlete to emulate the feats of Herakles.[24]

This may be cautious British empiricism on Collingwood's part, but it does raise a real point. Can we be assured that a possibility is a genuine one unless we see it actually exemplified under the conditions of historical existence in the world? Bultmann does in fact say that the Christian myth differs from the myths of the Hellenistic cults in that it refers to a definite historical figure, but he does not seem to think that this is very important. So we must ask whether theology can concern itself exclusively with the questions of existential possibility and ignore those of historical factuality? Can a philosophy of

---

23 L. Malevez, *The Christian Message and Myth,* trans. Olive Wyon (London: SCM Press, 1958), p. 157.
24 *Religion and Philosophy* (London: Macmillan, 1916), p. 53.

history which deliberately brackets the factual question be adequate
to the needs of theology? How are the questions of fact and possibility related? What is the minimum of factuality that Christianity
needs to get along with—if any?

A third point arises when we recall Jaspers' contention that in
Bultmann's thought *the contact with philosophy is too narrow*. We
have already seen, of course, that there is some justification for Bultmann's almost exclusive preoccupation with Heidegger, on the
grounds that the theologian interests himself in philosophy only
where zones of common interest occur. But if one philosopher is
permitted to be heard to the exclusion of all others, he may come to
exert an influence beyond what the theologian intended him to have.
Perhaps Bultmann has become aware of this danger, for it is noteworthy that in his Gifford Lectures[25] he makes only the briefest of
references to Heidegger and devotes much more attention to R. G.
Collingwood, of whom he goes so far as to say that "the best that is
said about the problems of history is, in my view, contained in the
book of R. G. Collingwood, *The Idea of History*."[26]

Yet it may be asked whether Bultmann's theology would not benefit from a still greater broadening of the philosophical horizon. Would
it not, for instance, be wise for the theologian to compare, supplement, and, if need be, correct Heidegger's analysis of human existence with the views of other existentialist philosophers, such as
Jaspers himself? More than that, does he not find zones of common
interest with philosophers who work in different traditions? In the
British Isles, for example, the contemporary philosophical interest is
not in existentialism but in logical empiricism. Surely the theologian
must take note of the work which philosophers are doing in the field
of linguistic analysis. If, like Bultmann, he talks about mythical language, existential language, analogical language, and so on, he must
ask about the structures of these different forms of language, and
show how they are connected together in his theology. In order to do
this, ought he not to pay attention to what the logical empiricists are
saying?

A fourth point is connected with Jaspers' accusation of *exclusive-*

---

[25] *History and Eschatology* (Edinburgh: The University Press, 1957).
[26] *Ibid.*, p. 130.

ness. It is true that the kerygma makes an absolute claim upon those who hear it, but does this mean that there can be no genuine knowledge of God apart from the Christian gospel? Bultmann's thought is ambiguous here. One can never enter into another religion as one does into one's own, but for this very reason it is impossible to deny that those who do enter into another religion may experience grace and revelation. Grace is not an exclusively Christian concept, and it will not do to say that the philosopher or non-Christian is self-sufficient, and lives out of his own resources. Jaspers has room for grace in his philosophical faith, and Heidegger too, in his later essays, can speak of Being as gracious toward men. The religions of India and of the Far East know the experience of grace. Bultmann does right to hold fast to the kerygma, but one may be loyal to one's own faith without being exclusive in the bad sense of denying that any other faith may reveal God to its adherents. Those who look to Bultmann for some liberalizing of kerygmatic theology would be glad to hear from him that he does not share the preposterous view of some kerygmatic theologians that outside of the Christian revelation there can be no genuine knowledge of God but only idolatrous imaginings.

The Theology of Rudolf Bultmann and Its Relation to Philosophy*

GÖTZ HARBSMEIER

The University of Göttingen
Göttingen, Germany

Rudolph Bultmann has been called the "father of existential theology." Our first task shall be a justification of this characterization.

I

To understand the distinctive relation between the theology of Bultmann and the philosophy of existentialism demands first of all historical orientation. An examination of Paul's Epistles discloses a fluctuating relationship between his Christian message and theology on the one hand and contemporary philosophy on the other. This relationship was sometimes friendly, stimulating, and helpful; then again it was one of rejection and enmity or suspicion and indifference, or was even regarded as satanic and idolatrous, evoking his serious warnings. Magnificent systems of theology, the basis of *philosophia perennis,* came into existence, but also systems in bitter opposition and conflict, each seeking control and predominance over the other. On some occasions final and absolute demarcations were established between their respective territories by rigid "anathemas" for dissenters. However, it never came to an enduring peace or a final parting.

* Translated by George Hackman.

It has never been definitely decided whether philosophy should be the guiding light for theology or whether it should carry its torch in the rear. It remains an open question which can only be answered in a concrete situation. One is continually asking whether this or that philosopher would not make a better theologian or this or that theologian a more thoughtful philosopher. Each generation of theologians is challenged to come to grips with contemporary and past philosophical thought, and this is even more true of philosophers in their dealings with theology.

II

It is characteristic of Bultmann that, in spite of a strong undercurrent of theological tradition, he has been able to keep himself aloof from every antiphilosophical trend. He would not join any school of thought which was either for or against theology in relation to philosophy, nor could he agree to a theological partnership with philosophy simply to enhance theological thought with arguments or proofs provided by modern philosophical thought.

For Bultmann theology and philosophy are, first of all, not two opposing giants, whose relationship or aloofness from one another one might dispute. Thus Bultmann is anything but the kind of dogmatician who would make existentialism the basis of his theology. In fact, Bultmann's concern in relation to the philosophy of existentialism is Christian freedom of thought, so that "whatever is true, whatever is honorable, whatever is just" will serve for the highest good in this area (Phil. 4:8). There is no specific principle in existentialism which Bultmann has sought out to serve him in his theological system. Only his conviction that here was true and factual thinking led him to accept the apparent challenge presented by the early work of Heidegger, *Sein und Zeit*. It is necessary to add here that Heidegger, too, on his part was decidedly influenced by Kierkegaard, Augustine, and Luther. Thus as a philosopher he was not completely divorced from theological insight.

III

Bultmann's chief problem is the relationship of "faith and knowledge." The intrinsic comprehension which dwells in faith, which is expounded by theology, can only find its fullest expression in rational thought and responsible comprehension. This is for Bultmann fundamental theological perception. He rejects a common theological tendency to convey thoughts about faith only through their own peculiar terminology and reasoning. He insists on the solidarity of the believer with all thinking men and demands a thoughtful account to everyone who requests it. This demand directs a believer who is concerned with theology to the insights which are fundamentally possible to all men and which are thought through by every responsible philosophy.

The motive, therefore, which Bultmann brought to philosophy was not to build a theology on the foundation of philosophical insights, but the obligation for a rational account of it. The motive is not one of the search for support through philosophy but one of the intellectual honesty and seriousness of the believer, i.e., the deliverance from exaggerated self-importance, as if the man of faith were the owner of supernatural and suprarational spirituality, and the believer were released from his obligation to the world. Bultmann wants to guard against misunderstood world-escapist and world-denying Christians by insisting on their obligation to give a reasonable and responsible account.

This responsibility of the Christian for thought and knowledge is by no means in opposition to the rightly understood Christian existence which must reject the world. Only when the Christian's relation to the world is rightly understood is his genuine denial of the world expressed in loving concern for his neighbor. Only thus is the proclamation of faith possible in the world. Only thus can the distinctive Christian character in opposition to the world be made reasonable, in the acceptance of which lies the salvation of man.

Philosophical reason and knowledge now have significance for faith, not as presuppositions or steps, but as the prevalent understanding of the world and self within which man interprets the saving grace offered to him. Thus man thinks, talks, and acts by his own value judgments. He is aware of himself and of the world in which he lives. Within his own thought and interpretation of his existence he must encounter the message of salvation.

How can this be made clear to him unless his existence can be formulated into explanatory language? How can he sense his own involvement if it is not made clear to him that the Christian gospel speaks to him in his particular life and circumstances? This life, philosophically explained, does not simply present a starting point which through the gospel is enhanced, crowned, and completed. The opposite is the case: it shall be taken from him and he shall receive the gift of a new life.

It is the same man who thinks, talks, and acts, the same one who has this self-awareness in the world, who shall be liberated into the New Being. As liberated being he will continue to speak the same language and to act in a thoughtful manner. Faith has created insight, thought, speech, and action which enable him to be aware of and to interpret his existence. His existence in faith is totally different than it would be without faith. He is indeed a New Being. The old has passed away. Nevertheless, he continues to think, speak, and act. Not only that, he continues to speak the same language, possesses the same intelligence quotient, and is dependent on the same conditions and presuppositions for his actions. He is the same man, but he thinks differently; he uses the same language, but has something different to say; he lives the same way, but his deeds are different when he believes. He will not be able to philosophize differently, but he will think differently when he believes. If he is a theologian, his manner of reasoning cannot escape the condition under which all men exist. In his philosophy he has to employ language which is also the language of unbelief.

Bultmann's interest in philosophy, be it Stoicism, Gnosticism, or Existentialism, is not in creating a synthesis between theology and the philosophical systems, but solely in the practical responsibility for thought in theology alone.

Theology is thought and speech about faith. It is also, of course, whether willingly or unwillingly, a profession whose tools are shared with philosophy. It does not matter for what purpose these same tools are also used in a particular philosophy. Without the earthen vessel of philosophical thought, there exists no genuine theology.

I V

But immediately the question arises "Which philosophy?" There are so many of them. For Bultmann it is not a question of choice as to which philosophy offers the most suitable premise and the least possible hindrance to theology. Rather it is a choice of the philosophy which best comes to grips with human existence. The criterion is not the nearness to the Christian faith but to existence itself. This nearness of a philosophy to the reality of everyday living and existence is of prime importance to Bultmann as a theologian. It is to this human situation that the message of the gospel must be directed.

To be sure, this is quite different from attaching it to a philosophy which has a special affinity to the Christian faith. Bultmann leaves no doubt in his theological utterances that there is no natural bridge from man's predicament and self-understanding to the Christian faith. For him there lies between the two a deep abyss of infinite qualitative difference which no amount of leveling can bridge. It depends on creating an understanding which is only possible by means of philosophical reasoning.

V

It is natural that there should be a point of contact between faith and the thought pattern of a particular generation. The fact is that man, whether he believes or not, knows something about God. Even in his contradiction of God, he knows whom he contradicts. He also knows about his own freedom, although he rejects it by his attachments to the world. He knows about his perverted existence, even though he willingly and knowingly yields to it. He knows that his life is not what it ought to be, but he strives desperately to maintain a status quo. He is aware of the challenge to make his life count for more, but he either rejects these demands for service to his fellow men or rationalizes them out of existence. He knows about love and forgiveness because he expects them from others, to whom he constantly remains in debt.

This insight into his true identity and his yearning to be free find a point of contact in the pronouncement of the Christian message. Therefore, the appeal of this message will fail unless there is reference to the knowledge concerning his true nature and existence. It is the foremost task of this message to formulate into language man's destiny and failure, to grip man by this self-understanding—that is, to enter into his philosophy of life. This message cannot proclaim intelligently God's acts of redemption if it does not issue from the starting point of man's predicament and God's intent. Even outside faith man stands in a certain relationship to God; it may be one of rejection or a process of conversion. Whoever analyzes correctly man's existence always indicates also a truth about man's relation to God. In some manner he always defines the lostness of man as long as he lives in contradiction to God. This fact must always be of interest to the theologian. This he must recognize. This does not mean that the wisdom of a philosophy ascends to the heights of a theology, but, rather, comprehends philosophical insights in the light of divine revelation.

This light of revelation makes the theologian a student of every genuine philosophy, as long as it properly interprets man's existence. It makes him a student—a critical student, doubtless, since he does not necessarily find existence presented from the viewpoint of the Good News. If the theologian does not know him whom he addresses, how can he talk with him? What has he got to say to him? How can he make it clear to him that the message is especially meant for him? Where else should a theologian learn reliably how man understands his existence, if not from the philosophers who expound these existential insights?

VI

The pursuit of existentialism by Bultmann is in the deepest sense biblical exegesis. Bultmann happened upon existential philosophy during his New Testament studies. He did not come to the Bible by way of philosophy; he discovered philosophy in the Bible. To be more precise, as a biblical exegete and interpreter he was aware of his task of having to weigh exegesis and interpretation in order to arrive at a satisfactory conclusion. As a result he became a follower of the philosophy of Heidegger. It was not a planned, deliberate process which drew him into this relationship. Bultmann's exegetical works, the *Commentary on John,* his *New Testament Theology,* his essays on *Faith and Reason,* as well as his sermons, represent existential exegetical experimentations. There may be better methods of interpretation; Bultmann has an open mind for other ways. For him there is no deliberate exclusion of other and better ways, but no one has shown him a method superior to the one he has so carefully analyzed and tested.

His connection with the existential interpretation may seem accidental, but it is netheles the result of thorough examination. It
became a concrete and critical issue during Heidegger's time at Marburg when Bultmann had to come to grips as a New Testament
exegete with Heidegger's work, *Sein und Zeit*. It was given to him
through the New Testament! When Heidegger describes man's existence as an existence for death and his ground of being as anxiety,
when he recognizes the existence of man in his historicity and his
determination as courage to be, when man's truth stands for affirmation in contrast to the general truth of the natural law, this must
concern the New Testament scholar, because he must ask himself
what these expressions concerning existence have to do with the
proclamations of the New Testament, which are also concerned with
existence.

Moreover, in regard to the Biblical proclamation Bultmann is convinced that God's claim upon man comes to him through his fellow
human beings, and also through the concern of man for those with
whom he is in daily contact. This concern has the authority of the demand, on the thinking of the theologian, not only then, and not because it is legitimately planned Christian thought, but only because it
is expected of me and challenges me to justify my fellow man through
love. This doesn't mean, as might be understood, to identify my thinking with God's will for me. It means to hear His call to me, to confront Him so that all justification is through Him. I must take the demand seriously, must test it and act upon it with the expectation that
here a man could speak the truth which also appears in the Gospels.
This is no more than what also happens in the Bible. Here too, Jesus'
disciples were not given heretofore unknown news about God, man,
and the world. Here too, unbelievers as well as Jews are taken at their
word, through which they disclose how much they already know
about reality and truth. This insight and the thinking of the Scribes
and Pharisees are not disregarded in their disputes with Jesus and
replaced by something new and different. Jesus speaks their language
and thinks their thoughts. He doesn't simply dismiss their ideas. He
thinks them out to their fundamental conclusion and doesn't give
them the excuse that they didn't have his explanation in order to
understand him. They could understand his logic. Paul reasoned and
spoke after his Damascus experience as he did before. His conversion

did not mean the rejection of his former pattern of thought and speech, but enabled him to make use of it in the service of the crucified Lord, whom he formerly persecuted. The change in Paul was not in the language which he had in common with Jesus, but in his confrontation with Jesus.

VII

In Bultmann's dealing with philosophy, the problem of language has received primary attention. The thought and speech of the preacher and theologian must suit the world. He does not mean by this the type of popular evangelism which uses a slangy approach to capture souls for Christ; he does mean, however, that the nature of faith does not require peculiar and unique language and ideology. It is not a matter of choice between two fundamental possibilities, where faith must make a decision for one, in confronting the language of unbelief. It is not a negation which he takes on himself. It is grounded solely in the saving act of God through Jesus of Nazareth, which makes itself understood in the language of the secular world. In this solidarity with the world, faith is anchored in love. Man's growing away from worldliness, which is intrinsic in faith, is expressed in his humanity and loving concern. It is the secular world, of which he is free and of which he frees himself, which erects ever new limits to understanding, ever new dividing systems of self-assertion and self-salvation. The spiritual man is free from these limitations, and at the same time applies his liberating insight to his hopes, his predicament, his fears, his innate sincerity, and his intense suffering—in the selfsame world, from which he cannot escape.

Bultmann is an existential theologian in so far as he attempts in the manner of existentialism to make the Christian faith reasonable, without, however, committing himself to any particular system of philosophy. His employment of this philosophy, to which he is not slavishly bound arises from a freedom of his which renders the encounter fruitful. He thereby follows the example of John or Paul in their time. He has no intention of making existentialism a permanent part of theology. However, he accepts the challenge which this discipline offers to theology and to the understanding of faith.

This undertaking has historic significance in this time and hour; it has brought rewards to Protestant, Catholic and Jewish theology, and will continue to do so—at the same time also bringing this philosophy to its fruition. Bultmann's undertaking can never be excluded from the history of theology or removed from the heritage of religious thought.

The Role of the Church in the Theology of Rudolf Bultmann*

———

HANS BOLEWSKI

Evangelical Academy
Loccum, Germany

The subject of the Church is seldom dealt with expressly in Bultmann's writings. But the question of what the Church is in its nature and its word, the question of what the Church is as a phenomenon of history and how this phenomenon is related to the other phenomena of history—these questions have largely determined his thought in both exegesis and the theology of history from his first writings down to the present. In his religio-historical as in his form-critical analysis he is always out to find dependences, analogies, points of contact, and adoption of material, in order to go on to extract against this background the specific character of a word or an attitude of the Church.

In a sense, of course, the whole of historical-critical theology has its orientation in the posing of the problem in this way. But Bultmann's quest to lay bare what is novel is distinguished by the especially sharp eye he has always had for the connections between historically contemporary phenomena, and by the special direction which he has found necessary to give to his quest precisely on the basis of such insight. It is quite another point of departure when Harnack states concerning the theology of Paul: "Strict teachings of the Pharisaic school, which had not been Hellenistically reworked,

---

* Translated by Paul E. Hoffman.

153

were among its presuppositions";[1] or when Bultmann, in his first great study of Paul,[2] comes to the conclusion that "the preaching of Paul consisted in part in forms of expression similar to the preaching of the popular Cynic-Stoic philosophers, like the classical diatribe,"[3] and points out at the same time that "the decisive difference is this: Epictetus does not know the living God, i.e., the God who guides nature and history according to his purposes, whose direction of peoples as of individuals is a work of bringing them up. He cannot know him because he lacks the concept of revelation."[4]

The question of revelation—i.e., the question of the truth of God concerning man, which is contained in the event which the Bible records—was at work in Bultmann's thought from the very start, although Bultmann himself apparently became aware of this only in the course of the theological controversies of the 1920's which arose in the wake of the publication of Karl Barth's first works. Because of this question of revelation, every phenomenon of history, according to Bultmann, must be examined as to its relativity, its temporal contingency, just as it must be examined as to the ultimate claim which, precisely in its contingency, it makes of him whom it confronts.

This way of posing the problem makes it necessary that the Church, as the mode in which Christian faith takes form in history, play a special role. Bultmann has explicated this problem primarily in terms of the Church of the New Testament and of early Christianity. But inherent in the problem as Bultmann poses it is that it goes beyond the merely historical question as to what was, and takes on decisive significance for the respective contemporary period in church history. And surely a characteristic of Bultmann's style of exegesis, as of his historiography, is that it always encompasses, precisely in its austerity, the contemporary setting of the problem and overcomes the distance of history.

Even the Primitive Church, though it did not "draw a boundary

---

[1] Adolf von Harnack, *Lehrbuch der Dogmengeschichte* I (Freiburg, 1886), 63.

[2] Rudolf Bultmann, *Der Stil der paulinischen Predigt und die kynisch-stoische Diatribe* (Göttingen, 1910) and "Das religiöse Moment in der ethischen Unterweisung des Epiktet und das Neue Testament," *ZNW*, Vol. XIII (1912).

[3] *Der Stil der paulinischen Predigt*, p. 107.

[4] "Das religiöse Moment in der ethischen Unterweisung des Epiktet," p. 181.

between itself, as a new religion, and Judaism,"[5] nevertheless developed, in baptism and even more so in its common meals, the beginnings of cultic forms of its own; it possessed in the "elders" a congregational office; and, "like the Old Testament–Jewish congregation," it found itself in need of "tradition, in which the history which founded it is preserved and made present."[6] In addition, it found itself in need of passing on the necessary "effective" offices and ministries—in other words, in need of succession. All these institutional forms are to be found in the Primitive Church, but undeveloped as yet, so that "the danger is still avoided of regarding the church as an institution of salvation which mediates salvation by virtue of its offices and sacraments."[7] However, this is the very way in which the Church is repeatedly tempted to misunderstand itself, in that it forgets the criterion appropriate to its nature; for "the appropriately instituted 'office' for the direction of the eschatological congregation" can "undoubtedly" only be "founded upon the proclamation of the word."[8] This can occur in institutional forms and within an institutional self-understanding different from that of the Primitive Church. The Hellenistic community, as an individual congregation, knew itself to be part of the total community, the *ekklesia*, the *soma tou Christou*. "The relation of the church to Israel's history is a peculiarly paradoxical one because the course of events from Jacob-Israel down to the present is not a continuous history but one broken by the eschatological occurrence in Christ."[9] And over against the world it possessed an exclusiveness which at times was in part determined by Stoic, but even more by Gnostic ideas. But basically "the eschatological-churchly consciousness is something completely unprecedented in the Hellenistic world."[10] This consciousness, however, can be dissolved into a merely historically understood idea of a third genus besides Jew and Gentile,[11] just as the Spirit is then no longer looked upon as an eschatological gift conferred upon

[5] Rudolf Bultmann, *Theology of the New Testament*, I, 53.
[6] *Ibid.*, I, 59.
[7] *Ibid.*, I, 62.
[8] *Ibid.*, I, 59.
[9] *Ibid.*, I, 96 f.
[10] *Ibid.*, I, 107.
[11] *Ibid.*, I, 108.

the Church as a whole, like the first fruits and the guarantee of the coming lordship of God, but in terms of the holiness of legendary Hellenistic *thei andres,* or in terms of the retreat from the world on the part of individual ecstatics and mystics.[12]

This does not mean, however, that the self-understanding of the Church as an eschatological entity excludes in principle the development of regulations or order within it. Quite the contrary. "No human society can have permanence in history without regulations," without order.[13] With this proposition Bultmann intervenes in the debate between Harnack and Sohm concerning the relation of Church and law, a debate which—in Bultmann's opinion—is still not settled.[14] While Sohm refuses to recognize the necessity of order for every human society, Harnack loses sight of the "self-understanding" of the Church and "understands its form and history from historical and sociological motifs alone."[15] The order of law, however, does come into conflict with the nature of the *ekklesia* when "law ceases to be regulative and becomes constitutive."[16] In the parallel existence of "congregational democracy" and the "aristocracy" of the Spirit-endowed[17] it is by no means simply questions of constitution which are at stake, but the very being of the Church. The question is, "In what form will the rule of the Spirit, or of Christ, realize itself in history"?[18]

At the beginning, at any rate, the Church "knows no office or law by which it is constituted as the church."[19] This sets in only with the attempt to trace the office of the *episkopoi* and *presbyteroi* back to the apostles in the book of Acts and in the Pastoral Epistles and ends up in the primitive catholicism of Clement I, according to which the apostles are represented as having been sent out by Christ to be the "organizers of the whole church."[20] In the course of this development, the new way of life led by the Christian is no longer "the

---

12 *Ibid.,* I, 163.
13 *Ibid.,* II, 95.
14 *Ibid.,* II, 95 f.
15 *Ibid.,* II, 96.
16 *Ibid.,* II, 97 f.
17 *Ibid.,* II, 98.
18 *Ibid.,* II, 99.
19 *Ibid.,* II, 104.
20 *Ibid.,* II, 107.

demonstration of the new (eschatological) existence" but "the condition for achieving future salvation."[21] And "the church has changed from a fellowship of salvation to an institution of salvation, even when, particularly when, it holds fast to the traditional eschatological conceptions."[22]

What is essential, in other words, is the extent to which the Church understands itself as an entity "Between the times," or to be more precise, whether it understands itself as an entity of history or an entity of the *eschaton*. It can continue to hold fast to its eschatological self-understanding as long as it proclaims to the world the salvation which has come about in Christ as the gift to man—already here and now—of the end of man's existence in history and of his concomitant anxiety. The Church gives up this self-understanding the moment it looks upon its task only in terms of history. This happens, however, not only when it makes a philosophy out of its teaching, or an instrument for the achievement of specific political or social goals out of its own institution, but also when it thinks of itself as the final precursor in history of an eternity beyond history. When this happens, faith in God and Christ is no longer the deposing of anxiety from its lordship over all human existence, but just the opposite: the transposing of anxiety to the realm of apparent transcendence, thus creating the problem of legalism, i.e., "a form of piety which regards the will of God as expressed in the written Law and in the Tradition which interprets it, a piety which endeavors to win God's favor by the toil of minutely fulfilling the Law's stipulations." It was precisely this against which Jesus' protest was raised.[23] And for Paul, therefore, "the ultimate purpose of the Law is to lead man to death and thereby to let God appear as God."[24] The understanding of the *ekklesia* which Paul draws from this decisively defines, in fact, the Church's being: "visible as a worldly fact, invisible—yet to the eye of faith also visible—as a thing of the world to come."[25]

This paradoxical understanding of the Church "between the times" became more or less lost, however, as early as the deutero-

---

[21] *Ibid.*, II, 113.
[22] *Ibid.*, II, 114.
[23] *Ibid.*, I, 11.
[24] *Ibid.*, I, 267.
[25] *Ibid.*, I, 308.

Pauline literature. "In most cases . . . the present is distinguished from the past as something made new by the coming of Jesus, or by his death and resurrection. Nevertheless, here the 'between-ness' of the present is conceived as that which determines only the chronology of the Christian situation and not its character; . . . ultimately, therefore, . . . only a temporary and preparatory period. Only where the Pauline tradition continues to work controllingly does the basic 'between-ness' come forth—radically in Ignatius. . . ."[26]

In the whole post-Pauline literature of the New Testament and in all the works of the Apostolic Fathers it is only Ignatius who constitutes an exception. Though he did not adopt the doctrine of the two aeons from which the "between-ness" originally was derived, and therefore thinks in terms of a Hellenistic dualism of flesh and spirit, life and death, the eschatological event nevertheless does happen for him in the eucharist when union with the flesh and blood of Christ occurs.[27] It is precisely for this reason that "the unity of the church and the unity of each congregation under the guidance of its one bishop is one of the chief concerns of Ignatius."[28] Although Ignatius' background does not lie in late Jewish tradition but in a thought context from which the Johannine writings (with which Ignatius has much in common) also came, "through him the problems clearly emerge which confronted a genuine appropriation of the Christian kerygma which had received its first theological explication at the hands of Paul."[29] "Ignatius learned from Paul to understand Christian faith as a truly existential matter,"[30] as an existential attitude or position (*eine existentielle Haltung*).

If faith is, in this sense, an existential *Haltung,* an existential attitude or position, then the form of faith in history, and thus also its relation to the Church as an institution, is of less importance than the way faith sees itself. Alongside the usual distinctions which are made in New Testament theology between various doctrinal types, it now becomes essential to note just how an author relates to the theology he himself propounds. Such a distinction can lead to the discovery of

---

[26] *Ibid.,* II, 199 f.
[27] *Ibid.,* II, 193.
[28] *Ibid.*
[29] *Ibid.,* II, 198.
[30] *Ibid.*

wholly new groupings within the literature of the early Church. Such divergent theologians as Paul, John, and Ignatius can be seen together, in contrast for example to Luke or the author of the Pastoral Epistles. The practical thought obtrudes itself that in a grouping of this kind we might have something like a criterion for genuine canonicity, with the other New Testament writings having come into the canon more or less by chance—or rather, through the church's apostasy from original Paulinism. Reform of the Church is on this basis conceivable, at any rate, as reform of the canon, with an existential attitude or position as the criterion. Or we could say, perhaps, that the present canon shows the Church *both* the possibilities *and* the dangers of its being the Church. We should not, of course, overlook the fact that in Bultmann's thought the usual distinction between *Haltung* and *Gehalt,* between the position taken and the content of that position, or, to put it in traditional dogmatic terms, between *fides qua creditur* and *fides quae creditur,* can no longer be maintained.[31] How the Church understands its existence "between the times" decides the Church's understanding of eschatology and therefore also its orthodoxy, so to speak. "The church remains true to its nature only if the dialectical understanding (of the relation of the here and the beyond, of the present and the future) remains alive in the church."[32]

If this is true, then the fundamental question is posed as to how the Church is to understand its existence "between the times" in the right way. "The primitive Christian community is aware of standing 'between the times,' viz., at the end of the old aeon and in the dawning (or at least immediately preceding the dawn) of the new."[33] But "can the believer understand his present in terms of that 'between-ness' when this 'between-ness' has been constantly extended until it is now almost 2000 years?"[34] That is a question that concerns the Biblical exegete as it has every individual believer ever since theology

---

[31] On this point, cf. Bultmann himself, "Zur Frage der Chrisitologie," *Glauben und Verstehen,* I (2nd ed., 1954), 80 ff.

[32] "Die Wandlung des Verständnisses der Kirche im Urchristentum," *Glauben und Verstehen,* III (1960), 141.

[33] "Der Mensch zwischen den Zeiten nach dem Neuen Testament," *Glauben und Verstehen,* III, 35.

[34] *Ibid.,* p. 36.

became aware in quite a new way—from the time, say, of Johannes
Weiss and Albert Schweitzer—of the importance and (compared with
modern thought) the foreignness of New Testament eschatology. The
exegete notes, however, that the places in the New Testament through
which one can hear disappointment over the nonoccurrence of the
Parousia are neither very numerous nor of great weight.

Nevertheless, eschatology never completely disappeared, and "universal (cosmological) eschatology" was not replaced by an individualistic view of man's continued life beyond death.[35] This was
possible—indeed, it became necessary—because especially in Paul
and in John[36] this "between-ness" is not understood as a change-
over from one mythical aeon to another, but because the old aeon is
seen as the aeon of sin, as the "basic attitude of the natural man who
cannot bear to live in insecurity in the presence of God,"[37] and
because the new aeon is understood as the aeon of grace to which
man "opens himself up in radical abandonment of self, i.e., in faith."[38]

So long as the Church in its kerygma holds fast in this way to this
understanding of the two aeons, by making every baptized person
certain of the Spirit as "the eschatological gift which here and now
transfers those endowed by this gift to eschatological existence,"[39] it
fulfills its task of being the Church in obedience. If, however, as in
the later phase of New Testament literature, it limits the possession of
the Spirit to special officeholders, it ceases in the Pauline sense (e.g.,
I Cor. 3:17) to be holy, i.e., the beginning of God's new time; the
holiness it then attains is the holiness of a cultic community or of a
mystery religion. It then has "in its institutions the Holy Spirit in its
grasp, as it were, and transmits the Spirit by means of the sacraments."[40]

In what happened in the New Testament period one can see,
apparently, a strangely fatal development. The Church shows itself to
be "an entity that does not belong to the world and that nevertheless
settles down in the world."[41] What is decisive for this process is that

---

35 *Ibid.*, p. 39.
36 *Ibid.*, p. 42.
37 *Ibid.*
38 *Ibid.*
39 *Ibid.*, p. 45.
40 *Ibid.*, p. 47.
41 *Ibid.*

"the paradox of the 'between-ness' hardly characterizes individual existence any longer, or characterizes it in the end only through the medium of the church in which the 'between-ness' has, as it were, been preserved."[42] It is quite decisive for the existence of the Church, therefore, that it make possible the confrontation of the existence of the individual believer and the kerygma. "The church is constituted by this kerygma."[43] "The church . . . is a word of Christ, who said: 'Whoever hears you hears me,' " as Bultmann is capable of saying in perfect agreement with a quotation from Luther's lectures on Romans.[44] It is this that gives the Church its relation to the world and lets its members remain worldly. "One may participate in the business and flux of the world." But at the same time there is the call of the kerygma to the conscious "distance of the 'having as having it not.' "[45]

This paradox of secularity and desecularization exists, however, only in relation to the existence of the individual believer, for the reason that it is the individual man in his ever-present quest for God whom the kerygma can and does confront. "In human existence an existential knowledge of God is alive as the quest for 'happiness,' for 'salvation,' for the meaning of the world and of history, as the quest for the intrinsic purpose of one's own existence."[46] Bultmann likes to appeal for support here to that famous sentence from Augustine's Confessions: *Tu nos fecisti ad Te, et cor nostrum inquietum est donec requiescat in Te.*[47] The question of the meaning of man's existence (which the believer can quite legitimately comprehend as a question concerning his existence before God) is, if it is put with genuine seriousness, an existential question, and the answer to this question is provided by the likewise existential kerygma. Science,

---

[42] *Ibid.*

[43] "Kirche und Lehre im Neuen Testament," *Glauben und Verstehen*, I, 180.

[44] "Echte und säkularisierte Verkündigung im 20. Jahrhundert," *Glauben und Verstehen*, III, 129.

[45] "Der Mensch zwischen den Zeiten nach dem Neuen Testament," *Glauben und Verstehen*, III, 48.

[46] "The Problem of Hermeneutics," *Essays, Philosophical and Theological* (London: SCM Press, 1955 [Eng. trans. of *Glauben und Verstehen*, II]), p. 257.

[47] *Ibid.*, e.g., or see "Entmythologisierung und Existenzphilosophie," *Kerygma und Mythos*, II (1952), 192.

particularly philosophy, which has its orientation in the quest for understanding and in the study of man, can throw light on why it is that this question arises, and it can provide the hermeneutical categories through which the mythological idiom of the New Testament can and must be interpreted in existential terms, without theology dissolving into philosophy simply on this account.[48]

Theology is always, therefore, "a movement of unbelief springing out and away from faith,"[49] a movement, however, which is necessary "in the concrete obedience of faith to the demand of a concrete situation,"[50] necessary for the sake of the kerygma, precisely in order that confrontation can take place with the person who is seeking after the meaning of his existence. For the presupposition for all of this is "that the question really apposite to the Bible—apposite, at least, within the realm of the church—is the question of human existence to which I am driven by the question which grips me existentially, the question of my own existence."[51]

That for such a confrontation with the kerygma—a confrontation which is apparently essential for man—there must be comprehensive planning of an institutional kind; that it also can and does come to a perversion and secularization of preaching;[52] and that because of this there is need for vigilance to see that in some way the institution of the Church corresponds to its purpose and mission, to see that the nature of the Church be the principle of its external form[53]—these are all matters on which Bultmann does of course reflect, but anyone looking to Bultmann for indications as to where to begin a reform of the Church will largely be disappointed. Everything that lies outside

---

[48] On the problematic character of this relationship (which we cannot go into here), see Heinrich Ott, *Geschichte und Heilsgeschichte in der Theologie Rudolf Bultmanns* (Tübingen: Mohr, 1955), esp. pp. 60 ff. See also Peter Biehl, "Welchen Sinn hat es, von 'theologischer Ontologie' zu reden?" *ZThK*, 1956, esp. p. 359.

[49] "Das Problem der 'natürlichen Theologie,' " *Glauben und Verstehen*, I, 312.

[50] *Ibid.*

[51] "Entmythologisierung und Existenzphilosophie," *Kerygma und Mythos*, II, 191.

[52] Cf., e.g., "Echte und säkularisierte Verkündigung im 20. Jahrhundert," *Glauben und Verstehen*, III, 122 ff.

[53] See on this point the essay (disappointing to anyone taking the announced title as his measure) by Friedrich Karl Schumann, "Um Kirche und Lehre," *Gesammelte Aufsätze und Vorträge* (Stuttgart, 1936), pp. 202–224.

the kerygma (something that is not limited, of course, to the preaching of the Church but that comprises also "the expression of Christian love between persons"[54]) falls under unbelief. Almost everything that Bultmann says of the Church applies to the Church as the context and object of faith, not to the Church as institution. In as recent a work as his latest major study on the relation of the primitive Christian message to the historical Jesus[55] he expressly underlined this in a footnote: "It is obvious that the 'church' here is not being viewed as an institution but as an eschatological event. It is not the guarantor of faith but is itself an object of faith. It is just as much a *skandalon* as the cross."[56]

But where do we get the right to designate two such different entities as this with the same word "church"? How can an eschatological event be at the same time an institution? How can the Church have a history? How are the Church's kerygma and the Church's external form related? Do only individuals raise the question of the meaning of their existence, or would not this question have to be raised with regard also to institutions, organizations and groups— even if something like this should lie beyond the horizon of questions posed by the philosophy of existence? Whether Bultmann has an answer for all these questions can only be stated after we look at what he says regarding the problem of human community with which he has dealt on numerous occasions. Here, too, eschatology plays a basic role. Indeed, the subject of eschatology and the Church represents in our century, and especially in Bultmann's thought, a continuation of the nineteenth-century subject of the Kingdom of God and the Church, a subject which Albrecht Ritschl brought to the foreground of theological debate.

"The new people of God has no real history, for it is the community of the end-time, an eschatological phenomenon."[57] It is hard to find a sentence that counters more sharply or more stringently than this the attempts that continually have been made since the period of

---

[54] "Echte und säkularisierte Verkündigung im 20. Jahrhundert," *Glauben und Verstehen*, III, 129.

[55] "Das Verhältnis der urchristlichen Christusbotschaft zum historischen Jesus," *Sitzungsber. Heidelberg. Akad. Wiss.*, phil.-hist. Kl., 1960, No. 3.

[56] *Ibid.*, p. 26, n. 80.

[57] *History and Eschatology*, p. 36.

German idealism to harmonize history, the Kingdom of God, and the Church. Bultmann himself took issue in the New Testament field with two such attempts at a continuation of a kind of Christian idealism: with Ernst Lohmeyer's essay of 1925 on the concept of religious community[58] and with Martin Dibelius' work of the same year on historical and suprahistorical religion in Christianity.[59] These two authors are charged either with offering feelings that cannot be legitimized on the basis of the New Testament or with offering a philosophy. With respect to Dibelius it is said, "the author is a romanticist, only that mixed into his romanticism is a dose of a modern philosophy of value."[60] And while Dibelius gives expansive treatment to the question of worship and cult in his chapter on the Church, Bultmann in sharp contradiction concludes: "The question of the church for present-day Protestantism is not a question of cult, but a question of theology."[61]

For Ernst Lohmeyer "the 'community of God' is . . . always solely oriented in intention toward the ultimate universal community which will be inaugurated by the eschaton. But this goal of eschatological universality and every stage along the way . . . are one and the same."[62] But it is precisely in the closing section on history and community (pp. 66–86) that, in Bultmann's view, Lohmeyer gives himself away: "Here we have that ancient Platonic dualism of ideas over against the world of appearances which shows up to orient the author's whole way of looking at things in the contradiction of norm and appearance, something that allows him to compare the realm of actuality with the norm of the absolute."[63] Not that it is illegitimate as such for the theologian to use philosophical categories. Philosophy may prescribe for theology, however, "neither the subject of its treatment nor the appropriate way of treating it. If philosophy is understood as the science of being (Sein), i.e., as the science whose

---

58 E. Lohmeyer, "Vom Begriff der religiösen Gemeinschaft," *Wissenschaftliche Grundfragen,* in R. Königswald (ed.), *Philosophische Abhandlungen* (Leipzig and Berlin, 1925), No. 3.

59 M. Dibelius, *Geschichtliche und übergeschichtliche Religion im Christentum* (Göttingen, 1925).

60 *Glauben und Verstehen,* I, 77.

61 *Ibid.,* p. 84.

62 *Ibid.,* pp. 2 f.

63 "Vom Begriff der religiösen Gemeinschaft," *ThBl,* VI (1927), col. 71.

task it is to check the concepts of being (*Sein*) with which all the positive sciences which deal with existent being (*das Seiende*) operate, then indeed philosophy can render theology an indispensable service."[64]

Bultmann's sharp contradiction calls to mind a similar reaction occasioned not quite a hundred years before by Schelling's Berlin lectures on the philosophy of history, of which Erich Frank reminds us in an extended footnote to his essay, "Letter and Spirit."[65] Attending Schelling's lectures were, among others, Engels, Kierkegaard, and Bakunin, who in their disappointment turned from idealism to a radical realism. It is no coincidence, perhaps, that in all three we find with a turning away from idealism a rejection of the Church in its form in history. And one is perhaps allowed the question whether, among the assumptions of a philosophy of existence that goes back to Kierkegaard (as we in fact find it in Bultmann), it is not just as natural to find the nonexistence of the Church in history as it is obvious to a no less modern theologian like Paul Tillich (who has his roots, of course, in quite another tradition of thought) that the New Being has an historical dimension. "The appearance of the Christ in an individual person presupposed the community out of which he came and the community which he creates."[66] The question of the Church is here directly connected with the hermeneutical question.

H. G. Gadamer, too, points out that Bultmann's proposition that "the interpretation of biblical writings is not subject to conditions different from those applying to all other kinds of literature"[67] is ambiguous, and that it is apparent, for example, that "modern hermeneutics as a Protestant discipline" is "as an art of scriptural exegesis related polemically to the dogmatic tradition of the Catholic Church and its doctrine of justice."[68] That means, however, that Biblical hermeneutics stands also, and precisely, within a tradition, and that it cannot naïvely and unreflectively look upon the categories offered by this tradition as a simple—if also critical—a priori, but

---

[64] *Ibid.*, col. 73.
[65] Erich Frank, *Philosophical Understanding and Religious Truth* (London: Oxford University Press, 1945), p. 168, n. 17.
[66] Paul Tillich, *Systematic Theology*, II, p. 156.
[67] "The Problem of Hermeneutics," *Essays*, p. 256.
[68] Hans-Georg Gadamer, *Wahrheit und Methode* (Tübingen, 1960), p. 314.

that existential interpretation (precisely in a time in which Christendom is itself beginning again to question its traditions critically for the sake of the one truth of God) ought also to be tested as to whether and to what extent it can contribute to a solution of the ecclesiological problem of the present day. To what extent, for example, can an order for the Church be legitimately drawn from the nature of the word and its tradition? This question is all the more pressing in that the understanding of such an order, to which Bultmann is constantly giving expression, presupposes—perhaps without wanting or realizing it—as the confrontation of the individual with the kerygma, a specific form of ecclesiastical order, viz., the distinction between an understanding and interpreting body of scribes and the large multitude of interested, and even larger mass of uninterested so-called laymen. But that amounts to a justification of the *status quo* in our churches, in which we can neither hold the existent order to be a proper order for the Church nor can we trust that it will continue for any length of time in our century. Is it then really impermissible to reflect upon the existence of the Church in history?

Bultmann himself did turn his attention in one of his essays to the "Forms of Human Community,"[69] whereby he pointed out that various forms of community should be distinguished: that which has been transmitted by nature, that which has developed in history, that which has its base in art and science, and that which has been founded by religion. I regret to admit that these distinctions, which may well have some traditional justification, I no longer understand. It is impossible for me to understand that deeply disturbing poem of Goethe's to Charlotte von Stein ("Destiny, why didst thou give no feelings thus to sense what's in the other's heart . . .") as an expression of "natural" community. Is it not rather the product of historical developments in which in our culture a man and a woman find it possible to discover one another, but also to lose one another?

In regard to all four types of community, mention is made, to be sure, of their degeneration, especially of the dangers to which they are exposed today: the prostitution of community in the totalitarian state; petrification and organized activity in science; orthodoxy in the

---

69 *Essays,* pp. 291 ff.

Church. But because God's grace brings man to himself, it "has liberated him for his neighbor."[70] But just where does this take place? One should think that it would take place in the Christian community, and the Christian community should concern itself to see that its members find it possible to live in and by such liberating freedom. But it seems as if it is supposed to be a particular danger for the Church "that the church—which is in its essence invisible— organises itself as an institution," whereas "in so far as it appears in visible form, it is always real only as *event*."[71] Can we so simply count on this happening also in the future, in view of the dangers to which all these forms of community are exposed? Must we not— recognizing, to be sure, the danger of convention and organized activity—use our minds to see to it that a church exists which in the continuity of history exists for men, so that men may find it possible to live in this world in the freedom that comes from God?

C. H. Dodd in the final section of his small book, *The Bible Today,* pointed out once again that in this question of continuity it is a matter of both the word *and* the Church. "Church and Bible are so closely bound together in our historical complex, that it is only common sense to expect the Bible to speak to us most clearly *in the context of the continuing life of the Church.* If we are to 'live ourselves into' the history which is God's revelation of Himself to men, we have no need to take a flying leap into a remote and alien past. The Church is heir to that history and makes us free of it."[72]

In response and contrast Bultmann asks: "Must not a theological understanding of history start from an understanding of the historical character (*Geschichtlichkeit*) of man (as of that which belongs to the nature of man's being), not, however, from the understanding of history as of a connected series of occurrences of the past?"[73] But must not a counterquestion be asked? How is the historical character of man to be grasped except within a history that is constantly in flux? This history has indeed its special quality, to the extent that

---

[70] *Ibid.,* p. 303.

[71] *Ibid.;* emphasis Bultmann's.

[72] C. H. Dodd, *The Bible Today* (Cambridge, 1948), p. 162.

[73] Rudolf Bultmann, " 'The Bible Today' und die Eschatologie," *The Background of the New Testament* (Cambridge, 1956), pp. 407 f.

without this history we would not be able at all to understand the kerygma. Here the Church, in Dodd's phraseology, stands over against history both as its heir and the thing that makes us free.

Here we are up against unsolved questions, questions which arise out of the methodology of an existential interpretation of the New Testament, questions as to the understanding of the origin and development of the New Testament concept of the Church as well as questions regarding the foundation, the purpose, and the mission of the Church in life's historical structures. Ernst Käsemann has pointed out that "the authority of the institutional ministry, a ministry that surrounds itself with executive organizations in the eldership, the diaconate, and the institutions of widows," arose "precisely on the soil of the Pauline mission field."[74] "This obvious inheritance from Judaism, mediated through Jewish Christianity as it fled from Palestine, is the bulwark behind which the church founded by Paul was able to maintain itself in the face of fanaticism."[75] And at the end of his historical account Käsemann poses the question: "Can it be that Paul, who throughout his lifetime fought against enthusiasm, did not succeed in providing a foundation for church tradition but succeeded only in disintegrating it, because he demanded too much of Christians and the fellowship of the church and for that reason himself incited to enthusiasm?"[76] Gerhard Ebeling has set up for his "Conversation with Rudolf Bultmann" certain "Theses on Ecclesiology" in which he would like to connect the question of ecclesiology to the quest for the historical Jesus. "Jesus as authoritative event, as the gospel in person, is the foundation of the church."[77] However, precisely because the Church is thus "the authoritative occurrence of the word" which concerns man as man and which makes him man, "the church refers not to the abstract individual but to man in the community of his humanity" (*seine Mitmenschlichkeit*).[78]

Those are theses that differ widely from Bultmann's, that in fact contradict them in part. And yet his approach maintains itself and

---

[74] Ernst Käsemann, "Amt und Gemeinde im Neuen Testament," *Exegetische Versuche und Besinnungen,* I (Göttingen, 1960), 129.

[75] *Ibid.,* p. 130.

[76] *Ibid.,* p. 134.

[77] Gerhard Ebeling, *Theologie und Verkündigung* (Tübingen, 1962), p. 97.

[78] *Ibid.,* p. 101.

even finds reconfirmation in them, the approach he brought to bear with such force in taking issue with Martin Dibelius, viz., his observation that for Protestantism the question of the Church is a matter of theology,[79] a theology, of course, which thinks existentially and for which the *engagement* in thinking is as essential as the outcome. In ecclesiology we today are presumably only at the beginning of a new way of working theologically, and we find ourselves unable to say whether in fact it will be one way or many ways. But there can be no doubt that out of the tremendous tensions which exist in theology today, very diverse escapes are possible. "The church is now the world." With this thesis Heinrich Schlier attempts to solve the question of the eschaton and history, and in doing so expresses the reason for his conversion to the Roman Catholic Church.[80]

From the outset, ecclesiology has never been in the central focus of Bultmann's work, but it could well be that he has provided the decisive impetus for continuing work on this question, which is one of the most tremendous of our time. In the few essays in which, apart from his directly exegetical works, he has expressed himself on the doctrine of the Church, he has brought infinitely more into flux than the many positivists whose works fill our average theological book lists. And I should, therefore, not like to conclude this brief critical presentation of the role of the Church in the theological thought of Rudolf Bultmann without expressing a word of gratitude to the man who has been for my generation something like our great preceptor and master in theological work. His thought and his work have accompanied me from the time of my first semesters at Marburg. Without the methodological schooling received through him I could not imagine myself in a position so caught up in the passionate issues of our day as that of director of an Evangelical Academy.

---

[79] See n. 59, above.

[80] Heinrich Schlier, "Kurze Rechenschaft," *Bekenntnis zur Katholischen Kirche* (Würzburg, 1955), p. 180.

The Event of Salvation and Word
in the New Testament

OTTO MICHEL
The University of Tübingen
Tübingen, Germany

It is an especial privilege for me to discuss with you here some important problems in our scholarly work. These are problems whose solution is still pending for the most part, but which concern us daily in Biblical exegesis.

It is understandable that dialectical theology, as heir of the "confessing" struggle and of the new reflection upon theology by Karl Barth, should largely predominate in the discussion. Hermann Diem has said, "What is not dialectical theology is simply not being read by us." That pertains especially to theological students. But dialectical theology has broken into a wing of Bultmann's methodology as well as of Barth's, and the leadership in method has shifted to Bultmann. His is a theology of existential interpretation. He takes his departure from the concept of human existence, which is so charged with meaning. From that perspective he assails those dogmatic categories which earlier appeared to be objective certainties, such as the Word of God, the canon of Holy Scripture, or the confessions of the Church, and discounts them as products of history belonging to the past. Anyone who appeals to them is suspected of seeking false security.

Of concern now is the individuality of human existence. The individual is supposed to find his own "self" with the help of Jesus, through his Word and call. Faith becomes an occurrence within human experience. The Scripture is to be understood in terms of the man who expounds it. It seems that existential theology has set itself the task of finding new concepts and ideas for Biblical statements which no longer satisfy. There are, to be sure, opposing theological movements which ask the abiding meaning of a Biblical concept and why the Bible is concerned not only with human existence, but also with history as the locus of encounter between God and man. These are questions which find existential interpretation wanting.

And further, alongside dialectical theology there remains the older alignment of Lutheran and Reformed theology. This confessional theology has renewed itself to some extent with Barthian motives. It has mustered its strength in opposition to the various existential movements and reaches for sure forms and certainties of faith that will survive the present spiritual crisis.

In the midst of these strong and diverse currents a few Biblically grounded theologians, each with his own approach, still have influence. Among them are A. Schlatter, M. Kähler, and other theologians of revelation dependent upon them. Of these I should like to speak first.

In the first place neither Schlatter nor Kähler is to be understood speculatively, Biblicistically, or as an eclectic theologian. The speculative influences of their time came from theological idealism, whose ideas were rooted in philosophical construction. Biblicism sought to concentrate on Biblical statements apart from the thought of the times, without grappling with the actual question of truth. As a way of synthesis may be regarded every attempt to sort out Biblical statements and to reduce them to a remainder which is still acceptable to modern man. None of these approaches has been overcome as yet, although each persists in another form than in the nineteenth century.

What made Schlatter and Kähler stand out was not only that they could speak of the living God and of his continuing works in the Church, but that they themselves came from the Church and led the way to the Church. Existentialism, on the contrary, evinces tension with the Church, its prevailing forms of piety, and its norms of spiritual life. Schlatter and Kähler, too, were critical of church piety, but not for the purpose of rejecting it; they still had a vital interest in revivalism and in Biblical certainties. Both dared to take seriously the basic motive of the Bible: its idea of revelation. Both knew of that reality which alone is adequate to receive the idea of revelation, namely, life on the plane of history.

The theology of Schlatter was noted for being revelation theology. It referred back to the decisive content of Holy Scripture concerning revelation and testified to Jesus as the center of the New Testament. Schlatter taught us to observe data, to see their connection and their significance—a procedure still valuable in exegesis. Thereby he wove the elements of creation, of faith, of redemption, and of consummation into a concept of revelation that was significant for an understanding of the Scripture. Although his focus was on revelation, he did not lose sight of concrete reality. The main object of Schlatter was a revelation theology and a realist theology in one.

Kähler began with the ideas of the Reformation. For him the Reformation doctrine of justification was the gateway to an understanding of both revelation and the Scripture. History opened itself most deeply in the encounter between God and man which Jesus Christ effected. In the Word—and the Word was for Kähler actual preaching—in which alone God disclosed himself, one encountered the crucified and resurrected Christ. By this encounter with the deed which Christ accomplished for us on the Cross, the Church became certain of its faith, and knew him to be the Lord of the Church. Therein lay certainty. Therein lay Christology. Kähler designated any statement about which scholarship contended, or which was disputed by it, as "historical." But what the living God had contributed to history was of "historic" importance. These two aspects lay on different levels, and sometimes appeared to be in conflict with each other. If anyone attempted to found the historic truth of the Bible upon historical data, he was suspected of apologetics.

From both these men we have received much of value. Neither took his conception from a philosophical or anthropological view, but from the works of God revealing himself to effect faith. Both hung with a final certainty on the statements of Scripture, which disclosed to them ultimate truth and yet concealed it also. Both were concerned with an experience of the living God, and not to delimit Him with critical thought. The way each of them expounded the Scripture was different, yet neither stressed any particular hermeneutical method except taking a Biblical statement seriously. Their problem was whether any Biblical statement could be ordered within an entire conception of revelation.

From Schlatter we should like to retain the courage to believe, to perceive reality undisguised, and to criticize false pretenses of the Church. We should like to retain also the confidence of Kähler in the living God and his Word. But we are not able to content ourselves today simply with the approach of Schlatter or of Kähler. The problem of hermeneutics has sharpened and intensified since their time. Historical-critical theology has developed its own method, and so strengthened the hand of scholarship that the older approaches of our fathers have had to give way. The picture of history for which Schlatter contended against his opponents, although still valuable in some respects, no longer applies. As for Kähler, he distinguished between historical data and their historic importance, a questionable and dangerous distinction to make. When Kähler said, "The historian can give no certainty regarding the question of salvation," the historian had to reply, "What must I do, then, if I can give no absolute certainty?" To be sure the historian can only give absolute certainty when he himself believes. But even when he believes, he will still be able to give absolute certainty only about an object of his research. But an historian can provide certainties, even though of another kind. These lie in his material. With full allowance for the problem of recognition, one cannot so subjectivize the question of what has happened that certainty about history is dissolved.

Where does one arrive when history is relativized? In his time it was Schlatter who opposed this tendency to relativize history. He knew the connection between the Old and New Testaments, and pointed out time and again that the roots of the New Testament lie in the Old. As professor of the New Testament, he lectured on the history of Israel, and wrote a book thereon. He traced the history of New Testament times, as did Emil Schürer before him. He wrestled with the problem of Judaism, aware that no one can know Jesus, Paul, or John until one has encountered Israel.

Yet a fact obtrudes which is painful to us: it was not given to these beloved teachers to take the political and cultural crisis, in which the Christian West had so long fallen, seriously enough for their students to acquire the prophetic power necessary for the church struggle and the postwar period. The apocalyptic character of our entire epoch had not yet broken through. Neither is existentialism as such, intent as it is upon individual existence, capable of grasping this character, but it contained the possibility of a religious and cultural criticism which was at least partially necessary. That was a possibility which dialectical theology received along with its main thesis from Kierkegaard. He taught that Biblical truth revealed and concealed itself in the dialectic of human existence, and could no longer be comprehended on the plane of space and time, but only in terms of its historic significance for the experience of man. The relation between the true God and the true man is antithetical; that is, what man recognizes of God and what God does stand in contrast to each other. Faith has to deal with this scandalous paradox. But as one follows Jesus, life is realized in his presence.

There is great strength in this position of Kierkegaard. It was Kierkegaard who, in the last analysis, brought our churches in Germany through the church struggle. Barth was the actual leader. His thought sustained resistance against the regime, provided certanity of faith, and shaped the theology of our "confessing church" synods. The elements which went into this theological resistance were not actually substantiated, but the theological statement as such was powerful. It embraced all areas of living and attempted to make the act of faith effective in them. Here was a position which, over against the regime, stood not only for a Biblical attitude, but also in behalf of an assailed and oppressed mankind. Regard for human existence lends itself to a new understanding of humanity. We may ask today whether in that respect one has grasped the essential content of the Bible. But it is good to keep in mind the part which that motive played in the situation.

In the Schlatter-Kähler tradition the severity of the conflict could only be endured when one admitted dialectical tenets, as did J. Schniewind. It seemed hard for Biblically-oriented movements to face the implication of truth in actual reality. In pietistic circles the Biblical heritage was expounded as having to do mostly with the individual. Kähler could say: "That the Bible is true, I recognize in Romans 7." But he could not discern the judgment which was coming upon our German people. With Schlatter it was still less possible. Herein lies the inadequacy of many pietistic circles. But one should not scold them; many official church circles found themselves in the same distress. After the war the prophetic-Biblical thrust broke up before the inner cleavage of the church, obliged to be culture-creative on the one hand, and culture-critical on the other. We may be confident, however, that God will make it possible for us to further endure the present crisis without succumbing to any compromise of Biblical truth.

What unites the exegete and the historian is the way of research which arose anew in the Enlightenment and was further developed in the nineteenth and twentieth centuries. Historical-critical scholarship, as it was refined in the school of form criticism by R. Bultmann and M. Dibelius, oriented us only toward a definite method. In the background, however, the heritage of the Enlightenment was continually bringing forth a new understanding of reality and truth. That is still going on. The question is whether historical-critical exegesis is to be carried on with reference to the actual material or whether other motives are to be admitted. Halle H. Gunkel, the father of form criticism, insisted vehemently that one should let himself be led by factual findings alone in form-critical analysis.

The consequence of existential interpretation has been to enlarge the research program of the historical-critical method into a search for truth, this time not with respect to ideas as in the nineteenth century, but rather with respect to the existential meaning of man. Thereby the exegete engages, to be sure, in conversation with the text, but in terms of his own understanding. He approaches the text with questions which incite it to speak, and then hears the answer, which surprisingly confirms his questions. The past of the text is perceived, but appears to be unessential for the present understanding. The present understanding is the main thing that happens. Thus a concept of understanding decides the outcome of our critical inquiry. In that way a method expands into a system of theoretical knowledge, of hermeneutics, of existential theology. I do not mean that form-critical analysis should not exercise its sharpest acumen, but that it should acquire its picture of history from a critical examination of the sources. It should take care not to infer its own favorite axioms, so that the sources can say something to it.

At this point the contrast with Schlatter and Kähler is obvious. They were concerned with a transmission of material that contained historic meaning, with the possibility that through the text history would remain living in every new setting. The matter impelled them, not actually a method. Their method was not rounded out, it was simply an adherence to statements that were not to be disputed.

Kähler could not quite make out with his concept of historic meaning; but seeing its limits did not subject it to doubt for him. Now, however, the question has arisen whether there is any basic possibility of making a theological assertion. Over and over again one torments himself with the question of how a Biblical statement can become authoritative in the present. But for Schlatter and Kähler the Word was at one and the same time an event, a share in the matter, and a transmission of a definite message that could not be detached from its content. Kähler took the Word to be the means of revelation by which God effected the personal encounter between man and himself. As means, the Word was still, therefore, full of content in its substance. According to existential interpretation, however, the Word becomes the starting point of understanding between an I and Thou. One looks into the philological and philosophical background of the Word, into the factors involved in conversation between the one speaking and the one spoken to. On these terms the Word is no longer what it was for Kähler. Of course we should learn the most we can from the questions which existential interpretation puts to the Word. But that should not lead us to go around or put aside the concepts and statements of Holy Scripture in their substance. And this danger is not slight. Where the concept of existence is made primary, it endangers the content of Holy Scripture. When hermeneutics becomes, in a definite methodological sense, the key to theology, theology descends to anthropology.

It is an urgent matter whether theology can still declare actual statements about God. The point of concern is not human existence, but the continuing conversation between God and man; we cannot allow this basic principle to be attenuated. The important thing about justification, for instance, is not being taught it or understanding it, but having it happen. In a time of apocalyptic decadence the Christian proclamation should not be robbed of its authority or impact. Biblical happening wants to persist, not merely to be perceived. Do I know that the living God daily judges, that he can lead someone to an abyss as well as approve the occurrence of faith? I do not want to interpret a text in such a way that afterwards the question "How do I find a merciful God?" is no longer there. I do not want to interpret a text in such a way that I no longer know who God is, who brought Israel to desolation. Once I referred in a lecture to the confession of

Pascal: to "the God of Abraham, Isaac, and Jacob, not the God of
the philosophers." Afterward in the discussion a theologian said,
"That confession to a God who is not a God of philosophers should
no longer be mentioned in Germany." Yet precisely this confession of
Pascal's must be articulated in Germany today. Our concern is that
theology should not be reduced to anthropology. To a large extent
existential interpretation has displaced the Evangelists to the margin,
subjected their theology to question, and put the theology of Paul in
the middle of the canon. But this severs the unity of the proclamation
in the New Testament. The final norm is the authority of Jesus of
Nazareth, not the self-unfolding of the human spirit. When we put
man's existential meaning foremost, although it does warrant consideration we relativize in the end those relations of man which are
decisive in Biblical thought: his relation to God in a concrete space-
and-time situation, his conduct in relation to his fellow men and over
against the mighty streams of his time. Any shortening of the perspective cuts off areas from the concern of scholarship. The history of
Jesus' time loses interest, and his place in the history of Judaism is
ignored. Theology always impoverishes itself—and even becomes a
curse—when it gives up its character as witness and understands
itself as spiritual meaning. To be sure it cannot show forth God, but it
should not deny Him either. At stake is the living encounter of Word
and man, of Word and history, of Word and creation. In this living
encounter lies the secret we have to testify.

I should like to say something now about the objection which the
New Testament itself brings to the method of existential interpretation.

(1) We should be impressed with how strongly the New Testament rests the occurrence of salvation upon the *Deus Praeveniens,*
upon the God who goes before. His *gratia praeveniens,* prevenient
grace, becomes very evident with respect to election. The same theme
was later important in different ways for Augustine and Luther. But it
is already tremendously potent in the New Testament. How, for
instance, does the oldest Gospel attempt to understand the relation
between God and Christ? The entire Gospel of Mark hinges upon the
relation between God and Christ rather than upon the relation of
Jesus to his disciples or upon the conflict of Jesus with the Jews. This
too is there, but the actual key to Mark is astonishingly the relation of

God and Christ. At the beginning: "A voice came from heaven, 'Thou art my beloved Son; with thee I am well pleased'" (Mark 1:11). That theme recurs in the Transfiguration (Mark 9:7), and finally in the Passion with the words, "My God, my God, why hast thou forsaken me?" (Mark 15:34). The oldest Gospel puts the secret of Jesus entirely in the hand of God. It understands the message from this apex first of all: "I have chosen you." The decisive fact is that God chose Him to be Christ in advance. In his election lies the beginning of Christology. I could almost say that his election by the voice out of heaven gives the purest original form of Christology.

When Paul explains his apostleship in Galatians 1:15, he goes back to God also: "When he who had set me apart before I was born, and had called me through his grace, was pleased to reveal his Son to me. . . ." There we have *eudokesen* also, "when it pleased God," even as in Mark 1:11, *eudokesa*. It means an "election." Here we strike the poverty of modern thought: one cannot imagine election. But in the New Testament the election takes place at the outset, as *gratia praeveniens*. Paul did not say that he came to faith at Damascus, but that God laid hold of him. That one's life can take an entirely other direction than one expected is puzzling and perplexing. But that is within the possibility of *gratia praeveniens*. And that is the decisive note in the New Testament. The process of salvation issued exclusively from God. If our method does not allow for that fact, then something is lost to the message. The act of God is described by setting it in a story and witness that was already familiar. The beloved son, the election which comes upon a person, the separation from a mother's womb—these are categories of the Old Testament, and were already present in the Old Testament before they were taken over in the New Testament. Light falls from the New Testament upon analogous processes in the Old Testament. The Psalmist, the King in Israel, the Prophet, Jesus of Nazareth, and Paul all belong to the same category of election. They are not individualists of faith. Their life is at the disposal of God. Whether it ends on the cross or by the sword, whether in Egypt as with Jeremiah, or we do not know where, is not important. But one thing was true of each life, it was entirely subject to God in the course of its history.

(2) Corresponding to *gratia praeveniens,* salvation originates prior to human preaching and acceptance. That sounds quite un-

modern, to be sure, but it is the testimony of the New Testament. From Romans 10:14–17 one usually hears just this much: "So faith comes from what is heard. . . ." How often that has been said in recent years, "faith comes from what is heard"—from preaching. But the whole of that verse says: "So faith comes from what is heard, and what is heard comes by the preaching [*rema,* word] of Christ." That means the starting point is not the preaching, as one usually over-looks, but rather the Word of Jesus. The Word which He himself spoke sustains the message. Our message has, therefore, a presuppo-sition—precisely that in Romans 10:17. So also, salvation originates prior to faith. Thus it is said in Romans 5:6, 8 that Christ died for us "while we were yet sinners." Salvation is accordingly not a function of sermon and faith, but rather derives from the prior Word and act of Jesus. Of course even as one can resist prevenient grace, one can also resist prevenient salvation. But the priority of salvation is Bibli-cal and is worked out especially in Romans 9 to 11.

(3) Now we face still harder problems. There is *the problem of the Word.* It pertains at the present time largely to the question of understanding. Certain expressions illustrate it, as: "In Jesus Christ faith becomes articulate," or "Jesus Christ is raised up in the Word." That means: the Word is that process through whose exposition the event is taken up into it; the actual event occurs together with the process of the Word. What, however, does the New Testament say to us about the Word? In the New Testament, Word and wonder belong together as signs of the activity of God. To be noted especially in the New Testament is the fact that the Word has the quality of a sign and manifests the glory of God, even as wonder. The creature is ad-dressed by the Creator in the Word. The preacher is the mediator through whom the Creator speaks. The Word is given to be obeyed. As the Word expects obedience, so also the sign expects faith. In a strict sense the Word is not concerned with being understood but with being obeyed. Amazingly enough, it is presumed in the New Testa-ment that the people who hear the Word that comes to them under-stand it. Whether they understand it rightly or not may obtrude here and there, but is not taken to be a problem. It is simply presumed in the New Testament that men understand the Word, even when they reject it. Perhaps the New Testament is not right about the matter, but that is an exegetical matter of fact. With respect to the Greek

Logos I agree that the Word requires to be understood correctly.
That is a primary concern in Greek thought. A word must be understood before it can be accepted. But strangely enough that is not a
concern either in the Old or New Testament. God did not say to
Jonah: "Now the first thing you do when you get to Nineveh is
consider how to be properly understood there." No, the important
thing was that he didn't shirk in his duty. That is the issue also in
Romans 10 and 11. Israel has been disobedient. It is admitted that
their zeal was "not according to knowledge" (Rom. 10:2). But
"have they not heard?" (10:18). "Did Israel not know?" (10:19).
Their failure to recognize the righteousness of God was not due to a
lack of understanding in the Greek sense, but to a hardening of heart.
Romans 1 finds men "without excuse; for although they knew God
they did not honor him as God. . . ." (Rom. 1:20–21). They do not
honor God because they refused to recognize Him.

(4) Finally, there is the *problem of the historical*. First, Luke
wants to create a certain order in the accounts so that Theophilus
may be secure in the things of which he has been informed. The very
mention of security with reference to Biblical data inflames some
people to a white heat. Luther set security over against certainty.
Surely Luke never thought of that distinction. His object was not to
be an historian in the sense that thereby faith could be inferred from
fact. As one who was well acquainted with catechetical instruction
for baptism at that time, around A.D. 80, he knew the source of faith.
But in view of questions concerning the life of Jesus, he felt compelled to undertake historical inquiry. What he accomplished—and it
was vastly important—was to get hold of many new sources. That
was no easy matter. It is still not the case today that one only needs
to buy a ticket to Jerusalem and then new sources will turn up. In
Jerusalem one doesn't find anything at first, perhaps a few old jars,
but no untapped sources of information. It is not so simple to get a
Jew to speak. It should be much more appreciated what an extremely
difficult task it was to acquire these traditions out of Palestine, and to
work them together so that not only a new Gospel came into being
but also a first church history.

Then take Paul. In Galations 1 and 2 he attempts to give an
account of one historical aspect of his past life, how long and why he
was in Jerusalem. He cannot rest his case upon historic meaning. He

must go back to historical fact. One asks why historical data are relevant in the New Testament, except to compose a biography or to secure faith. They are adduced to protest either a devaluation of historical material or its distortion from some point of view. Paul had to contend with just such a distortion. He recognized his dependence upon the church in Jerusalem, but not so that he must concede to it. In protest he appeals to the historical situation. What took place quite casually, and is subject to verification, shows otherwise.

Our concern is with historical processes which must be retained for the sake of faith, processes which are verifiable which faith has not produced, which do not only take on historic meaning but which enter into historical fact. These processes are at work in the New Testament. One cannot dismiss them as historicizing. Some matters are verifiable, such as the inscription on the Cross, not in the interest of faith but as objective data. The historical approach contends for objective data, not only for views of history. It is time that we take the problem of the factual seriously in our own life also. The factual is not to be set down as irrelevant. There is so much scorn in "Can one be saved by the factual?" Yes, one can. For the factual contains the metaphysical. Christianity depends upon historical fact. We must say, "If Christ were born in you a thousand times, and never once in history, you would be lost." A Christ who did not live, who did not die for me, is no Christ in whom I can believe.

This is naturally very difficult for us as Germans to accept. We struggle against the historical because the historical is so painful. It is that way in each of our lives also. Facts are brutal, for they do not let us speak for them. In 1918, and again in 1945, we were brought low. That is not a point of view but a brutal fact. In theology also there is a continual struggle against the brutality of facts. This morning we read for our devotions an account in the Old Testament from II Kings 22. The book of the Law had been found. It threatened judgment upon Israel. In that hour, churches and Christians would gladly read in their Bible: "If we believe, repent, and obey, then judgment will not come upon us, and Israel will escape doom." How wonderful if the Bible said that. To the pious, penitent king is said: "Because your heart was penitent, and you humbled yourself before the Lord. . . . your eyes shall not see all the evil which I will bring upon this place" (II Kings 22:19–20). For Judah, however, the text is unrelenting. That is the Bible in its brutality—concerned, to be sure, with individual life, but with collective judgment also. Beyond that it thinks, in universal-historical terms, of a new heaven and a new earth. Our life so coheres in history that it cannot be resolved into single moments or situations. The past is not gone. It is still there in the present. And the future is already partly determined in the present. These simple Biblical realities are obscure not only in Germany but in the whole world. Everywhere one attempts to dissolve and to dismiss the past, to reduce history to existence. But the Bible does not play along. The past of those twelve years is still with us, reformed of course, but it works further in the partition of our people. To think otherwise would fit in with the romanticism of Germany, but not with the Bible. For there, thousands of years are affected in advance. "Therefore as sin came into the world through one man . . . so death spread to all men." (Rom. 5:12) The consequence of Adam is still really present. We would deal trivially with the Scripture were we to suppose that the Lord Jesus Christ had lifted us out of it. That would please a jubilant mankind which is ready to march with song and dance into another catastrophe. The heritage of Adam is all the more dangerous because it is so often overlaid with a Christian veneer.

The event of salvation and of Word are not separable from each other, as though there were an event of salvation without an event of Word. Nor may they, despite their close relation, be identified, as though the event of Word subsumed the event of salvation.

I have not wanted to be apologetic in what I have said. But I do want to let mankind, and the history of which we are a part, stand in the light of the Word of Scripture. And I would like to have my life, and the life of my people, and the life of my church so stand as it appears in the light of the Old and New Testaments. I cannot do that if I leave out of consideration basic concepts and relationships in the Bible. My concern is that the substance of Biblical statement should be left intact. Accordingly I will try to submit myself humbly to Paul, Matthew, Luke, and to that one whom the Germans do not like—to James. Then I will learn to be a Christian. Then, moreover, the prospect for the present would look different.

The Consequences of Bultmann's Theology for Ethics

————— ◄◆► —————

HEINZ-HORST SCHREY
Teachers Training College
Heidelberg, Germany

INTRODUCTORY REMARKS

As the problem of ethics is closely interwoven with soteriology and anthropology, it is not possible to isolate Bultmann's ethics from the rest of his theology. For this reason there may be some overlapping with other parts of this book. For the same reason I could refrain from expounding each of the notions as they occur, since these may be explained in greater detail elsewhere in this book. It has been my effort to focus attention on the problem of human action and Christian life as seen by Bultmann. The picture will resemble a mosaic, pieced together from different sources, since in Bultmann's work we find no comprehensive systematic treatment of ethics. The study of what Bultmann has to say on ethics has resulted, however, in the insight that he deals with the central aspects of this subject in a remarkably consistent and systematic way.

LIBERAL PROTESTANT THEOLOGY AND ITS SHORTCOMINGS

Let us begin with Bultmann's discussion of some of the presuppositions of liberal theology. It conceives of Christianity as an intramundane phenomenon, subject to the laws of social psychology whereby the "scandalous" character of the Christian belief is smoothed over. Inasmuch as it assumes that God discloses himself all through the processes of history, it is a kind of "historical pantheism." The ethical aspect of liberal theology is the assumed identity of secular professional work and divine worship; all work as such is a fulfillment of the divine command. Bultmann confronts[1] this subtle form of secularism with the central idea of Reformation theology, justification by faith. He finds that there is no immediate way to serve God besides faith, which is a conviction that God is the supreme supramundane entity, and he questions all human effort in its attempt to please God and to identify cultural activities with the purposes of the Kingdom of God. Professional work can only be regarded as serving God when humans are convinced that it lacks this quality in itself—when it does not give us the satisfaction of deserving God's grace by our own human merits. There is no way of establishing a position before God by human effort. Man cannot but hear the Word of God as the *skandalon* convicting him of his sin and his insurmountable distance from God.

The major point of criticism, however, is another one: liberal Protestantism derives certain ideals of secular action from faith. It uses the concepts of love and of the Kingdom of God as normative for attitudes like socialism or pacifism. Bultmann denies any direct relation between human action and the Kingdom of God. Social efforts—antimilitarism, temperance, etc.—may be necessary for the good of mankind; they are, however, all possibilities within the framework of human sin, and cannot, therefore, bring about God's Kingdom on earth. Whoever makes that claim for such activities does not realize the *skandalon* of the Word of God which is the absolute judgment on any human activity. It shows that back of all human action lies the intention of self-vindication (*Selbstbehauptung*). This is what the idea of original sin really means: man vindicating himself to make himself like God. The confrontation with God's Word places God in the center, and man can no longer continue his *experimentum medietatis* (Augustine), his attempt to place man in the center of the universe. Liberalism regards Christian existence as a succession of stages in personality growth from low to high, while dialectical theology does not reflect on the psychological side of faith, but

---

[1] In his essay "Die liberale Theologie und die jüngste theologische Bewegung" (*Glauben und Verstehen*, I, 5).

conceives of justification as a dialectical togetherness of sin and grace, judgment and forgiveness.

BULTMANN'S THEOLOGICAL STARTING POINT: THE DOCTRINE OF JUSTIFICATION BY FAITH

Bultmann is primarily a theologian and no philosopher. Philosophy has a subsidiary task in his thought, as a means of expressing the Christian message in terms of modern language. The position Bultmann takes concerning the problem of ethics is centered in the Reformation doctrine of justification by faith. Insofar, his thought is a renewal of Lutheran theology, applied to the situation of modern man. The strength of this position is in its sobering effect, its disillusioning realism over against all kinds of naïve or enthusiastic equations between God and man. Thus it is not an antiquated part of theology, devoid of all meaning for modern man, but the very center from which the reality of man must be understood. Justification by faith means for Bultmann in the first place—and here he follows the line of Lutheran theology—forgiveness of sin as an historic event, real in Jesus Christ.[2]

Man lives in self-deception as long as he is not confronted with God, the "wholly Other" (R. Otto). He cannot recognize himself as a sinner as long as he has no idea of what God really is: the demanding God who fully claims man's existence for himself. Ethics has its ultimate motivation in God who claims man's existence. Only when confronted with God can man realize the source of his ultimate responsibility.[3] To speak of God means at the same time to speak of man as being claimed by God. God's judging Word convicts man of sin, and offers forgiveness at the same time. Thus man before God is "sinner and just at the same time." It is the paradox of the Christian faith that there is no progress from one to the other, since in God's judgment the justified man remains the sinful creature forever. Justification does not alter man's moral structure, and justice is no supernatural quality to be demonstrated in good works.

---

[2] Cf. "Das Problem der 'natürlichen Theologie.'" *Glauben und Verstehen,* I, 307.

[3] Cf. "Welchen Sinn hat es, von Gott zu reden?" *Glauben und Verstehen,* I, 33.

At this point Bultmann has to counter an argument: If man realizes that he is a sinner and nothing but a sinner before God, how can he be the subject of moral action at all? How can there be ethics? Isn't the result of this the final annihilation of human action? Bultmann answers by reflecting on what the ethical demand in connection with the idea of God really means. When God reveals himself as the ultimate reality behind any demand on man and his existence, there can be no question as to whether man should act and talk or not. The confrontation with God is a "must"—not to be understood as a natural necessity, but as a free deed, coming out of man's existence. This is what Bultmann calls obedience. The very nature of obedience is commitment to a "must" out of free decision.

Decision is a central conception in Bultmann's thought. It marks the commitment of human will facing the alternative of good or bad, of self-centeredness or obedience toward God. Paul can speak of the Christian's new life as life in the spirit. Does this exclude the importance of decision for the Christian? By no means, for the spirit is no magical influence of an impersonal power. Spirit becomes real in personal decision. Even the Christian is not spared decision, but he is no longer the slave of sin and he is free from the urge for recognition and from dread.[4]

THE IDEA OF FREEDOM

Here we have reached the point at which we have to examine Bultmann's idea of freedom. He emphasizes that the idea of freedom is the highest and noblest asset of Western civilization.[5] The Western conception of freedom contains two elements of divergent origin: the Greek concept of the free citizen and the Christian idea that freedom is no integral part of human nature, but an event happening when one is confronted with a magnitude that demands decision. The Stoic philosopher claims freedom for every human being, since he has the faculty of reason, and with the use of his reason frees himself from the bondage of passions and worldly lust. For Paul freedom also

---

[4] Cf. "Christ the End of the Law," *Essays*, p. 36: faith is itself obedience; p. 59: Paul is also able to designate faith as obedience because, in this very renunciation of one's own achievements, it is a radical submission to God.

[5] "The significance of the idea of freedom for Western civilization," *Essays*, pp. 305–325; on the relation of freedom and grace, cf. "Grace and Freedom," *Essays*, pp. 168–81; *Theology of the New Testament*, Vol. I, Part II, pp. 330–52.

implies independence from the lower values, from fate and death. This leads us to the intricate problem of anthropology. Christian ethics presupposes a different conception of what man really is from the Greek concept of man. For the Greek philosopher, man is a self able to control himself by the innate power of his reason. The Christian conception of man is, according to Bultmann, a self as historic existence, i.e., as a being that becomes real in concrete decisions encountering other men or destiny. This is what might be called the existentialist trend in Bultmann's thought. Man cannot be described in static terms as having a certain definable quality or character, but he gains his character by qualifying himself in his decisions. Here we face the problem of freedom. In making decisions, man is not as free as he imagines himself to be; he is tied down by his past. Bultmann uses this term in a specific sense: as the general attempt of man to assert himself and to make something out of himself. The "past" of man is his attempt at self-vindication before God—in Pauline terminology, the establishment of his own "righteousness." This is the real meaning of sin.[6] To speak of the attempt at human self-realization as the "past" means, at the same time, to know a "future" which is quite different from that other way.[7] This future is not within the scope and reach of natural man; it is an encounter with divine grace, given to us in Jesus Christ. Here the dialectic nature of the Christian concept of freedom is apparent, since the bondage to Christ is the "law" that frees man from his former self and opens him up for the future and for a free encounter with all men. Thus freedom from the former self shows the very quality of love.

ESCHATOLOGY AND ETHICS

Freedom is not only a negative concept, freedom from something, but a steady intention to let loose and not to fix oneself on positions

---

[6] Cf. "Christ the End of the Law," *Essays,* p. 47: real sin does not consist in individual transgressions of the law at all, but in the basic attitude of man—his striving to establish his own righteousness and to glorify himself in the presence of God.

[7] Cf. "Christianity as Eastern and Western Religion," *Essays,* p. 224: His future is *his* future, not standing before him as the image of an ideal to which he more and more conforms in an upward struggle, but a future which is to be chosen in responsible decision, with the risk of attaining to himself or losing himself.

already attained in the past. Bultmann calls this intention *faith*.[8] It is
identical with the eschatological situation called for by the revelation
of God in Christ. This encounter with Christ is a critical situation for
man, since he is to decide whether he is to believe in the mission of
the Son or not.[9] This is the specific difference between any form of
mystical or philosophical self-realization and the Christian way of
becoming a self. The paradox of gaining one's self by giving it up in
self-commitment and sacrifice (Matt. 16:25) is only possible for man
when he encounters God as self-giving love. Being rendered a "Thou"
toward God, man can become a "self." Thus revelation has no intel-
lectualistic connotations, but means an existential act of receiving
one's self in radical loneliness from God's grace. In the eyes of the
world this act of *Entweltlichung*[10] resembles nihilistic despair, yet it
is different because the Christian knows of the "other side of despair," the communion with God. This term is not used by Bultmann;
he describes, however, its inherent truth in terms of modern existentialism. He prefers to speak of the "truth of existence,"[11] of which
even the philosophers know and at which they aim, but which does
not find real fulfillment except in the communication with God
through Christ.

Bultmann's ethics is not only existentialist in its terminological
framework, but also Christocentric in its essence. The eschatological
expectation is not confined to the consummation of the world at the
end, but means a new relation to the present world: man is no longer
an organic member of the cosmos, linked up with it in an inseparable
intimacy of relations. In faith, the unworldliness of human existence,

---

[8] Cf. "Forms of Human Community," *Essays*, pp. 291–304.

[9] Cf. "Die Eschatologie des Johannes-Evangeliums," *Glauben und Verstehen*,
I, 134–52; "The Understanding of Man and the World in the New Testament
and the Greek World," *Essays*, p. 85: in Jesus Christ the destiny of every man
is decided. He is the eschatological act of God; Commentary on the Gospel
of John, pp. 192 f.: Jesus, God's present Revealer, is the eschatological judge.

[10] This term has been rendered in English by "withdrawal from the world,"
but this seems to convey that Paul means the Christian shall leave this world
and withdraw into some sort of monastic existence. What he means is not
this, but an inner aloofness from the world, even though it is to be used,
knowing that its shape is waning (I Cor. 7:31).

[11] Cf. "Forms of Human Community," *Essays*, p. 303: the community
established by faith and by God himself (i.e., the Church) fulfills what is
planned and intended in all human community.

the transcendence of the human self over against the world, has been discovered, which finds its expression in a new ethical attitude toward the world; as Paul worded it in I Corinthians 7:29 ff.: to use the world as not abusing it. This is no Gnostic abrogation of the world as the prison of the soul, but a dialectical synthesis of Old Testament faith in God the Creator and New Testament insight into the preliminary character of this world (*Vorläufigkeit*). The consequence of this attitude is a radical profanization of the world. It is no longer conceived of as a divine entity, as in Greek pantheism, but as an object which is at the disposal of man's faculties, to be brought under human domination by science and technique.[12] Thus modern science and technology are, in the last analysis, an outcome of the Christian ethic of the "as though," a fruit of eschatological ethics. In the history of Christianity this has led to a new relation to the transcendent world as well. Monastic asceticism is the Catholic way of realizing Christian aloofness from the world; asceticism within the world, with its participation in commerce and industry is the Protestant way.

Christianity has, according to Bultmann, brought into the world a new understanding of general human possibilities, the recognition of the problematic nature of man and of the importance of decision within historic existence. Bultmann emphasizes again and again that the Christian way of life is not materially different from the way any human being lives. Faith neither reveals new insights into the transcendent world—this is what Gnosis and mysticism do—nor does it confer novel human moral possibilities other than every human being possesses. The newness of faith, and consequently of the Christian way of life, lies in a new interpretation of human existence, a new understanding of human nature and the world. This understanding is not only an intellectual affair, but existential understanding which results in commitment and obedience, in sacrifice and love. Human action does not change its character as work within a world of objects and men, done under the premises of regularity and causality; even

---

[12] Cf. "The Understanding of Man and the World in the New Testament and in the Greek World," *Essays,* p. 88: From Christianity there comes no protest against secular science, because the eschatological understanding of the world is not a method of explaining it. . . . Christianity demands that science and *politike techne* really should be secular.

Christians have no other way of acting and living in this world. The only difference is the new understanding: they know that their work is not meaningful in itself or in the socially useful effect it may have, but as a deed of obedience; just as the meaning of giving does not lie in the gift as such, but in the loving-kindness of the giver and his act of giving.[13]

THE NATURE OF THE DIVINE IMPERATIVE

In the beginning of this essay we stated that ethics for Bultmann has its motivation in God who claims man's existence. What does this term "claim" mean? Is it a moral ideal, an "ought" which is to be rendered real by action? Is it a goal toward which man has to advance in more or less steady progress? Bultmann denies this idealistic conception of the ethical norm and defines it in terms of the existential "I-Thou" relationship. The gap between *Sein* und *Sollen,* "being" and "ought," cannot be bridged by successive progress toward the moral ideal, but by acting as such (*Vollzug der Tat*). A state of moral perfection can never be reached, because man is always under the claim and the authoritative demand of the present moment. This present demand is at the core of the I-Thou relationship, in which moral action comes to its full realization. Human action always concerns the community of men. There is a difference between cultural and ethical action. Cultural action aims at the perfection of some sort of work—technical, artistic, or scientific—and concerns itself with the world of objects, while ethical action aims at the Thou and springs from the primary togetherness of I and Thou. This is what the Christian conception of the "neighbor" means. He is not to be looked for as if the I were a lonely subject in empty space and had to seek contacts with some other lonely subject *a posteriori.* Inasmuch as man lives in a world of primary togetherness, he is an historic creature (*geschichtliches Wesen*), and not merely "natural."[14] Therefore, seeking out the neighbor as a possible object of action is

---

[13] Cf. "Zur Frage des Wunders," *Glauben und Verstehen,* I, 222.

[14] Back of this distinction between nature and history lies the philosophy of Neo-Kantianism (Rickert, Windelband). Bultmann's conception of history, however, stems from existential philosophy (Heidegger) and distinguishes between "historical" (*historisch*) and "historic" (*geschichtlich*).

wrong, because it treats the neighbor as a "what-is"[15] to be treated and acted upon, as though he were a phenomenon of this world— material to be shaped. This would mean that the I-Thou relationship could be "manufactured." It is typical of Greek ethics that it considers man as material to be shaped according to an ideal, like a piece of art. Thus ethics becomes in fact education or educational cybernetics.

THE NATURE OF THE GOOD

How does Bultmann answer the question, crucial for any moral theology seeking after the nature of the good: "What am I to do?" Can there be a material answer to this question? Can the moral theologian give a practical answer, a sort of pastoral counseling about what the "right" or the "good" is in a given moment? Bultmann follows the line of Kantian thought and denies this possibility. Even notions like justice, truthfulness, purity, etc., are only concerned with the formal structure of ethical action. Bultmann denies the possibility of a material ethics (M. Scheler, N. Hartmann) as a legitimate philosophical question. This would mean to preconceive the structures and situations of life as a pattern in the mind. Such an attempt would mean trespassing on the limits set for philosophical thought as well as a gross misunderstanding of human existence. Moral philosophy would thus reduce human existence to a status of timelessness. Moral action would then have its real meaning in its effect, in the goal to be reached by moral action, not in the process of acting (*Vollzug*) as such. As human existence is togetherness in time and history, material preconceptions of good do not take seriously the true character of the human I-Thou relationship. Thus, the answer to the question "What shall I do?" cannot be given in general, but must be left to the individual and to the challenge of the moment, to the momentary relationship to the Thou.[16] This does not mean that Christian ethical action is left to the vagueness of momentary velleity, to arbitrariness

---

[15] Here I follow the usage of Heidegger's translators who render *Vorhandenheit* by "what-is"; cf., e.g., D. E. Roberts, *Existentialism and Religious Belief,* 1957.

[16] Cf. "Das christliche Gebot der Nächstenliebe," *Glauben und Verstehen,* I, 235.

on the part of the acting subject, for it stands under the categorical imperative "Thou shalt love thy neighbor as thyself."

THE MEANING OF LOVE

Is the "love commandment" an answer to the question "What am I to do?" Yes and no! This commandment is not an answer in that it is not concerned with the result of action, with a material aim to be reached, or an ideal to be performed. Neither the Sermon on the Mount nor the chapter on love in I Corinthians 13 gives a concrete description of what the deeds of love really are like. Love is not a value to be made real by action, but a practical and "historic" understanding of what my neighbor—i.e., any man who is connected with me in a given moment of time and a given situation of life— needs, and what is to be done for him. Thus love, in a way, is a positive answer to the question of what to do, because love discovers the method of action needed right now, and is the governing force behind our action. Bultmann stresses the naturalness of the love commandment. It is no Christian specialty, because the neighbor has always been there, and therefore the love commandment is not unknown to mankind. Inasmuch as togetherness is a general human structure, everyone should know the love commandment. This sounds like a parallel to natural theology: there is within the very structure of human nature a law innate, and therefore not unknown to man, as there is a certain knowledge of God, because there is an ontological relationship between God and man. Is Bultmann a follower of natural theology or natural-law theories? Not in the usual sense of the word, because Bultmann speaks of structures which are open to human insight even without faith, but he speaks of them with the understanding that they are being perverted and distorted by human failure.[17]

Man perverts his essential structure by a persistent abalienation from the very meaning of his existence (*Verfallen in Uneigentlichkeit*). Applied to the idea of love this means a persistent misunderstanding of what love should be. Greek ethic conceives of love as a virtue which has its source in the dignity of man. The Christian conception of love does not interpret it as a virtue or as general philanthropy, or

---

[17] Cf. "The Question of Natural Revelation," *Essays,* pp. 90–118: There Bultmann points out that "every phenomenon of history is ambiguous" (p. 105), and therefore does not have the quality of divine revelation.

as an innate quality of the perfect man or as an emotional feeling. Love in Christian interpretation is not a quality in man, but a mode of human togetherness. Its reality cannot be described in an isolated way, but lies in the proper functioning of human encounters. Thus Christian love is exactly the opposite of Greek *eros*. *Eros* looks after its own interests, seeks its own perfection and satisfaction. Love in the Christian sense is the inversion of natural man's direction in life. Thus it is service and sacrifice, overcoming the self, not self-vindication. No abstract or ideal value is the motivation of love, but the reality of the neighbor as close to me, no matter how good or bad he is. The question "What shall I do?" cannot be answered theoretically, but only by pointing to the questioner's own self: as thyself! This is not only a utilitarian rule by which the spheres of interest between the I and the Thou are marked, but it makes the questioner conscious of the fact that he does not really know what love is, because he does not really love. To know about love is not theoretical, but existential knowledge. Thus the question of human good involves the entire human being and lays it bare in its actual lack of love. Love belongs to the matters that can only be understood in existential terms, not as work or property, not as a "what-is" to be pointed out. The actuality of love is always ambiguous and insecure: open to misinterpretation, and thus hidden from the eyes of the world in its very essence; infinite in its fulfillment, yet never at the point of perfection; not possible as an object for reflection. The question about love, or what love really is, points to the questioner himself, in so far as he is supposed to understand himself as being loved. Love cannot only be understood by the very act of loving; one must also have the experience of being loved. This experience, however, partakes of the same ambiguity as active love toward one's neighbor; it can only be received in faith. Love in the deepest sense of the word is not motivated by casual and fragmentary experiences of love in human togetherness, but ultimately in the experience of love which excludes any distrust and ambiguity, i.e., in the infinite love of God who is real in human life and encounters man in the loving-kindness of his forgiving word. Thus love as a reality in our lives is what Bultmann calls an eschatological event, since this love becomes real only in the encounter with Christ. Love is the mark of the new life in God and for one's neighbor. Therein lies the dialectical attitude of the Christian toward the world and his life in the world that nothing in itself is worthless or valuable. In the light of the love commandment anything that otherwise would be considered worthless can become significant, and the things great in the eyes of the world may be evil or insignificant as far as the divine world is concerned. Faith and the demand for love disclose the dual character of all things as capable of serving either evil or good.[18]

THE PROBLEM OF INSTITUTIONS

What Bultmann has been trying to do in his analysis of the ethical is to find the essential difference between genuine and perverted human existence, between the true understanding and the misinterpretation of good. Thus, he does not concern himself so much with communal life. When he does so in his essay on "Forms of Human Community," he proceeds in the same manner. He distinguishes between four forms of human community: natural groups such as marriage and family, tribe and *Volk;* historical groups such as comradeship, institution, nation; group life that is instituted by art and science; religious group life. All of these forms of communal life can either be genuine expressions of true personality—for only persons who are a "self" can have genuine communal experience, since community is conditioned by the will to freedom and responsibility, truth, and readiness for sacrifice and self-commitment—or they can degenerate into forms of sheer conventionalism and organization, in which men wear masks and lose their "selves" in the dominance of mankind (das Man). Bultmann mentions life in the modern big cities and in the totalitarian state as forms of perverted social pseudoexistence. In the above-mentioned essay the humanist trend in Bultmann's thought shows best, because his criticism of the pseudo forms of human communal life does not seem to be guided by special Christian insights, but by a general philosophical distinction between what characterizes genuine and perverted existence (*Eigentlichkeit—Uneigentlichkeit*).[19]

---

[18] Cf. "Adam, Where Art Thou?" *Essays,* pp. 119–132.

[19] Cf. "Humanism and Christianity," *Essays,* pp. 151–67; Bultmann thinks highly of the humanistic curriculum and pleads for reading Plato in high school. He rejects the suspicion that the humanist belief in God is nothing but a preformation of atheistic unbelief. "How can this be asserted by anyone who has read Plato!" (Reported in R. Lennert, "Immer noch: der evangelische Religionsunterricht in der Schule," *Die Sammlung,* VI [1951], 253 f.)

Bultmann is rather skeptical of the possibility of a "Christian institution."[20] What about the Church as religious institution? Bultmann states that all genuine community life is rooted in faith, and the Church is the community of those who are called by God, believe, and bear witness. Yet, the community of faith is transcended by the community of love which tries to include all men. As soon as the Church becomes an institution it tends to become perverted, for it is by nature a spiritual community and therefore invisible, and can but exist *in actu,* i.e., when people listen to the Word and believe in it. Orthodoxy and dogma are greater dangers for the Church than conventionalism and organization. The Church is invisible, because it is founded on faith and "kerygma," not on any worldly phenomenon to be seen. It is visible only to faith and obedience.[21]

CONCLUSION

It has been said that every theology that makes use of a certain philosophical terminology not only interprets the message of the Bible, but also introduces categories into the interpretation which might change the meaning of the text.[22] The eye, focused on certain perspectives, only perceives what fits into the system of philosophical categories and is easily blinded toward everything that falls outside the system. Thus it is rather difficult to find the starting point for genuine criticism, because any such criticism might be exposed as a gross misunderstanding of the real meaning of what Bultmann said. Let us, however, try to examine some of Bultmann's major concepts.

1. *Historicity of Human Existence.* Bultmann emphasizes that human existence is different from mere "nature" or "what-is" (*Vorhandenheit*) by its historicity (*Geschichtlichkeit*). The I-Thou rela-

---

20 Cf. "Das christliche Gebot der Nächstenliebe," *Glauben und Verstehen,* I, 240, n. 1. You can be a tailor or shoemaker and prove that you are able to make clothes or shoes. You cannot in the same sense demonstrate love. Neither are there Christian institutions, education, schools, states, etc. What a loving and a non-loving person do can have the same outward appearance. School, state, etc., can become an object of the labor of love (I Thess. 1:3). My own translation. H-H.S.

21 Cf., "Kirche und Lehre im Neuen Testament," *Glauben und Verstehen,* I, 153–187.

22 Cf. "Für und wider die Theologie Bultmanns." Denkschrift der ev.-theol. Fakultät der Universität Tübingen, 1952, p. 21.

tionship and decision in the present moment are among the marks of
man as a historic being. Historicity to Bultmann is the very core of
the ontological structure of human existence. Accordingly, all ethical
concepts are reduced to this structure. Then the question arises as to
whether this philosophical reduction is capable of expressing the full
meaning of ethics. The attempt to reach a sphere of sheer ontological
structures means to leave the concept of historicity behind and to
penetrate into the realm of ahistoric generalizations. Can historicity
be severed from the historical, or isn't its truth also true in history?
And doesn't the passing on of truth as well as its incorporation into
tradition point to history? Thus the ontological cannot be severed
from the ontic (to use Heidegger's terminology). It seems the special
task of ethics is to point out the way in which the historical existence
of man becomes concrete in the situations of life. Thus the Ten
Commandments are concrete interpretations of what the general
structure of the I-Thou relationship really means in man's communal
life. Ethics can hardly be reduced to a formalistic scheme of relation
and situation, but should reach down into the real behaviour in a real
world.[23]

2. *The Invisibility of Faith and Love.* It is a part of Bultmann's
Lutheran heritage that he emphasizes the invisibility (*Unanschaulich-
keit*) of faith and love. Again the attention is focused solely on the
isolated existence before the transcendent God. Thereby, however,
the concern for real man in real history is lost. There is, under the
ultimate judgment of God, only the alternative of sin and grace—the
latter understood as forgiveness of sin. Neither sin nor grace can be
made visible. There again the problem of historicity arises. Historical
man does not live only in the *nunc aeternum,* in the face of the
ultimate, nor does he exist only in the present moment; but he lives in
the continuity between Now and Then, in a world in which his
actions are neither affairs of his inner life nor done with reflection on
the establishment of the self before God. They are outward deeds and
follow the rules of proximate aims. The fact that the Christian has to
live in history, as does every man, makes the problem of the conduct

---

[23] Cf. W. Kamlah, *Christentum und Geschichtlichkeit* (2nd ed., 1951),
p. 21 ff: the elimination and remotivation of *Geschichtlichkeit.*

of life urgent. Christians have historically been distinguished from other people by avoiding certain practices and living a certain style of life. The fact that the prophecy of the approaching end of the world was not fulfilled raises the problem of ethics. So it seems a distortion of the truth when Bultmann claims that the post-Pauline theology in the New Testament understands Christian obedience as good works necessary for salvation.[24] Isn't the question of the practical concretion of the imitation of Christ (*Nachfolge*) a legitimate one? Can the missionary witness of the Church and pastoral care do without it? There has emerged in the West a "Christian historicity" (*christliche Geschichtlichkeit*), because under the influence of Christian ideas, especially the idea of love, institutional life in Western society, particularly law, has undergone changes which are discernible to historical research. It is true that all this has *not* brought about the Kingdom of God, and Bultmann is right in disillusioning naïve equations within liberal Protestantism, but it has changed the way of life in a visible way, even in a secularized society. If such secularization is visible and can be laid open by historical research, faith and love cannot only be invisible, in spite of their inherent ambiguity.

3. *The Concept of Eschatology.* Bultmann understands eschatology as the "as-though-not" attitude of the Christian in his relation to the world. This leads to a withdrawal from the world (*Entweltlichung*). This conception presupposes an interpretation of eschatology as the "eternal now" of God's judgment on all creation, without any account of the New Testament idea of the future revelation of God's glory and its anticipation of this glory in Christ. Here Bultmann's perspective comes close to idealism, because the real *Ausstand* of the future does not play any part; thus essential features of what the New Testament understands by eschatology seem to be cut out. It seems as though fear of mythology and the inauguration of the process of demythologizing eschatology did destroy the actual time dimension in eschatology. If the time dimension of the future is taken seriously, eschatology could have even different consequences for ethics from those Bultmann points out: the Christian not only keeps aloof from the sinful world, but has to act in the old world in the light of the new. Jesus has promised that his fol-

---

[24] Cf. *Theology of the New Testament*, Vol. II, chap. viii, pp. 203, 223.

lowers would do the works he did and even greater than these (John 14:12). Thus eschatology has not only the negative aspect which is emphasized by Bultmann, but also the positive one of building up signs of the new world of God which has become real in Christ. There are dangers in doing this, and therefore Luther did not agree with the *Schwärmer* (fanatics) of his time. On the other hand, does not the noble aloofness of Bultmann's concept of eschatology lead to a quietism which is no less dangerous? To take the concept of historicity seriously means also to run the risk of such worldly realizations of eschatological existence as the light that shineth in the world and the salt that salteth the meat (Matt. 5:13 f.).

4. *The New Self-understanding as the Core of the Ethical.* The model situation for Bultmann seems to be the individual who has to decide one way or the other—the Kierkegaardian "either-or" situation. This certainly is an important aspect of ethics. Man, in the final analysis, stands under ultimate obligation to God, but also under the conditions of society. He is not only the isolated individual in the sense of Abraham being called to kill his son and thus perfecting the "teleological suspension" of ethic, but he is also the member of institutions and has to live in pre-given institutional structures. Thus not only sacrificial and forgiving love is his norm, but "he must also come to terms with the problem of establishing tolerable harmonies of life on all levels of community under conditions set by the fact that men are sinners."[25] The ethical problem seen in its real historical setting seems to have two levels: the level of the ultimate norm, with which Bultmann is concerned, and the level of the proximate norm of justice. Does the Reformation doctrine of justification by faith in the form of *iustitia forensis* (i.e., grace as the word of forgiveness, not as *iustitia effectiva,* effective in the lives of the believers) do justice to the ethical problem of how the Christian is to live in historical time? Bultmann admits that life in institutions can become an object for the labor of love, but this idea is not followed up to make the point that love should find its historical realization, even in the public realms of industry and politics, as the regulative force of justice which tends to become injustice. The isolated individual seems to be the model even

---

[25] Quoted from Reinhold Niebuhr, "The Problem of a Protestant Social Ethic." *Union Seminary Quarterly Review,* XV (Nov. 1959), 2.

when Bultmann speaks of the forms of human community, because the fulfillment of the self (*Eigentlichkeit*) is the criterion for the "good society."[26]

5. *The Impact of Demythologizing for Ethics*. Finally may I conclude with a suggestion which attempts to draw a parallel in the realm of ethics to Bultmann's idea of demythologizing the New Testament message? He emphasizes that the presuppositions of thought have changed since New Testament times, and therefore the present generation has to do away with what he calls mythological elements in New Testament thought patterns. This method might also be applied to the patterns of social and ethical thought. Not only the presuppositions of thought, but also the conditions of society have changed since New Testament times. Ideas which might have been true in a primitive society with its intimacy of communal life cannot simply be transferred to the conditions of an anonymous mass society in which division of labor and social stratification have made things more difficult and less perspicuous. For example, the idea of the value of real property is suited to conditions in a simple society in which property is a means of subsistence for its owner. In a modern capitalistic society, however, the reality of property has changed to anonymous monetary forms. Under such conditions the application of the ancient ideas to the new forms of reality becomes questionable.

---

[26] This criticism agrees with that of E. Käsemann who finds that Bultmann gives expression to the New Testament idea of the Lordship of Christ over the world only in the sphere of ethics, especially in the I-Thou relationship. Bultmann's identification of theology and anthropology might result in a modified individualism, as world and history are reduced to the behavior of individuals to one another. "The moment of decision is strongly emphasized as though history rests solely upon it; this does not do justice to the reality of history which always implies either disintegration or order [*Verfallenheit— Getragenheit*] for man" (E. Käsemann, "Neutestamentliche Fragen von heute," *ZThK*, LIV [1957], 14). This implies the further question whether Bultmann's emphasis on anthropology does not absorb the whole of theology into some sort of ethical behaviorism. A good example of what I mean is his interpretation of the Cross of Christ. According to Bultmann it has its sole meaning in the imitation of Christ, as the instigation for the follower of Christ to bear his own cross willingly; cf. "Neues Testament und Mythologie," *Kerygma und Mythos*, I, 42: to believe in the Cross means to take up the Cross of Christ as one's own—to be crucified with Christ. Here, the dread of mythology obstructs the view of the significance of the Cross as the once-happening event which makes our salvation possible, as, e.g., the Epistle to the Hebrews emphasizes.

If theological ethic tries to uphold ancient social norms under different conditions of life, it tends to become ideology, an instrument of what Karl Marx called "false consciousness." Therefore, in ethics there is a parallel task to demythologizing which may be termed deideologizing (*Entideologisierung*). I talked these problems over with Bultmann and he has agreed on the urgency of this task, even though he has not undertaken it himself. In the field of ethics, theology is under the same obligation as in the field of Biblical interpretation: to wrestle with the mystery of reality. The promise is given unto us that we would not be without divine blessing.

Bultmann's Relationship to Classical Philology*

FRIEDRICH MÜLLER

The University of Marburg
Marburg, Germany

The language of the New Testament is Greek, the Greek spoken in the Mediterranean world in the first century after Christ. The study of literary monuments from this period is a responsibility of classical philology, for this discipline is no longer limited to the strictly classical period (from Homer to Demosthenes) but is also concerned with writings from the following thousand years. For the third period of this literary epoch (A.D. 500–1300) there has, indeed, developed a special science—Byzantine studies—that deals with the pictorial art and culture in general. However, within the middle or Hellenistic period classical philologists have hitherto been content to let theologians deal with Christian literature. This is particularly true of the writings of the New Testament, which are treated by classical philologists almost as if they are taboo.

There are several reasons for this hesitancy on the part of classical philology, the most obvious being the fact that these writings have been the purview of a special science, theology. Furthermore, the study of New Testament writings is not possible without a thorough knowledge of Palestinian and Hellenistic Judaism. But the most important reason is the fact that the New Testament writings have

---

* Translated by Arne Unhjem.

been regarded as revelation literature that must be understood as the "Word of God." As a rule the classical philologist is not prepared to accept this claim, especially if he has made himself at home in the world of Homer, the tragedies, or Plato. But because of this hesitancy among classical philologists, New Testament theology has a double reason for venturing into the domain of classical studies. And in a study of Rudolf Bultmann's theology it is thus not only the man himself but also the subject matter that justifies a consideration of his relation to classical philology.

For a New Testament theologian such a relation can become truly productive only if he is willing to treat the New Testament writings philologically, just as he would other literary works. Readiness to do this presumes both a certain historical insight and a religious conviction that the New Testament as the "Word of God" has been subjected to the fate of everything that "becomes flesh"—the process of history. This means two things: (1) that the writings of the New Testament, regardless of their genuine origin and unique use, have an historical beginning like other writings, since they were written down by people conditioned by a given historical situation; (2) that the transmission of these writings also was subjected to the same historical conditions that have affected other literary works, because it was accomplished by people who understood and copied the documents according to their own abilities and convictions even when they felt themselves enlightened and guided by the Holy Spirit.

The theologian may hear the "Word of God" in the New Testament and seek to make this Word audible, but he will perceive as his God-given task and responsibility the duty to understand the origin and transmission of the New Testament in terms of historical contingency—thus to hear more clearly therein the Word of God, which is more than history. It is this attitude which not only justifies but makes imperative the kind of positive relation to classical philology that has always been characteristic of Bultmann's work.

The understanding of a literary work always begins with the understanding of individual words. Only the conjunction of understood words can give the meaning of a proposition, just as from the conjunction of meaningful propositions there emerges the meaning of the whole work. Thus the history of classical philology obviously begins with the clarification of word meanings, beginning with Homeric poetry. This clarification of words (glossology, etymology, semantics, lexicography) is always the first and fundamental task of all philology.

Bultmann's contributions to the study of New Testament words may be seen in Gerhard Kittel's *Theologischen Wörterbuch zum Neuen Testament,* including such important words as *aletheia* (truth), *elpis* (hope), *lupe* (sorrow), *merimna* (anxious care), and above all *pistis* (faith)—all, of course, with cognate verbs and nouns. The starting point here is always Greek usage (with proper distinction between classical and Hellenistic meanings) and Old Testament usage down to Hellenistic Judaism (Philo). The analysis of Old Testament usage is as a rule done by Old Testament scholars in this dictionary, but the treatment of the classical and Hellenistic Greek is always done by Bultmann himself. It is only against this kind of background that the language of the New Testament can be understood: only this kind of comprehensive analysis will make it possible to understand New Testament words in their own sense rather than according to their Greek meaning or the meaning they have assumed in our own language, into which they have been adopted from the Greek and subjected to our own historical conditions.

This clarification of words is bound to benefit classical philology. Of course, this is true also of other contributions to Kittel's dictionary besides those by Bultmann. But when a seminar in classical philology will invariably refer to Kittel for the elucidation of Greek words, this is in large measure due to Bultmann's articles in the dictionary.

Bultmann's *Theologie des Neuen Testament* is also essentially a study of words, an analysis of all the important terms in the New Testament here considered in their context; in the context of individual writings and groups of writings; in relation to the thought of the author, their place of origin, their environment, and the historical development that has modified them. His ultimate concern, however, is always with subject matter. Bultmann takes his starting point in the central, eschatological dimension in the preaching of Jesus, the "Kingdom of God." He examines the kerygma in the Primitive Church of Paul and John, and the ethical problems of the organized Christian community. In all this, Bultmann's main concern is to describe the historical revelation of the Christian faith as it is transmitted to us in the New Testament. Philological problems of a purely historical nature are always secondary for Bultmann. Rather they belong in an "Introduction to the New Testament."

Thus the classical philologist finds himself instructed by Bultmann's New Testament theology both through his comprehensive historical analysis of New Testament words and through his treatment of the subject of faith in the primitive and ancient Church. Here the philologist can learn much to aid his own understanding of the Hellenistic environment.

This is particularly true of two smaller works by Bultmann, *Die Gnosis* and *Das Urchristentum im Rahmen der antiken Religionen.* The main topic here is Hellenism, but the latter work also contains a chapter entitled "The Greek Heritage" which deals with the Greek *polis,* Greek science, and the Greek world view. He has even devoted a special treatise to this essentially classical Greek cultural domain, "Polis and Hades in Sophocles' *Antigone.*" In this essay Bultmann has enunciated the valid and important conclusion that the *nomos* which Antigone obeyed was not just the ancient family duty to honor the dead; and thus the problem of the drama is not simply the tension between the *nomos* of the *polis* and the *nomos* of family tradition. Rather, "the traditional custom represents the challenge of Hades only as an altogether dreadful beyond." "What Antigone held up against Creon was . . . the awareness that human existence and indeed the existence of the *polis* are limited by the enduring power of Hades," by "the power from which genuine justice springs and by which all human legal statutes are evaluated." However, the "power of death" is for Antigone the "power of darkness and dread, even when she knows that down there she will come into her own." "The redeeming meaning of death has only negative connotations. It is not the case that she expects from death a new and genuine life." This remains the essential difference between Greek and Christian "eschatology."

Classical philology is the immediate beneficiary of this analysis in Bultmann's treatise. But his ultimate purpose in this effort to interpret Sophocles' *Antigone* is to shed light on what is unique in the Christian faith.

Within the New Testament the four Gospels are the essential documents of revelation for the Christian faith. It would be much simpler if there were only one gospel, free of internal contradictions.

But we have to deal with differences and even contradictions that are apparent in the four Gospels. We will not succeed in this if we concentrate only on explaining the individualities of the four gospel writers. Their dependence on each other as well as their individualities force us to posit as intermediaries between the original preaching of Jesus and the writings of the Evangelists both an oral and a written tradition, inspired by the teachings of Jesus before his death and by Christian preaching afterward. The supreme task of all New Testament theology is to recover from our scriptural sources (and the traditions they are based on or point to) the preaching of Jesus in its original purity. (To assume that one can accept responsibility for this as a task that is uniquely one's one is only foolishness, naïveté, or conceit.)

Bultmann's contribution to this task is to be found primarily in his *Geschichte der synoptischen Tradition,* in which he follows the *Formgeschichte* method first used by H. Gunkel and his followers, and in which he continues the studies begun by M. Dibelius (*Formgeschichte des Evangeliums*). Here, in much the same way, he is seeking to discover the original elements of the Gospels and attempts to separate them from the traditions which the gospel writers had used. He does this by examining the motives which must have inspired the earliest transmission of the gospel accounts. In this study the notion of "form" is sociological, rather than the aesthetic one that is used as a rule by classical philologists in the study of the Platonic and Aristotelian traditions. The concern is thus not with *Formgeschichte* in the literary and critical manner of philology, but is mainly with subject matter, with the content of New Testament tradition: the preaching of Jesus and the Christian faith. Here Bultmann accepts as the basis for his study the virtually unanimous judgment of all contemporary literary criticism of the Synoptics, namely, that the Gospel of Mark and a collection of sayings of Jesus (no longer preserved) were the sources for the Gospels of Matthew and Luke— the Gospel of Mark being subsequently re-edited.

In this work Bultmann is less interested in the problems pertaining to the literary form of the Gospels in the sense of style criticism. His major preoccupation is with the content and meaning of the Gospels.

The first example of a brilliant combination of interest in both matter and form can be found in Bultmann's commentary on the

Fourth Gospel, that of John. The immediate concern here, too, as in his study of the Synoptic Gospels, is to recover the tradition that culminates in the Gospel as we have received it. But the problem here is not only to deal with the elements that were transmitted by tradition to the Evangelist. Here the focus of attention is on the concepts and ideas of the important spiritual movement that is commonly called Gnosticism. This movement had its origin in Iran (Zoroaster), but as it spread to Palestine it developed, as Bultmann has cleverly deduced, a separate form of Judaic Gnosticism. This has since been verified by the Dead Sea discoveries. In our Gospel of John we have a unique document reflecting the absorption and transformation of this Judaic Gnosticism by Christianity.

The immediate accomplishment here, too, pertains to subject matter; and classical philology has much to gain from Bultmann's commentary on the Gospel of John—as well as from the little monograph on Gnosticism that was the by-product of his work on the Gospel of John. Here the classical philologist can learn to detect beneath the religious and moral cast of Judaic thought, feeling, and action quite a different world view. This view did not arise on Greek soil but came from Indo-European sources (among us it has experienced a late blooming in the anthroposophical movement). It resembles Greek thinking enough to be frequently confused with it; but it is in truth quite different, and Bultmann, with his thorough knowledge of Greek thought, has been able to demonstrate this.

His exposition of the *logos* concept at the beginning of the Gospel of John provides a vivid example of this. This concept is assigned a central meaning by Heraclitus, too, in the beginning of his partially preserved work. A similar emphasis was given later to the *logos* in the Stoic world view, and the concept was later absorbed into Christian thought after both of these modes of thought had become closely affiliated in Alexandrian Judaism (Philo). However, the *logos* of Heraclitus and Stoicism was an immanent cosmic principle which made possible the harmony between the microcosm and the macrocosm. In Gnosticism the *logos* is not just a cosmological principle but also has soteriological significance, and it is in this twofold character that it is absorbed into the Gospel of John. The inner nature of the *logos* does indeed change as it is applied to Jesus Christ: it becomes separated from sheer speculation and becomes a part of history. Even so, the Gospel of John is so saturated with speculative concepts, ideas, and thoughts stemming from the Gnostic or Gnostic-Judaic tradition, that if it were to be received and interpreted as a strictly historical document this could lead only to grotesque misinterpretation. For instance, if the story of the wedding in Cana were interpreted in terms of such a "realistic theology," there would emerge an image of Jesus that would turn his *ecce homo* into pure blasphemy.

But interpretation of the content of the Gospel of John is only one side of the task which confronts the theologian. There is also the interpretation of its literary form, and here Bultmann has shown that this form can be understood only on the basis of three suppositions: (1) that the Evangelist himself depended on written Gnostic sources; (2) that an editor of the original text of the Gospel made additions to it; and (3) that in the copying of this Gospel later, a certain disarrangement of its content occurred.

One would avoid disturbing simple minds if, instead of undertaking such a drastic interpretation of the Gospel of John, one could simply accept the transmitted form of the Gospel as the work of the Holy Spirit and allow himself to be immediately inspired by the Spirit in his understanding of the Gospel. The alternative to this is the approach of the theologian who, since he is familiar with what has happened to other ancient literature, dares not ascribe to the Holy Spirit and the effect of God's special revelation what he on the basis of other experience can explain as the natural consequence of the *history* of the Word of God (what in theological language is meant by saying that "the word became flesh"). A classical philologist would regard the discernment, creative imagination, and attention to essentials with which Bultmann proceeds throughout his commentary on John as the work of the Holy Spirit—preferring this to a naïve acceptance and the confusion of the merely historical with what is eternal. This is not to deny that Bultmann's achievements must also be regarded as historical, and are therefore both subject to criticism and liable to become outmoded. Even the most superior achievement in the field of philological criticism is limited precisely by the fact that it proceeds from a given historical basis.

Bultmann's commentary on the Gospel of John is indeed something more and something other than critical philology. The Gospel of John itself is not only an historical document but a source of new and living faith for today. To ensure that this result becomes an actuality is the fundamental hermeneutical task with which the Gospel confronts the theologian. To say this, does indeed assume a concept of hermeneutics that goes beyond the usual definition of this task. Theoretically Bultmann (in his essay on *Das Problem der Hermeneutik*) does not go beyond the common definition, which regards hermeneutics as concerned exclusively with interpretation. But the impressive example he has given in the commentary on the Gospel of John shows that in practice he has undertaken to define the task of hermeneutics in a new and much more profound way. For the classical philologist this new hermeneutics practiced by Bultmann— *interpretatio*—is already anticipated in the speech by Diotima, Socrates' teacher, in Plato's *Symposium* (202e). Here, to engage in hermeneutics is to be involved in mediation. If this is to be carried out properly, the mediator must not only have a correct understanding of the past but must also understand the present in which the past is to be effective once more. The central concern in the entire New Testament as well as in the Gospel of John is the kerygma of Jesus Christ. To transmit this kerygma to the contemporary hearer in such a way that he can hear it as a fresh message is possible only if the hearer is addressed in a manner that makes him feel that he understands himself. In order to remove the accidental and arbitrary elements that cling to the interpreter in his role as mediator and distort his hermeneutical work, Bultmann has resorted to the kind of analysis of contemporary man's self-awareness that he has found most profound and helpful: Martin Heidegger's existential analysis of man's being. Without doubt the tremendous influence exerted by Bultmann's commentary on the Gospel of John is due to the fact that his interpretation concerns itself not only with the Gospel as such but also with the hearer, for whom the interpreter has developed a new sense of responsibility.

Even the classical philologist whose ultimate commitment is to Plato will regard his task not only as interpretive "understanding" but as "mediation," not only as historical research but as an attempt to make the ancient writers come alive with their own historical "vitality" (cf. York von Wartenburg: letter to Dilthey, February 11, 1884). But classical philology would surrender its role if it were to engage in speculation instead of adhering to the historical method.

For this reason philology is barred from the road which Bultmann follows in his hermeneutics. Only if there can be discovered in ancient thought a principle that is similar to the kerygma of the New Testament—i.e., a central principle that is not only intrinsic to ancient thought but is inherently powerful, and meaningful to us either in terms of our relationship to the past or for our own situation —can the philologist assume the hermeneutical role of the mediator. We are indebted to Werner Jaeger for the discovery and description of such a principle, the Greek notion of *Paideia*. While the kerygma, faithful to its eschatological origin, seeks to liberate man from the bondage of an existence understood in terms of finite immanence, the *Paideia* attempts to awaken within man powers that will enable him to find fulfillment in just such an existence. The kerygma and the *Paideia* are thus essentially different principles. The kerygmatic Christianity of the theologian and the *Paideia* humanism of the classical philologist do have something in common, for both envision the possibility that a steady existential orientation will take the place of a pluralistic existence that always implies relativism and nihilism. The realization of this possibility depends on whether the kerygma answers the individual's understanding of his existence and the *Paideia* answers the individual's mode of living.

But do not both of these possibilities entail the danger that the proffered orientation becomes dogmatic monism, so that both kerygma and *Paideia* become ossified slogans that prevent an intimate relationship to the gospel and ancient thought? Both kerygma theology and *Paideia* philology are referred back to the historical matrix from which they came. The kerygma is constantly seeking new deliverance from the historical, mythological understanding of being in the New Testament by means of a "demythologizing" interpretation, and only thus escapes the ever new danger of either being identified with or dissolved by the historical element. On the other hand, the Greek notion of *Paideia* achieved its completely conceptualized understanding first in Plato but was present in a nonconceptual way in all of Greek antiquity. For this very reason there was less danger that *Paideia* humanism would turn into a form of monism or "programmatic humanism." But it was able to escape this danger completely only where it became affiliated with kerygmatic Christianity.

Yet, is such an affiliation really possible? Are not the kerygma and the *Paideia* not only essentially different, but also mutually contradictory principles?

The kerygma does indeed seek to extricate man from the bonds that tie him to this finite world; but, on the other hand, it also binds him to this world in demanding that he make his own interests identical with those of his neighbor. The message of Jesus and thus the heart of the kerygma can be fully comprehended only in the double commandment to love God totally and love one's neighbor without reserve. But in the sense of the message of Jesus the neighbor is always a concrete neighbor in an equally concrete situation. It is only in the realm of the *Paideia* that he becomes a human being who, as *zoon politikon,* is to fulfill his destiny in the human community, and thus also appeals to our "political" responsibility. For this very reason kerygmatic Christianity is involved in an ever new and positive relationship to *Paideia* humanism. In this sense Bultmann himself has always admitted being a humanist, and he has constantly advocated the preservation and requirement of a special form of this humanism in the education of young people in the classical *Gymnasium.*

On the other hand, the humanist ought not to seek a positive relationship to Christianity merely because true humanism never can bring the human being to his highest level and the *humanum* is thus always referred to a *divinum;* rather, this relationship must be sought because the Christian kerygma is always able to save the *Paideia* from hardening into a monistic dogma. It remains to be seen whether classical philology will also prove useful for Bultmann's theology by helping a *Paideia* relationship to ancient thought in general and a corresponding understanding of our own life to replace an existential interpretation bearing Heidegger's imprint. This interpretation is of limited effectiveness today even though it grew out of a lively relation to Greek thought. In any case, Bultmann's life work has made possible a new relationship between kerygmatic theology and classical philology, one that promises to be fruitful in the future.

Bultmann on Judaism

SAMUEL SANDMEL

Hebrew Union College
Jewish Institute of Religion
Cincinnati, Ohio

I

It is my opinion that Rudolf Bultmann is not only the greatest New Testament scholar of our day, but also one of the truly great of all times. In details here and there I would exercise the prerogative of disagreement with him, but I believe that I have learned more from him than from any New Testament teacher and that he has shaped my judgments more than any other. The one personal contact, when he lectured at Vanderbilt where I taught, was a week of unbroken pleasure.

The fact is, however, that my opinion on Dr. Bultmann's portrayal of Judaism in his writings constitutes the most serious area of my disagreement with him. Presently I shall specify this in some detail. Yet certain words of prologue are necessary, for I should not want my disagreement to appear simply as a parochial Jewish protest, such as have had to be made about other scholars, and which are justified and with which I associate myself. The comments I make on Dr. Bultmann's scholarship are almost entirely in a different realm.

The typical Jewish protest against New Testament scholarship is this—that in the various lives of Jesus in the nineteenth century, scholars, albeit unconsciously, tended to write the "biographies" of Jesus as if they had no belief in his divinity. Consequently they seem

211

to have sought, even desperately, to discover some human achievement for him. Since Apocrypha, pseudopigrapha, and translations of
rabbinical literature have, for at least the past three centuries, established a general congruency of the teachings of Jesus wih the
Judaism of his times, it was impossible to separate Jesus from that
Judaism on the basis of substance; instead, a separation was made on
quite another basis, by depicting the Judaism of the age of Jesus as
cold, arid legalism, indeed, as mechanical and devoid of heart.
Prophecy, so we were reminded, was by then a thing of the past, and
the trivia of legalism, with cut-and-dried doctrines of reward and
punishment, had supplanted the warm charismatic religion of the pre-
exilic luminaries. Accordingly, Jesus arose in the midst of this religious sterility, so the scholarship asserted, to restore to Judaism the
religious heart which it had lost. (One needs to note the margin of
difference between Jesus as the incarnate Logos as in the Fourth
Gospel, and a Jesus as, one must say, a somewhat lofty enthusiast.)
The net effect of the contrast drawn between an arid Judaism and, as
it were, a fervent Judaism preached by Jesus was to set Jesus over
against Judaism rather than within it. A Jesus at variance with
Judaism was a repeated motif in the nineteenth century. This is a
startling reversal of the judgment of all but the Marcionites in the
early Church, for the early Church held that Jesus, and the Church
also, was the continuation of Judaism. This nineteenth-century trend
in New Testament scholarship was brilliantly described by George
Foote Moore in "Christian Writers on Judaism," in the *Harvard
Theological Review* in 1921.

Three late-nineteenth-century writers, Weber, Bousset, and
Schuerer, were the principal objects of Moore's devastating strictures.
Here we can confine ourselves to Schuerer's chapter, "Life under the
Law," in his *A History of the Jewish People in the Time of Jesus
Christ*,[1] as an epitome of the procedure of nineteenth-century scholars. In Schuerer's one-sided and unsympathetic portrayal, the Law
was a burden under which Jews groaned, for it stifled both creativity
and religious spontaneity. As a burden, the Law represented to Jews
something simultaneously repelling and compelling; any Jew with any

---

[1] In Div. II, Vol. II, pp. 90–125, in the English translation.

sense, we might infer, would have been pleased to get out from under. So much for Schuerer.

The God of the Jews was not so much transcendent (a favorable word) as remote (an unfavorable one). He was no factor in the lives of people, for He never entered in as a favorable force in the day-to-day existence. He was the fierce and fearful disciplinarian, and never the loving, solicitous, tolerant, and forgiving father.

It was such portrayals, travestying rather than depicting Judaism, which called forth a series of Jewish protests. Whenever I reread these, I am compelled to agree with the bill of particulars in them; when I find in these protests a sporadic bitterness, such as in the just contention that most Christian scholars have known rabbinical literature only from compendia and through translations, I lament that the tone of nineteenth-century Christian scholarship called forth from Jews a tone equally lamentable. Some of the infelicitous, indeed ugly tone of nineteenth-century Christian scholarship abides into our day, as, for example, in the *ICC* commentaries on the New Testament. The contrast in tone between the *ICC* and the *Moffatt* series as regards Judaism is notable; so too, the *Interpreter's Bible* has very largely, but not quite completely, avoided the distortions, and has, indeed, brought matters to a better balance. Where imbalance persists, the explanation seems to be in the persistence of aspects of the heritage from nineteenth-century scholarship, or in the misdirection caused by Strack and Billerbeck's *Kommentar zum Neuen Testament aus Talmud und Midrasch*. This compendium is staggering in its size, and more than one scholar who has never read a full page in a rabbinical text has been grossly misled. (Note how I too become condescending and superior at this point.) I have elsewhere discussed Strack and Billerbeck at some length,[2] and I see no purpose in beating the same dog over and over again. Let me simply summarize by saying that Strack and Billerbeck do not approach rabbinical Judaism properly, and hence the scholar who relies upon them is misled.

The works of Bultmann to which I here allude are *Jesus and the Word* and *Primitive Christianity*. I have used these in my personal

---

[2] In my "Parallelomania," *Journal of Biblical Literature,* LXXXI (1962), esp. pp. 8–11.

study much less than three others, *The Theology of the New Testament, Das Johannesevangelium,* and *Geschichte der synoptischen Tradition.* But my wish here is to discuss a certain main line in Dr. Bultmann and not to produce a plethora of details.

I have found not one ugly sentence about Jews or Judaism in the writings of Bultmann which I have read. I do not see him in the same way as Israel Abrahams[3] necessarily looked at Schuerer. My differences with Bultmann are academic and not personal; they are the differences which emerge from two individuals' understanding and interpretation, and are not denominational in the sense of Jew versus Christian. It is my belief that at some crucial points his viewpoint turns incorrect; at no point have I found even the incorrect viewpoint vicious.

II

In *Jesus and the Word,* Bultmann has a chapter entitled "The Historical Background for the Ministry of Jesus." In it, he speaks of the Law "which properly has only this meaning: to release man from the world, to separate him from any interest in an independent cultural development, and to humble him in obedience to the transcendent power of God" (p. 17). I must comment that the first phrase says too much; the Law did not mean release from the world but guidance and direction *within it.* The second phrase strikes me as very inappropriate, for it raises as an issue something which seems to me scarcely to have entered into the ken of Jews; it is a modern construction, not an ancient Jewish one. The third phrase elicits my disagreement only in its formulation; I should put it, rather, in this way: that the meaning of the Law was to *raise* the Jew in obedience to the living immanence of the transcendent God.

Bultmann sees in that Judaism a balance between the Law and hope. He says, "In rabbinical Judaism after the beginning of the Christian era the hope retreats more and more into the background. . . . The rabbinical Judaism finally rejected the apocalyptic, leaving it to Christianity, and concentrated on the Law." I comment that Christianity, too, eventually so retreated from the apocalyptic as

---

[3] In *Studies in Pharisaism and the Gospels,* 2nd ser., "The Yoke," pp. 4–14.

virtually to abandon it, and that it is most inappropriate to limit hope exclusively to the apocalyptic. I would insist that it was the apocalyptic that Judaism abandoned, not hope, and that Judaism abandoned it and Christianity retreated[4] from it for the same reasons, namely the sad experiences arising out of the apocalyptic. Predictions made too clearly and too specifically led to frustration or to disaster rather than to well-being; and this same thing is attested in Christendom as well as in Judaism.

But this summary of Judaism as comprising law and promise, obedience and hope, seems to me to be much too nimble. Perhaps this arises from an understandable need on the part of Bultmann to compress, or even from a use of terms in some special way. Yet the suspicion arises that it derives from an unconscious setting of the stage, from a preparation as by a playwright to explain Jesus, rather than from an endeavor to depict Judaism without regard to Jesus.

I am by no means certain that the movements of John the Baptist and of Jesus were "essentially unpolitical" (p. 25). There is not sufficient evidence either to affirm or deny. A stronger case can be made for a political aspect to Jesus' movement than for John's; See the Gospel of Mark and the Book of Acts. Certainly whatever political aspect there was to Jesus' movement was almost completely winnowed out in developing Christian thought.

Bultmann's contrast between the eschatology of the prayer in the "Eighteen Benedictions" and a passage from the Lord's Prayer (pp. 41–42) is hardly apt, for here Bultmann has succumbed in both cases to arbitrary selection. And I must not refrain from expressing my opinion that, on pages 44–45, in discussing the coming of Gentiles into the kingdom of God, the scholar has given way to the homiletician, for here it seems to me that Bultmann has faltered. So, too, his contrast (pp. 91–92) between the "demand of the law" and "the demand of God" is either homiletics or else a confusion of Jesus with Paul; in Judaism the Law was deemed God's demand, and to divide these as Bultmann does into two differing demands is quite untrue to Judaism. The Jewish formula for a "benediction" declares

---

[4] The virtual abandonment of eschatology is an example. Cf. C. H. Dodd, *The Parables of the Kingdom,* and Martin Werner (Eng. trans.), *The Formation of Christian Dogma,* especially pp. 31–119.

that God is blessed for He "has *sanctified us by his commandments* and commanded us to. . . ."

A clue, however, to Bultmann's procedure is to be found (p. 155) in his statement: ". . . Jesus stands within the limits of strict Judaism, and differs from it not because he presents especially original ideas about God and the world, but because he apprehends the Jewish conception of God in its purity and consistency." Whether this conclusion is tenable or not (and I think it is not) is scarcely the point in this essay. The true point is that, unlike Schuerer, Bultmann has not conjured up some reprehensible Judaism against which to contrast Jesus. Rather he seeks to find in an admirable Judaism a Jesus whom he finds even more admirable.

So much for *Jesus and the Word.* Turning to *Primitive Christianity,* we may advert to his statement (p. 60): "By binding herself to her past history, Israel loosened her ties with the present, and her responsibility for it. . . ." Two comments are in order. First, if what Bultmann is saying is correct, it would be as applicable to Christianity as to Judaism; and, in fact, in view of the dualism present in so much of even "orthodox" Christianity, it would be even more applicable to Christianity than to Judaism. Second, Bultmann is incorrect. Granted there is some sense in which loyalty to a past dilutes the confrontation of the present, in normative Judaism present and future were deemed to be intimately and inseparably connected with, not isolated from, the past. The passage in the Passover Haggadah says this clearly: "In each generation a man must regard himself as though he himself has been redeemed from Egypt." Furthermore, the statement (again p. 60) that there was no possibility of science and art among Jews, is only partially correct, and the partial correctness rests on a basis different from the one Bultmann gives. In respect to the plastic arts, it was the accrued objection to depicting the human form which tended to stifle sculpture and painting; decoration, though, did take place. As for science, enough evidence is available about the understanding of astronomy to suggest that lawyer's literature—which is what the rabbinical literature is—is scarcely evidence for or against the existence of science. I do not dispute Bultmann's description here, but his explanation of what he has described.

Again, in the area of what Bultmann seems to see as history, one reads his statement that since "proselytes actually had to join the Jewish community," this is "another instance of the way Israel was cutting itself adrift from history." Not at all! The proselyte was simply admitted into the community and *into its history*. The documents would not sustain Bultmann at this point, nor would logic; the would-be proselyte was invited to become part of the historically centered community.

Bultmann's statement on page 62 reveals his most serious misunderstanding, and, in fact, some continuing partial bondage to Schuerer and Bousset. According to Bultmann, the Bible in synagogue worship "was no longer primarily a historical record of God's dealing with his people, but a book of divine Law." To conserve space I must here condense my objections. First, Law and Bible never were as identical as Bultmann supposes; in the Jewish view the Bible *contained* laws, but was not interchangeable with them, as witness the Psalms and the Prophets. Bultmann forgets that Haggadah was as important to the rabbis as Halakah; he truly misses the point about Jewish legalism. In his view, apparently, the legalism was virtually the entirety of Judaism; in point of fact, the legalism was directed toward clarifying the ambiguities and uncertainties of Scriptural legalism; it is methodologically unsound to use a people's clarifying legalisms as if they exhaust the total dimensions of a people. When Bultmann goes on to say that "life was alienated from history," he is saying something which every pericope in rabbinical literature would refute. And he completely distorts Judaism in saying that the holiness sought for was designed to be "above all worldly interests and ideals." Quite the contrary; in so far as such modern terminology conforms to ancient documents, the Jewish quest was to have holiness permeate worldly interests and ideals, not rise above them. No, there was no effort to separate sanctity from life, but rather to sanctify life.

My purpose in picking on these details in Bultmann is not for their own sake, for there is truly very little involved in them in themselves, and it would be a very minor consideration whether or not Bultmann has phrased his analysis felicitously. These details, however, serve him as a sort of prologue to the contrast toward which he is heading, namely, the *obedience* in Judaism and the *radical obedience* which he conceives of as characterizing Jesus.

He defines radical obedience as involving "a personal assent to the divine command"; he ascribes to Judaism what he calls a "formal obedience." I doubt whether the ancient rabbis, or Jesus, or his disciples would have understood the distinction. Would not obedience *to all the forms* exemplify and demonstrate radical obedience? Or does "personal assent" imply an exemption from the formal? I find no reality in Bultmann's words here, and absolutely no applicability in them either to rabbinical Judaism or to Jesus.

In these pages in his book (pp. 50–71) Bultmann is setting the stage for his consideration of Jesus; to put it clearly, he is stacking the cards—this by describing a Judaism that never existed so that he can set a special view of Jesus over against it.

True, he insists that "the proclamation of Jesus must be considered within the framework of Judaism" (p. 71). But at this point we again encounter the strange paradox that the scholar who more than anyone has taught us how little of Jesus is authentic in the Gospels, now finds him there abundantly. It is outside the realm of this essay to deal with that topic. Yet I must go on to say that in dealing with the Sermon on the Mount (p. 72) Bultmann abstains from reflecting a common view that Matthew, not Jesus, was its author; and he is dead wrong in asserting that the Sermon contrasts the Law and the will of God, for the Sermon is *a new law, more rigid than Moses';* and it is certainly not to be summarized nimbly as the will of God. Moreover, Bultmann's special pleading leads him to say that "without contesting the authority of the Old Testament Jesus discriminates between its various aspects." This statement is quite irresponsible, and does violence to the Sermon, with its formula, seven times repeated, "You have heard it said, but I say to you," and six of the seven quotations are Old Testament quotations.[5]

Bultmann seems to me at his best in interpreting Judaism when it is Hellenistic rather than rabbinical Judaism to which he addresses himself. I have some competency in Philo;[6] I regard Bultmann's essay in *Primitive Christianity* (pp. 94 ff.) as a truly brilliant achievement.

---

[5] The seventh (Matt. *5:43–48*) is likewise intended as a scriptural quotation; the "quoted" passage simply is absent from Scripture.

[6] See my *Philo's Place in Judaism.*

III

Having conceded, it seems to me, what the facts require, that Bultmann is never guilty of an offending attitude toward Judaism, I must go on to comment further on what seems to me the major infelicity. It derives from manner and disposition, not from basic assessment. It is Bultmann's tendency to create his own categories and to superimpose these on Judaism, or else to make Judaism fit into them. All too often these categories can be applied only by forcing Judaism into them. It seems to me that they do not arise from what a study of Judaism yields, but rather represent Bultmann's special subjective conception. It is not to Judaism alone that he applies this procedure, but he does so to Christianity too.

To my mind this procedure involves mostly a debit, for even when distortion is free from malice, it is nevertheless distortion. But it would be grossly unfair to a magnificent scholar to leave this allegation unmodified. I am not charging Bultmann with a capricious, that is, thoughtless, creation of categories, but with an arbitrary creation of them—this in the etymological sense of the word arbitrary. He has studied the material thoroughly; he has pondered it carefully. It is thereafter that he has not resisted the tendency to supply categories which are simultaneously true and untrue to the material. He has devised terms and labels for utterances which are intuitive, unrestrained, and devoid of inner consistence. He has made quasi-systematic a body of ancient thought which is notably unsystematic. It is not that he has betrayed material by putting it into the wrong categories; it is that he has put into categories of today thought which defies putting even into ancient categories.

The Judaism which emerges from his pages is too sharply defined; it is too crystal-clear; it is too highly focused.

Yet, paradoxically, I must state that his procedure, much as I have reservations about it, contains its own admirable illumination. He has devised categories (such as promise and hope) that I think I would never have dreamed of, certainly not in his way; but in my scrutiny of the material, in the light even of those of his categories which I feel I must reject, I find myself gaining some new insights and responding to nuances which I have previously failed to notice. So penetrating is Bultmann's weighing of the material that he who studies Bultmann, and disagrees here and there, has the sense (so at least I do) of having penetrated further and better because of him.

Certain scholars, especially very young ones, seem to me to put an undue premium on whether another scholar is right or wrong. We discern this especially in the book reviews which younger scholars write. For them certainty is ready at hand, and a minor error (such as a wrong reference not caught in proofreading) is as heinous a sin as mayhem or murder. Most scholars outgrow such juvenility. In the highest rungs of scholarship, especially in the humanities, there is no such thing as right or wrong; we are all acquainted with that class of scholar "who never gets a footnote wrong or an idea right." Scholarly differences are often matters of individual mood and temperament; there is no book on Paul which I admire quite as much as that by Machen, a fundamentalist, with whom I almost completely disagree.

Respecting Professor Bultmann, I repeat that I count myself as one of his disciples. What I have written in my first paragraph in assessment, I have often and repeatedly expressed in the spoken word. The area wherein I, as it were, agree, is enormously large; the area wherein I differ is small, restricted. It is to me a source of continuing gratification that I regard his views on Judaism as sometimes incorrect, but never improper; sometimes out of balance, but never unbalanced; sometimes too neat, too pat, too apt, but never hateful and hating.

The Old Testament and Its Significance for Religious Instruction

HANNELIS SCHULTE
Ziegelhausen über
Heidelberg, Germany

I

"Why do we read the Old Testament? What significance do these old stories have for us?" These are questions with which the teacher of religion has to struggle when he has just told the Old Testament stories and starts reading them in the Bible with his students. What is his answer? Has he an answer that is both reasonable and convincing? And when he refers to the Church, by what authority does he do so? What is the attitude of the Church toward the Old Testament? She inherited it from ancient tradition; she preaches on passages from the Old Testament; she might talk about its great significance for Christian or even for European art and literature. Is this, however, an answer to the question why today, within the Christian Church, we read the Old Testament and preach on its passages?

In Germany, during the regime of Hitler, this problem became urgent because some people wanted the Christian Church to get rid of the Old Testament. As a "Jewish book," as a "collection of stories about cattle dealers and bagnio panders," it was openly despised, and in some parts of Germany its use was not permitted for religious instruction. So anybody who wanted to stand up for his faith defended the Old Testament—because it was evident that after the

221

attack on the Old Testament the attack on the New Testament was to follow. But generally speaking, the Confessional Church (*Bekennende Kirche*) was more eager to defend the Old Testament with her back to the wall than to go into details as to why she could not abandon it.

Of course we heard several reasons cited for this: (1) The Old Testament contains the religion in which Jesus was brought up, so that we cannot understand his words properly without knowing the Old Testament. (2) The Old and the New Covenants belong together as do law and gospel. (3) The Old Testament—according to Luther —"fosters Christ" and contains the prophecies and promises whose fulfillment he is. These are reasons enough—but are they an answer; are they well-founded and perspicuous?

(1) It is questionable to talk of the knowledge that the Old Testament gives us and to say that without it we might not be able to understand the message of Jesus and of the Epistles of the New Testament. For by the same line of argument, how can we comprehend the New Testament without a knowledge of the terms of Gnostic belief, of the ideas of Hellenistic religion, and perhaps about the Dead Sea Scrolls as well? And yet we do not employ these as texts for sermons nor do we grant them any authority within the Church. (2) What about the conception of the Old and the New Covenants? There arises the question whether the Old Covenant means anything to us—on the grounds that it is abrogated by the New. Did not Luther call the Old Testament Law *"der Juden Sachsenspiegel"* (the Jewish code of law), for which we had better substitute our European tradition of law and our own knowledge of good and evil? (3) Finally, what is the meaning of the statement that "the Old Testament fosters Christ"? Are we supposed to understand this *allegorically* (on one occasion in the United States I heard it proclaimed that Moses struck the rock and water came forth); or *typologically,* e.g., Adam—First Man, Christ—Last Man; or *Messianically,* as fulfillment of the prophecies? Does this really mean restricted to the prophecies? Or how else can we understand it?

II

Now at this point Bultmann joins the discussion with his lecture, "Prophecy and Fulfillment":[1] "Evidently, in all these cases [i.e., of Messianic prophecies] the New Testament authors do not gain new knowledge from the Old Testament texts but read out of them or into them things they already know."[2] The same is true for allegorical and typological exegesis. Bultmann continues: "But are we as theologians allowed to do so? Are we allowed to avoid the scandal of the Cross by preaching it as being ordered and prophesied by God long ago? Or can we not only overcome it by comprehending its meaning, its significance for us?"[3] If this is true, the scheme of prophecy and fulfillment tempts us to walk the easier way, i.e., to explain the Cross by a theological theory, so that we do not become aware of the harder way to realize the Cross in our own life. Should we not, therefore, abandon that scheme? "Or is there any legitimation for its theological use, which says that the Old Testament Jewish history is Prophecy, fulfilled in the story of the New Testament Church?"[4] Bultmann answers: It is Prophecy, but only in the inner discord, the breakdown of that history.[5] For when we fail under the inner discordance of our existence, we are prepared for the occurrence of the grace of God, whose strength is made perfect in our weakness (II Cor. 12:9).

This occurrence of grace leads us to understand our failure as a promise, for this failure destroyed us and so made it possible for God to act in us. "The conflict of being created for God and called to God, and yet of being imprisoned in secular history,"[6] is clearly to be seen in the history of Israel. Bultmann explains this point through three terms, the first of which is the *Covenant*. A nation in its empirical history may fulfill the Covenant of God when its duties consist only of certain rites and ceremonies, or of a fixed order of life, but it is impossible to keep the Covenant when the moral commitment of each

---

[1] Rudolf Bultmann, *Essays, Philosophical and Theological* (London: SCM Press, 1955), pp. 182 ff.

[2] *Ibid.*, p. 187.

[3] *Ibid.*, p. 205.

[4] *Ibid.*, p. 205.

[5] *Ibid.*, p. 207.

[6] *Ibid.*, p. 207.

member is requested. This latter, however, is the prophetic demand. The prophets of Israel spurn the outward fulfillment of the ceremonies and ask for inner and moral obedience. Thus the covenant becomes an impossibility—i.e., the covenant of which the prophets speak cannot be realized under empirical conditions but can only be created by God. This covenant is nothing else than the New Testament Church as the group of those who are chosen by God.

It is the same with the idea of the *Kingdom of God,* which becomes within the Old Testament and Jewish creed more and more a hope for the future, because it seems impossible to believe in it as a present reality. Only in the New Testament is the Kingdom of God understood as the hidden victory of faith. The prophetic demand for a *People of God* was also doomed, because it could not possibly be carried through into politics. For no nation is able to be both "People of God" and nation in history.[7]

What are the conclusions regarding Bultmann's view of the Old Testament? (1) In this connection he looks at it chiefly as an historical document. (2) He understands it as a paradigm of human existence. (3) He shows us that the Christian Church is always to be reminded of the fate of Israel, because she is always tempted to transform into human organization what can only be a gift of God. Only by overcoming those temptations does she in faith become the Christian Church.

Now we have to deal with the first two points: What does it mean to understand the Old Testament as an historical document and as a paradigm of human existence?

III

Reading Old Testament texts with his students, the teacher has to face certain difficulties. According to the schedule of the Church of Baden for example, the reading starts with the prophets, with the special objective of prophecy and fulfillment. But, because the reading of the old-fashioned Lutheran version of the Old Testament presupposes a lot of good will on the part of the students, it is not

---

[7] *Ibid.,* p. 207; cf. Rudolf Bultmann, *Primitive Christianity in Its Contemporary Setting* (New York: Meridian Books, 1956), chap. ii, "God and the Nation."

advisable to start with the most difficult section, the prophets. Only Jeremiah and Jonah might be acceptable at the start. I therefore prefer to begin with a series of stories from the books of Samuel or the Kings. Once the class gets used to the language and style, the pupils are eager to engage in this reading. In this connection the teacher may discuss the historical accuracy of the Old Testament source criticism, etc. This discussion, however, does not contribute greatly to the religious experience of the students.

If therefore the teacher is not satisfied, Bultmann's arguments about Old Testament anthropology may inspire him to go on. Perhaps he tries to compare the Old Testament with the *Iliad* in this respect. Men and women, especially in the older sources of the Old Testament, are no moral models and no heroes as in Greek literature. Man is not seen as a work of art to be formed after an ideal. There is nothing like the characteristic Greek term *kalos kagathos* (i.e., one who has goodness and beauty—the gentleman) or the Greek idea of "virtue" (*arete*) as the disposition for "work" (*ergon*); there is nothing like *eros,* the desire or longing for the ideal.[8] If all this is absent, what is it that motivates the behavior of all these men whom we meet in the Old Testament stories? They are men faced by a challenge—not faced by the demand of an ideal which tries to form their personality, but by the challenge of the community in which they live. This community asks its members to live together in peace, to deal justly with their neighbor, for the community needs righteousness on the national order.[9] Man is therefore not seen in the Old Testament as a personality but as a "social being." That is his destiny according to God's will. Even the special call addressed to an individual orders him to act for the nation—for example, the mission of Gideon: "Go in this thy might, and thou shalt save Israel from the hand of the Midianites" (Judg. 6:14). Not the perfect, but the obedient man is right according to God's will.

In reality man is not proceeding step by step to perfection by overcoming his weakness, but again and again gives offense to the order of the community and God's guidance by stubbornness and ingratitude. "Sin is murmuring over his, that is, God's guidance up to

---

8 *Ibid.,* p. 47.
9 *Ibid.,* p. 48.

now and failing to trust in his future care; sin is ingratitude and faithlessness, it is lack of confidence, the opposite of the fear of God and of faith which is the trustful waiting for God."[10] Man therefore depends upon the expiatory sacrifice and the hope that his sin will be forgiven.

If the teacher of religion is able to discuss with his students—for example, in connection with the stories of Saul and David—one or another of these ideas, he gains much for the reading of the New Testament. For: *"This, that is the Old Testament view of life, is the same as that of the New Testament,* the same as the Christian in contrast to the Greek, humanistic or idealistic view of life."[11] For the structure of faith and justice, grace, sin, and forgiveness is the same in the Old Testament as in the New Testament. The Old Testament makes us understand more clearly even than the New Testament that God's demand and his grace occur not in special religious situations but in the ordinary situations of our life, in the special "worldly" requirements of our existence.

I V

It is for a fruitful reading of the prophetic books that one first studies the historical books. But now the teacher is confronted with another difficulty. I remember the violent opposition I once met when I read the prophet Amos in a holiday camp. The girls wanted to hear something of concern to their personal life, not about justice in political life. When we once read Jeremiah 32 (the story of buying the field in Anathoth), a pupil asked me: "What is the use of these words about the nation's future? They mean nothing for the individual, who has to live through all these terrible events and to die."

This shows a correct understanding. The words of the prophets are spoken to a nation: they are political preaching. Their commands are given to the individual only as he is a member of this nation. The hope they promise is first of all political hope for Israel. To this nation we do not belong.

We cannot be compared with Israel as a nation—for we want to be

---

10 *Essays,* pp. 322 ff.
11 *Ibid.,* p. 324.

a modern state which grants freedom of creed to its subjects.[12] Nor
are we Israel as a church—for "the church is not a sociological unit,
a national or cultural community, linked together by the continuity of
history, but she is constituted by the message of God's forgiving in
Christ and is the community, constituted by this message, preaching
and belief. . . . To him, who belongs to the church, the history of
Israel is passed and finished."[13]

Is it then of any value to read the prophets of Israel in Christian
religious instruction? We have first to realize that the reluctance of
our pupils to read the Old Testament is justified. They do not know
why they dislike it and are often not able to express their feelings, but
they have the impression that it is a story with almost no relation to
themselves. For this reason the teacher should not treat the Old
Testament as an authority that cannot be questioned.

Today it is quite usual to demonstrate the authority of the Old
Testament by understanding it as a steppingstone to the New Testament in the history of salvation or, as may often be heard, a witness
to the magnificent actions of God. Of that Bultmann warns us
emphatically. For consequently the New Testament too would be
understood as a part of the history of salvation; for example, we may
be tempted also to regard the story of Christ and the work of the
Apostles as such "magnificent actions of God," which culminate in
Jesus Christ as "the unit of time." That means that we look back on
those actions of God as on past events. There God showed his power
—or Jesus Christ his kingdom—and from this we conclude that he is
able to do such works among us today. If this is the case, the story of
Christ is only *our* "exodus from Egypt," and just on the same level
with the Old Testament in spite of all other differences. "The mes-

---

[12] Today we see that Israel still manifests the same contradiction which
began with the prophetic message long ago: it tries to understand itself as
God's community and at the same time as a modern state. Is it possible to
combine these two ideas? To give an example: the state of Israel is open to
every immigrant who professes the Hebrew religion. The government reflects
the demand of orthodox Jews that the immigrant promise to keep the many
strict religious laws; it does not want immigrants of Jewish descent who are
not of the Jewish faith—for example, Christian Jews. In my opinion this is
a compromise which does justice neither to the idea of God's people nor to
that of the modern state.

[13] *Ibid.*, p. 333.

sage," however, "of God's forgiving grace in Jesus Christ is not a historical record about a past event, but it is the *preaching word of the church,* speaking now to everybody as God's word, and in which Jesus Christ is present as the 'word.' "[14]

Not God's past actions but his present acting is important for faith:

In the Old Testament, message and history are at first separated. History is what the nation went through, out of which it comes to the presence of the message, and the message of the prophets or the law speaks to this present situation. The present is associated with the past, when the now occurring message reminds of the past history, in this way brings it into presence and continues it. The message of Christian preaching and the story it tells coincide, are one. The story of Christ is not past, but occurs through the preaching message.[15]

Once again: What is the value of reading the prophets of Israel or the other parts of the Old Testament? Certainly the history of Israel is, as history of *Israel,* without any meaning for the Christian faith, but it is significant for us as *history.* In this view, religious instruction is in a better position than the sermon, because it may deal with problems with which the sermon as a direct message of God cannot deal. We are now discussing what I should like to call "the discovery of history by Israel," so we have to go back again to the writing of history.

As far as we know, the Yahwistic source, supposedly leading from Genesis 2 to I Kings 12:19[16] and written at the end of the tenth century B.C.,[17] is the oldest historical writing which has been preserved. While the Greeks presented us with science when the Ionian philosophers began to ask about the *arche,* we owe historical writing to Israel.[18] But the important question is the way in which history is understood. While the Greeks inquire about the laws of nature, Israel discovers human freedom. However, we do not find this term in the

---

14 *Ibid.,* p. 332.

15 *Ibid.,* p. 292.

16 G. Hoelscher, *Geschichtsschreibung in Israel,* p. 32.

17 C. A. Simpson, *The Early Traditions of Israel* (London: Oxford University Press, 1948).

18 *Primitive Christianity,* p. 15.

Old Testament—"freedom" as a word is completely unknown there.[19] Even when the historian wants to show those decisions of man that influence history, he talks about the interference of God in history. He may talk about this interference in a mythological way—for example, saying that the angel of Yahweh comes to a person and gives him an order—or in a more elaborate way as in the story of Absalom's rebellion. Here the story is told in strict interdependence of cause and effect, but when it comes to the climax, where Absalom's decision involves success or failure of his rebellion, the story is suddenly interrupted: "For the Lord had appointed to defeat the good council of Ahithophel . . ." (II Sam. 17:14). The historian is not yet able to call the contingency in history human freedom or decision, but talks about God's interference instead.

Moreover the Old Testament historian even dares to make the idea of the national union of Israel the thread of his account, so that he presents the Judean tradition of the migration from Egypt as the history of the whole of Israel and makes Moses the leader of all twelve tribes.[20] Why does the historian do this? Because, after the breakdown of David's kingdom following Solomon's death, the restoration of national union has become the most urgent task. The historian writes for the sake of that national task—in other words he understands that an active role in history is a mission given to his people. Therefore "the Old Testament understands history not as the causal progress of human beings or thoughts, as the progress of humanity, of culture or mind, but as God's action, which gives to all men their destination and task."[21]

"If we find here [that is, in the history-writing of Israel] an interest in knowledge, then it is an interest to know oneself, and the historian calls his nation to the judgment of itself, reminding it of God's actions in the past and of the behavior of the nation. This message is at the same time the call to responsibility towards the future that will bring salvation or ruin."[22] This discovery of history is therefore at the same time the discovery of the historical destination of man: "within the Bible man is understood in his historical

---

[19] *The Presence of Eternity* (New York: Harper & Brothers, 1957), p. 97.
[20] Cf. Hoelscher, *op. cit.*, and Simpson, *op. cit.*, both *passim*.
[21] *Glauben und Verstehen*, I, 323.
[22] *The Presence of Eternity*, p. 18.

destination, formally expressed: in his present he is qualified by his past and challenged by his future."[23] So far we have discussed our subject primarily with reference to the historians of the Bible. The destination of man is, however, expressed in the message of the prophets of Israel. "The prophets have their significance not in representing the very heights of noble humanity or as *homines religiosi,* but in calling their nation and demanding of them a definite behavior ordered by God, in which they prove faithful to their history given by God."[24]

The prophetic message does not aim at a separate religious domain nor at the protection of man or nation against menace from a supernatural world; therefore the teacher has a good starting point here for the discussion and criticism of religion. The severe words with which Hosea, Amos, Isaiah, and Jeremiah lash the offering ceremonies— where, behind the correct performance, disobedience and dishonesty are hidden—are as distinctive as possible, as are the harsh phrases by which Hosea, Amos and Jeremiah try to arouse their nation out of the security induced by its consciousness of being elected.[25] This means: God is not on the side of religious people against the atheists or heathen; even *religion* has to be opposed for God's sake. In this way the teacher may show his pupils that modern criticism of religion has authorization and significance.

This discussion leads to the other problem, Christianity and the other religions. (1) The formal comparison of religions will show that nothing like the prophets of Israel is to be found in any other religion. Certainly many religions know prophetism in the sphere of the mantic, which is not alien to the Old Testament, but the prophets of Israel go far beyond that. (2) When we ask about the nature of religion there is the answer that only in the Bible is the freedom of God from religion maintained, because it preaches God's love even of the nonreligious domain, of the whole world, of which he is the creator.[26]

---

[23] *Ibid.,* p. 100.

[24] *Glauben und Verstehen,* I, 323.

[25] *Primitive Christianity,* pp. 37 f.; 49 ff.

[26] Not without reason, D. Bonhoeffer refers to the Old Testament for the nonreligious interpretation of Biblical terms (*Widerstand und Ergebung,* esp. pp. 225 ff.). On this point and on the relation of Bonhoeffer's and Bultmann's thought see the lecture of G. Ebeling, "The Nonreligious Interpretation of Biblical Terms," in *ZThK,* LII, esp. pp. 333–40.

That leads us to the question concerning the relation between the prophets and Jesus. Was Jesus one of them, as modern Jewish thinkers like to assume? From the point of view of the history of religion there is no objection to this statement. Jesus was called by God as the prophets were, and understood himself as sent to Israel. He taught about righteousness in the relation between a man and his neighbor, and his implication for the political situation may have been greater than we see it now in the New Testament. He attacked the pious hypocrisy of the religious leaders and tried to set free the actual relation to God, then chained by law. Yet the witness of the New Testament speaks of Jesus as the Son of God, as the Image of God, etc., and that means—nonmythologically interpreted—the identification of God's action with Jesus' and of Jesus' action with God's.

Jesus' action is strictly understood from the view of revelation: whatever he says or does is word and action of the Father . . . the "word of God" as spoken by Jesus does not give—as the prophetic word does—the knowledge of the actual historical necessity in the light of God's demand. If it did, it might be expressed by the idea of calling and inspiration—this word is rather not to be distinguished from his personality: revelation occurred in the wholly historical appearance of a man once and forever, so that the reaction to him is the decision about life and death forever for all men.[27]

The third series of questions which arise from reading the pre-exilic prophets are those about "political preaching." Bultmann's view is that the prophets attack the worldly kingdom because it does not answer the old theocratic ideal and cannot but destroy the old family order. Since the prophets are not able "to formulate the idea of God's nation in such a way that it might be realized under the worldly kingdom,"[28] their demand is Utopian, whereas "their demand of right and justice in itself might agree with the laws of any sound government."[29]

But I do not see that the prophets' criticism principally attacks the idea of a kingdom, of armaments, or of fortification and military treaties. Hosea warns of "making kings," and Isaiah of certain military measures and treaties. But here the protest is aimed at the trust

---

[27] *Das Evangelium des Johannes,* 11th ed., p. 189, to John 5:19.
[28] *Essays,* p. 202.
[29] *Primitive Christianity,* p. 44.

in such treaties and measures, and not at military and political efforts as such. The question is whether salvation comes from these efforts or whether they are provisional human actions from which one might abstain. Especially with Jeremiah, it is quite evident that his demand, "Come under the yoke of Nebuchadnezzar!" (e.g., Jer. 27:12), and later on, "Yield to the princes of the king of Babylon!" (e.g., Jer. 38:14 ff.)—i.e., his direct political commands—are not at all Utopian. As far as we can see, they give the realistic judgment of the situation, contrary to the Utopian plans of the war party and its prophets. If we do not see as the background the ideal of God's nation but the special political situation, the commands of the prophets are not to be called Utopian—unless we want to say the same about any obedience of faith. Or is the individual, met by the demand to trust God, in principle in a different situation from that of the king or the whole nation? The economic security of his own life and the well-being of his family will raise the same questions for the individual and ask him for the same decision: whether he dares to trust in God. In the eyes of the man who calculates only the economic and military factors, the obedience of faith will always be Utopian.

There is another objection to Bultmann's arguments: it may be that many of the prophetic denunciations of foreign nations are in their traditional form incorrect or ambiguous, but as a whole we are not allowed to reject them completely as incorrect. That means, the challenge of the prophetic word is based not only on the ideas of God's nation and Covenant, but on the belief that God is creator and master of history—a view which Bultmann stresses in other connections.[30]

Out of this arises the question—which Bultmann as far as I can see does not ask—whether today the Church with her message is in the same situation toward the nations as the prophets were, and is obliged to approach them with her message about God's justice and righteousness. Thereby the prophetic sayings of the Old Testament gain a direct significance and authority for the Church. God's demand for justice among men and nations in the Old Testament refers to other economic, social, and political conditions, but by preaching on these texts we will become aware that they not only agree with our

---

30 *Ibid.*, pp. 15 f.; 20 and *passim*.

situation in so far as they state that there is a demand of God, but they also help us find concrete answers to our problems. Again and again the basic structure of human and political attitude is the same. Nevertheless we have to realize that thereby we preach law and not the gospel. In such a sermon we ought not to forget to state that love is the fulfillment of law and that the demand to perform justice is too heavy a burden for man, so that it makes him perhaps humble, but in most cases indifferent, desperate, or convinced of his own righteousness. Then only the gospel can help, and now we are in the situation of failure, which makes men listen to the gospel.

That the Old Testament as law is the preliminary witness for the preaching of the gospel, Bultmann explains with great skill.[31] But this necessary function of the Law may be performed even by other ideas, if they only elucidate the "thou shalt."[32] But it is for historical reasons that we use the Old Testament in this respect. "So there are only *pedagogic reasons,* when in the Christian church the Old Testament is used to make man conscious of the fact that his life is under God's demand, . . . and when the prophets' demands remain alive in Christian preaching, because in them, as nowhere else except in the teaching of Jesus, the imperative of the divine command resounds with unequaled emphasis and clarity."[33]

I am willing to admit that in so far as the Law is the preliminary message of the gospel and has a task of convincing, we only use the Old Testament for pedagogic reasons. But with regard to the political preaching I do not see where else but from the Old Testament the Church may get the order and a basis for her message. Of course you may deny this prophetic mission of the Church. But when you agree with it, because it deals with the salvation or destruction of our world as God's creation, the Old Testament acquires a significance exceeding that which Bultmann likes to concede to it. For with regard to its prophetic message the Old Testament is unique, not related to or replaceable by any concept of law.

---

[31] *Essays,* pp. 319–22.

[32] Insofar, it was not altogether wrong when the *"deutsche Christen"* (DC) wanted to substitute the *"Nomos* of the German Nation" for the Old Testament. But actually the "ethics" of the Third Reich supported the "right of the stronger" and glorified the "struggle for existence." That has nothing to do with God's demand.

[33] *Ibid.,* pp. 321 f.

V

Why is the Old Testament still alive in the Christian Church? We
will try to find a comprehensive answer. Bultmann distinguishes two
ways in which the Old Testament is significant for us. First, because
it belongs to our tradition, to the history from which we come. "Only
in critical discussion with the Old Testament, may its result be positive or negative, can we elucidate the view of life which guides our
intention and action within our own history."[34] In this respect religious instruction is very important for the interpretation of the Old
Testament in the Church; and on the other hand the Old Testament is
very significant for religious instruction, because it leads to a view of
life which is determined by this concept of history.

Second, we have to ask how the Old Testament is given us as
God's word that we are to hear and to obey. We have to deal with the
meaning of the Old Testament for the message of the Church. Before
we answer this question, we want to see how Bultmann relates the Old
Testament to the New Testament. According to him, we are wrong in
seeing the difference in such a way that in the Old Testament, law, in
the New Testament, grace is predominant. In the Old Testament, too,
the grace of Israel's election precedes and establishes law.[35] The Old
Testament, too, knows about faith, mercy, and God's forgiveness.[36]
"Yet the Israelite, although he may know about forgiveness, again
and again turns his hope to salvation, which is either understood as
political or as eschatological and more universal salvation. (Therefore the Jew nowadays still may say to the Christian: It is not possible that the Messiah has already come, for the world still needs
salvation.) But the meaning of the message, which preaches Jesus
Christ to be the very action of God, is that grace is nothing but
forgiveness, and that makes man new and strong."[37]

The Old Testament knows about the possibility of forgiving in
hope, the New Testament witnesses to it as something that happened
and is happening. Because of this restriction, because it has not got

---

[34] *Ibid.*, p. 324.
[35] *Ibid.*, p. 326 f.
[36] *Ibid.*, p. 327 ff.
[37] *Ibid.*, p. 331.

Jesus who is the "Word of God,"[38] the Old Testament is not directly the Word of God. Yet we may preach it. How is that possible?

What are we doing when we preach on an Old Testament text? First, we as the hearers of the word transfer it from the old situation to our situation. But then we interpret it with the trust and strength of our Christian faith, for example as the fulfillment of all that is told there in hope or as demand. "Faith therefore seizes the Old Testament and dares—in strength and with the right of faith—to direct the Old Testament sayings, once not spoken for us, to us, so that our situation is elucidated and we understand the words of Christ, spoken to our situation."[39]

"But when the Old Testament is received as God's word into the message of the church, the absolutely necessary condition is: 1) that the Old Testament is used in its original meaning, and without its original relation to the people of Israel and their history, that is without any allegory; 2) that the Old Testament is only received in so far as it is actually a promise, for example as it prepares the Christian understanding of existence. In so far we may say that Christ speaks already in the Old Testament."[40]

---

[38] *Ibid.*, pp. 292 f.
[39] *Ibid.*, p. 336.
[40] *Ibid.*, p. 336.

Contemporary Interpretation of the Gospels as a Challenge to Preaching and Religious Education*

MARTIN STALLMANN
The University of Göttingen
Göttingen, Germany

The preaching and teaching of the Church have always been influenced by scientific exegesis; the characteristic feature, however, of contemporary interpretation of the Gospels, on which attention is focused in the following pages, is that it raises fundamental questions about the nature of Christian proclamation and instruction and about the proper understanding of their place and role in church life.

This modern interpretation of the Gospels is inseparably associated with the name of Rudolf Bultmann. If one were to date its beginnings, one would have to refer to the articles Bultmann wrote during the middle 20's and to his *Jesus* (1926); its later development was accompanied by numerous publications by him. Yet one cannot call it a "Bultmannian" interpretation of the Gospels, for the approach and method developed in his exegetical work are not confined to a school of disciples, but dominate, at least as a problem, the entire German exegetical effort in so far as it is devoted to the New Testament, and have long since become familiar to the current theological generation even without Bultmann's direct influence.[1] In addition, both as

---

* Translated by Paul W. Meyer.

[1] Among those students of Bultmann who have turned to New Testament research, there is scarcely one who has not contributed to the interpretation of the Gospels: G. Bornkamm, H. Braun, H. Conzelmann, E. Dinkler, E. Fuchs, E. Käsemann, P. Vielhauer, and (from the perspective of systematics)

regards details of historical inquiry and in the extremely significant question of the "historical Jesus," such differences exist among the representatives of current gospel interpretation as to preclude the use of Bultmann's name as a general label. Despite these differences, however, one point of unity remains; church proclamation and religious instruction are compelled by this new exegesis to undertake serious self-examination.

I

Ever since the beginnings of New Testament research, the historical character of its documents has become ever more apparent. So far as the Gospels are concerned, this development took a decisive turn with the advent of form criticism. The differentiation of traditional from editorial materials and the quest for the literary types and *Sitz im Leben* of the individual pericopes, which were characteristic of this new method, produced no infallible criteria for determining "genuine" tradition, especially none for distilling an authentic tradition about Jesus. Instead, they compelled the further development of a *traditionsgeschichtliche* method which would not be satisfied simply to document changes as they occurred in the process of tradition but would press on to examine the motives behind such change.[2] The changes incurred by the tradition at the hands of the several Evan-

---

G. Ebeling. Of course these men continue to a degree the work of M. Dibelius, E. Lohmeyer, J. Schniewind and others. That the work of other scholars, such as W. G. Kümmel, W. Marxsen, J. M. Robinson, or E. Schweizer, belongs here also, goes without saying. The point is that the contemporary development is not a matter of a "school" or even of a sharply defined group of scholars. The label "kerygmatic theology" is occasionally used in a polemic sense, but only indicates that these writers are concerned with understanding the content of the New Testament as proclamation. What is characteristic of this group, however, is that in this effort the resources of historical research— historical criticism above all—are fully utilized, whereas the designation "kerygmatic" would apply also to such a treatment of the texts as is exemplified by G. Wingren, who expressly ascribes kerygmatic character to the material but whose own *heilsgeschichtliche* interpretation of the New Testament remains relatively untouched by historical criticism (*Die Predigt* [1955], p. 187 and *passim*).

[2] Alongside M. Dibelius' *Formgeschichte des Evangeliums* (English title: *From Tradition to Gospel*), the book most often cited in all gospel exegesis is Bultmann's *Die Geschichte der synoptischen Tradition* (*History of the Synoptic Tradition* [1921; 3rd ed., 1957]), a work which has never been superseded.

gelists turned out to depend not only upon varying distance in time
from the tradition's origins nor upon the differences long recognized
to exist between the Jewish-Christian and Gentile-Christian, or Palestinian and Hellenistic, churches. It was recognized that the Evangelists themselves had consciously shaped the tradition and given it
literary form. Their individual habits in editing and organizing the
material betrayed definite theological motives in such a way as to
bring more clearly to light the unique theological character not only
of the Fourth Gospel but also of the first three Gospels.[3] The
following observations regarding the Gospel of Mark will serve to
illustrate the nature of these theological motives.

As is well known, the confidence with which earlier investigators
had hoped to lay bare behind the Marcan Gospel a substratum
of reliable historical information about Jesus was first shaken by
W. Wrede's book, *The Messianic Secret of the Gospels* (1901). He
was the first to focus attention upon the procedures of the second
Evangelist, because he sought to explain the curious way in which the
latter incorporates the "injunctions to silence" into his narrative. No
one whose attention has once been called to it can fail to be
impressed by what Wrede observed and then traced to the theory of
the "Messianic secret." On the one hand, the Evangelist unmistakably treats the career of Jesus as the arena in which the final conflict
between God and the demonic powers takes place. He tells of
exorcisms and healings in which this struggle is victoriously carried
through; even the so-called "conflict narratives" (Mark 3:1–6, 22–
30; 2:1–12), which are connected with healing miracles and which
culminate in a saying of Jesus, portray the same drama. On the other
hand, wherever Jesus' authority comes clearly into view, it is sup-
pressed with a command to silence. Jesus does not wish recognition
as Messiah; he encounters profound misunderstanding not only from
the people but from his very disciples (4:40 f.; 6:52; 8:16 ff.; 9:10,
32). Even his parables are intentionally enigmatic; they are aimed at
rendering their hearers obdurate, and they are explained only for the

---

[3] Cf. Bultmann's characterization of the individual Gospels in *Tradition*, pp.
362 ff., and in his *Theologie des Neuen Testaments* (1953), § 54, pp. 464 ff.
For the separate Gospels, cf., for Luke: H. Conzelmann, *Die Mitte der Zeit*
(1954; 3rd ed., 1961; English title: *The Theology of St. Luke*); for Mark:
W. Marxsen, *Der Evangelist Markus* (1956); for Matthew: G. Bornkamm
et al., Überlieferung und Auslegung im Matthäusevangelium (1960).

benefit of the disciples (4:10 ff.). This combination of the theme of the manifestation of Jesus' Messianic authority with the motif of the Messianic secret imparts to the Evangelist's presentation a uniquely contradictory flavor. The aptness of M. Dibelius' characterization of the Gospel of Mark as "a book of secret epiphanies" is widely recognized.

To explain these features Wrede drew upon pragmatic historical considerations. He held that Mark needed to explain to his readers why Jesus was believed to be the Messiah only after Easter; to meet this need, Mark put forth the theory that Jesus himself did not wish to be recognized as Messiah and for that reason had in fact not been. In actual fact, Jesus' earthly career had possessed no observable Messianic traits. It was in the gospel account that his activity on earth was first represented as that of the Son of God. In producing this representation, however, Mark was not able without resulting contradiction to combine the historical actualities of Jesus' career—and what was remembered of them—with the conceptions of Jesus' Messianic authority which had in the meantime become current in the Christian community. In contrast to this position of Wrede, more recent exegesis attempts to interpret the secrecy motif by means of more theological considerations. It regards "the theory of the 'Messianic secret' no longer as a purely literary phenomenon but as a materially necessary expression of a faith in a Messiah who is distinguished by his 'incognito.' "[4] J. Schniewind has gone so far in stressing the significance of the Messianic secret as to define Synoptic exegesis in general as its elaboration.[5] This is related to his attempt to understand the Messianic secret as history rather than as a theory of the Evangelist; departing from Wrede's formulation of the concept, Schniewind found "Messiahship as a mystery" proclaimed in every pericope of the gospel.[6]

---

[4] Bultmann, *Tradition*, p. 373.

[5] J. Schniewind, "Zur Synoptikerexegese," *ThR*, N. F., II (1930), 186.

[6] J. Schniewind, *Das Evangelium nach Markus, NTD*, I (1933), pp. 40, 54, and *passim;* "Messiasgeheimnis und Eschatologie," *Nachgelassene Reden und Aufsätze* (1952). Practically nowhere in German research is historicity in the proper sense assigned to the Messianic secret; yet this is widely done among English New Testament scholars. Cf. the survey given by H. Conzelmann in *RGG* (3rd ed.), III, col. 621. For a critique, cf. Bultmann, *Theologie* § 4, 4, pp. 32 f.; Conzelmann, *op. cit.,* col. 632 f.; W. Marxsen, "Messiasgeheimnis," *Evang. Kirchen-Lexikon,* II (1958), col. 1311 ff.

For the majority of scholars the Messianic secret, in the sense in which Wrede identified it as a technique employed by the second Evangelist for his exposition, remains an historical problem. Its solution depends upon the general picture of Christian origins which the historian draws from the sources. Yet an interpretative solution is required if the Gospel of Mark is to be made intelligible enough so that it will have something to say to the man of today. This example is particularly well suited to illustrate the relationship in which the reconstruction of past history stands to the interpretation of the New Testament documents in the latest phase of gospel exegesis: the reconstruction does not exist in a realm of its own which can be considered or just as well ignored, but serves instead as an indispensable aid in exegesis.[7] The Messianic secret is no longer regarded as a theory by which Mark attempted to reconcile authentic traditions about Jesus with the Church's beliefs regarding the Christ. It is more readily intelligible on the supposition that the tradition was already shaped by the Church's faith when it reached Mark and that Mark, in applying the secrecy motif to it, was interested in giving expression to a particular understanding of revelation.[8] Even before Mark the Hellenistic Church had come, by means of the exorcism and miracle narratives, to represent Jesus as invested with divine power, a *theios aner* who identified himself by his deeds as Son of God.[9] For Mark as well, the title "Son of God" is the primary predication of sovereignty. In his Gospel, it is God himself who applies the title to Jesus at the Baptism and the Transfiguration. The demons, too, know it belongs to him, yet they and those who are healed are forbidden by Jesus to "reveal" him. What they cry out, no one else hears. After Peter's confession and the Transfiguration, even the disciples are enjoined by Jesus to remain silent regarding his identity. When Jesus himself acknowledges it before the Sanhedrin, he is condemned to death for doing so. The only human being to call Jesus Son of God in the entire Gospel of Mark is the centurion after the crucifixion, and he does so not because as a Gentile he had occasion to observe anything special about Jesus' divinity in the moment of his dying, but rather because

---

[7] Bultmann, *Theologie,* "Epilegomena," pp. 470 f.

[8] H. Conzelmann, *ZThK,* LIV (1957), 293–295.

[9] Bultmann, *Theologie,* §12, 3, pp. 128 f.

the Evangelist wishes to make it clear that Jesus' divine sonship is revealed at the point of its most profound concealment, Jesus' victory over the powers won in the moment of his death. In contrast to his narrative tradition, the Evangelist seeks with his secrecy motif to validate just such a faith, which, like the Pauline theology,[10] regards precisely the unknown, misunderstood, condemned, and crucified Jesus as the Son of God. Because Mark can do this only with effort and not without violence, his editorial hand becomes recognizable to us, and with it also his theological motivation. His aim is to attest the fact that the victory of the Son of God cannot be known or ascertained by criteria drawn from a human notion of what constitutes divine superiority but is concealed under a directly opposite set of terms.

II

When the Messianic secret is understood in such terms, an affinity between Mark and John becomes apparent. As Bultmann has pointed out, the Johannine portrayal of Jesus' ministry can be understood as a continuation and elaboration of Mark's secrecy theory.[11] The difference lies only in the fact that John consistently understands the concealment as based upon revelation itself: the entire human ministry of Jesus of Nazareth is a revelation of his divinity precisely by creating offense; revelation is revelation only by calling human criteria for divine action into question; for John it is precisely Jesus' "exaltation" on the Cross which is the high point of revelation.

One cannot deny, of course, the fact that Mark treats the tradition about Jesus quite differently from John, who obviously does with it pretty much as he likes. The impartial reader finds himself closer in Mark to the historical tradition and is compelled here, as in the case of the Synoptics generally, to regard their tradition as indispensable for the recognition of Jesus' identity as Son of God. That Jesus is the Son of God is by all appearances subject to documentation by a whole series of miraculous events, which are presented within a biographical framework along with certain chronological and geo-

---

[10] J. Schreiber, "Die Christologie des Markusevangeliums," *ZThK*, LVIII (1961), 154 ff.

[11] Bultmann, *Theologie* § 46, 5, pp. 394 ff. and *Glauben und Verstehen*, II (1952), 260 ff.

graphical indications. Very quickly the reader discovers to his sur-
prise that Jesus' contemporaries did not know who really encountered
them in spite of all the things that transpired before their eyes. But
this is just the Evangelist's way of making clear that no universally
accepted criteria are available which can be applied to Jesus as the
Son of God. The presupposition for knowledge of him as such is his
Resurrection (Mark 9:9). No one can be expected to believe in him
as the Son of God until after Easter. Easter here does not stand for a
given fact in the advancing course of world history, but opens up a
new possibility for speaking about Jesus, namely the mode which
Mark himself employs. Mark is aware of writing after Easter, in a
fashion made possible only by Easter. That Jesus, whom eyewitnesses
did not recognize despite all his miracles, in whom the disciples did
not believe, whom the world's authorities condemned to death,
should be the one in whom God has acted and still acts, is something
that could be asserted only after God himself had substantiated this
life as his own Word. Mark expects his readers to believe in God's
action in the life of Jesus, but the point of reference he offers them
for this faith is only his own word to them and not the reliability of
eyewitnesses. He does not expect his readers to know Jesus as the
Son of God on the basis of his reports; he demands that they
recognize him for what he is, even though Mark's own account
expressly denies the existence of any unambiguous objective evidence
to support this demand. His account thereby repeats the challenge
posed for faith by the Cross of Jesus: to believe in God's presence at
the point where the hiddenness of his revelation is maintained.

This peculiarity of the Evangelist's historical narrative we have
been describing is often referred to as its "kerygmatic" dimension. By
this is meant that what the Evangelist wishes to say is not communicated to the reader by way of information, indoctrination, or instruction, but by a kind of proclamation, i.e., by an appeal which elicits
reaction and decision. Kerygma refers to a word which has become
personal address and which as such condemns unbelief and establishes faith. The kerygmatic character of his Gospel involves Mark
both in adhering to the central assertion of his miracle narratives,
namely that Jesus is the Son of God, and at the same time in
qualifying the manner in which Jesus had acted out his divine sonship
according to the tradition. The content of his message is only the

assertion that the man Jesus of Nazareth is God's Son. *How* this was so is not intended to have any basic bearing on Mark's proclamation. How is the pagan centurion under Jesus' Cross supposed to be aware of the human or "superhuman" nature of the crucified? What prompts Mark to write a gospel at all is not a desire to recall how Jesus' divine nature manifested itself everywhere in his earthly actions, but the fact that Jesus' human life must be *proclaimed* to be the locus of divine action if it is to be *believed* as such. The occasion for Mark's writing is provided in the fact that the prior tradition had so completely deified Jesus' earthly activity, as though every spectator must have discerned his identity. This tendency is what Mark opposes when he introduces the secrecy motif into the narrative tradition. Faith does not consist for him in simply heeding what is universally accepted as God's action, but penetrates behind such appearances and lives, in fact, by overcoming the natural human distaste for what is not perceptible and apparent; that is why it is dependent upon the summons of preaching contained in the Gospel. Herein lies the eschatological character of Jesus' life for Mark, for this life does not simply confirm what men have always expected of God but overturns the whole system of human criteria and conceptions, of human desires, claims, and hopes. Man's system must be destroyed if man himself is to be redeemed.

All of the Evangelists have as their aim the assertion of this eschatological dimension in the life of Jesus and accordingly write in a kerygmatic, proclamatory vein. To this end they have in various ways subordinated the Church's tradition about Jesus to their proclaiming intent. It is perfectly clear they never supposed God's redemptive action in Jesus' earthly career to be something they could simply pass on in the form of historical narrative. They narrate, but each Evangelist attempts in so doing to illustrate in the clearest way possible the decision of faith which his proclamation calls for. That they employ narrative at all is due only to the fact that their message affirms the humanity of Jesus of Nazareth to be revelatory, but each Evangelist is free to present the manner and style of this humanity in his own way. The fact of the humanity itself, "the fact that eschatological salvation has become historical,"[12] is what each one in his

---

[12] Bultmann, *Theologie*, § 54, 3, pp. 470 f.

own way illustrates in his narratives. This same central assertion is made by Paul, without any illustrative material, as the central core in the story of Jesus.[13] The early Christians "were agreed that the history of Jesus was constitutive for faith because the earthly and the heavenly Lord are the same";[14] yet they held this conviction in such a way that they "allowed most of the historical events of Jesus' life to slip into oblivion and to be supplanted by the message."[15]

In view of all this, it is perfectly understandable that the impartial reader of the Gospels should come to the conclusion that their aim is to undergird Christian faith with historical reports and validate preaching with history. The truth is, however, just the reverse; the Evangelists begin with the certainty of Easter faith and on this basis put traditional narratives to the service of preaching. Their narratives are relevant and important only to the extent that they can be passed on with this kerygmatic purpose. "The Synoptics have not combined historical narrative and kerygmatic Christology in order to prove the latter from the former, but in order *vice versa* to 'demonstrate' the Messianic character of Jesus' life by causing the light of kerygmatic Christology to play upon it."[16] Modern exegetes of the Gospels have on the whole been surprised at the remarkable discovery which has crowned their labor, at the fact that "historical criticism has not emerged as it originally expected with the historical Jesus but instead has come upon the early Christian kerygma as the primary *datum* of the gospel tradition."[17] Along with this amazement goes a serious effort to make the methodological revisions required by such a discovery.

---

[13] *Ibid.*, § 33, 1, p. 289. Since 1929 at least, Bultmann has repeatedly pointed out that Christian proclamation can only concern itself with the fact of Jesus' historicity and cannot rest upon any particular historically ascertainable details of his activity, e.g., *Glauben und Verstehen*, I (1933), 205 ff., 265 ff. Recently he has defended this thesis once more in the face of attempts to validate the Christian kerygma by demonstrating its continuity with the "historical Jesus"; *Das Verhältnis der urchristlichen Christusbotschaft zum historischen Jesus* (Sitzungsber. Heidelberg. Akad. Wiss., phil.-hist. Kl., 1960, No. 3).

[14] E Käsemann, "Das Problem des historischen Jesus," *ZThK*, LI (1954), 141.

[15] *Ibid.*, p. 129.

[16] Bultmann, *Das Verhältnis der urchristlichen Christusbotschaft*, p. 13.

[17] Käsemann, *op. cit.*, p. 131.

III

New Testament scholars have often themselves formulated the theological consequences of their historical research and their interpretation of the Gospels. One result is that the Christology of the early Church, a target of historical criticism from its beginnings, has been subjected to extraordinarily sharp scrutiny. The titles for Jesus which appear in the New Testament do not make objectifying statements about Jesus' nature or describe his abstract attributes. They rather acknowledge his meaning for faith and single him out as the eschatological event—which is not a predication made of him on the basis of definite and demonstrable characteristics but designates what he is in proclamation, and only there.[18] Patristic Christology thus finds itself under attack not only in the normal course of fresh historical discovery but also in the name of the purity and unity of the faith called for by the kerygma. The Christian message does not require first a faith prepared to subscribe to certain assertions about Jesus' essential nature, and then another faith by which the sinner confesses to justification by grace; it does not consist of a stage of indoctrination followed by another in which faith in its proper sense is finally called for.[19] The redemptive event cannot be objectively described in order then to be subjectively appropriated. All such objectivations belie the fact that Christian proclamation invites faith in the living God as man's salvation and not in propositional truths. If faith is to be kept pure, it cannot look for salvation to be realized anywhere but in the proclamation in which God authenticates himself in his Word.[20]

Along with the repudiation of such dogmatism, a further result of the contemporary trend is the rejection of the methods of liberal theology, which hopes by historical verification to arrive at the object of faith. Modern research has destroyed the notion—together with all the false hopes it engendered—that historical inquiry can produce a

---

18 Bultmann, *Glauben und Verstehen,* II, 246 ff.

19 Bultmann, *Theologie,* § 33, 4–5, pp. 295 ff.

20 "The redemptive event is only present in the word of preaching, the word of address and claim and promise," Bultmann, in citing II Cor. 5:18 f., *ibid,* p. 297.

reliable account of Jesus' personal history, or that a relationship of memory can be established with Jesus' life or message or ministry in order to provide a basis for faith.[21] An historically traceable continuity exists between Jesus' message and the preaching of the early Christians, but no continuity between the humanity of Jesus and the Christ of proclamation exists which can be conveyed by tradition and exhibited by historical investigation. Nothing that can be observed in Jesus' career or uncovered by historical inquiry can explain the fact that Jesus the preacher turns out to be the Jesus Christ proclaimed by faith. Christian preaching about the eschatological presence of God in the man Jesus of Nazareth cannot be proved historically.

On the positive side, this more recent interpretation of the Gospels appeals repeatedly and expressly to the Reformation teaching about *fides ex auditu* and to the general Reformation understanding of the Word of God. The distinctive insight of Reformation theology, that salvation is imparted through the spoken word, reappears in the contemporary "identification of word-event and redemptive-event."[22] In this sense Bultmann has expressly claimed that the Reformers' doctrine of justification naturally leads one to resist every attempt to objectivate God's salvation, to make his action visible or subject to the determinative power of cognition. He who wishes to believe in God as his God cannot and must not seek authentication for the word of address. "For the ground and the object of faith are identical."[23]

I V

Our survey of recent gospel exegesis shows, without further ado, how it has served to emphasize the church's preaching as the sole support of faith, a result which is reconfirmed at every point in the actual execution of exegetical analysis. What takes place in proclamation is the judgment and mercy of God, the dawning of God's day and faith's "today"; in it the One is present who reconciles men with God.

The significance of this new emphasis only becomes clear when

---

[21] Bultmann, *Glauben und Verstehen,* I (1938), 245 ff.
[22] G. Ebeling, *Wort und Glaube* (1960), p. 431; cf. pp. 326 ff. and *passim.*
[23] R. Bultmann, in H. W. Bartsch (ed.), *Kerygma und Mythos,* II (1952), 207.

one considers the change it involves in the relationship between exegesis and preaching.[24] In the period of orthodoxy, the role of exegesis was to distill from the text the dogmatic truth contained therein and to deliver this to the preacher, who in turn was to teach it to the congregation and use it as a basis for his exhortation. The historical approach to the New Testament, interested in the background environment of the text, asked of exegesis only that it identify the original meaning or the "historical kernel" of a given passage; it fell to the preacher to seek the eternal meaning of this ancient material and to establish and communicate its "practical" bearing on his contemporaries. Such "practical" exposition, oriented around contemporary needs and problems or the issues of the moment, became all too easily divorced from methodological and scholarly analysis. In addition, within the development of the scientific disciplines, a "purely historical" approach, seeking to arrive at its conclusions in purely objective fashion without any presuppositions, turned out to be a fiction. Historical tradition needs to be analyzed critically. The analyst, however, is motivated not just by curiosity regarding past occurrence but also by an interest in what the human beings mentioned in the tradition experienced and how they understood themselves as a result of those experiences. Because modern man is moved by questions of his own history, he seeks to establish an existential contact with the tradition; in the dialogue which results he receives insight into the decisions which confront him in his own history.

On this understanding of man's relation to tradition rest the aims of an "existentialist interpretation,"[25] which interprets documents of past history in the light of human existential possibilities. Such an interpretation seeks thus to illumine the self-understanding which manifests itself in historical testimony that contemporary man finds himself personally addressed by his encounter with the past and compelled to response.

---

[24] Cf. G. Ebeling, "Wort Gottes und Hermeneutik," *Wort und Glaube* (1960), pp. 319 ff.; E. Fuchs, *Zur Frage nach dem historischen Jesus* (1960), pp. 55 ff. and 405 ff.

[25] Bultmann, *Glauben und Verstehen,* II, pp. 231 ff.; *Kerygma und Mythos,* II, 189 ff. Cf. also E. Fuchs, *Hermeneutik* (1954), pp. 55 ff. and *passim;* "Zum hermeneutischen Problem in der Theologie," *Die existentiale Interpretation* (1959).

It is a mistake, though a common one, to suppose that such interpretation attempts to bridge the gap between the text and preaching in the same way as did the earlier dogmatic or historical exposition. This is to misunderstand not only this interpretation but even more the nature of proclamation. Existentialist interpretation regards itself as scientific exegesis like the others; it discloses but it cannot create the bearing of a given text upon the reader's existence. Its function is not to bring proclamation, God's speaking, into being but rather to aid it in finding its proper language.[26] As G. Ebeling has formulated it, exegesis deals with "proclamation that *has* taken place"; preaching is "proclamation that *is* taking place." The latter is not so much exposition of the text as "putting it into execution," i.e., a carrying out of the proclamation intended by the text.[27] *What* is preached is not the text itself but Jesus Christ as the living Lord. The encounter with proclamation that *has* taken place, be it by historical reconstruction or by existentialist interpretation, invariably has the effect of law; I can only accept the fact that I must believe if I am to be saved. But preaching that *is* taking place is gospel; it calls for faith by offering it to me as a gift; it solicits and invites me to believe.[28] When this happens, the word spoken in the Church's preaching is known to be the work of God himself. Scientific exegesis helps the preacher *not* to stand in the way of this divine work; and in this critical role, by cutting off all would-be attempts to actualize or distribute a past salvation, it is indispensable to the preacher today. To repudiate the historical approach and to appeal directly to the witness of the Gospels, on the grounds that they were after all intended to be read as testimonies of faith, may seem to enhance their authority but really does not. Actually this only establishes the authority of a blindly accepted tradition and disturbs that real congruity with the witness of scripture which is in fact indispensable for the preacher. Modern exegesis of the Gospels has made it clear that an interpretative repetition of the text is not by itself the

---

[26] Bultmann, *Kerygma und Mythos,* II, 189. Cf. his *Das Verhältnis der urchristlichen Christusbotschaft,* pp. 18 ff.

[27] Ebeling, *Wort und Glaube* (1960) p. 347.

[28] Bultmann, *Das Verhältnis der urchristlichen Christusbotschaft,* p. 25, n. 79.

preaching of the Word of God. It can be said, of course, that the Evangelists all "repeat" the gospel, but they do this by narrating, in a fresh way, traditional material that has come to them as kerygma, not by reproducing or repeating in their own words a past occurrence or a traditional version thereof. They know their own authority derives not from their individual and personal piety but from the fact that they themselves have been visited by God's address. This visitation sustains their preaching as it sustains preaching generally in every age. Hence preaching has its origin in the experience of hearing the Word of God, has its place in the Church, and has its ground and warrant and authority in God's real presence in the Holy Spirit. This is the reason for the preacher's custom of closing his sermon with "Amen," to express his confident hope in divine endorsement.

Modern gospel exegesis thus entails in the first place a *formal* definition of the preaching task. Exegesis does not supply the content of preaching or hold preaching in a state of helpless dependence upon its results. In particular details, of course, exegesis has always contributed materially to preaching; but what preaching urgently needs is to secure from that proclamation which the Gospels expressly claim to be, an understanding of its own task and with this a criterion for its own integrity. It cannot be simply taken for granted that what poses today as preaching is really Christian proclamation. Preachers are always prone to accommodate themselves to the needs of the times or of their congregations and to get involved in the moral and religious stresses with which they deal. In so doing, there is the danger of superficially evaluating these needs and supposing they can be met either by dispensing a bit of advice drawn from Christian dogmatics or ethics or a Christian world view, or else by recalling certain exemplary figures from Christian history. When this happens, it is forgotten that the Church's real treasure is the Word of God, and as a result man's need for this Word goes undetected. To avoid such "secularization,"[29] whether threatening or actual, preaching needs to be continually reminded by the New Testament of the task of proclamation, namely to provide a vehicle in human expression for God himself in his judgment and mercy.

---

[29] R. Bultmann, "Echte und säkularisierte Verkündigung im 20. Jahrhundert," *Glauben und Verstehen,* III (1960), 120 ff.

V

The redefinition of preaching required by the New Testament, including the Gospels, affects also the relation between preaching and
religious education. Where faith is understood in terms of assent to
propositional or dogmatic truths, the difference between preaching
and teaching is only one of procedure: the sermon communicates
single truths, whereas religious instruction seeks, by means of a
logically and systematically organized series of lessons, to introduce
the pupil to the entire body of Christian doctrine. So far as the
training of children goes, this kind of instruction has been almost
everywhere replaced with lesson material dominated by the Biblical
narratives. This latter type of curriculum has become increasingly
divorced from preaching, if for no other reason than because the
personality features characteristic of the age levels of children and
young people are taken into account. More important, however, is the
confidence with which psychological insights are applied within it to
plan a graded course of instruction which will realize with maximum
certainty of success the goal of leading the child from simple perception through reasoned concepts to applied principles of behavior.
What is determinative for the relationship of such graded instruction
to preaching is the fact that it is aimed at the effect produced in the
pupil; it is intended to bring about the subjective appropriation of the
objective and historically transmitted material of Christian faith. The
attempt is to cultivate Christians pedagogically by employing Biblical
materials as a means for the development of "personal Christianity."
The history of God's dealings with man is thus supposed to set in
motion a new history of man's dealings with God. In the presentation
of the Biblical narratives, the teacher projects himself and his pupils
into the Biblical story; in the subsequent discussion and engagement,
sometimes referred to as the stage of "proclamation," the pupils
project the sacred story into their own lives.[30]

Now this pedagogical procedure can be followed as long as the
graphic portrayal of historical events from which it starts is undisturbed, but it becomes impossible the moment historical truth poses
critical questions and casts any doubt on this portrayal—regardless of

---

[30] G. Schmidt, *Katechetische Anleitung* (1946), p. 66.

whether such doubt is entertained only by the teacher or also awakened at a given point in the pupil. In either case, no apologetic resources suffice to restore again the historical credibility required wherever religious instruction rests upon the authority of vivid factuality.

Religious education has hesitated to face the consequences of historical criticism. It continues widely to believe in the possibility of teaching as though the authority, and hence also the historical statements, of the Bible remained unchallenged. Where historical studies are recognized, it tries to utilize them to convey a modicum of historical fact and thus to sustain the notion that it can impart the fundamentals of Christianity by confronting the student with events and documents out of the past. But where, as a result of historical research, the kerygma turns out to provide the creative reality and the molding power of Christian tradition, an education which is aimed in such a manner at a formative encounter with history loses its force. Inexorably pedagogy is pursued more and more by the question of what the appeal to Jesus is supposed to mean for Christian proclamation. Once Jesus is no longer revered as a personality, as an example, as a moral hero, as a teacher of eternal truths, as the founder of a new piety, or as a religious martyr, what is the nature of his claim? On what does its unconditional force rest? What can serve to make clear its warrant?

In line with all that has been said so far, religious education is driven at this point to refer to preaching. The question about the meaning of the early Christian kerygma can be answered pedagogically only by reference to the Church as the place where the scandal of God's incarnation and the Revealer's crucifixion is currently perpetuated. Such reference is not to the Church as an institution, as though the latter could in any way contribute to the credibility of the gospel or to the support of truth. Mobilizing such sociological factors as congregational *esprit* or church membership is no more capable of nourishing religious instruction than is organizational contact with ecclesiastical commissions. The point of orientation for religious education is not the Church as a buttress of faith but the Church as itself an object of faith. For it is in the unpretentious word event of preaching that contact with Jesus of Nazareth as the guarantor of God's truth is concretely established. Religious education cannot ask of the Church more than this concrete actualization of the kerygma. It must not allow itself to be enticed into bypassing the sermon in the search for an independent appropriation of the gospel.

The task of religious education is defined in the person of the sermon listener. He wants to understand what the Christian message attributes to him and what happens to him in faith. The content of the message is not a mythical account of a miraculous act performed by God to save humanity but the truth which sets this man free from falsehood and delusion. It brings him light and life, so that he can comprehend himself anew in it. He can thank God for it, and he can ask in prayer to be upheld in the truth. The religious education of youth is to a particularly high degree a training in language; it deals with the concepts and ideas which the worshipper encounters in sermon and liturgy, in song and prayer. The task of interpreting this language involves teaching the student to discriminate; his attention is thus called to the strange language of preaching and with it to the strange claim couched therein.

Thus recent gospel exegesis affects the *formal* definition of the task also of religious instruction. As in the case of preaching, the importance of this conclusion should not be underestimated. Christian education, too, is in need of a critical standard which will enable it to become confident of its own integrity. Without such a standard it is tempted to find in success the verification of its methods, or else, in the absence of success, to doubt its own possibilities, to withdraw in resignation, or to grasp in despair at goals and methods which have allegedly been proved to be better. But scholarly exegetical investigation cannot be expected to provide more than a formal definition of the Church's educational task. It cannot prescribe methods or techniques for the execution of this task. The educator must not suppose that he has only to simplify and pass on to his students the interpretation offered by the historical scholar, a view that was prevalent early in this century when the *religionsgeschichtliche Schule* enjoyed its vogue. Nor on the other hand does contemporary gospel exegesis translate the reader back over the centuries, and thus set the educator, and anyone else who wishes, free to make of the "original" gospel what they please. It produces historical results, to which at any given stage it assigns the truth of probability. Christian education is not directly interested in these. But the discovery of the kerygmatic character of the texts and an understanding of what the concept "kerygma" at any point involves can never by divorced from an historical-critical analysis of the texts and is in fact reached only in the course of methodical exegesis. Exegetical analysis, in turn, depends upon certain conditions of its own which religious education cannot usually meet. On the other hand, the religious educator does not find his path marked out for him by the preacher, as though he had only to repeat or impress upon his pupils the work of the latter. The path which commends itself on internal grounds as the only right one is not marked out in advance for him at all. Education consists of exposing oneself to questions. What makes possible an inventive and yet conscientious search for new pedagogical possibilities is in the long run a loving devotion to the questioning pupil, the ceaseless effort to do justice to his questions, and an unrelenting candor on the part of the teacher about his own questions.

When religious education and homiletics face the challenge posed by the contemporary exegesis of the Gospels, when preacher and teacher in the course of following this exegesis encounter the kerygma and awaken to the unlikely suggestion that contemporary men are called upon to carry out this proclamation, then they will sense why Luther ended his preface to the Shorter Catechism of 1529 with the following words: "Therefore take note, O pastor and preacher, our office has become quite different from what it was under the Pope. Now it has become serious and beneficial, but in return it consists of much effort and labor, much danger and tribulation, and very little of reward and thanks in this world. Yet Christ wills to be himself our reward, if we but labor faithfully" (W. A. 30, I, 320).

II

REPLY TO INTERPRETATION
AND CRITICISM BY
RUDOLF BULTMANN

Reply*

RUDOLF BULTMANN
Marburg an der Lahn, Germany

Where shall I begin to answer the questions directed to me in the various essays, and in what order shall I take them?

Because the discussion of my theology was launched through the problem of demythologizing, I think I should begin with the article which treats this theme in particular. Because this problem is closely connected with my understanding of history, it seems natural to turn next to the articles concerning this aspect of my work. This in turn is closely connected with the interrelationship of history and philosophy; therefore I will have to respond next to those articles dealing with my understanding of philosophy. Next, I must concern myself with the articles about special questions of New Testament interpretation. And finally I must address myself to the essays dealing with the consequences of my theology for religious education and for the Church's preaching.

1. *Reply to Günther Bornkamm, "The Theology of Rudolf Bultmann."* Bornkamm says correctly that my theological work stems from two roots: (1) historical-critical research; (2) so-called dialectical theology, especially that of Karl Barth and Friedrich Gogarten. In fact, I have seen and still see it as my task to bind into a unity the intentions at work in that tradition and this movement. The possibility of doing this seems to me to be offered in a deepened

---

* Translated by Howard C. Kee.

understanding of the historicity of human life as it has been disclosed
to me, especially in the work of W. Dilthey, Count York, and Martin
Heidegger.

I can only be grateful for the characterization which Bornkamm
gives of my theological work; to it I need add nothing. It offers also a
correction of the misunderstandings with which Bornkamm expressly
takes issue in his account of the discussion which my work has
evoked. To this also I have nothing to add. I emphasize here only his
repudiation of the misunderstanding according to which I have turned
theology into anthropology and delivered up the Christian faith to
subjectivism. He rightly rebuts the charge that I deny the *skandalon*
(offense) of the once-for-all (*ephapax*) Romans 6:10.

His recognition of my fidelity to the tradition of the Reformers is
most clearly evident in his characterization of the reaction to my
work on the part of Catholic theology, which sees in my theology the
consistent carrying through of Luther's theology to the point of
absurdity. It is precisely in this carrying through, Bornkamm says,
that there is posed for Protestant theology the decisive question
whether it will turn back to a traditional metaphysic and to an
objectivizing understanding of revelation in order to provide a supposed certainty for faith.

Bornkamm rightly says that, with full appreciation for my theological intention, questions nevertheless remain open. Of course, he
limits himself to some subjects on which theological work must
always remain open: the themes of world, time, and history. I can
only say that to this list belongs also the relationship of faith to
destiny and to nature. But probably in Bornkamm's mind this is
already included under "world" and "history."

2. *Reply to Edwin M. Good, "The Meaning of Demythologization."* I appreciate the clarity and understanding with which Good
describes the meaning of demythologizing and characterizes its hermeneutical intention and importance. He sees correctly that the
presupposition of any interpretation is the preunderstanding which
has guided the question. Now the question directed at the New
Testament is, "How does the New Testament understand human
existence?" The appropriate interpretation, therefore, is existentialist.
Even though for such an interpretation I seek to show the fruitfulness

of the ontological analysis of Heidegger, I do not thereby make myself dependent on the philosophy of Heidegger, as Good clearly recognizes, since the goal of my existentialist interpretation is the existential understanding of the New Testament. To my delight, Good adduces Luther as a witness in behalf of this approach to interpretation. Also, Good recognizes the relevance of viewing as eschatological both the understanding of Christian existence achieved through my interpretation and the understanding of faith as decision for the future—free from any objective guarantee—on the ground of the encounter with the grace of God. The question, then is not whether, but how to demythologize.

This is the point at which Good's questions come in. The first is whether my definition of myth is correct, inasmuch as I conclude that any direct speaking of God is mythological, and therefore impossible. He asks whether I do not myself use mythological concepts when I speak of the action of God and his transcendence. I should like to reply that talk which concerns the activity of God is analogical. It seeks to express that the being confronted by God has its origin in God alone and that man in his relations with God is only the passive, the receiving one. The case is similar in speaking of the concept of the transcendence of God. God is not beyond the world in a spatial sense, but beyond the world within which I find myself, which I seek to grasp through my thought and searching and can in this way comprehend, to which I belong in my natural life, which I myself establish through my will and plans. If I may put it sharply, God is beyond the world which I myself am. I can also say that God's otherworldliness means that he in relation to my world is nothingness, just as to those without faith he must appear as nothing. But I must say further that the God who is beyond the world encounters me in my world—where what I receive is as a pure gift—above all in man's living with his fellow man. But also he encounters me in that which shakes me to the depths, that is, which brings me to naught and precisely thereby frees me from myself and thus from the world. My understanding of myth will not prohibit me from speaking of God in images, for instance in songs which praise God, thank him, or ask of him. In a word, the existential meaning of symbolic language must be grasped.

Good's second question is whether the phenomenological analysis

of existence is possible without faith, inasmuch as it strives to see
man as he really is. Does it not therefore presuppose faith? Here one
must make a differentiation. The existentialist analysis as Heidegger
has presented it is only possible since and because there has been in
history such a thing as Christian faith. Heidegger himself is influenced
by Paul, Augustine, Luther, and Kierkegaard. However, the understanding of human existence first achieved through faith can be
secularized and existentialist analysis carried on without faith. Can,
then, only faith recognize the question of authenticity or inauthen-
ticity of existence? Another question naturally concerns the *realization* of authenticity. On that matter only faith has the answer.

The third question is whether the historical Jesus has not been
eliminated through the kerygmatic Christ, since the latter is proclaimed only as an eschatological phenomenon. To this I should like
to reply: (1) the proclamation of the historical Jesus must be
absorbed by the kerygma, even if, as Luther thought, it is only the
proclamation of the law. There is after all no understanding of the
gospel without the law—the law in the radical form in which Jesus
proclaimed it. (2) Faith stresses the paradoxical identity of an
historical event and the eschatological event. If the historical Jesus
were eliminated, then the paradox would be destroyed and the
kerygmatic Christ would be reduced to a mythological figure.

The fourth question is whether or not I ignore the Christian
fellowship—the Church—when I understand faith as the encounter
of the individual with God. Is not the encounter with God possible
only in the fellowship where faith in God is living and preached? Here
I agree with Good. Faith is faith in the Word of God which
encounters me through the preaching of it, and preaching occurs only
in the Church. Even if I were to say that the Word of God can
encounter me in the Bible apart from its actualization in the empirical
church, I should still have to add that the Bible is given to me only
through the church tradition. However, I should now have to say also
that the preaching of God's word encounters me only as an individual, and as an individual I must respond. As no one can die for
me, so no one can believe for me. Yet, just as God's speaking to me
reaches me from within the community—that is, from the Scripture
which is transmitted through the community—in the same way it calls
me into the fellowship. I should like to add: the preaching of the

community enables me to participate in the eschatological event that has its origin in Jesus. This eschatological event is, in its paradoxical identity with the historical event, never a bygone event, but it is fulfilled again and again in the preaching of the Church. Just as certainly as the Church is a phenomenon in world history, it is at the same time an eschatological phenomenon.

3. *Reply to H. P. Owen, "Revelation."* In the first part of his article, Owen describes impartially and accurately my understanding of revelation. I am especially grateful that, in view of misunderstandings, he shows how my concept of myth and demythologizing is determined by my understanding of revelation—in that I understand myth as an attempt to objectivize God and his action, and that from this viewpoint I come to the task of demythologizing.

There is one thing, however, that I miss in his characterization of my concept of revelation, and it is indeed a decisive matter. He does not take sufficiently into account my thesis that the Christian faith asserts that an historical event—that is, Jesus' launching of his ministry, his activities and his fate—is the eschatological event. This omission explains why he subjects my understanding of revelation to a criticism which is in part expansion, in part contradiction.

He thinks he should first raise the objection that I, in dependence on Kant, Schleiermacher, and the liberal theology of the nineteenth century, do not see subjective faith in its connection with its objective basis, and that as a result I view preaching as the act of revelation. But, as I have tried to show, the danger that the hearing will be understood as a merely subjective action of the hearer is avoided if the preaching is so understood that in it the eschatological event (Jesus Christ) is being fulfilled constantly in the present. In the encounter that is brought about through the preaching there is achieved a new self-understanding, which is at the same time the recognition that it is the action of God.

That such recognition can be displayed in theological statements, I do not deny. I nevertheless pose the question as to what extent such statements of traditional dogmatics are a legitimate presentation of the knowledge of God which is disclosed in faith. It is my view that traditional dogmatics should be interpreted existentially as well.

Neither do I deny that God bears witness to himself in nature, or

that non-Christian religions were and are partially a revelation of
God. But I think that this can only be expressed as a judgment of
Christian faith. One can in fact say this: the non-Christian questions
concerning God and the efforts to provide an answer show that God
"reveals" himself even outside the Christ event and Christian preaching. But I think that the idea of the revelation of God must be so
strictly understood that one may designate as revelation only the
thinking about, reflecting upon, and encountering of, God's action,
which cannot be directed by man, but which reaches man as an event
from beyond himself and beyond everything within the perspective of
Christian faith.

Owen's chief objection to my position is that I deny the epiphany
of the divine in the historical Jesus. In response to this I can only
point to the paradox mentioned above (and in other essays in this
book), that is, to the Christian faith's paradoxical identification of an
historical event with an eschatological event. From my side I can only
ask Owen the question: What is there about the historical Jesus that
lifts his incognito and allows him to be seen as the epiphany of the
divine? Are there objective criteria for this? Such criteria could be
exhibited only by objectivizing historical science. And is faith in Jesus
Christ as historical event dependent upon historical science?

4. *Reply to Heinrich Ott, "Rudolf Bultmann's Philosophy of
History."* Ott presents my conception of history and of historicity in a
manner which displays understanding. He sees correctly that it does
not lead to nihilism if one refuses to make the question concerning
the meaning of history one which concerns the meaning of the entire
course of history. Then the meaning of history lies in the present and
can at any time be found in it. Even though Ott's presentation is thus
far accurate, I must add two observations:

(1) When I have said that any moment has within it the possibility of being an eschatological Now, I have spoken of the *ontological* possibility. That Ott has not distinguished this from the *ontic*
actualization is perhaps my own fault. In my *History and Eschatology,* to which Ott has made reference throughout, I have not made
clear the distinction between the ontological possibility and the ontic
actualization as it takes place in Christian faith. Only when this
distinction is clearly in view will it also be fully clear (as Ott has

actually correctly observed) that my presentation of the historicity of human existence (*Dasein*) does not seek to provide a historical-philosophical undergirding for the Christian faith, but rather to show that the revelation of God focuses on the reality in which we live. To Ott's statement that this reality can thus be more deeply understood, I should add that the insight into the historicity of *Dasein* (being there) can also understand revelation as the Word which strikes reality.

(2) Ott is of the opinion in his concluding critical section that my understanding of history is trapped in an individualistic outlook when I say that the meaning of history is contained in the moment of any particular decision. He thinks there is a contradiction involved when I speak of the responsibility which man has toward the heritage of the past as well as toward the task posed for him by the future. But have I ever left any doubt that the responsible decision which is to be made at any given moment is a decision related to both past and future? Ott should have made this point right at the outset when he was presenting my view of historicity. It is part of the ontological understanding of history.

To Ott's presentation of my view of hermeneutics I have nothing to add. We are obviously of one mind when Ott explains my concept of preunderstanding as grounded in a living relationship to the thing which is being interpreted and when he sees the overcoming of historical positivism in the recognition that any historical phenomenon has its own future in which it proves itself to be what in fact it is.

In this connection, however, I must deal with the charge that I have not clarified the meaning of historical causality, which obviously is to be distinguished from the causality of natural events. As a matter of fact, I have not done that expressly. I think I have done it indirectly, however, in that I have said that the true subject of history is man, and we can speak of history in the true sense only in an instance where the subjects of the event are men, who, as beings of consciousness and will, are differentiated from nature. Thus I can simply say that the causality of history is human will, which calls forth actions, which in turn set in motion historical events. I am using the term "actions" in the wider sense to include human reactions to accidental occurrences, and therefore to events which do not originate in the will. But such reactions are nevertheless also actions. I could express it in the terminology of Toynbee: they are responses to a challenge. Of course it is clear that the motives of willing and acting are different and may grow out of very different situations. However, that implies no differentiation of causalities. Basically, one may say that the causality of history is the conscious and willing action of man. One could ask whether the concept of causality is not primarily an *historical* matter. Is not the understanding of a natural event as causally conditioned a secondary matter derived from what man experiences with regard to the intentions and consequences of his own will and action?

The decisive question which Ott directs to me is this: "Is it a 'mere boundary conception' if I speak of the end of history in which the meaning of all historical events will be perceptible? Or must one reckon ontically, i.e., actually, with such a qualified end of history, that is, with an end in which the meaning of all events is revealed?"

In fact, I do not reckon with such an end. If I say that the question concerning the meaning of history is meaningless because the meaning can be revealed only at the end of history, I have in view the question concerning the meaning of history which presents a teleological understanding of history, that is, the question concerning the meaning of the whole course of history. My objective is to throw this very question concerning the meaning of history back on the question concerning the meaning of the present—of this moment.

I would not know in what sense one could say that the meaning of history "is revealed" at its end. For whom, then would it be revealed? Certainly not for God. For the final generation of men? For the last historian? Certainly not. For whom then?

Ott is of the opinion that an end of history, a "last judgment," would not fall within the circle of vision of an historian, but "must be thought of as the ontological presupposition for the historical-ontological way of speaking of the future dimension of all that is historical." The ontological presupposition, however, could only consist in the fact that the *possibility* of an ultimate understanding of the meaning of history could be conceived at its end. In my opinion, one can no more speak of this possibility as ontologically realizable in a "last judgment" than one can speak in general of the end of history as an ontic fact.

To speak ontologically of the future dimension of all that is historical leaves open the possibility of an endless continuation of history. The affirmation that to an historical event belongs its future cannot imply that the meaning of the event can ever be definitely recognized, but states that its meaning becomes clearer. From this there follows the challenge to seek after the meaning of events (for example, the death of Socrates, Caesar's crossing the Rubicon, Luther's posting of the theses, the disintegration of the unified culture of the Middle Ages) in any given present, and thereby to preserve critically the heritage of the past with a view to any given future. In this sense, any historical phenomenon can only be viewed from a particular historical viewpoint. There remains the question concerning the meaning of individual historical phenomena and epochs. Even if the interpretation changes in the course of time, and even if misunderstandings are not excluded, the interpretation of an event is by no means merely appended to it in external fashion, as Ott assumes. It is the event itself which evokes interpretation with the aim of being understood and thereby demands the decision which bears responsibility for the future.

I do not see that it follows from this that man must believe in *a* meaning of history which actualizes itself more and more in its own process. The responsibility for the progress of humanity, of justice and freedom in the relationships of men and nations, which Ott rightly stresses, presupposes the validity of justice and freedom. By this is also presupposed a meaning of human action—not, however, "the idea of the meaning of history as a whole nor a faith in this meaning." That would seem to me to represent a falling back into a teleological view of history, and the same would be true of the concept of the providence of God as Ott understands this term. Actually, Christian faith believes in a hidden meaning of all history in the presence of God, but not, however, in the sense that during the course of history a hidden redemptive plan is actualized. Faith, therefore, does not believe in a redemptive history which is somehow bound up within world history, to the actualization of which men contribute by virtue of human freedom.

5. *Reply to the essay of Paul S. Minear, "Rudolf Bultmann's Interpretation of New Testament Eschatology."* Since the question

concerning the understanding of eschatology is so closely related to the understanding of history, it may be appropriate for me, in conjunction with my response to Heinrich Ott, to answer the questions posed by Paul Minear.

Minear's presentation of my interpretation of eschatology in the Greek world as well as in the Old Testament, in Judaism, in the New Testament, and in the beginnings of the Church, is clear and correct. He sees rightly that my interpretation is shaped by the question: In what way and to what extent is an eschatology cosmologically and therefore mythologically conceived, and how closely does it correspond with the understanding of the historicity of man? Minear also sees rightly that I reject any cosmological eschatology because it does not correspond to the historicity of man. However, he considers my interpretation, especially of the New Testament, to be in error because my way of putting the question is wrong and because it rests on an inadmissible distinction between nature and history—indeed, on a dualistic conception of reality. This, Minear implies, is a metaphysical presupposition.

To this I must first say that the distinction between nature and history is, as such, not a metaphysical proposition, but a simple phenomenological statement which does not in itself say anything concerning the relationship of the two different realms of nature and history. The distinction itself is clear, inasmuch as the methods of research in nature and history are different, unless one seeks to understand the history of mankind in the sense of a thoroughgoing materialism, which is surely not Minear's objective.

Obviously, both nature and history can be viewed in different ways. Natural science views nature in an objectivizing way and involves man only in so far as he is himself a natural being. Thus natural science disregards the way in which nature encounters specifically human life, what nature means for real human life, how man is oppressed by nature, how he uses it, how he dominates it and takes possession of it. But if one considers these factors (that is, how nature encounters man), then one must speak of a reciprocal action between nature and history. But how one can move from this perception to a cosmological eschatology I frankly cannot see.

Similarly, history can be viewed in different ways: first of all, in an objectivizing manner in so far as it presents the picture of a chain of events unfolding in the course of time, which is understandable as a chain of cause and effect. The causality of this chain is not an absolute, but only a relative determination, because the will and action of men proceed out of their own decisions. These decisions are always conditioned, yet always free—conditioned in so far as they are always grounded in situations which are simply given; free, however, in so far as man is at any time free to decide what he will allow to be the basis for his willing and acting, unless, of course, one understands history from the standpoint of a thoroughgoing materialism.

On the other hand, history can also be understood as the range of possibilities for human self-understanding, which range is disclosed precisely in man's decisions. Through them, one can see that man not only stands within a historical course of events but is himself historical. It is then a question of the extent to which he is conscious of his own historicity, that is, how far he is conscious of being able in his history to gain or to lose his authentic existence—precisely in his decisions. In this striving for authentic existence (for the "meaning" of his life), which moves every man whether consciously or unconsciously, is disclosed the challenge under which he as man, stands. He is given the task to be authentic and to gain his authenticity within the situations which condition his life.

Since these situations are given also through nature, which is not separable from history but bound up with it in reciprocal action, it is not true that an existentialist anthropology destroys the connection with nature, as Minear supposes. The crux of the matter is the extent to which man is conscious of his responsibility in his decisions, or the extent to which he pushes off responsibility on historical or natural conditions. His responsibility is always responsibility for the world and its future, as Gogarten has so often stressed. A cosmological eschatology would reduce this responsibility; indeed, it would permit such responsibility to vanish entirely. To speak of responsibility before God "in the last judgment" means neither responsibility for the world nor for the future, but the responsibility of a single individual for himself.

If one speaks of man's responsibility for himself, this only means that man should seek to gain authenticity for his existence and that this is his responsibility before God. The abandonment of a

cosmological eschatology and the historicizing of eschatology means
that for man any moment has the possibility of being an eschatological moment. As Christian faith sees it, man can realize this
possibility whenever, through God's forgiving Word, he is freed from
himself—from the old self which by definition has always forfeited its
authenticity. As a free man he can encounter any future confidently
and therefore hopefully, since the freedom which faith has given him
is not a possession, but is ever received anew. In this sense, faith is
conscious of God's permanent future. For faith the world has re-
gained its character as creation; faith need no longer wait for a
renewal of the world through cosmic catastrophes. Also for faith
there is no dualism, since the fact that freedom must be won anew
does not have its ground in a dichotomy which splits reality asunder,
but in the fact that the old self must always be overcome again.

One can say that the dualism which Minear charges me with is
present in the New Testament in so far as the world is viewed as a
realm under the dominance of demonic powers and Satan. In so far
as that is the case, what is also to be expected is man's liberation
from the world through its being transformed by a cosmic catastrophe. That is not the case, however, either with Jesus or in the
theological explication of Christian existence which has been given by
Paul and John. The liberation from the world does not consist in a
transformation of nature, but in the fact that "this" world, which has
gained its character through men who have succumbed to evil, is
finished for the one who by faith in the word spoken by God in Jesus
Christ has become a new creature and has found freedom. (II Cor.
5:17, Gal. 5:1, John 8:32 and 36). In this sense Christ has subdued
both nature and history.

6. *Reply to K. E. Løgstrup, "The Doctrines of God and Man in
the Theology of Rudolf Bultmann."* Since Løgstrup's article is
concerned with my relationship to both history and philosophy,
perhaps my answer to him may serve as a transition to the discussion
of those articles which deal specifically with my relationship to
philosophy.

Løgstrup begins with the assumption that in my theology nihilism
is a presupposition, indeed, an essential element of faith. His assumption is based on the fact that I say that man in faith is conscious of

his nothingness. In knowing of his nothingness, the world appears to him as darkness, as the harsh limitation of life. Faith consists, as Løgstrup interprets my position, in the recognition of limitation, in the decision that precisely in limitation one encounters the demand of God.

In response to this, Løgstrup says that God's power is at work not only in our limitedness, but also within our limited life in "the unfolding of our life." In this unfolding, in our relationship of man to man, the phenomena of mutual human love occur. In these situations, we do indeed experience our limitedness, not however as limitation through the darkness of nothingness (*Nichts*) but through our neighbor (*Nächsten*). The demand of God consists in the recognition of the ethical command.

Now Løgstrup does not assert that I fail to recognize this aspect of the divine demand, since in spite of the nihilistic character of my concept of faith I recognize that there are in human life "analogous situations." The relationship of man to man in mutual love, in mutual forgiveness, is analogous to the relationship of man to God. Since I acknowledge such analogous situations, there runs through my theology a peculiar contradiction.

To that charge, I have two things to say. (1) I cannot say, as Løgstrup does, that in recognizing the ethical demand we recognize *realities* of the good in human life. I think, rather, we recognize only *possibilities*. I do not deny that these possibilities are created and given and that as "given" they have their positive meaning. Nor do I deny that there are possibilities the realization of which is not only demanded but which can also become event. If one were to hold the fulfillment of such a demand as basically impossible, then it would be the case—as Løgstrup rightly says—that no genuine decision would be possible. The world would then be nothing more than a relative matter because—and on this point Løgstrup is not mistaken—man is always being tempted, and often yields to the temptation, to understand what has been given to us, not in its character as demand, but rather to regard it as that which is at his disposal. The evil will operates always in contradiction to the created goodness of life. The fulfillment will come to completion only if man is freed from self-seeking, which means when he becomes a new man. Basically, then, my nihilism consists of this, that I say the old self must come to naught before God since it is he who makes the world nothing and makes it appear as darkness because it is he who fails when confronted with the possibilities which are at the same time given and demanded.

(2) Løgstrup considers it a contradiction in my theology that I understand the demand of God as on the one hand the acknowledgement of my nothingness and on the other, an ethical demand. It is my thought, however, that in the seeming contradiction there appears in reality the dialectic of man's relationship to the world. The "No" to the world implied when one declares its nothingness and the "Yes" to the world implied when one acknowledges it as God's good creation belong together. One cannot exist without the other. The world becomes nothing when I, as the old self, make it nothing. I can, however, only make it nothing if in itself it is not nothing.

I believe that Løgstrup and I are not so far removed from one another as may at first appear. Perhaps we stand in opposition to each other only through the fact that he ignores the dialectic of man's relationship to the world, and attributes nihilism to me because he understands the nothingness with which we are here dealing in an absolute instead of in a relative sense.

Nevertheless, it seems to me questionable whether we can agree on the question concerning *the relationship of Christian preaching and philosophy*. Løgstrup says, rightly, that the concepts which indicate the relationship of man to man are available for philosophical thinking. If the demand which is perceptible in them can be made philosophically comprehensible as a demand of God, he asks why this is not also true of the concept, God. I acknowledge that the concept of the ethical demand does lie within the competence of philosophy. I also admit to Løgstrup that Heidegger's analysis of human coexistence, which recognizes only objective, impersonal relationships, is too narrow. However, the question remains: How does philosophy come to speak of God and interpret as God's command the ethical demand which faith understands as the command of God? For philosophy it is enough to speak of the imperative ethical demand, and for that no concept of God is required.

On one point I should like to go still farther than Løgstrup: I would say that philosophy knows not only that man is limited through the ethical demand, but also that he is limited through his finiteness. But unlike faith, philosophy need not understand these limitations as being imposed by God.

Even if I were to concede there might be a philosophy which speaks of God and interprets by means of the God concept both the limits which arise through the ethical demand and those which arise through man's finiteness, these are still merely concepts which fall within the competence of philosophy. Philosophical analysis cannot do more than develop the concept of existence (as authentic or inauthentic) and to this extent point out the ontological structure of *Dasein,* which is the presupposition for the ontic actualization of existence. Of course, the ontological presupposition is discernible only on the ground of actual ontic life. But philosophy as existentialist analysis nevertheless does not have at its disposal the ontic actualization. Philosophy does not have at its disposal the existential encounters of man and man which happen in any given moment. Something analogous is to be said about the relationship of man and God. Even if it is presupposed that philosophy can develop the concept of a God, it cannot thereby bring about the encounter of man and God. At the most it can bring to consciousness the question of God. It is not the God concept, but God's address in his Word which establishes the encounter of man with God. And this is at any time an event.

7. *Reply to Shubert M. Ogden, "The Significance of Rudolf Bultmann for Contemporary Theology."* Positive evaluation and criticism are combined in Ogden's arguments. He is of the opinion that my theological work requires further development.

Ogden sees the positive achievement of my work as twofold: (1) in my understanding of history as the Word which addresses the present; (2) in my employment of the philosophy of existence in a way that is fruitful for the development of a theological method. Ogden describes fittingly my relationship to liberal theology, and with similar accuracy he characterizes the intention of demythologizing. The latter is not to be regarded as an apologetic means, but as an effort to interpret the content of the New Testament message. It seeks to show what the New Testament says about the existence of man before God, and about man's relationship to the world. Demythologizing is therefore a hermeneutical procedure which consists in the existentialist interpretation of the New Testament. Ogden observes correctly that I seek to utilize for this purpose Heidegger's analysis of human existence as it is presented in *Being and Time,* without thereby converting the statements of the New Testament into a philosophy.

Ogden considers the call for demythologizing and for existentialist interpretation to be an achievement from which there cannot be any turning back, but he wants to develop my intentions further and to carry them through more consistently than I have done. With this I am basically in agreement. The question is only whether my intentions really lead to those consequences which Ogden holds to be necessary.

The first inconsistency which he thinks he finds in my position is that I do not carry through the demythologizing of Christology with sufficient consistency because I declare that the authentic existence of man is made possible only through God's action in Jesus Christ. It would be false to deny that the "possibility in principle"—which I in fact do not contest—could become a "possibility in fact" without faith in Jesus Christ as the decisive act of God. God's liberating act may occur everywhere, even if at the same time it is decisively revealed in the Word which Jesus speaks and which he is.

The decisive question, therefore, is this: Is the statement mythological that God reveals himself in Christ in such a manner that the possibility in principle can become the possibility in fact? Here, I think I must take issue. That statement does, of course, contain a paradox, namely, that an historical event (Jesus Christ) is at the same time an eschatological event. I do not believe that one can characterize the latter as mythological. Ogden and I are agreed that in myth the divine action is directly identified with phenomena within the world, but this is not the case with my statement. My statement means that an historical phenomenon to which nothing by way of miracle adheres is for human existence a decisive event. If historical phenomena in general can have the character of address (and here again I believe that Ogden and I are in agreement), then it is hard to see why *an* historical event cannot be regarded as *the* ultimate definitive address. This is precisely what I have in mind when I describe the historical event of Jesus Christ as the eschatological event.

The mythical character is taken away from this event when I say,

"This event as an eschatological event cannot be exhibited, rendered visible, or objectively established. It is only present as address." That means the eschatological occurrence continues to take place in the preaching, in the address which proclaims. The preaching, therefore, participates in the paradox, since it is always the word of man and at the same time is to be understood as God's address. Similarly, the church in which preaching takes place is, on the one hand, a visible phenomenon of world history, and on the other hand, in its authentic sense, an invisible eschatological occurrence.

The second criticism of Ogden concerning my theology is that my existentialist interpretation restricts itself to the categories of Heidegger's analysis of existence. For this reason, it is not possible for me to speak directly of God, but I content myself with speaking only analogically of God. But Ogden charges me now with not carrying through the thought of analogy with sufficient consistency. He says that I limit myself basically to speaking only indirectly of God in that I speak of man and the possibilities of his self-understanding in relation to God. Ogden is of the opinion, on the contrary, that what is required is a philosophical theology which speaks directly of God and his action, but without thereby falsely objectifying him. This philosophical theology Ogden finds in the work of Charles Hartshorne, who, without denying that God is always subject and never object, is nevertheless of the opinion that it is possible to represent the structure of God's essence objectively.

I do not consider such a philosophical theology possible. It is only possible to make God the object of conceptual thought in so far as the concept "God" can be objectively explicated. Indeed, that must be the case since theology must be able to say what it means when it speaks of God. Theology must therefore clarify in a conceptual way—for example, the concepts of transcendence, of omnipotence, of the presentness of God, the concepts of grace and forgiveness. This cannot mean, however, that theology speaks directly of God and of his activity. It cannot speak of God as he is in himself, but only of what he does for us.

8. *Reply to John Macquarrie, "Philosophy and Theology in Bultmann's Thought."* The question which Macquarrie addresses to me is how I understand the relation of theology and philosophy. This

question is evoked by the fact that on the one hand my theological thought is influenced by the philosophy of existence, specifically that of Heidegger, and that on the other hand I maintain the kerygmatic character of theology. Macquarrie now asks, "Is there a contradiction here, or is it a matter of a synthesis of theology and philosophy?" He is of the opinion that the latter is the case, and he shows this by expounding my concept of preunderstanding. Basically, preunderstanding is the understanding of one's own existence which can be clarified conceptually through philosophy. To this end, I use the concepts of authentic and inauthentic existence and of history and historicity developed by Heidegger in his *Being and Time*. Macquarrie sees accurately that I do not, in this way, make theology at all into a philosophy of existence and that I do not set aside the kerygma, which is for philosophy a *skandalon* (offense). Macquarrie has made his point especially through his clear noting of the criticism which Karl Jaspers has brought to bear against me. The philosophical analysis of existence has for me only propaedeutic significance, and prejudges nothing concerning the existential life of the individual. Philosophy leaves fundamentally free the possibility of a word spoken to man from beyond. It offers, however, the possibility of speaking of Christian existence in a language which is comprehensible today. I can only be grateful for this interpretation of my intention.

However, Macquarrie also directs critical questions to me. The first is this: My understanding of Christian faith is oriented in a one-sidedly anthropological way. He defends me effectively against the charge of subjectivism. He thinks, however, that my theology requires an ontological basis such as Tillich provided in distinction from me. Here I can only confess that I myself cannot conceive of an ontological basis. Should theology speak in scientific fashion of the mode of being of God? I don't think that this is Macquarrie's intention, but what then?

Further, Macquarrie objects to my understanding of history. He thinks that my existentialist interpretation of history ignores the factual character of historical events and thus also of the actual history of Jesus. Here I must reply that I do not regard the factual character of history and of Jesus as in any way irrelevant for faith and for theology. I say, rather, Christian faith declares the paradox that an historical event (precisely, Jesus and his history) is at the same time an eschatological occurrence. If the historical fact were stricken out, then the paradox would be abandoned. There is no existentialist interpretation of history at all which ignores the factual occurrence. I can also say that the existentialist interpretation of history attempts to answer the questions that the factual history in which we are entangled poses for us.

The third objection of Macquarrie is that I orient myself in one-sided fashion to the philosophy of Heidegger. I ought to take into account also other philosophical views, especially those of logical empiricism and linguistic analysis. I acknowledge my one-sidedness. Heidegger's analysis of existence has become for me fruitful for hermeneutics, that is, for the interpretation of the New Testament and of the Christian faith. I am willing to be shown whether other theologians can make fruitful use of other philosophies for herme-neutics, and I will gladly learn from them. Thus far, I am aware only of Ogden's attempt to utilize the philosophy of Charles Hartshorne for theology. I have already given my response to Ogden's position.

Finally, Macquarrie takes exception to the exclusiveness with which I state the absolute claim of the Christian kerygma and do not recognize that there is genuine knowledge of God outside of the Christian faith. Now I do not deny that there is an understanding outside of Christian faith as to what God is and what grace is. I am convinced that Augustine's words, "Our heart is restless until it rests in Thee," are true for all men. In all men, explicitly or implicitly, the question concerning God is a living one. The exclusiveness of the kerygma consists in the fact that it provides the answer to this question by offering the right to say "God is my God." From the standpoint of faith, it can of course be said that in all human questions concerning God, God reveals himself.

9. *Reply to Götz Harbsmeier, "The Theology of Rudolf Bult-mann and Its Relation to Philosophy."* Harbsmeier's understanding of the relationship of my theology to philosophy is similar to that of Macquarrie. He sees that my point of departure is from the fact that faith contains an understanding and that it is the task of theology to develop this understanding in suitable conceptuality, that is, in the achievement of rational thinking and speaking. Thus it is, in fact, as Harbsmeier formulates it, the problem of language which motivates

my theology. Theology is basically the thinking and speaking of faith, and for this philosophy is required.

Philosophy is the exposition of the understanding of man's existence that manifests itself in his thinking and speaking. Theology must know man and his understanding of existence if it is to speak in a way that can be understood. The man on whom it focuses its attention is a thinking and speaking man and his manner of thinking and speaking remains the same even with respect to faith. Indeed, the believer thinks and says different things from the nonbeliever, but not in a different way. The commonality of faith and the world consists in the fact that faith speaks with the same language as unfaith; and the believer is held fast in this commonality by love. The question can only be, "Which is the philosophy that offers the appropriate conceptuality to explain the understanding of existence which is expressed in thinking and speaking?" Harbsmeier observed quite rightly that my theology does not become dependent on a philosophical system by my seeking to make fruitful use of the concepts of the so-called philosophy of existence, particularly of Heidegger's analysis of existence in *Being and Time*. I learned from him not *what* theology has to say, but *how* it has to say it, in order to speak to the thinking man of today in a way that he can understand.

10. *Reply to Hans Bolewski, "The Role of the Church in the Theology of Rudolf Bultmann."* I am glad I am in agreement with Bolewski that the Church must be understood as an eschatological phenomenon. Obviously, we are also one in our way of posing the question as to how the Church understands its being "between the times," just as we are agreed that the Church is constituted through the kerygma. On the other hand there is a difference between Bolewski and me on the question of the way in which the essence of the Church can become the law by which its outward form is shaped.

The question is: How can an eschatological phenomenon be at the same time an institution? How can it have a history? To this I should first like to reply that the basis for this is the paradox that an historical event is at the same time an eschatological event. This paradox is declared by the Christian faith. The eschatological event that has its origin in Jesus Christ continues to fulfill itself as eschatological event in the preaching of the Church and in faith which responds to the preaching. This event, however, at the same time has been an historical event ever since its origin in the historical Jesus. It runs its course in the historical process of the history of the Church.

This paradox is the basis for the question as to the meaning of the essence of the Church as an historical entity with its institutions, organizations, and the congregations. Its meaning lies in this fact: that the necessary condition for the essence of the Church is that it is always realizing itself in time as an eschatological phenomenon. Otherwise, the eschatological occurrence would be misunderstood as something that occurred beyond history, and therefore beyond man, who has to lead his life within history.

I am just as strongly of the opinion that the Church, precisely in consequence of this paradox, has a history and that therefore its proclamation lives from the historical tradition (and on this point I agree with Tillich, Gadamer, and Dodd). In consequence I am unable to see that any concrete order for the Church can be deduced from its essence as eschatological phenomenon, apart from the one demand that the order must stand in the service of the proclamation of the Word. It is in the preaching of the Word that the eschatological occurrence takes place.

Certainly in the framework of theology, homiletics is necessary as a doctrine of preaching. However, no homiletics can transmit to an individual preacher a method which guarantees to him that his sermon will be genuine proclamation, any more than there can be a church order through which it is guaranteed that the Church in any particular historical form achieves its authentic meaning: to be the scene of the eschatological occurrence. At the same time, however, the necessity exists for the Church to reflect in any given moment how the church order serves the meaning of the Church, i.e., to proclaim the eschatological event.

I admit that such reflection receives too short treatment in my theological work. It seems to me, however, that the problem is again and again posed anew and a new solution demanded. Responsibility for this must be borne by those whose task it is directly or indirectly to care for the order of the Church.

Such reflection has not been my concern, and I concede to Bolewski that I have thought in one-sided fashion—about the individual person and his relationship to the kerygma and not about the

community. I cannot see, however, how the existentialist interpretation of Scripture and of the kerygma can contribute to a solution of
ecclesiological problems, because I am of the opinion that the
solution must be left up to the one who bears this specific concrete
responsibility. On this account, I cannot see that, as Bolewski thinks,
my view of the way in which kerygma and the individual man stand
in relation to each other presupposes a specific form of church order.
At least, I thought—and think—that I have left complete freedom
with respect to the question of order as it corresponds to any
particular situation and responsibility. I confess, however, that ecclesiology has not stood in the midpoint of my work, and so I can
only be grateful to be reminded of this lack in my work.

11. *Reply to D. Otto Michel, "The Event of Salvation and Word
in the New Testament."* Michel offers a critical assessment of my
existentialist interpretation of the Bible. He recognizes a relative
justification for it, but he would like emphatically to specify its limits.
He places over against a theology for which the question concerning
the individuality of human existence is dominant a theology for which
history is the place of encounter of God and man. In this way, the
danger would be avoided that theology would become anthropology.

In so far as Michel thinks that he is aiming at my existentialist
interpretation by this criticism (he does not say so expressly), I
should have to object that he overlooks the fact that I stress
emphatically the paradox that the eschatological event which has
occurred in Jesus Christ is at the same time an historical event. I
never intended to cut loose faith from history or to reduce the
historical event to the existential life of man. What Michel says
concerning *gratia praeveniens,* and in his further remarks that *salvatio* precedes faith, is my intended meaning as well. I have never
understood faith otherwise than as the answer to the word by which
God addresses man, a word that encounters man in history.

When Michel says that the event of *salvatio* must never be reduced
to the Word, he can only say that because he misunderstands the
presence of the eschatological event in the Word. If, however—as I
think—the Word in the New Testament, as in the preaching of the
Church, is the eschatological event, then what happens precisely in
the Word, if it is heard in faith, is *salvatio.* I cannot recognize any

antithesis between the understanding of the word and obedience, since there is no genuine understanding of the word which is not at the same time obedience.

12. *Reply to D. Heinz-Horst Schrey, "The Consequences of Bult-mann's Theology for Ethics."* The problem of my theology upon which Schrey fixes his attention is my understanding of the relationship of Christian faith to human life. He presents first my understanding of the teaching of justification through faith. Since justification cannot alter the moral structure of man, who can only be *justus et peccator* forever, there can be no ethic which is grounded in faith. The believer stands under the demand of God and fulfills his obedience in any moment by his decisions. These are not determined by an ethical theory, but are called for through the relationship of I and Thou. They stand under the demand of love, which demand is an eschatological event because it arises out of the receiving of the love of God. A precise *what* love is cannot be specified, but must at any moment be discovered in the historical situation. Since this demand is always present and new in any present, it does not contain a program of cultural or social ideals. There is no such thing as an ethic of concrete commandments (*Materialethik*).

Against this point of view Schrey directs critical questions. My view of the historicity of human life is oriented to the schema of the ontological structure of human being as the analysis of existence (specifically Heidegger's) has traced it out. But can this view fully perceive the meaning of ethics if indeed it reduces ethics to the formal schema of historicity? Must not an ethic take as its theme also the behavior demanded of man in the real world and must not therefore Christian faith also devise Christian institutions in the framework of which man's activity may follow its course?

My answer is that Schrey is quite correct in his assertions that in faith the Christian is not isolated as an individual self and that his personal historicity cannot be cut loose from the history in which he stands. As a human being he bears responsibility not only for himself but also for the world. I think that this responsibility belongs also to the obedience which man owes God and which is included in the command to love. The neighbor whom the Christian is to love is always a man who finds himself in a specific historical and social situation. The I-Thou relationship exists only in concrete situations. On this I am in complete agreement with Schrey. However, the command to love gives no concrete directions for carrying out this responsibility. For this purpose man has the faculty of reason—in order to recognize what is demanded in any particular situation, what actions under the given conditions of society can imply good or evil for his neighbor.

Certainly the Christian, as one who believes and loves, has the obligation to seek means by which social existence may gain a form in which a genuine human personal life is possible. He is, therefore, also responsible for institutions in which a life of freedom and responsibility is possible, and for the ordering of social existence through justice and righteousness. Just as the believer must surely bear this obligation, so it is equally true that these demands are, as such, not specifically Christian, but are rather general human demands. Where such demands are guaranteed or carried out through institutions, these are by no means Christian institutions, no matter how much the Christian is responsible for enforcing the demands. Perhaps one may say that faith and love are made manifest only in so far as there are Christians who, acting in faith and love and guided by their reason, take upon themselves responsibility for the world. This, however, can only be recognized indirectly. But that the world has won a new form because faith and love exist in history is a highly problematical proposition.

The consequence of eschatology for ethics at most can be stated to be the effect that the believer, whose existence as eschatological is something *"new,"* accepts responsibility for the world with a new urgency. Thus one may say that eschatological faith has not only a negative but also a positive importance for the world. However, an ethic cannot be derived from eschatology.

I am entirely in agreement that the demythologizing of the kerygma must go hand in hand with a deidealizing of ethics. Because ethical ideology of the past, for example the concept of private property, rests upon past historical conditions, what is now required is an ethic which corresponds to the conditions of present-day life.

13. *Reply to Friedrich Müller, "Bultmann's Relation to Classical Philology."* In Friedrich Müller's article, two things are of basic

importance for me: (1) Müller sees that the interpretation of the New Testament must be carried out according to the method of historical-philological research as it has been developed in classical philology. This method must be used by theologians for whom the New Testament is thought of as the Word of God, since the Word of God is an event which has entered into history; in history it has, so to speak, "become flesh." It is attested in writings which are documents of history and which first of all must be made understandable as such. Precisely to this end, the theological interpreter requires the historical-philological method. On this Müller and I are entirely in agreement. And if in his opinion he is able to show that classical philology can also receive impulses and directions from my interpretation, then I can be glad and feel that the commonality of our work, which I have always felt, has been confirmed.

(2) The second matter which seems to me essential deals with hermeneutics. Interpretation is also hermeneutics, which teaches one to understand the text in the sense that the "hermeneut" is at the same time the mediator, as Müller makes clear through his reference to the Diotima speech of Socrates. That means that the interpretation does not limit itself to making understandable the past as such, but is to show the relation of the past to the present; that is, it is to make the past, in its own historical "vitality," active in the present.

Thus far I am entirely in agreement with Müller. But now he points to a decisive distinction between the understanding of the hermeneutical mediator function in classical philology and in the interpretation of the New Testament. The distinction lies in this: that the interpretation of the New Testament has as its goal the exposition of the kerygma, which classical philology does not and cannot know, since its work of mediation has another goal—that of *Paideia,* as Müller makes clear through his reference to Werner Jaeger.

Now Müller sees quite rightly that an analogy exists in the respective goals of the two disciplines and that in spite of every distinction there is no opposition. When the kerygma draws man out of his ties within the world, it nonetheless also points to man's tasks within the world. In order to fulfill these, he needs paideutic humanism. I am glad that Müller and I arc at onc on this point.

Nevertheless I do have one small critical observation to make with regard to Müller. When scientific interpretation of the New Testa-

ment has the task of making the kerygma clear, then it can only point
out an historical phenomenon which is to be drawn from the New
Testament writings. As scientific interpretation it is not itself
kerygma; it does not preach itself. Preaching is the task of the
Church; scientific interpretation has to be watchful so that the
Church's preaching corresponds to the content of the kerygma as it is
drawn from the New Testament writings.

14. *Reply to Samuel Sandmel, "Bultmann on Judaism."* It is not
easy for me to weigh agreements and differences in the discussion
with Sandmel. In any case, I am glad there is a wide-ranging
agreement about the question concerning the character of Judaism in
the time of Jesus and the relationship of Jesus to Judaism. Sandmel
knows that I have often enough stressed the fact that Jesus was a
Jew. One dare not overlook the fact, however, that Judaism at the
time of Jesus was not a completely homogeneous entity, and that
there were within it distinctions, such as those between the Pharisees
and Sadducees, or those between the teaching of the Law and
apocalyptic. The Qumran texts have shown us that there were even
opposing viewpoints.

On just this basis, therefore, Sandmel is exactly right when he
considers it to be one-sided—even false—to characterize Jewish piety
simply as legalism. Above all, one must keep in mind that Judaism
offered plenty of room for the discussion of legal questions, and
Sandmel's reference to the expansion of Halakah through the Haggadah is in this respect very important. Such a discussion shows that
the exposition of the Law was a problem, but it shows at the same
time that a one-sided legalistic understanding of the Law was always
a possibility which found its representatives. It is also erroneous—
and on this I agree with Sandmel—to suppose that the pious Jew
considered the Law as a pressing burden. Even Paul did not understand liberation from the Law as being freed from a pressing burden,
as, for example, Philippians 3:4–8 clearly shows. For the consciousness of the Jew there is, of course, no opposition between the Law
and the will of God. However, when the exposition of the Law was
under discussion, then the implication is that the question was a living
one as to the manner and extent that the written Law was the
expression of the will of God. This is what is under discussion in the

antitheses of the Sermon on the Mount (Matt. 5), even if we understand the Evangelist to be responsible for the formulation of the antitheses.

Sandmel charges me with differentiating the radical obedience which Jesus demands from the obedience which consists in the formal fulfillment of the Law. He thinks that any obedience must be radical. But what does radical obedience mean? By this expression I understand an obedience which does not simply submit to the commandment on the ground of its authority transmitted through the tradition, but which takes possession of the commandment in such a fashion that it affirms of itself its demand. To put it another way, radical obedience is obedience which understands.

Now it cannot be denied that in Judaism, at least to a large extent, obedience was conceived of as a formal thing. This is clearly stated in the expression of Rabbi Jochanan ben Zakkai: "Neither does a dead man make one unclean, nor does water make clean, but the Holy One has said, 'I have firmly established a law. I have established a decree. You are not permitted to transgress my decree, which stands written.' " Also it cannot be denied that in Judaism both completely ritual commands (such as the commands of cleanliness and sabbath purification) and ethical demands were counted as divine commands. A comprehending obedience is, however, only possible with respect to ethical commandments, and in this sense Jesus demands radical obedience. I do not contest that some rabbinical words have been transmitted in which there is expressed a comprehending obedience. Nowhere, to my knowledge, is the comprehending obedience so radically formulated as in the preaching of Jesus. Of course, the Law demands the sanctification of all of life, but so long as this sanctification is demanded and striven after by ritual as well as ethical performance, then I must abide by my judgment that such sanctification does not direct man into historical life, but rather removes him from it.

This is closely connected with another point of difference between Sandmel and myself, namely, that concerning the relationship of Judaism to history. Sandmel knows how often I have stressed that the Israel of the Old Testament, in distinction from the Greeks, possessed a consciousness of history and of the historicity of man. Now I believe that this consciousness was not lost in Judaism—particularly in the apocalyptic tradition—but retrogressed, indeed became depraved, as was true also in primitive Christianity. I can, of course, recognize that this consciousness is given expression in the words which Sandmel cites from the Passover Haggadah, but I cannot see that the accepting of proselytes into the Jewish community is evidence for this historical consciousness. Did the proselytes really participate in the actual history of Israel? Were they not, rather, accepted only into a religious community based on ritual? If it is said that by this means they became sons of Abraham, as the early Christians understood themselves to be, then one could speak of their becoming a part of the *Heilsgeschichte* (history of salvation). But neither in Judaism nor in early Christianity was *Heilsgeschichte* understood as actual history.

Genuine historical consciousness includes consciousness of the tasks which grow out of history. Can the recruiting of proselytes pass for such a consciousness? Historical consciousness contains knowledge of one's responsibility toward the world and the shaping of it. Judaism had no more consciousness of this than did Paul and primitive Christianity in general. Therefore, I am led to the judgment that Judaism has severed itself from the world through the consciousness of its being different from all the other peoples. The mere fact that the Law directs the Jews to lead their life *in* the world cannot be considered evidence that they possess a consciousness of responsibility *for* the world. Neither can one say that Judaism has understood the transcendence of God as his immanence in the world. But one must say—and on this point I think I am again in agreement with Sandmel—that Judaism did not develop any dualistically motivated asceticism. Even though, as I see it, one cannot deny that traces of dualism have entered into Judaism (for example, in a certain part of the Qumran texts) and into early Christianity, faith in God as the Creator has overcome dualism.

15. *Reply to Hannelis Schulte, "The Old Testament and Its Significance for Religious Instruction."* In replying to the arguments of Hannelis Schulte, I limit myself to the subject of the importance of the Old Testament for religious education. Its meaning for the Church's preaching as a whole is a very comprehensive issue, which H. Schulte has treated only as an appendix. Therefore, I limit myself

to a few short observations on this subject. Even though my intention diverges from her own, H. Schulte has factually and accurately represented my view of a special question: namely, in what manner the Church can and should take over the political preaching of the prophets. I readily concede that the Church should take up again the political preaching of the prophets in so far as this preaching proclaims the demand for right and justice as God's demand. The responsibility of the Church for political life consists in the preaching of this demand. I cannot acknowledge, however, that the Church can raise concrete political demands as the prophetic preaching once did.

Naturally, H. Schulte is right when she stresses at the conclusion that both for the Church and for religious education the Old Testament is important because it belongs to the tradition out of which we live and the history from which we have come. The study of the Old Testament guides us, therefore, in the understanding of our own history.

The most important element in the article of H. Schulte, however, is what she says concerning the method of religious education. I can see that instruction in the Old Testament should begin with the history of Israel, and therefore should be carried out in such a way that the Old Testament is understood as an historical document. Instruction in this manner leads one to understand man as an historical being, that is, in the contradiction which is characteristic of all human existence as well as in the demands under which man stands as under the demands of God. He should understand them as the demands which he has to fulfill in the worldly tasks of his natural life, above all in his social life. H. Schulte has made this clear in a skillful way by showing how the Old Testament understanding of man contrasts with the Greek.

On this basis, religious instruction can make the preaching of the prophets comprehensible as a preaching which does not demand a specifically religious pattern of behavior, but which is a call to responsibility for historical life. In this way, the prophetic criticism of religion can be made understandable in so far as religion misunderstands the authentic demands of God and supposes that it can achieve the fulfillment of these demands through ritual worship.

The way in which H. Schulte makes clear the originality of the prophets in the history of religion seems to be fruitful for religious instruction. Occasionally she refers in an instructive way to the relationship of the Old Testament to the New, especially in connection with the preaching of Jesus. On the whole, one may say that she shows the way by which religious education can make the Old Testament understandable as the preparation for the understanding of Christian existence. She does so precisely while repudiating the traditional view that the history of Israel is to be considered as a preparatory stage in the *Heilsgeschichte*.

16. *Reply to Martin Stallmann on "Contemporary Interpretation of the Gospels as a Challenge to Preaching and Religious Education."* For a theologian whose chief task is the illumination of the New Testament, it is a pleasure to see how Stallmann shows the way which leads from scientific research of the Gospels to preaching and instruction. This was made possible because scientific research led to the recognition of the kerygmatic character of the gospel accounts. This made it possible to observe that the Gospels present the humanity of Jesus as the place of the divine action and that the history of Jesus is, therefore, eschatological in character.

Stallmann sees that in opposition to dogmatic Christology and in contrast to the life-of-Jesus research of the nineteenth century, what is decisive is the "That" of the humanity of Jesus. He sees that between the historical Jesus and the Christ who is preached after Easter there exists an historical continuity, although no continuity between the humanity of Jesus and the Christ who is preached. The "That" of the humanity of Jesus belongs in the kerygma, and perhaps Stallmann would have been able to formulate it more clearly through the statement that the Easter faith asserts the paradox that the historical event is at the same time an eschatological event.

Stallmann sees quite rightly the consequence for preaching and instruction. The exposition of the text must lead to an existential encounter with the text. This objective is served by the existentialist interpretation, the meaning of which Stallmann accurately represents. The existentialist interpretation as a scientific task is to be differentiated from preaching, in so far as existentialist interpretation teaches one to understand the text as proclamation which itself *occurred,* while in the sermon the text is proclamation which is in any given moment *occurring* anew. Perhaps Stallmann has exaggerated the difference between existentialist interpretation and preaching. Cannot the existentialist interpretation also be an indirectly occurring proclamation? For Stallmann correctly recognizes that through the presentation of an understanding of existence in history, the possibility of one's own understanding of existence is called into question and occasions a decision.

It is true in the case of religious instruction that on the ground of truthfulness the kerygmatic character of the text must not be separated from the complex of historical-critical questions. In a word, the pupils must be given the opportunity to ask questions. Only in this way can they find the way to an understanding of the text for themselves. A single, correct way which can be pointed out in advance does not exist; on this point I can only agree with Stallmann.

Bibliography of the Publications
of Rudolf Bultmann to 1965*

Abbreviations:

   ChrW = Christliche Welt.
   DLZ = Deutsche Literaturzeitung.
   OLZ = Orientalistische Literaturzeitung.
   RGG = Die Religion in Geschichte und Gegenwart.
   ThBl = Theologische Blätter.
   ThLZ = Theologische Literaturzeitung.
   ThR = Theologische Rundschau.
   ThWB = Theologisches Wörterbuch zum Neuen Testament.
   ZKG = Zeitschrift für Kirchengeschichte.
   ZNW = Zeitschrift für die neutestamentliche Wissenschaft.
   ZThK = Zeitschrift für Theologie und Kirche.
   ZwZ = Zwischen den Zeiten.

Key to German Words:

   Auflage = edition
   Ausgabe = version
   Besprechung = review
   Ders. (*derselbe*) = the same author
   Ergänzungsheft = supplement
   Festschrift für = publication in honor of
   kurze Anzeige = short report
   Lieferung = part
   S. (*Seite*) = page
   s. (*siehe*) = *see*

---

* The list of the publications of Rudolf Bultmann to 1954 was compiled by Walter Baumgartner, Erich Dinkler, and Hans Siebeck, and appeared in *Theologische Rundschau, Heft 1* (Tübingen: J. C. B. Mohr [Paul Siebeck], 1954). Professor Bultmann has brought the list up-to-date, for which gratitude is here expressed.

Sammlung = collection
Übersetzung = translation

1908

"Licht vom Osten" (Bespr. von Ad. Deissmanns gleichbetiteltem Buch).
Monatsschrift f. Pastoraltheologie, V, 78–82.
"Die neutestamentliche Forschung 1905–07." Ibid. 124–32, 154–64.
Heinrici, Lit. Char. d. ntl. Schriften, *ChrW*, XXII, 378.

1909

Besprechung von:
Handcommentar zum N.T. IV, Evang., Briefe und Offenbarung des
Johannes, 3. Aufl. *ChrW*, XXIII, 814.

1910

Der Stil der paulinischen Predigt und die kynisch-stoische Diatribe.
(Forsch. z. Rel. u. Lit. d. A. und N.T. 13). Göttingen: Vanden-
hoeck u. Ruprecht.
Besprechung von:
Die Bibel ausgewählt (Inselverlag). *ChrW*, XXIV, 90 f.
Ziller, Die moderne Bibelwissenschaft und die Krisis der evangelischen
Kirche. Ibid. 689.
J. Weiss, Jesus im Glauben des Urchristentums. Ibid. 861.

1911

"Die Schriften des Neuen Testaments und der Hellenismus." (Über das
Handbuch zum N.T. hrsgg. von H. Lietzmann.) *ChrW*, XXV, 589–
93.
Besprechung von:
Ad. Deissmann, Paulus. Ibid. 1178.

1912

"Das religiöse Moment in der ethischen Unterweisung des Epiktet und
das Neue Testament." *ZNW*, XIII, 97–110, 177–91.
"Vier neue Darstellungen der Theologie des Neuen Testaments." (Bespr.
der neutestl. Theologien von Holtzmann, Weinel, Feine und
Schlatter). *Monatsschr. f. Pastoraltheol.*, VIII, 432–43.

1913

"Was läßt die Spruchquelle über die Urgemeinde erkennen?" *Oldenburgisches Kirchenblatt*, XIX, 35–37, 41–44.
Artikel: "Urgemeinde." *RGG*, V.
Besprechung von:
P. Rosegger, Mein Weltleben. Neue Folge. *ChrW*, XXVII, 1188 f.
C. Lemonnier, Ein Dorfwinkel. Ibid. 1192.

1914

"Einleitung" (in das N.T.). Bespr. von Werken von Feine, Wendland, J. Weiss, Norden. *ThR*, XVII, 41–46, 79–90.
Antwort auf Feines Erwiderung. Ibid. 125–30.
Besprechung von:
L. Pirot, L'oeuvre exégétique de Théodore de Mopsueste. *ThLZ*, XXXIX, 363 f.
G. A. van den Bergh van Eysinga, Die holländische radikale Kritik des N. T.; *ChrW*, XXVIII, 643 f.
E. Klostermann, Die neuesten Angriffe auf die Geschichtlichkeit Jesu. Ibid.
A. Schweitzer, Geschichte der Leben Jesu-Forschung, 2. Aufl. Ibid.
    J. Weiss, Synoptische Tafeln. Ibid.
W. Bauer, Das Leben Jesu im Zeitalter der neutestl. Apokryphen. Ibid.
Kurze Anzeigen von:
H. Gunkel, Reden und Aufsätze. *ThR*, XVII, 90.
W. W. Jaeger über Norden, Agnostos Theos. Ibid. 163 f.
W. H. S. Jones, A note on the vague use of theos. Ibid. 164.
Neutestl. Studien für G. Heinrici. Ibid. 360.

1915

"Neutestamentliche Theologie" (Bespr. von J. Behm, Der Begriff *diatheke* im N. T.; E. Lohmeyer, Diatheke). *ThR*, XVIII, 264–67.
Besprechung von:
Aufhauser, Antike Jesus-Zeugnisse. *ThLZ*, XL, 260.
J. Behm, Die Bekehrung des Paulus. Ibid. 356.
Kurze Anzeige von:
Fr. Barth, Einleitung in das N. T. *ThR*, XVIII, 147.

1916

"Biblische Theologie" (des N. T.). (Bespr. von A. Pott, Das Hoffen im N. T.; G. Wetter, Charis; Ders. Phos; Ders. Die Verherrlichung im Johannesevangelium). *ThR*, XIX, 113–26.

"Von der Mission des alten Christentums." (Über Harnack, Mission und
Ausbreitung des Christentums etc., und H. Lietzmann, Petrus und
Paulus in Rom). *ChrW*, XXX, 523–28.
Besprechung von:
J. Kögel, Zum Gleichnis vom ungerechten Haushalter. *ThLZ*, XLI, 525.
E. Stange, Die Eigenart der johanneischen Produktion. Ibid. 532–34.
W. Köhler, Die Gnosis. *ChrW*, XXX, 38 f.
C. Barth, Die Interpretation des N. T. in der valentinianischen Gnosis.
Ibid.
H. Weinheimer, Geschichte des Volkes Israel, II. Ibid. 434.
Die ältesten Apologeten, herausgeg. von E. J. Goodspeed. *Berliner philol.
Wochenschr.*, XXXVI, 129–31.
G. Wetter, Phos. Ibid. 1172–75.

1917

"Die Bedeutung der Eschatologie für die Religion des N. T." *ZThK*,
XXVII, 76–87.
"Vom geheimnisvollen und offenbaren Gott." (Predigt.) *ChrW*, XXXI,
572–79.
Besprechung von:
J. Sickenberger, Kurzgefaßte Einleitung in das N. T. *ThLZ*, XLII, 44.
H. Schumacher, Christus in seiner Präexistenz nach Phil. 2, 5–8. Ibid.
338 f.
Ch. Burrage, Nazareth and the Beginnings of Christianity. Ibid. 364.
J. v. Walther, Die Sklaverei im N. T. Ibid. 467 f.

1918

Besprechung von:
Th. Soiron, Die Logia Jesu. *ThLZ*, XLIII, 246.
J. Wrzol, Die Echtheit des 2. Thess. Ibid. 268.

1919

"Die neutestamentliche Forschung im 20. Jahrhundert." *Oldenburg. Kir-
chenblatt*, XXV, 115–16, 119–22.
Besprechung von:
K. Deissner, Paulus und Seneca. *ThLZ*, XLIV, 5.
F. Bauer, Paulus. Ibid. 5.
Fr. Spitta, Die Auferstehung Jesu. Ibid. 124 f.
M. Dibelius, Die Formgeschichte des Evangeliums. Ibid. 173 f.
W. Classen, Leben Jesu. *ChrW*, XXXIII, 468 f.
Handbuch der klassischen Altertumswissenschaft, VII 2, 2 (Geschichte
der griech. Literatur, II, 5. Aufl.). Ibid. 550.

1920

"Die Frage nach dem messianischen Bewußtsein Jesu und das Petrus-Bekenntnis." *ZNW*, XIX, 1919/20, 165–74.
"Religion und Kultur." *ChrW*, XXXIV, 417–21, 435–39, 450–53.
"Ethische und mystische Religion im Urchristentum." Ibid. 725–31, 738 bis 743.
Besprechung von:
H. Cladder, Unsere Evangelien. *ThLZ*, XLV, 198.
P. Ketter, Die Versuchung Jesu nach dem Berichte der Synoptiker. Ibid. 199.
K. L. Schmidt, Die Pfingsterzählung und das Pfingstereignis. Ibid. 199 f.
J. Behm, Der gegenwärtige Stand der Frage nach dem Verf. des Hebräerbriefes. Ibid. 247.
I. Maiworm, Bausteine der Evangelien zur Begründung einer Evangelienharmonie. Ibid. 267 f.
E. Stange, Paulinische Reisepläne. Ibid. 293.
K. L. Schmidt, Der Rahmen der Geschichte Jesu. *Wochenschrift für klass. Philol.*, XXXVII, 209–12, 241–47.

1921

Die Geschichte der synoptischen Tradition (Forschungen z. Rel. u. Lit. des A. u. N. T., NF 12). Göttingen: Vandenhoeck u. Ruprecht. (2. Aufl. 1931.)
"Ed. Meyers Werk über die Evangelien," *Literaturblatt der Frankfurter Zeitung* vom 3. April.
"Die neueste Bestreitung der Geschichtlichkeit Jesu." (Über A. Drews, Das Markusevangelium als Zeugnis gegen die Geschichtlichkeit Jesu.) Ibid. vom 12. Oktober.
Besprechung von:
R. Knopf, Einführung in das N. T. *DLZ*, XLII, 254 f

1922

"Karl Barths Römerbrief in zweiter Auflage." *ChrW*, XXXVI, 320–23, 330–34, 358–61, 369–73.
"Gott in der Natur." Ibid. 489–91, 513 f., 553 f.
"Unruhe und Ruhe." Ibid. 569 f.
"Vom Beten." Ibid. 593 f.
"Vom Schicksal." Ibid. 609 f.
"Aus der Geschichte des Christentums." (Über Werke von Ed. Meyer, R. Schütz, R. Woerner, Frz. Meffert.) *Literaturblatt der Frankfurter Zeitung* vom 9. Juni.
Besprechung von:

K. Deissner, Paulus und die Mystik seiner Zeit. *ThLZ*, XLVII, 193 f.
    ZNW, XIX, 1919/20, Heft 2. Ibid. 194–96.
K. Deissner, Religionsgeschichtliche Parallelen. Ibid. 215.
A. Reiss, Das Selbstbewußtsein Jesu. Ibid. 215 f.
R. Schütz, Apostel und Jünger. Ibid. 271–73.
Brun-Fridrichsen, Paulus und die Urgemeinde. Ibid. 273 f.
H. Leisegang, Pneuma Hagion. Ibid. 425–27.

1923

"Der religionsgeschichtliche Hintergrund des Prologs zum Johannes-Evan-
    gelium." *Eucharisterion,* Festschrift für Gunkel, II, 3–26.
Besprechung von:
G. Bert, Das Evangelium des Johannes. *ThLZ*, XLVIII, 175–77.
E. Friedell, Das Jesusproblem. Ibid. 177.
R. Jelke, Die Wunder Jesu. Ibid. 177 f.
R. Knopf, Einführung in das N. T. 2. Aufl. Ibid. 294–396.
G. Dalman, Orte und Wege Jesu. 2. Aufl. *ThBl*, II, 123–25.
A. Huck, Synopse der drei ersten Evangelien. Ibid. 150 f.
E. Thurneysen, Dostojewski. *ChrW*, XXXVII, 325.
W. Zündel, Jesus in Bildern aus seinem Leben. Ibid. 556 f.
W. Bousset, Wir heißen euch hoffen. Ibid. 789.
J. Lepsius, Das Leben Jesu. *Literaturblatt der Frankfurter Zeitung* vom
    11. Mai.

1924

"Die liberale Theologie und die jüngste theologische Bewegung." *ThBl*,
    III, 73–86.
"Das Problem der Ethik bei Paulus." *ZNW*, XXIII, 123–40.
Besprechung von:
J. Gr. Machen, The Origin of Paul's Religion. *ThLZ*, XLIX, 13 f.
Ed. Norden, Die Geburt des Kindes. Ibid. 319–23.
H. Lietzmann, An die Korinther I. II. An die Galater. Ibid. 366–69.
H. Hartmann, Jesus, das Dämonische und die Ethik. *ThBl*, III, 162 f.
Fr. Preisigke, Vom göttlichen Fluidum nach ägyptischer Anschauung; Die
    Gotteskraft der frühchristlichen Zeit. Ibid. 185 f.
L. Fendt, Gnostische Mysterien. *ChrW*, XXXVIII, 487 f.
Ad. Deissmann, Licht vom Osten. 4. Aufl. Ibid. 488–90.

1925

Die Erforschung der synoptischen Evangelien. (Aus der Welt der Re-
    ligion, 4.) Gießen: Töpelmann (2. Aufl. 1930).

"Die Bedeutung der neuerschlossenen mandäischen und manichäischen Quellen für das Verständnis des Johannesevangeliums." *ZNW*, XXIV, 100 bis 146.

"Das Problem einer theologischen Exegese des N. T." *ZwZ*, III, 334–57.

"Welchen Sinn hat es, von Gott zu reden?" *ThBl*, IV, 129–35.

"Der christliche Sinn von Glaube, Liebe, Hoffnung." (Skizze eines Vortrags.) *Zeitschr. f. den evang. Religionsunterricht*, XXXVI, 170–72.

Besprechung von:

E. Fascher, Die formgeschichtliche Methode. *ThLZ*, L, 313–18.

W. Gemoll, Das Apophthegma. Ibid. 343 f.

J. Bestmann, Zur Geschichte des neutestl. Kanons. Ibid. 372.

M. Dibelius, Der Brief des Jakobus. *DLZ*, XLVI, 335 f.

Eitrem-Fridrichsen, Die Versuchung Christi. Ibid. 1982–84.

W. F. Otto, Der Geist der Antike und die christliche Welt. *ChrW*, XXXIX, 41–43.

Schriften der Jüdisch-Hellenistischen Literatur in deutscher Übersetzung 3, 4. Ibid. 375.

Ad. Bauer, Vom Judentum zum Christentum. Ibid. 375.

Angelos I. Ibid. 661 f.

G. Krüger, Der Historismus und die Bibel. Ibid.

E. Peterson, Was ist Theologie? Ibid. 1061 f.

Die apostolischen Väter I (Samml. ausgew. kirchen- u. dogmengeschichtl. Quellenschriften II 1, 1). Ibid.

Epistula Apostolorum (Kl. Texte für Vorles. u. Üb. 152). Ibid.

Pistis Sophia, übers. u. herausgeg. v. C. Schmidt. Ibid. 1164.

1926

Jesus. (Die Unsterblichen I.) Berlin: Deutsche Bibliothek. (2. Aufl. 1929; Übersetzung ins Schwedische 1928, ins Dänische 1930, ins Japanische 1933, ins Englische 1934.)

"Das Wesen der dialektischen Methode." *ZwZ*, IV, 40–60.

"Geschichtliche und übergeschichtliche Religion im Christentum" (Über das gleichbetitelte Buch von M. Dibelius). Ibid. 385–403.

"The New Approach to the Synoptic Problem." *The Journal of Religion*, VI, 337–62.

"Die evangelisch-theologische Wissenschaft in der Gegenwart." *Abendblatt der Frankfurter Zeitung* vom 27. Sept. und 11. Okt.

"Wilhelm Heitmüller." *ChrW*, XL, 209–13.

"Die Reform des theologischen Studiums und des kirchlichen Prüfungswesens." (Über die betr. Denkschrift der Greifswalder Fakultät.) Ibid. 422–28.

"Karl Barth: Die Auferstehung der Toten." *ThBl*, V, 1–14.

"Urchristliche Religion" (Bericht über die Literatur 1919–1925). *Archiv f. Religionswiss.*, XXIV, 83–164.
"Urchristentum." (Über Ed. Meyer, Ursprung und Anfänge des Christentums III.) *Literaturblatt der Frankfurter Zeitung* vom 23. Mai.
Besprechung von:
W. Bauer, Das Johannesevangelium. 2. Aufl. *ThLZ*, LI, 246 f.
Ad. Deissmann, Paulus. 2. Aufl. Ibid. 273–78.
Fr. Preisigke, Wörterbuch der griech. Papyrusurkunden, 1. Lief. Ibid. 491 f.
A. Frövig, Das Sendungsbewußtsein Jesu und der Geist. Ibid. 543–45.
W. Bussmann, Synoptische Studien I. *DLZ*, XLVII, 1587–89.

1927

"Analyse des ersten Johannesbriefes." Festgabe für Ad. Jülicher, 138–58.
"Das Johannesevangelium in der neuesten Forschung." *ChrW*, XLI, 502–11.
"Zur Frage der Christologie." (Über Em. Hirsch, Jesus Christus der Herr.) *ZwZ*, V, 41–69.
"Vom Begriff der religiösen Gemeinschaft." (Über das gleichbetitelte Buch von E. Lohmeyer.) *ThBl*, VI, 66–73.
Besprechung von:
W. Schauf, Sarx. *ThLZ*, LII, 34–37.
M. Dibelius, Geschichte der urchristlichen Literatur. Ibid. 80–83.
H. Windisch, Johannes und die Synoptiker. Ibid. 197–200.
P. Fiebig, Der Erzählungsstil der Evangelien. Ibid. 226–28.
J. Sickenberger, Kurzgefaßte Einleitung in d. N. T. Ibid. 321 f.
J. Aufhauser, Antike Jesus-Zeugnisse. Ibid. 339.
E. Lohmeyer, Die Offenbarung des Johannes. Ibid. 505–12.
L. Köhler, Das formgeschichtliche Problem des N. T. Ibid. 578–80.
E. Jung, Die geschichtliche Persönlichkeit Jesu. Ibid.
A. Reatz, Jesus Christus. Ibid.
K. Refer, Der Heiland. *Literaturblatt der Frankf. Zeit.* v. 17. April.
W. Bousset, Apophthegmata. Ibid. v. 11. Sept.
Artikel: Aurelius; Briefliteratur, urchristliche, formgeschichtlich; Brun, J. L. Bugge, Chr. A. *RGG*, 2. Aufl., I.

1928

"Untersuchungen zum Johannesevangelium," A (*Alétheia*). *ZNW*, XXVII, 113–63.
"Die Eschatologie des Johannesevangeliums." *ZwZ*, VI, 4–22.
"Die Bedeutung der dialektischen Theologie für die neutestamentliche Wissenschaft." *ThBl*, VII, 57–67.

"Urchristentum und Staat." *Mitteil. des Universitätsbundes Marburg,* Nr. 19, 1–4.
"Der Glaube als Wagnis." *ChrW,* XLII, 1008–10.
Besprechung von:
W. Bousset, Die Religion des Judentums, 3. Aufl. *ThLZ,* LIII, 250–54.
E. Klostermann, Das Markusevangelium. Ibid. 544–46.
O. Schmitz, Die Bedeutung des Wortes bei Paulus. Ibid. 563–67.
W. Schlatter, Das große Kapitel von der Totenauferstehung. Ibid. 605.
M. Johannessohn, Das biblische *kai egéneto* und seine Geschichte. Ibid. 568 f.
Festgabe für Ad. Deissmann. *ThBl,* VII, 125–29.
G. Kittel, Die Probleme des pal. Judentums und das Urchristentum. *Gnomon,* IV, 297–305.
K. A. Busch, Das Lukas-Evangelium. *ChrW,* XLII, 228 f.
J. Behm, Die mandäische Religion und das Christentum. Ibid. 393.
W. Bousset, Apophthegmata. Ibid. 1041 f.
Artikel: Ebioniten; Eidem, E.; Evangelien, gattungsgeschichtlich; Frey, J.; Fridrichsen, A. J.; Fröwig, D. A.; Gleichnis und Parabel II, in der Bibel; Grass, K.; Heidegger, M.; Jeremias, Kundsin, Lindblom, Literaturgeschichte, biblische 1, 3. *RGG,* 2. Aufl., II.

1929

Jesus. 2. Aufl. (s. 1926).
Der Begriff der Offenbarung im N. T. (Samml. gemeinverständlicher Vorträge 135). Tübingen: Mohr.
"Die Bedeutung des geschichtlichen Jesus für die Theologie des Paulus." *ThBl,* VIII, 137–51.
"Zur Geschichte der Paulus-Forschung." *ThR,* N. F. I, 26–59.
Besprechung von:
Ad. Schlatter, Der Glaube im N. T., 4. Aufl. *ThLZ,* LIV, 195 f.
Fr. Büchsel, Der Geist Gottes im N. T. Ibid. 196–203.
Fr. Büchsel, Johannes und der hellenistische Synkretismus. Ibid. 203–205.
H. Windisch, Der Sinn der Bergpredigt. *DLZ,* L, 985–94.
W. Rust, Die Wunder in der Bibel, 1. 2. *ChrW,* XLIII, 36 f.

1930

Die Erforschung der synoptischen Evangelien. 2. Aufl. (s. 1925). Englische Übersetzung in: *Form Criticism.* Chicago–New York, 1934.
"Untersuchungen zum Johannesevangelium," B. *ZNW,* XXIX, 169–92.
"Urkristendom och religionshistoria." *Svensk Teol. Kvartalskrift,* VI, 299 bis 324 (deutsch in *ThR,* N. F. IV, 1932).

"Aimer son prochain, commandement de Dieu." *Revue d'Histoire et de Philosophie religieuses,* X, 222–41 (deutsch in *Glauben und Verstehen;* s. 1933).

"Die Geschichtlichkeit des Daseins und der Glaube." *ZThK,* N. F. XI, 329 bis 364.

"Mitarbeit an der Straßburger Revue d'Histoire et de Philos. rel.?" *ThBl,* IX, 251–52, 360–62.

Besprechung von:

Th. Zahn, Grundriß der neutestl. Theologie. *ThLZ,* LV, 107–10.

W. Jaeger, Die geistige Gegenwart der Antike. Ibid. 169–71.

E. Lohmeyer, Grundlagen paulinischer Theologie. Ibid. 217–23.

E. Lohmeyer, Der Brief an die Philipper; Kyrios Jesus. *DLZ,* LI, 774–80.

E. Barnikol, Die vorchristliche und frühchristliche Zeit des Paulus; Die drei Jerusalemreisen des Paulus. *ZKG,* XLIX, N. F. XII, 90 f.

A. von Harnack, Einführung in die alte Kirchengeschichte. *ChrW,* XLIV, 182 f.

Artikel: Mosbech, H.; Mystik IV, im N. T.; Mythos III B, im N. T.; Noachische Gebote; Offenbarung IV, im N. T.; Pastoralbriefe; Paulus. *RGG,* 2 Aufl., IV.

1931

Die Geschichte der synoptischen Tradition. 2. Aufl. (s. 1921).

Besprechung von:

A. von Harnack, Die Bezeichnung Jesu als "Knecht Gottes" etc. *ThLZ,* LVI, 97 f.

K. Schoch, Christi Kreuzigung am 14. Nisan; J. Schaumberger, Der 14. Nisan als Kreuzigungstag und die Synoptiker. Ibid. 272 f.

U. v. Wilamowitz-Mœllendorf, Die *katharmoi* des Empedokles. Ibid. 338 bis 340.

M. Goguel, Au seuil de l'Evangile. Jean Baptiste. Ibid. 345–48.

H. Lietzmann, Ein Beitrag zur Mandäerfrage. Ibid. 557–80.

A. Schweitzer, Die Mystik des Apostels Paulus. *DLZ,* LII, 1153–58.

R. Liechtenhan, Paulus. Ibid. 1393 f.

Artikel: von Schrenk, E.; von Stromberg, A.; Torm, Fr.; Urgemeinde; Westberg, Fr.; Wetter, G. P. *RGG,* 2. Aufl., V.

1932

"Römer 7 und die Anthropologie des Paulus." *Imago Dei,* Festschrift für G. Krüger, 53–62.

"Urchristentum und Religionsgeschichte." (Über K. Holls gleichbetitelte Schrift.) *ThR,* N. F. IV, 1–21 (s. 1930).

"Jesus der König, der kein König war." (Über R. Eislers Werk: *Jesous Basileus* etc). *Literaturblatt der Frankfurter Zeitung* vom 24. Jan.
Besprechung von:
K. Mittring, Heilswirklichkeit bei Paulus. *ThLZ*, LVII, 156–59.
Schmid-Stählin, Gesch. der griech. Lit., 1. Teil, 1. Band. Ibid. 291 f.
E. Benz, Das Todesproblem in der stoischen Philosophie. Ibid. 387 f.
W. Bussmann, Synoptische Studien II. *DLZ*, LIII, 2257–60.
E. Barnikol, Personenprobleme der Apostelgeschichte; Johannes Markus, Silas und Titus; Römer 15, letzte Reiseziele des Paulus, Jerusalem, Rom und Antiochien; Der nichtpaulinische Ursprung des Parallelismus der Apostel Petrus und Paulus. *ZKG*, LI, III. F. II, 554 f.
R. Reitzenstein, Die hellenistischen Mysterienreligionen, 3. Aufl.; Die Vorgeschichte der christl. Taufe. *Hist. Zeitschr.*, 145, 372–76.

1933

Glauben und Verstehen. Gesammelte Aufsätze. Tübingen: Mohr.
"Gott ruft uns." (Predigt.) *Neuwerk*, XIV, 70–81.
"Zur Frage des theologischen Studiums." *Montag-Morgenblatt der Frankfurter Zeitung* vom 2. Jan.
"Die Aufgabe der Theologie in der gegenwärtigen Situation." *ThBl*, XII, 161 bis 166.
"Der Arier-Paragraph im Raume der Kirche." Ibid. 359–70.
Besprechung von:
E. Klostermann, Das Lukasevangelium. *ThLZ*, LVIII, 70 f.
O. Michel, Paulus und seine Bibel. Ibid. 157–59.
W. Bussmann, Synoptische Studien III. *DLZ*, LIV, 241–45.
Artikel: *agalliaomai, agnoeo, aidos, aischynomai, aletheia, aniemi, aphemi, ginosko. ThWB*, I.

1934

Form Criticism (s. 1930).
"Comment Dieu nous parle-t-il dans la Bible?" *Foi et Vie*, XXXII, 263–74.
"How does God speak to us through the Bible?" *The Student Work 1934*, 108–12.
"Der Glaube an Gott den Schöpfer." (Predigt.) *Evang. Theologie*, I, 1934/35, 175–89.
"Neueste Paulusforschung." *ThR*, N. F. VI, 229–46.
Besprechung von:
W. F. Howard, The Fourth Gospel in Recent Criticism. *ThLZ*, LIX, 68–71.

J. E. Carpenter, The Johannine Writings. Ibid. 87–89.
E. Stauffer, Grundbegriffe einer Morphologie des neutestl. Denkens. Ibid. 211–15.
O. Kietzig, Die Bekehrung des Paulus. *DLZ*, LV, 1154–59.
H. D. Wendland, Die Eschatologie des Reiches Gottes bei Jesus. Ibid. 2019 bis 2025.
J. Wobbe, Der Charis-Gedanke bei Paulus. Ibid. 2308.
H. Lietzmann, Geschichte der alten Kirche, I. *ZKG*, LIII, III. F. IV, 624 bis 630.
E. Barnikol, Mensch und Messias. Phil. 2. Ibid. 632–36.

1935

"Polis und Hades in der Antigone des Sophokles." *Theol. Aufsätze für Karl Barth*, 78–79.
Atrikel: *deloo, eleos, elpis, eulabes, eufraino, zao. ThWB*, II.

1936

"Jesus und Paulus." In: *Jesus Christus im Zeugnis der Heil. Schrift und der Kirche* (Beih. zur Evang. Theol. 2), 68–90.
"Die Bergpredigt Jesu und das Recht des Staates." *Forschungen und Fortschritte*, XII, 101 f.
"Der Sinn des christlichen Schöpfungsglaubens." *Zeitschr. f. Missionskunde und Religionswissenschaft*, LI, 1–20.
"Predigt über Act. 17: 22–32." *Bekenntnis-Predigten*, 21, 14–26.
"Neueste Paulusforschung." *ThR*, N. F. VIII, 1–22.
Besprechung von:
Schmid-Stählin, Geschichte der griech. Literatur, 1. Teil, 2 Bd. *ThLZ*, LXI, 303 f.

1937

"Reich Gottes und Menschensohn." (Über R. Ottos gleichbetiteltes Buch.) *ThR*, N. F. IX, 1–35.
"Hirsch's Auslegung des Johannes-Evangeliums." *Evang. Theologie*, IV, 115–42.
Besprechung von:
W. Luther, "Wahrheit" und "Lüge" im ältesten Griechentum. *ThLZ*, LXII, 245 f.
H. Odeberg, 3. Enoch or The Hebrew Book of Enoch. Ibid. 449–53.
J. Sundwall, Die Zusammensetzung des Markusevangeliums. *DLZ*, LVIII, 1133–36.
L. Bieler, Theios Anér I. II. *ZKG*, LVI, III. F. VII, 640–43.

1938

"Das Verständnis von Welt und Mensch im Griechentum und im N. T."
(Skizze eines Vortrags.) *In Extremis,* 9–24 (s. 1940).
Artikel: *thanatos, hilaros, kauchaomai. ThWB,* III.

1939

"Johannes Weiss zum Gedächtnis." *ThBl,* XVIII, 242–46.
Besprechung von:
H-D. Wendland, Geschichtsauffassung und Geschichtsbewußtsein im
N.T. *ThLZ,* LXIV, 252–56.
H. Lietzmann, Geschichte der alten Kirche, II. *ZKG,* LVIII, III. F. IX,
260–66.
Sundkler-Fridrichsen, Contributions à l'Étude de la Pensée Missionnaire
dans le N. T. *OLZ,* XLII, 302 f.
Coniectanea Neotestamentica II. Ibid. 437–39.

1940

Christus des Gesetzes Ende. (Zusammen mit H. Schlier; Beiträge zu
Evang. Theologie 1.) München: Lempp.
"Das Verständnis von Welt und Mensch im Griechentum und im N. T."
ThBl, XIX, 1–14.
"Johanneische Schriften und Gnosis." (Über E. Percy, Untersuchungen
über den Ursprung der johanneischen Theologie.) *OLZ,* XLIII,
150–75.
Besprechung von:
E. Hirsch, Die Auferstehungsgeschichten und der christliche Glaube.
ThLZ, LXV, 224–46.
M. Dibelius, Paulus auf dem Areopag. *Gnomon,* XVI, 334–36.

1941

Das Evangelium des Johannes. (In Meyers Kommentar.) Göttingen:
Vandenhoeck u. Ruprecht.
Offenbarung und Heilsgeschehen. (Beitr. z. Evang. Theologie 7). Mün-
chen: Lempp.
"Die Frage nach der Echtheit von Matth. 16, 17–19." *ThBl,* XX, 265–79.

1942

Besprechung von:
A. von Jüchen, Jesus und Pilatus. *ThLZ,* LXVII, 26.
W. Nestle, Vom Mythos zum Logos. Ibid. 146–48.

Schmid-Stählin, Gesch. der griech. Literatur, 1. Teil 3. Bd., 1. Hälfte.
    Ibid. 148 f.
C. M. Edsman, Le baptême de feu. *Gött. Gel. Anz.*, CIV, 202–206.
Artikel: *lype, merimnao, nekros. ThWB*, IV.

1943

Besprechung von:
K-H. Volkmann-Schluck, Plotin als Interpret Platons. *ThLZ*, LXVIII,
    203 bis 205.
J. Schmidt, Ethos. Ibid. 205 f.

1944

"Zum Thema: Christentum und Antike." *ThR*, N. F. XVI, 1–20.
"Zur Frage der wissenschaftlichen Ausbildung der Theologen." Studien-
    betreuung der Kriegsteilnehmer der Martin-Luther-Universität Halle,
    November.

1945

"Adam, wo bist du? Über das Menschenbild der Bibel." *Die Wandlung*,
    I, 22–33.
"Das Leben in zwei Welten." *Predigt.*

1946

"Anknüpfung und Widerspruch." *Theol. Zeitschr.* (Basel), II, 401–18.
"Das Verhältnis der Universität zu Antike und Christentum." Berichte
    des Planungs-Ausschusses der Philipps-Universität Marburg zur
    Neugestaltung der deutschen Hochschulen, 20–27.

1947

Exegetische Probleme des zweiten Korintherbriefes. Symbolae Biblicae
    Upsalienses, 9.
"To love your Neighbour" (Übers. von "Aimer son Prochain," s. unter
    1930). *Scottish Periodical,* 1, 42–56.
"Glossen im Römerbrief. *ThLZ*, LXXII, 197–202.
Besprechung von:
Wilfred L. Knox, St. Paul and the Church of the Gentiles. *ThLZ*, LXXII,
    77–80.
P. Brommer, Eidos et Idea. Ibid. 79–82.
Wilh. Oehler, Zum Missionscharakter des Johannesevangeliums. Ibid. 169
    bis 1170.

Werner Georg Kümmel, Verheißung und Erfüllung. Ibid. 271–74.
Georg Wünsch, Evangelische Ethik des Politischen. Verkündigung und
Forschung, *Theologischer Jahresbericht* 1942/46, 1946/47, 253–66.

1948

Theologie des Neuen Testaments. 1. Lieferung. Tübingen: Mohr (Sie-
beck).
"Humanismus und Christentum." *Studium Generale,* I, 2, 70–77.
"Zur Geschichte der Lichtsymbolik." *Philologus,* 97, 1–36.
"Bekenntnis- und Liedfragmente im ersten Petrusbrief." Coniect. Neotest.
XI, in honorem Antonii Fridrichsen, 1–14.
"Gnade und Freiheit." *Glaube und Geschichte,* Festschr. für Fr. Gogarten,
7–20.
"Neues Testament und Mythologie" (aus: *Offenbarung und Heilsgesche-
hen,* s. unter 1941) und "Zu Schniewinds Thesen," in *Kerygma und
Mythos.* Hamburg: Reich u. Heidrich, S. 15–53 und 135–53.
"Adam, wo bist du?" (aus: *Die Wandlung,* s. unter 1945). *Lebend. Wis-
senschaft,* 10. Heft. Stuttgart: Kreuz-Verlag.
"Heilsgeschichte und Geschichte." Über O. Cullmann, Christus und die
Zeit. *ThLZ,* LXXIII, 659–66.
Artikel: *oiktiro. ThWB,* V.

1949

Das Urchristentum im Rahmen der antiken Religionen (Erasmus-Biblio-
thek), Zürich: Artemis-Verlag.
"Weissagung und Erfüllung." *Studia Theologica* (Lund), II, 1–24 (s.
unter 1950).
"Das Christentum als orientalische und als abendländische Religion."
Schriften der Wittheit zu Bremen, XVIII, 4.
"Zu Schniewinds Thesen" (s. unter 1948) in "Entmythologisierung."
Stuttgart: Evang. Verlagswerk.
"Für die christliche Freiheit." *Die Wandlung,* IV, 417–422.
Besprechung von:
O. Cullmann, Les premières confessions de foi Chrétienne, *ThLZ*
LXXIV, 40–42.

1950

Das Evangelium des Johannes. 2. Aufl. (s. unter 1941). Gött.: V. u. R.
Le Christianisme primitif dans le cadre des religions antiques. Übers. von
Das Urchristentum im Rahmen der antiken Religionen (s. unter
1949). Paris: Payot.

"Das Problem der Hermeneutik." *ZThK*, XLVII, 47–69 (s. u. und unter 1951).

"Ursprung und Sinn der Typologie als hermeneutischer Methode." *Pro Regno et Sanctuario*, Festschr. für G. van der Leeuw, 89–100. Abgedruckt in *ThLZ*, LXXV, 1950, 205–12.

"Die Bedeutung der alttestamentlich-jüdischen Tradition für das christliche Abendland." Welt ohne Haß, Aufsätze und Ansprachen zum 1. Kongreß über bessere menschliche Beziehungen in München. Berlin, Hamburg, Stuttgart: Christian-Verlag, 43–54.

"Das Problem des Verhältnisses von Theologie und Verkündigung im Neuen Testament." *Aux Sources de la Tradition Chrétienne*, Festschr. für M. Goguel. Neuchâtel-Paris, 32–42.

"Weissagung und Erfüllung." Abdruck aus *Studia Theologica*, II (s. unter 1949), *ZThK*, XLVII, 360–83.

"Hermeneutikkens Problem, I." Aus *ZThK*, XLVII, 1950. S. o. unter 1950), *Tidehverv*, XXIV, 86–93.

Geleitwort zur Neuauflage von Ad. v. Harnack, "Das Wesen des Christentums."

Besprechung von:

K. Prümm, Religionsgeschichtliches Handbuch für den Raum der altchristlichen Umwelt. *ThLZ*, LXXV, 481–84.

M. Pohlenz, Der hellenische Mensch, Ibid. 596–600.

H. Herter, Platons Akademie. Ibid. 732–33.

R. Harder, Eigenart der Griechen. *Gnomon*, XXII, 343–48.

1951

Theologie des Neuen Testaments. 2. Lieferung. Tübingen: Mohr (Siebeck).

Jesus, 3. Aufl., Tübingen: Mohr (s. 1926 und 1929).

Theology of the New Testament Vol. I. New York, Charles Scribner's Sons.

"NT u. Mythologie etc." in *Kerygma u. Mythos*, I (s. 1948), 2. Aufl.

"Das christologische Bekenntnis des Ökumenischen Rates." *Schweizerische Theol. Umschau*, XXI, 25–36. Gleichfalls in: *Evangel. Theologie*, XI, N. F. VI, 1951/52 1–13.

"Hermeneutikkens Problem," II (s. unter 1950). *Tidehverv*, XXV, 8–12.

"Theologie und Glaube" (Ein Brief). *Unterwegs*, V, 273–74.

"Die kirchliche Redaktion des ersten Johannesbriefes." In Memoriam Ernst Lohmeyer 189—201. Stuttgart: Evangel. Verlagswerk.

1952

Das Evangelium des Johannes, 3. Aufl. (s. unter 1941).

Glauben und Verstehen, II. Ges. Aufsätze. Tübingen: Mohr (Siebeck).

Theology of the New Testament I. London: SCM Press.
"Gnosis" (Besprechung von Dom Jacques Dupont, La Connaissance religieuse dans les Épitres de Saint Paul). *Journal of Theological Studies,* New Series, Vol. III, Part 1, S. 10–26.
"Humanism and Christianity." *Journal of Religion,* XXXII, Nr. 2 S. 77–86.
"Zum Problem der Entmythologisierung." *Kerygma und Mythos,* II, 177–208.
"Der Mensch zwischen den Zeiten." *Man in God's Design* (Studiorum Novi Testamenti Societas), 39–59.
"Zur Auslegung von Gal. 2, 15–17." *Ecclesia semper reformanda* (Sonderheft der Ev. Theologie, Ernst Wolf zum 50. Geburtstag), 41–45.
"Das deutsche Volk und Israel." *Merkur,* VI, Heft 12, S. 1111–15. (Antwort auf Leo Baeck "Israel und das deutsche Volk" Ibid, Heft 10, Seite 901–11).
"Gnosis" (Bible Key Words from Gerh. Kittels Theol. Wörterb. zum NT), (s. oben unter 1933 Artikel *ginosko*).

1953

Theologie des Neuen Testaments, 3. Lieferung. Tübingen: Mohr (Siebeck).
Das Evangelium des Johannes (s. unter 1941), 4. Aufl.
"Ignatius und Paulus." *Studia Paulina,* S. 37–51, in Honorem Johannis de Zwaan. Haarlem: De Erven F. Bohn N. V.
"Zum Thema: Christentum und Antike." *ThR,* N. F. 21, S. 1–14.
"Die christliche Hoffnung und das Problem der Entmythologisierung." *Unterwegs,* VII, S. 257–64.
"Weihnachten," *Neue Züricher Zeitung* vom 25. Dez., Blatt 1.

1954

Theologie des Neuen Testaments (s. unter 1953), 2. Aufl.
Das Urchristentum im Rahmen der antiken Religionen (s. unter 1949), 2. Aufl.
Glauben und Verstehen, I (s. unter 1933), 2. Aufl.
"Die christliche Hoffnung und das Problem der Entmythologisierung" (s. unter 1953), Rundfunk-Vortrag und Diskussion mit G. Bornkamm, Fr. K. Schumann. Stuttgart: Evang. Verlagswerk.
"Antwort an Karl Jaspers." *Theol. Zeitsch.* (Basel), S. 81–95. Ebenso in *Merkur,* VIII (75), S. 415–26 und in *Kerygma und Mythos,* III, S. 47–59, sowie in: Karl Jaspers—*Rudolf Bultmann, Die Frage der Entmythologisierung,* S. 57–73, München: Piper-Verlag.

"Ist humanistische Bildung zeitgemäß?" *Die alte Schulglocke* Nr. 8.
Besprechung von:
H. J. Schoeps, Theologie und Geschichte des Judenchristentums. *Gnomon,* XXVI, 177–89.
"History and Eschatology in the New Testament." In: *New Testament Studies,* I, 5–16.
C. H. Dodd, The Interpretation of the Fourth Gospel. *New Testament Studies,* I, 77–91.
Bemerkungen zu dem Aufsatz "Der Auferstandene" in *Der evangel. Erficher.* 98–100.
Artikel: *peitho, penthos, pistis. ThWB,* V.

1955

"Wissenschaft und Existenz." In: *Ehrfurcht vor dem Leben,* Festschrift für Albert Schweitzer zum 80. Geburtstag, 30–43.
"Echte und säkularisierte Verkündigung." *Universitas,* 699–706.
"The Transformation of the Idea of the Church in Early Christianity," *Canadian Journal of Theology,* 73–81.
Theology of the New Testament, II. Trans. Kendrick Grobel. London: SCM Press.
L'Interprétation du Nouveau Testament (Sammlung verschiedener früher publizierter Aufsätze). Paris: Aubier, Éditions Montaigne.
Essays, Philosophical and Theological (Übersetzung von *Glauben und Verstehen,* II (s. unter 1952). London: SCM Press.
"Zum Thema Christentum und Antike." *ThR,* XXIII, 207–29.
Vorwort zu Erich Frank, *Wissen, Wollen, Glauben.* Zürich: Artemis-Verlag.

1956

Das Evangelium des Johannes. 4. Aufl. (s. 1941). Göttingen: Vandenhoeck u. Ruprecht.
Primitive Christianity in Its Contemporary Setting (Übersetzung von *Das Urchristentum im Rahmen der antiken Religionen,* s. 1949). New York, Meridian Books.
Marburger Predigten. Tübingen: J. C. B. Mohr (Paul Siebeck).
" 'The Bible Today' und die Eschatologie." In: *The Background of the New Testament and Its Eschatology,* Festschrift für C. H. Dodd, 402–408. Cambridge: The University Press.
Besprechung von Dom J. Dupont, "Essais sur le Christologie de St. Jean." *ThLZ,* 33–35.

1957

Die Geschichte der synoptischen Tradition. 3. Aufl. (s. 1921).
Das Evangelium des Johannes. 6. Aufl. (s. 1941).
History and Eschatology. Edinburgh: The University Press. Das gleiche
    Buch unter dem Titel *The Presence of Eternity.* New York: Harper
    & Brothers.
"Der Mensch und seine Welt nach dem Urteil der Bibel." *Deutscher
    Pfarrertag in Marburg/Lahn,* Sept. 1957, S. 10–18.
"Allgemeine Wahrheiten und christliche Verkündigung." *ZHTK,* 244–54.
"In eigener Sache" (Besprechung von R. Marlé, "Bultmann et l'interpréta-
    tion du NT"). *ThLZ.,* 241–50.

1958

Theologie des Neuen Testaments. 3. Aufl. (s. 1953).
Die Geschichte der synoptischen Tradition. 4. Aufl. (s. 1921).
Geschichte und Eschatologie (deutsche Ausgabe von *History and
    Eschatology,* s. 1957). Tübingen: J. C. B. Mohr (Paul Siebeck).
Jesus and the Word. (engl. Ausgabe von *Jesus,* s. 1926 bzw. 1934). 2.
    Aufl. New York: Charles Scribner's Sons.
Jesus Christ and Mythology. New York: Charles Scribner's Sons.
"For Freedom and Responsibility." *Christian Century,* 967–69.
Der Gedanke der Freiheit nach antikem und christlichem Verständnis.
    Pforzheim. (Nicht im Buchhandel, aber s. 1959 in: Glauben und
    Verstehen.)
"Das Befremdliche des christlichen Glaubens." *ZThK,* 185–200.

1959

Das Evangelium des Johannes. 7. Aufl. (s. 1941).
Glauben und Verstehen, Ges. Aufsätze, III. Tübingen: J. C. B. Mohr
    (Paul Siebeck).
Lizenz-Ausgabe der Theologie des NT. 3. Aufl. Berlin: Evangel. Verlags-
    anstalt.
History and Eschatology. (Japan. Übersetzung, s. 1957).
"Adam und Christus nach Röm. 5." *ZNW,* 481–86.
"Erziehung und christlicher Glaube." In: *Martin Heidegger zum 70.
    Geburtstag,* 175–79.
"Zur Frage nach den Quellen der Apostelgeschichte." In: *New Testa-
    ment Essays in Memory of T. W. Manson,* 68–80. Manchester:
    The University Press.

"Ein neues Paulus-Verständnis?" Besprechung von J. Munck, "Paulus und die Heilsgeschichte." *ThLZ*, 481–86.

1960

Die Erforschung der synoptischen Evangelien. 3. Aufl. (s. 1925). Berlin: Töpelmann.

Primitive Christianity in Its Contemporary Setting (engl. Übersetzung von *Das Urchristentum im Rahmen der antiken Reiligionen*, s. 1949 u. 1956). Fontana Library.

Jesus Christ and Mythology (s. 1958). London: SCM Press.

Jesus Christ and Mythology (Japan. Übersetzung, s. 1958). Tokyo: Shinkyo Shuppansha.

Das Verhältnis der urchristlichen Christusbotschaft zum historischen Jesus. Sitzungsber. Heidelberg. Akad. Wiss., Phil.-hist. Klasse, 3. Abhandlung.

"On Behalf of Christian Freedom" (deutsch "Für die christliche Freiheit" in: *Die Wandlung*, s. 1949). In: *The Journal of Religion*, XL, 1, S. 95–99.

"Das deutsche Volk und Israel." In: *Besinnung und Umschau*, II, 1 (s. 1952).

Existence and Faith. Ed. and trans., S. Ogden. Shorter Writings. New York: Living Age Books.

"Reflexionen zum Thema Geschichte und Tradition." In: *Weltbewohner und Weimaraner*, Festschrift für Ernst Beutler, 9–21. Zürich: Artemis-Verlag.

"Ein Wort über Bildung." In: *Strix, Schülerzeitung des Alten Gymnasiums in Oldenburg*, LX, Nr. 1, 4–6.

1961

Glauben und Verstehen, I, 4. Aufl.; II, 3. Aufl. (s. 1933, 1952).

Die Erforschung der synoptischen Evangelien. 4. Aufl. (s. 1925).

Das Verhältnis der urchristlichen Christusbotschaft zum historischen Jesus. 2. Aufl. (s. 1960).

Das Urchristentum im Rahmen der antiken Religionen (Japan. Übersetzung, s. 1949). Tokyo: Shinkyo Shuppansha.

Die Geschichte der synoptischen Tradition 5. Aufl. (s. 1921).

"Das Verhältnis des urchristlichen Christuskerygmas zum historischen Jesus." In: *Der historische Jesus und der kerygmatische Christus*, 233–35. Berlin: Evangel. Verlagsanstalt.

"Das Verständnis der Geschichte in Griechentum und Christentum." In: *Der Sinn der Geschichte*, 50–65. München: Beck.

"Optimismus und Pessimismus in Antike und Christentum." In: *Universitas*, XVI, 8, S. 811–33.
"Zum Problem der Entmythologisierung." In: *Il Problema della Demitizzazione*. Roma: Istituto di Studi Filosofici.

1962

Das Verhältnis der urchristlichen Christusbotschaft zum historischen Jesus. 3. Aufl. (s. 1960).
Glauben und Verstehen, III (s. 1959).
"Das Urchristentum im Rahmen der antiken Religionen" (s. 1949). In: *Rowohlts deutscher Enzyklopädie*.
"On the Problem of Demythologizing" (s. 1961). *The Journal of Religion*, 96–102.
"Zur Interpretation des Johannesevangeliums" (Besprechung der Bücher von W. Thüsing, *Die Erhöhung und Verherrlichung Jesu im Johannesevangelium*, und von D. E. Holwerda, *The Holy Spirit and Eschatology in the Gospel of John*). ThLZ, 1–8.
Besprechung von Schubert M. Ogden, *Christ without Myth*. *The Journal of Religion*, 96–102.
Ergänzungsheft zur Geschichte der synoptischen Tradition (s. 1921).
Briefwechsel zwischen Dvoracek, v. Campenhausen, und Bultmann. In: *Communio Viatorum*, Prag.
"Jesus Christ and Mythology" (Japan. Übersetzung, s. 1958).
"Zur Frage einer philosophischen Theologie." In: *Einsichten*, Festschrift für Gerh. Krüger, 36–39. Frankfurt: Klostermann.
"Das Verständnis der Geschichte in Griechentum und Christentum" (s. 1961). In: *Politische Ordnung und menschliche Existenz*, Festschrift für E. Voegelin, 59–70. München: Beck.

1963

Exegetische Probleme des zweiten Korintherbriefes (s. 1947). Darmstadt: Wissenschaftliche Buchgesellschaft.
The History of the Synoptic Tradition (engl. Übersetzung von *Geschichte der synoptischen Tradition*, s. 1921). Oxford: Blackwell.
Jesus (Japan. Übersetzung, s. 1926).
Theologie des Neuen Testaments I (Japan. Übersetzung, s. 1948, 1951). Tokyo: Shinkyo Shuppansha.
"Ist der Glaube an Gott erledigt?" (Über John A. T. Robinson, *Honest to God*). In der Wochenschrift *Zeit* VII, Nr. 19, S. 18.
"Der Gottesgedanke und der moderne Mensch." ZThK, 335–48.
"Zum Problem der Entmythologisierung. In: *Kerygma u. Mythos*, VI, 1, S. 16–19 (s. 1961).

1964

Geschichte und Eschatologie, 2. Aufl.

Jesus Christus und die Mythologie (r. 1958). Hamburg: Furche-Verl.

Der alte und der neue Mensch in der Theologie der Paulus (Drei Anfgabe aus der FNW 1924, aus Imago, Festschr. für G. Krüger 1932, aus ZNW 1959). Darmstadt, Wissenschaftl-Buchgesellschaft.

Der Sinn unserer Weibnacht. Suddendsche. Freiburg, Feuilleton zu Weihnachten, Dec. 1964.

1965

Theologie des Neuen Testaments (r. 1948. 1951), 6. Aufl.

Index of Subjects

action, 190, 263 f.
Acts of the Apostles, 156, 215
alienation, 192
altruism, 89 f., 193
anathemas, 144
analogia entis, 5, 18
analogy, theory of, 124 f., 259, 273
anthropology, 66, 73, 89, 140 f., 176 f., 187, 199, 258, 278
anthroposophy, 206
Apocalypse, 46, 70, 75, 214 f., 282
Apocrypha, 212
Aristotelianism, 205
art, 216
asceticism, 189, 284

baptism, 155
being, 131, 141, 164 f.
Benediction, 215 f.
"between-ness," 157–161
Beyond, the, 84
Bible, 172, 217; *see also* New Testament, Old Testament
Byzantine studies, 201

Cambridge Platonists, 48
canonicity, 159
categories, 80 ff., 195, 219
categorical imperative, 192
catholicism: *see* Roman catholicism
causality, 57 f., 263 f., 267
Christ event, the, 30 f., 38, 70 f., 121 f., 126, 138, 278
Christianity Today, 28
Christliche Welt, Die, xx
Christology, 120, 123, 178, 245, 272

Church, the, 39, 75, 171, 195, 224, 251 f., 260, 276 ff., 285
community, religious, 163–167, 194, 198 f., 225
congregational democracy, 156
Confessional Church, xxi, 4, 25, 174, 222
confessional theology, 170 f.
Copernicanism, 14, 17
cosmology, 66–72, 75–82, 266
Covenants, 222 ff.
Cross, the, 32 f., 38, 135, 199, 223
Cynic philosophers, 154

Dead Sea scrolls, 206, 222
decision, 29, 31 f., 39, 60, 92–97, 99, 186, 263
deideologizing, 200, 280
demythologizing, xii f., xxv, 8 ff., 110–116, 126, 199 f., 209, 257–261, 271 f.
desecularization, 11
deutero-Pauline literature, 157 f.
dialectrical theology, xxiv, 170, 174, 184 f., 257 f.
dogma/dogmatism, xviii, 47 f., 195, 261
dualism, 77 f., 268, 284

Easter, 242, 286
ecclesiology, 168 f., 278
education, 251 ff., 284–287
election, 178
empiricism, 128, 142, 275
encounter, 48 f., 59, 63, 260
Enlightenment, 175

311

ephapax, 12, 258
Epistles, 222
eros, 193, 225
eschatological event, 189 f., 260 f., 278
eschatology, 30 f., 155–160, 153, 187 ff., 197 f., 215, 265–268, 280
ethical demand, 88 f., 93, 101, 150, 186, 269 f.
ethics, 233, 279 f.
eucharist, the, 158
evangelical church, 28
exclusiveness, 142 f., 275
exegesis, 23, 29, 130, 139, 149, 153, 236 f., 247 ff.
existence, 8, 11, 132, 140, 162, 271
existence, authentic, 133 f., 194, 260, 267, 274
existence, limitation of, 88
existence, meaning of, 85, 113 f., 146 ff., 161, 163, 188, 263
existential theology, 144, 171
existentialism, xii, xv, 24–29, 45, 106, 116, 128–131, 138, 142, 144–147, 188, 260, 271 f., 274, 276
existentialist interpretation, 15, 114 f., 120–123, 126, 158, 166, 175, 177, 247 f., 258 f., 271 f., 286 f.

faith, 12, 19, 31 f., 34, 36 f., 83 ff., 89, 91, 94–97, 145 f., 147, 179, 188, 196 f., 243, 245, 260, 262
fallenness of man, 133 f.
forgiveness, 91, 100 f., 185
form, 205
Fourth Gospel, the, 78–82, 212; *see also* John: Gospel of John
freedom, 53, 167, 186 f., 228 f., 268
fundamentalism, 30
"Für und wider die Theologie Bultmanns," 195
future, the, 57, 187, 263, 265

Gifford Lectures: *see* Bultmann, Rudolf: *History and Eschatology*
Gnosticism, 12, 75, 78 f., 147, 155, 189, 206 f., 222
God, acts of, 43, 227 f.
God, concept of, 46, 102 f., 124, 126, 193, 213, 259, 273
God, futurity of, 79

God, Kingdom of: *see* Kingdom of God
God, man's relation to, 42, 99 f., 147 f., 176 f., 185 f., 269 f.
God, will of, 218
God, word of: *see* Word of God
good, the, 191 f.
good works, 197
Gospels, 204 f.
grace, 21, 32, 93, 143, 223, 234, 275

Hades, 204
Haggadah, 217, 282, 284
Halakah, 217, 282
Hellenism, 155 f., 203 f.
Hellenist cults, 141
hermeneutics, 8 f., 22–25, 29, 54 f., 114, 165, 173, 176, 208 f., 263, 271, 275, 281
historicity, 52 f., 62, 66 f., 72–77, 167, 195 f., 198, 258, 262, 267, 279
historiography, 67, 154
history, 6 ff., 71 f., 180 f., 228, 258
history, consciousness of, 283 f.
history, interpretation of, 37 f., 135, 172 f., 257, 274 f.
history, meaning of, xvi, 38 f., 56 ff., 74, 106, 264 f.
history, philosophy of, 141, 153, 262–265
Hitler regime, xxi, 221
Holy Spirit, the, 160, 202, 207
holyness, 160, 217
homiletics, 277
humanism, 194, 209 f., 281

idealism, 124, 164 f., 171, 197
ideology, 200
images, 40, 112
imperative, divine, 190 f., 270
Incarnation, 32
individualism, 170 f., 199
Interpreter's Bible, 213
invisibility, 196 f.
irrationality, xvi f.
Israel, 226 f., 285

Jesus, event of: *see* Christ event, the
Johannine writings, 158

Judaism, 69 f., 155, 168, 173, 201, 282 ff.
Der Juden Sachsenspiegel, 222
judgment, 33; *see also* Last Judgment
justification by faith, 12, 172, 184 ff., 198, 246, 279

Kantianism, 191
kerygma, xii, xv, 32, 43, 131, 138 ff., 143, 161, 203, 208 ff., 242 ff., 253, 260, 274 f. 281 f.
kerygma theology, 12, 237
Kingdom of God, 163 f., 184, 197, 224
Kings, Book of, 225
knowledge, 44, 49, 86, 145 f., 229

language, 151, 252
Last Judgment, 58, 73, 122, 264, 267
law, constitutional, 156 f., 187, 233
Law, Mosaic, 212 ff., 218, 222, 282 f.
legalism, 157, 217, 282
Liberal Protestantism, 47, 197
liberal theology, xxiv, 108–111, 183 f., 245, 261, 271
liberalism, 26 f.
limitations, 90 f., 269
linguistic analysis, 35, 142, 275
literalism, 25 f.
Logos, 180, 206
Lord's Prayer, 215
love, 89–92, 150, 192–197, 269, 279 f.
Lutheranism, 171, 185

man, meaning of, 24; *see also* existence, meaning of
Marcionites, 212
Marxists, 64
meaning, 59, 62 f.
Messianic secret, 81, 238–241
methodology, xii ff., 107 f.
ministry, 168
miracles, 241 f.
Moffatt series, 213
monism, 209
myth, 9 f., 35, 45, 111–115, 259, 261
mythology, 25 ff., 66 ff., 197, 199, 266

nature, 78 ff., 266
Neo-Kantianism, 190
neo-orthodoxy, 21

New Testament, 10 f., 113 ff., 133 ff., 149 f., 160, 168, 177–180, 199, 201 f., 211, 222, 226, 258 f., 281
nihilism, 52 f., 83–86, 89, 188, 268 f.
nothingness, 84 f., 269 f.

obedience, 88, 179, 186, 217 f., 279, 283
objective environment, 78 f.
Old Testament, 68, 155, 178, 181 f., 203, 218, 283–286
omnipotence, 86, 102 f.
ontic actualization, 262
ontological analysis, 29, 132, 259, 279
ontological possibility, 263 f.
ontological structure, 196
organization, 194 f.
original sin, 184
orthodox theology, 109
orthodoxy, 159, 166, 195

pacifism, 184
Paideia, 209 f., 281
pantheism, 184, 189
Parousia, 71 f., 160
past, the, 187, 216
Pastoral Epistles, 156, 159
Pentecost, 32
personality, 60 f.
Pharisees, 282
phenomenology, 29, 36 f., 259 f.
philology, 280 ff.
philosophical faith, 136
philosophy, 45 f., 99–103, 257, 268–271
physis, 48
pietism, 174
piety, 157
Platonism, 164, 205
polis, 204
political preaching, 231 f., 285
positivism, 56
preaching, 43, 48, 99 ff., 151, 179, 228, 245–249, 252, 260 f., 273, 277, 284, 286
present, the, 44, 52, 105 f., 262
preunderstanding, 7, 14, 23 f., 55, 139, 258, 263, 274
primitive Christianity, 72 f., 155, 159
promise, 80 f.
prophecy, 223

Prophets, 217, 224 ff., 230 f., 285
proselytes, 217, 284
providence, divine, 64, 265
Psalms, 217

Qumran texts, 282, 284

rabbinical literature, 213
reality, 175, 263
realization, 260
reason, 146, 186 f., 280
redemption, 33, 38, 70, 148 f.
reductionism, 28
reform, 162
Reformation, 17, 172
Reformation theology, 246, 258
relativism, 76
religion, 85 ff.
religions, Eastern, 143
religious instruction, 250–253, 284 ff.
responsibility, 62, 267
Resurrection, 33 f., 38, 242
revelation, 14 ff., 19, 54, 137 f., 141,
    143, 149, 154, 171 f., 241, 258,
    261f.
revivalism, 171
righteousness, 92, 187
Roman Catholicism, 4, 9, 17 ff., 47,
    156, 165, 258

Sadduccees, 282
sacraments, 155
salvation, 75 f., 122, 146 f., 155, 157,
    178 f., 197, 278 f.
scholarship, 220
science, 112 f., 119, 166, 189, 216,
    266
secularism, 184
secularization, 161 f., 197, 249
self-knowledge, 53
self-realization, 188

self-understanding, 49, 139, 148, 156,
    198 f., 247, 261
Sermon on the Mount, 218, 283
sin, 187, 225 f.
skandalon, 11, 163, 184, 258, 274
socialism, 184
spiritual man, 134, 151
Stoics/Stoicism, 147, 154 f., 186, 206
subjectivism, xvi ff., 258
symbol, 112
symbolic language, 259
Synoptics, 238 f.

Ten Commandments, 196
terminology, 203
theism, 124
Theologische Rundschau, xxiii
Tradition, 157 f., 166, 234, 237 f.,
    247 ff.
trust, 100 f.
truth, 175

unbelief, 162 f.
Utopianism, 232

voluntarism, 85

Weltanschauung: see world view
Wholly Other, the, 185
word meanings, 202 f.
Word of God, 14, 43, 202, 207, 235,
    246, 249, 260, 278 f., 281
world view, 26, 94–97
world, relation to the, 97 ff., 146, 188
    f., 258
worship, 164

Zeit, Die, xxv
"zones of common interest," 130, 137,
    142 f.
Zwischen den Zeiten, xxiv

Index of Names

Abraham, 198, 284
Abrahams, Israel, 214
   Studies in Pharisaism and the Gospels, 214
Absalom, 229
Adam, 182
Amos, 226, 230
Antigone, 204
Aquinas, Thomas of, 106
Augustine, 49, 145, 177, 184, 260, 275
   Confessions, 161

Baillie, John
   The Idea of Revelation in Recent Thought, 42
   The Sense of the Presence of God, 122
Bakunin, 165
Barth, Karl, xxii–xxiv, xvii, 4 f., 14, 16, 18, 23, 42, 50, 104, 108, 110, 127 ff., 140, 154, 170, 174, 257
   R. Bultmann: ein Versuch ihn zu verstehen, 12, 25, 128, 140
   Kirchliche Dogmatik, 14, 25
   Der Römerbrief, xxiii, 129
Bartsch, H. W., xxv
   Kerygma and Myth, xxv, 25, 110, 112, 121
Baumgartner, Walter, xxii, 289
Baur, Ferdinand Christian, 5
Becker, Carl, xxiii
Biehl
   "Welchen Sinn hat es, von 'theologischer Ontologie' zu reden?" 162
Billerbeck, 213

Blanshard, Brand, xvii
Bolewski, Hans, 276 ff.
Bonhoeffer, Dietrich, 230
   Widerstand und Ergebung, 230
Bornkamm, Günther, xxiii, 37, 236, 257 f.
   Jesus von Nazareth, 117 f.
   Überlieferung und Auslegung im Matthäusevangelium, 238
Bousset, Wilhelm, xxi, 212, 217
Braaten and Harrisville
   Kerygma and History, 108
Braun, H., 236
Brunner, Emil, xi, 42, 115
Buber, Martin, xii
Budde, Karl, xxii
Buddha, 44
Bulgakoff, 42
Bultmann, Arthur, xix
Bultmann, Rudolf
   Commentary on John, 149, 214
   Essays, Philosophical and Theological, 46
   Die Exegese des Theodor von Mopsuestia, xx
   Existence and Faith, 41
   Faith and Reason, 6, 15, 33 f., 37, 38, 149, 229, 244
   Die Gnosis, 204
   History and Eschatology, 8, 51 f., 66, 76 ff., 142, 262
   History of the Synoptic Tradition, xxi, 205, 214, 237
   Jesus and the Word, 37, 110, 213–216

315

Bultmann, Rudolf (*Continued*)
  Jesus Christ and Mythology, xxiii,
    6, 29, 111, 117 f., 236
  Offenbarung und Heilsgeschehen,
    xxv
  The Presence of Eternity, xxiii, 30,
    38, 229
  Primitive Christianity, 4, 37, 66,
    204, 213, 216 ff., 230
  Der Stil der paulinischen Predigt
    . . . xx, 154
  Theology of the New Testament, 4,
    29, 33, 37, 45, 66, 134, 149, 155,
    203, 214, 238, 245
  This World and the Beyond, 116
  "Adam, Where Art Thou?" 194
  "Die Bedeutung der Eschatologie
    für die Religion des Neuen
    Testaments," 65
  " 'The Bible Today' und die Escha-
    tologie," 31, 167
  "The Case for Demythologization,"
    25, 27, 111, 130
  "Christ and the End of the Law,"
    186
  "Christianity as Eastern and West-
    ern Religion," 187
  "Das christliche Gebot der Näch-
    stenliebe," 191, 195
  "The Christological Confession of
    the World Council of Churches,"
    48
  "The Concept of Revelation in the
    New Testament," 41
  "Concerning the Hidden and the
    Revealed God," 41
  "Echte und säkularisierte Verkün-
    digung" 161, 249
  "Entmythologisierung und Exist-
    enzphilosophie," 161
  "Die Eschatologie des Johannes-
    Evangeliums," 188
  "Forms of Human Community,"
    166, 188, 194
  "Grace and Freedom," 32, 186
  "Humanism and Christianity," 194
  "Ist voraussetzungslose Exegese
    möglich?" 23
  "Kerygma and Myth," 12, 42
  "Kirche und Lehre im Neuen
    Testament," 161

Bultmann, Rudolf (*Continued*)
  "Die liberale Theologie und die
    jüngste theologische Bewegung,"
    184
  "Der Mensch zwischen den Zeiten,"
    159, 161
  "Milestones in Books," 129
  "New Testament and Mythology,"
    3, 8, 131, 199
  "Polis and Hades in Sophocles' An-
    tigone," 204
  "The Problem of Hermeneutics,"
    22, 139, 161, 165, 208
  "Prophecy and Fulfillment," 223
  "The Question of Natural Revela-
    tion," 162, 185, 192
  "Das religiöse Moment in der ethi-
    schen Unterweisung des Epiktet,"
    154
  "The significance of the idea of
    freedom for Western civiliza-
    tion," 186
  "Der Sinn des Mythos," 32
  "The Understanding of Man and
    the World in the New Testa-
    ment," 188
  "Das Verhältnis der urchristlichen
    Christusbotschaft zum histori-
    schen Jesus," 119, 163, 244
  "Die Wandlung des Verständnisses
    der Kirche im Urchristentum,"
    159
  "Welchen Sinn hat es von Gott zu
    reden?" 185
  "Zur Frage der Christologie," 159
  "Zur Frage des Wunders," 190
Buri, Fritz, 16, 128, 129
  "Entmythologisierung oder Ent-
    kerygmatisierung der Theologie,"
    128

Caesar, 56, 265
Calvin, John
  Institutes of the Christian Religion,
    49
Camus, Albert, xii, 107
Castelli, Enrico, xxv
  Problema della Demitizzazione, xxv
Clement of Alexandria, 127
Clement I, pope, 156
Cohen, Hermann, xxii

Collingwood, R. G., 53, 61, 141, 142
  The Idea of History, 142
  Religion and Philosophy, 141
Conzelmann, H., 37, 236, 239
  The Theology of St. Luke, 238
Croce, Benedetto, 61
Cullmann, 47

Dahlmann, H., xxiii
David, 226, 229
Demosthenes, 201
Dibelius, Martin, 164, 169, 175, 237, 239
  Formgeschichte des Evangeliums, 205, 237
  From Tradition to Gospel, 237
  Geschichtliche und übergeschichtliche Religion im Christentum, 164
Diem, Hermann, 170
Dilthey, W., 208, 258
Dinkler, Erich, 236, 289
Dodd, C. H., 31, 167 f., 277
  The Bible Today, 167
  The Parables of the Kingdom, 215

Ebbinghaus, Julius, xxii
Ebeling, Gerhard, 118 f., 168, 237
  "Conversation with Rudolf Bultmann," 168
  "The Nonreligious Interpretation of Biblical Terms," 230
  Theologie und Verkündigung, 109, 168
  "Wort Gottes und Hermeneutik," 247
  Wort und Glaube, 246, 248
Engels, 165
Epictetus, 154

Farrer, Austin, 26
Frank, Erich, xxii, 55, 165
  Philosophical Understanding and Religious Truth, 165
Friedländer, Paul, xxiii
Friedrichsen, Anton, xxiii
Fuchs, E., 37, 236
  Hermeneutik, 247
  Zur Frage nach dem historischen Jesus, 247
Fuller, R. H., 42, 67, 110

Gadamer, Hans-Georg, xxii, 165, 277
  Wahrheit und Methode, 165
Gideon, 225
Goethe, J. W. von, 10, 166
Gogarten, Friedrich, xxii, xxiv, 4, 257, 267
  Demythologizing and History, xxv, 29
  Entmythologisierung und Kirche, xxv
  "Die Krisis unserer Kultur," xxiv
Good, Edwin M., 258–261
Greig, J. C. G., 139
Grobel, K., 70, 134
Gunkel, Hermann, xx, 175, 205

Hackman, George, 144
Harbsmeier, Götz, 275 f.
Harnack, Adolf, xx, 26, 153, 156
  Lehrbuch der Dogmengeschichte, 154
  What is Christianity? 26
Hartmann, Nicolai, xxii, 191
Hartshorne, Charles, 125 f., 273, 275
  The Divine Relativity, 125
  The Logic of Perfection, 125
  Man's Vision of God and the Logic of Theism, 125
  Reality as Social Process, 125
Harvey, Van, xxv
Harvey, Van A. and Ogden
  "Wie neu ist die Neue Frage nach dem historischen Jesus?" 118
Hebert, 42
Hegel, 64, 104, 127
Heidegger, Martin, xxii, xxiv f., 8, 29, 32, 36, 39, 100 ff., 118, 123 f., 126, 131–135, 139, 141 f., 149, 190, 208, 210, 258 ff., 270, 273 ff.
  Being and Time, 28, 102, 116, 129, 131, 145, 150, 272, 274, 276
Heitmüller, Wilhelm, xx, xxi
Henderson, Ian, 30
  "Myth in the New Testament," 30
Hepburn, Ronald, xiii f., 35
  "Demythologizing and the Problem of Validity," 35
Heraclitus, 206
Herakles, 141
Herrmann, Wilhelm, xx, xxii, 16, 47, 109

Hermann, Wilhelm (*Continued*)
  *The Communion of the Christian
    with God,* 109
Hoffman, Paul E., 153
Hölscher, Gustav, xxii
  Geschichtsschreibung in Israel, 228
Homer, 201, 202
  Iliad, 225
Hosea, 230 f.
Hughes, Philip Edgcumbe
  "Myth in Modern Theology," 28

Ignatius of Loyola, 158 f.
Isaiah, 230 f.

Jaeger, Werner, 209, 281
James, 182
Jaspers, Karl, xxv, 16, 25 f., 34, 40,
    131, 136–139, 142, 274
  Die Frage der Entmythologisierung,
    xxv, 136
  Myth and Christianity, 29, 40
  The Perennial Scope of Philosophy,
    136
Jeremiah, 225, 230, 232
Jesus, xxiii f., 44 f., 50, 85, 117, 150 f.,
    173, 215, 231, 237 f., 240–246,
    260, 262, 286
Jochanan ben Zakkai, Rabbi, 283
John the Baptist, 215
John the Evangelist, 10 f., 38, 72,
    74–79, 134, 159, 268
  Gospel of John, 188, 205–208, 238,
    241
Jonah, 225
Jülicher, Adolf, xx, xxii
Justin the Martyr, 127

Kähler, M., 171–176
Kamlah, W.
  Christentum und Geschichtlichkeit,
    196
Kant, 47, 261
Käsemann, Ernst, 37, 168, 199, 236
  "Amt und Gemeinde im Neuen
    Testament," 168
  "Neutestamentliche Fragen von
    heute," 199
  "Das Problem des historischen Je-
    sus," 244
Kee, Howard C., 257

Kegley and Brètalli
  Reinhold Niebuhr, 111
Kierkegaard, Sören, 5, 45, 66, 90, 102,
    145, 165, 174, 198, 260
  The Sickness unto Death, 102
Kinder, Ernst, 108
Kittel, Gerhard, 203
  *Theologisches Wörterbuch zum
    Neuen Testament,* 203
Körner, J.
  Eschatologie und Geschichte, 12
Krüger, Gerhard, xxii
  Einsicht und Leidenschaft, 10
Kümmel, W. G., 237
Künneth, Walter, 108, 119

Lanterno, E. H., 110
Lennert, R., 194
Logstrup, K. E., 268–271
Lohmeyer, Ernst, 164, 237
  "Vom Begriff der religiösen Ge-
    meinschaft," 164
Löwith, Karl, xxii
Luke, 159, 182
  Gospel of Luke, 180, 205, 238
Luther, Martin, 12, 17, 43, 56, 90,
    101, 145, 161, 177, 180, 198, 222,
    258 ff., 265
  Catechism, 253
  Treatise on Christian Liberty, 31

Macquarrie, John, xxi, xvi, 273 ff.
  An Existentialist Theology, 29, 116,
    131
Malevez, Father L., 140 f.
  The Christian Message and Myth,
    26, 141
Manheim, Ralph, 136
Marlé, R., 18
Mark, Gospel of, 177 f., 205, 215,
    238–243
Marx, Karl, 200
Marxsen, W., 237
  Der Evangelist Markus, 238
  "Messiasgeheimnis," 239
Matthew, 182, 218
  Gospel of Matthew, 205, 238
Melanchthon, 17
Meyer, Paul W., 236
Michel, D. Otto, 278 f.
Minear, Paul S., 265–268

Moore, George Foote
  "Christian Writers on Judaism,"
    212
Mopsuestia, Theodore of, xx
Moses, 229
Müller, Friedrich, xxiii, 280 ff.
Müller, Karl, xx

Natorp, Paul, xxii
Newman, Cardinal, 47
Niebuhr, Reinhold, xi, 107, 111 f.,
    115 f.
  "The Problem of a Protestant So-
    cial Ethic," 198
Niebuhr, Richard R., 34
  Resurrection and Historical Reason,
    34, 38
Nielsen, Niels C., Jr., 51
Nygren, Anders, xi f.

Oepke, A.
  "Entmythologisierung des Christen-
    tums," 26
Ogden, Schubert M., xii, xxv, 41, 271
    ff.
  Christ Without Myth, 111, 121
  Existence and Faith, 106
  "Bultmann and the New Quest,"
    118
  "Bultmann's Demythologizing and
    Hartshorne's Dipolar Theism,"
    123
  "The Lordship of Jesus Christ," 122
  "The Understanding of Theology in
    Ott and Bultmann," 118
Ott, Heinrich, xxiv, 118 f., 262–266
  Geschichte und Heilsgeschichte in
    der Theologie Rudolf Bultmanns,
    xxiv, 7, 162
Otto, Rudolf, xxii, 185
Owen, H. P., xiv, 261 f.
  Revelation and Existence, 41

Pascal, 49, 177
Paul, 10 f., 18, 29, 37, 48, 72–80, 134,
    139, 150–59, 168, 173, 178, 182,
    186, 215, 244, 260, 268
  Corinthians, 189
  Epistles, 144
  Galatians, 180 f.

Paul (Continued)
  Philippians, 282
Peter, 240
Philo, 203, 206, 218
Plato, 10, 194, 202, 208 f.
  Symposium, 208

Rade, Martin, xx
Rathje, Johannes, xx
  Die Welt des freien Protestantis-
    mus, xx
Resse and Freeman
  Process and Divinity, 123
Rickert, 190
Ritschl, Albrecht, 47, 104, 163
Roberts, D. E.
  Existentialism and Religious Belief,
    191
Robinson, James M., xxv, 104 f., 117,
    237
  A New Quest of the Historical Je-
    sus, 34, 37 f., 104
Robinson and Cobb
  The Later Heidegger and Theology,
    118
Robinson, Bishop John A. T., xxv
  Honest to God, xxv
  The Honest to God Debate, xxv

Samuel, 225
Sandmel, Samuel, 282 ff.
  "Parallelomania," 213
  Philo's Place in Judaism, 218
Sartre, xii
Saul, 226
Scheler, M., 191
Schelling, 165
Schlatter, A., 171–176
Schleiermacher, 47, 261
Schlier, Heinrich, xxiii, 169
  "Kurze Rechenschaft," 169
Schmidt, G.
  Katechetische Anleitung, 250
Schniewind, J., 44, 174, 237, 239
  "Messiasgeheimnis und Eschatolo-
    gie," 239
  "Zur Synoptikerexegese," 239
Schreiber, J.
  "Die Christologie des Markusevan-
    geliums," 241
Schrey, Heinz-Horst, 279 f.

Schürer, Emil, 173, 212–217
  A History of the Jewish People in
    the Time of Jesus, 212
Schulte, Hannelis, 284 ff.
Schumann, F. K.
  "Um Kirche und Lehre," 162
Schweitzer, Albert, 65, 160
Schweizer, E., 237
Siebeck, Hans, 289
Simpson
  The Early Traditions of Israel, 228
Smith, L. P., 110
Socrates, 44, 56, 265, 281
Soden, Hans von, xxi, xxii
Sohm, 156
Sophocles
  Antigone, 204
Stallmann, Martin, 286 f.
Stanyon, J. Sandys, 109
Stein, Charlotte von, 166
Stochholm, Johanne M., 83
Strack, 213
Strack and Billerbeck
  Kommentar zum Neuen Testament
    aus Talmud und Midrasch, 213

Täger, Friedrich, xxiii
Tatian, 127
Temple, 42
Tertullian, 127
Theophilus, 180
Thielicke, Hellmut
  "The Restatement of New Testa-
    ment Mythology," 36

Throckmorton, B. H., Jr.
  The New Testament and Mythol-
    ogy, 39
Thurneysen, xxiv
Tillich, Paul, xi f., 26, 107, 112, 115,
    141, 165, 274, 277
  Systematic Theology, 111, 122, 165
  Dynamics of Faith, 111
Toynbee, Arnold, 264
Troeltsch, Ernst, xxiv, 5

Unhjem, Arne, 3, 201

Vielhauer, P., 236

Weber, 212
Weiss, Johannes, xx, 65, 160
Werner
  The Formation of Christian Dogma,
    215
Wieman, Henry Nelson, xi
Williams, Charles, 40
  The Descent of the Dove, 40
Windelband, 190
Wingren, G., 237
  Die Predigt, 237
Wrede, W., 239
  The Messianic Secret of the Gos-
    pels, 238
Wyon, Olive, 141

York von Wartenburg, Count, 208,
    258

Zoroaster, 206

Format by Sidney Feinberg
Set in Linotype Times Roman
Composed, printed and bound by American Book–Stratford Press, Inc.
HARPER & ROW, PUBLISHERS, INCORPORATED